After the Cure

STUDIES IN GOVERNMENT AND PUBLIC POLICY

After the Cure
Managing AIDS and
Other Public Health Crises

Martin A. Levin and Mary Bryna Sanger

 University Press of Kansas

Published by the University Press of Kansas (Lawrence, Kansas 66049), which was organized by the Kansas Board of Regents and is operated and funded by Emporia State University, Fort Hays State University, Kansas State University, Pittsburg State University, the
University of Kansas, and Wichita State University.

Library of Congress Cataloging-in-Publication Data

Levin, Martin A.
    After the cure : managing AIDS and other public health crises / Martin A. Levin
and Mary Bryna Sanger.
        p. cm. — (Studies in government and public policy)
    Includes index.
    ISBN 0-7006-1022-7 (alk. paper) — ISBN 0-7006-1023-5 (pbk. : alk. paper)
        1. Communicable diseases—United States—Prevention—History. 2. Communicable
diseases—Government policy—United States—History. 3. Aids (Disease)—United
States—Prevention—History. 4. Aids (Disease)—Government policy—United
States—History. I. Sanger, Mary Bryna. II. Title. III. Series.

RA643.5.L48 2000
362.1'969'0973—dc21   00-022178

British Library Cataloguing in Publication Data is available.

Printed in the United States of America

10 9 8 7 6 5 4 3 2 1

The paper used in this publication meets the minimum requirements of the American
National Standard for Permanence of Paper for Printed Library Materials Z39.48-1984.

Contents

Preface vii

Acknowledgments xix

1. Taming the Management Beast: Approaching Management
   with Strategic Skepticism 1

2. The Successful Management of Polio 29

3. The Swine Flu Immunization Program 50

4. The Clinton Administration's Childhood Immunization Policy 73

5. Controlling Reemergent TB: Successful Management
   of an Impossible Job 95

6. Predicting the Future from the Past: The Early Mismanagement
   of the AIDS Crisis 119

7. Scenario Building: The Day After an AIDS Vaccine Is Discovered 141

8. Curing the Disease: Prospects for Improving the Management
   of Public Health Initiatives 176

Notes 205

Index 239

Preface

With Allen S. Kamer

The development of an effective AIDS vaccine will not be the beginning of the end. Rather, it will only be the end of the beginning. In the near future we will pick up the morning newspaper to read that an effective AIDS vaccine has been developed. But because management matters, the discovery will not be the cure; bright ideas are not enough. Thus, we propose general executive strategies and specific advance ameliorative actions.

Unless we act now—well before that vaccine is fully developed—the joy of that day will be tempered by the aftershock of serious implementation problems and management delays. The day after an AIDS vaccine is developed will only mark the start of the next and equally difficult stage, the implementation of the campaign to inoculate all Americans with the vaccine.

We predict a pattern of implementation marked by management problems and delays resulting from many serious conflicts: scientific controversy and competition over the vaccine's effectiveness and safety; threats of lawsuits over side effects and demands from the manufacturers and developers for indemnification from lawsuits; professional and institutional timidity and conflict among health care providers; tensions between treatment and prevention advocates; tensions over priorities for groups and individuals receiving the vaccine; tensions between private interests and the public interest; and media sensationalization, especially of rare cases.

More specifically, from the moment of discovery of an AIDS vaccine, even before the predictable production and distribution problems arise, controversy is likely to rage among scientists and professionals over its safety and effectiveness. The FDA will feel pressure from some groups, as it has in the past, to move the vaccine to market quickly. Others are likely to try to delay authorization. AIDS activists may, as they have done in the past, press for either speed or delay or both and at different times. A striking case of their delaying efforts is our analysis in the next section of the blocking of the gp120 vaccine from going forward. In this instance they pressed—successfully—against even moving into phase III trials for this promising vaccine. And Chapter 6 shows the same effective pressure from AIDS activists in the bathhouse closings, needle exchange, and FDA approval cases.

There will be threats of lawsuits: some by those who fear getting AIDS from the vaccine, others by those who fear other side effects. Fears about side effects will be widespread for several reasons, including the fact that at the very least there probably will be some negative side effects, as there typically are in any complex medical intervention. And there may be times in the vaccination process, such as its early stages, when there will be a significant number of side effects, albeit a small percentage of the overall cases.

These problems also are likely to be greater if, as we suggest in Chapter 1 is the likely case, the best AIDS vaccine available is—unlike most vaccines for childhood diseases—less than 100 percent effective. This is the case with several vaccines, such as the hepatitis B vaccine, which has an effectiveness closer to 65 percent. But the most significant problem is likely to be that whatever the degree of actual side effects or their risk, in the course of these and other conflicts, they will be distorted and sensationalized. These are some of the clear lessons of our analysis of both the swine flu vaccine debacle in Chapter 3 and vaccines for childhood diseases in Chapter 4.

Even more problematic, the manufacturers will want the federal government to indemnify them from these suits before they produce the vaccine. To say the least, this indemnification will not occur automatically, which our swine flu analysis again illustrates. There will be protracted conflicts, and during the ensuing delay, more people will contract AIDS. The dynamics of public relations may significantly complicate the vaccine's implementation. For example, drug and insurance companies will fear criticism and negative media coverage both for delaying the vaccine's release or for any later side effects. Thus, companies might be moved to defend themselves by publicly emphasizing the vaccine's possible risks, which would undermine public confidence even before it hit the market.

Delays will arise not only from concern about the safety and wisdom of using a new vaccine but also from professional and institutional timidity. Concern for individual careers may create disincentives for participating in a risky, large-scale inoculation program. Conversely, professional ambitions may result in competing approaches to inoculation aimed at building public reputations, which will, in turn, exacerbate conflict and delay. For example, the goal of reinforcing awareness of preventive medicine and vaccinations underlay the push by the Centers for Disease Control (CDC) and its head, Dr. David Sencer, to use the swine flu vaccine in an immediate, universal inoculation program in 1976.

But a dozen years later, as New York City health commissioner at the beginning of the AIDS epidemic, Dr. Sencer strongly constrained governmental responses to the new epidemic. He did not move to regulate bathhouses, accurately suspected as playing a major role in transmitting the virus, lest he be criticized for too aggressive government action, as he had been after the swine flu scare. Many viewed this delay as significantly adding to the spread of AIDS in New York.

There also will be tensions between treatment and prevention advocates. AIDS victims—those who already have the disease or who are HIV-positive—and their organizations, especially those in the gay and minority communities, understandably will be more immediately interested in treatment rather than prevention activities. Indeed, we see the same patterns among others already suffering from a disease, such as breast cancer victims. Thus, they probably will resist shifting funds from their treatment to a universal inoculation campaign. By contrast, those who are not HIV-positive—the large majority, although less well organized than the current victims, will want most funds devoted to prevention modes such as a vaccine.

In addition, underlying tensions exist between this majority population without the disease and most HIV victims because of the subtext of racial and sexual orientation differences overlaid with putative moral judgments. This animosity is likely to heighten these funding conflicts and make compromise more difficult, especially in the short run.

And there will be tensions over priorities for groups and individuals receiving the vaccine. The public as a whole is likely to disagree about how it should be done and with what priorities. Key groups will especially disagree, ranging from at-risk communities to parents of middle-class teenagers, the federal and local governments, and the institutions administering the vaccine.

The nature of these tensions is reflected in the questions that will be raised and indeed will need to be resolved—in the short run. Some of these questions include who should get the vaccine first: Should the first priority be the populations at greatest risk, such as gay men, members of minority communities, and IV drug users? Or should it go to those who can pay for it out of their own pocket or through insurance? Should teenagers be given a high priority because of their potential sexual activity and because our society generally wishes to give priority to the protection of children? If so, should minority teenagers be given priority? Should preadolescent children be given priority because they will be teenagers soon?

Who will pay for those who can't afford the vaccine? Who will compensate the institution for administering it to those who can't afford it? Who will ensure that everyone gets it? How will the workers who are administering the vaccine be protected? How will they be paid?

The crowning source of conflict will be media sensationalization, especially of rare cases. With the approval of an AIDS vaccine, the media will make a problematic situation worse by fueling public fears. Exceptional incidents, such as a health care worker becoming infected in the course of her duties, will inevitably occur, and the media will sensationalize them. Then, by repeating such stories frequently, they will make the atypical seem typical.

This description is not hypothetical. In 1991 the media constantly repeated the story of the Florida dentist who allegedly gave AIDS to his patients.[1] Such coverage was evidence of the media's inability to make the distinction between something being possible—in this case, becoming infected through a health care provider was possible although highly improbable—and something being probable. In this instance there was a very low scientific probability of becoming infected because, first, the nature of the HIV virus is very fragile and short-lived outside the body, and, second, the way that it is most likely to be transmitted is through sexual contact, sharing unclean intravenous needles, or blood transfusions.

Ultimately, the media did a poor job of educating the public by failing to explain that the risk of getting AIDS from health care providers was highly improbable in general and almost impossible in this case on the face of it. Instead, they failed to distinguish important facts about the Florida dentist's AIDS infections, namely, that five of his patients—with very disparate socioeconomic and lifestyle patterns—contracted AIDS at about the same time. Scientists have suggested since then that such a pattern of infection is very unlikely to happen as an accident, such as through unclean dental instruments, because the virus is most usually transmitted directly either from blood to blood or through sexual contact. All other types of transmission are, thankfully, very difficult (especially because the HIV virus is very delicate and does not survive for long outside a blood source) and thus unlikely.

These conflicts and management problems are likely to have a discouraging effect on a shaky public consciousness. Ultimately, the public probably will embrace the vaccination program, although slowly and partially. Ordinary citizens take their cues from public health and scientific professionals and the media, whose hesitancies and conflicts will be reflected in public opinion.

Existing myths about AIDS and how it is transmitted will further heighten fears that will impede a vaccination program. In particular, people are likely to have irrational fears about a vaccine for their teenagers and children. Again, this pattern has already been apparent, such as when parents kept their children from going to school with AIDS victim Ryan White.

We are not suggesting that under current conditions an AIDS vaccine will never be successfully implemented. In the long run, or perhaps in the medium run, it ultimately will be fully implemented. But these management conflicts will create serious delays that at the very least are likely to result in incomplete vaccination of the target population for a significant period of time. During this time of delay and incomplete vaccination, many more will contract the disease and eventually die, and many billions of dollars will be spent on their treatment.

Moreover, these are the conflicts and management problems likely under *ideal* scientific conditions—a disease that is susceptible to the development of a vaccine with close to 100 percent effectiveness, as polio was. But, as we explain in Chapter 1, because of the nature of the HIV virus, especially its ability to mutate quickly, this result is not likely. Diminished effectiveness will only exacerbate the types of conflicts, public controversies, and management problems described here.

Finally, management problems will also make the vaccine's implementation much more expensive. We are a rich nation. However, the opportunity cost of what will be at least hundreds of millions of extra dollars will be funds forsaken for other health care programs, including those analyzed here, such as TB and childhood diseases, or for AIDS treatment and education programs, or for other problems for the disadvantaged groups most vulnerable to AIDS.

All these conflicts will discourage the public from embracing the vaccination program. Thus, even after an effective AIDS vaccine is developed, many billions will continue to be spent on treatment, and many Americans will continue to contract the disease and will die from it.

We base these predictions on two sources: first, a general model of public management and implementation and its problems that is detailed in Chapter 1; and second, the implementation and management experiences of the other contemporary public health cases that we analyze in Chapters 2–7, including the ultimately successful but initially troubled 1950s polio immunization program, the 1970s swine flu debacle, the 1990s controversial childhood vaccine initiative, and the recent management successes of dealing with the past decade's reemergent TB.

But we emphasize at the outset that these predictions are just the first step in what ultimately is our approach for designing a successful national vaccination program and for ending AIDS. We are not merely offering the pessimistic warnings of a Jeremiah; rather, we proffer the positive counsels of a Joseph—a proactive and anticipatory executive. Namely, we propose, in the proactive approach of strategic skepticism and advanced ameliorative action, a strategy of anticipating the inevitable management conflicts and delays and then taking actions in advance to ameliorate them and head them off.

There is no magic bullet; discovery is not the cure. We must start our effort to design better policies for dealing with AIDS and these other large-scale public health threats with this recognition. Even breakthrough vaccines and treatments cannot by themselves cure diseases. But more effective management strategies can make a difference—they can help silver bullets hit their targets. Conversely, ineffective implementation of even the best scientific breakthroughs can severely limit the good they can do.

The crises created by these dangerous diseases involve complex forces. But our analysis of the lessons of polio, swine flu, TB, childhood diseases, and AIDS show that public executives can do much better than they have. Indeed, as we will discuss, even small improvements in the management of these public health programs can have significant positive impacts, because the discovery is not enough. This is true whatever the discovery may be—the vaccine for AIDS or swine flu or antibiotics for TB. Even methadone, which many in the 1960s heralded as the miracle treatment for heroin addiction, confronted great implementation challenges.

During the 1960s developed nations' big cities experienced a heroin epidemic. But by the middle of that decade, a substitute opiate—methadone—was synthesized, and it had almost none of heroin's pathological side effects. As with

AIDS, however, the discovery was only the beginning: methadone was not self-executing, just like an AIDS vaccine will not be self-executing.

As we have discussed elsewhere, the development of methadone as a substitute opiate did not automatically or immediately reduce the heroin problem, but it ultimately contributed to a lessening of the problems associated with that drug. And now methadone maintenance is part of a broad arsenal of weapons used against the scourge of heroin. Yet its first and modest local successes were only achieved through an executive like Gordon Chase, New York City's health services commissioner under Mayor John Lindsay. He was responsible for many outstanding health care innovations, including the nation's first legalized abortion clinics and the first large-scale screening and treatment program for lead paint poisoning. But his real breakthrough contribution was moving beyond clever policy choices: he used his managerial skills and strategies to bring together rapidly the means, resources, organizational relationships, and cooperation necessary to launch and sustain a radical program like methadone maintenance in the face of much opposition.

The strategies we propose for achieving better policies to deal with these health crises are predicated, therefore, on the concept of executives acting, like Chase, first with strategic skepticism—the ability to anticipate and predict what will go wrong in the implementation process and be attuned to conflicting interests and their likelihood of delaying, and even resisting, implementation. Based on this anticipatory style of identifying, analyzing, and managing potential obstacles, these executives can then take advance ameliorative actions—developing and implementing strategies in advance to be better able to surmount such problems or at least circumvent them.

More important than providing a set of blueprints, we develop a way of conceptualizing the management role: approaching management challenges with strategic skepticism informed by preemptive scenario building is the executive strategy most likely to reveal the potential minefields and arm program managers for remedial action. Management of complex systems is seldom routine. But as we will discuss, in this way, generic threats to program implementation can be anticipated, identified, and analyzed in advance in order to take such ameliorative action.

Management matters; it is where policy succeeds and fails. In social policy, bold choices catch the eye of politicians and the public, but they are not automatically or easily implemented. Similarly, in science, breakthrough discoveries do not in themselves cure diseases.

Indeed, the following chapters show the independent importance of management even when safe and effective treatments and vaccines are available. Even so, most public health executives, like other public executives, focus almost exclusively on the initial policy choices and thus usually meet with limited success. As we have argued elsewhere, policy choices are point decisions and are fundamental. But having a goal and a vehicle to achieve it are not the same as creating and sustaining the actual apparatus, both human and technical, to launch, steer, and see it through. Success depends on line decisions—complex processes of assemblage, coordination, and bargaining among many independent actors that take place after the initial point decision. These line decisions are the multiple and critical implementation steps that give life to the larger ideas generated by a policy decision.

If an effective vaccine were available tomorrow, as we suggested at the outset, it would face considerable obstacles. Indeed, as we show in Chapter 7, even the day before a vaccine is developed is likely to be difficult because there are two sets of major disincentives to the discovery process beyond the scientific obstacles. First, the implementation process for an AIDS vaccine will be fraught with management and implementation problems, which will create very significant disincentives for the discovery process because implementation and discovery are linked. Indeed, the policy-administration distinction is a false one. Thus, to the extent implementation is expected to be difficult, this will impede the discovery process because it will create disincentives for those entering that process. Their reluctance will result from their judgment about the difficulty of reaping the benefits from their investment because of managerial obstacles.

A second set of disincentives for potential developers springs from a combination of the high costs and comparatively low profits that characterize the vaccine business. Compared to other products that pharmaceutical companies develop and market for chronic illness, vaccines are generally less profitable. In Chapter 5 we describe how, in recent years, these disincentives had in fact discouraged vaccine development for childhood vaccines. Potential developers abandoned the research and development effort, and a number of companies withdrew from the vaccine market entirely.

The scenario for an AIDS vaccine initiative presented in Chapter 7 is based on the experience gained from similar initiatives for polio, swine flu, TB, and childhood diseases and informed by strategic skepticism. Through the use of scenario building and stakeholder analysis, we paint a picture of management conflict and implementation delay frustrating the efforts to bring a lifesaving vaccine to millions. Further evidence of the likelihood of this picture becoming reality is the fact that over twenty years have passed since the swine flu debacle, and the AIDS epidemic is well into its second decade in the United States. But as described in Chapter 6's four case studies, the early efforts to deal with the AIDS crisis indicate the current incapacity of public and private agencies to effectively and proactively confront the obstacles that typically undermine management success. Thus, we now can conclude that our analyses and predictions are, sadly enough, compellingly realistic rather than merely hypothetical.

The irony—and indeed the strength—of these analyses and predictions is that the same predictions about the difficulty of the implementation of an AIDS vaccine might have been made a decade ago. But at that time, ten years after swine flu and relatively early in the AIDS epidemic, one would have assumed that if AIDS continued to claim many lives and resources for the next decade, something "would give"; that the implementation process for an AIDS vaccine would become less difficult with this passage of time and the increased human and financial tolls. But at the time of this writing in 1999, after almost fifteen years of such losses, there does not seem to be any convincing evidence that the difficulty of implementing of an AIDS vaccine would be any less this year, or any year in the near future, than it might have been a decade ago.

Evidence of the difficulty of maintaining compliance and wide distribution of the protease treatment we describe in Chapter 6 suggests the continued difficulties we face. Other experiences provide additional support for the implementation problems we predict. Some of them preceded protease, such as the gp120 vaccine.[2] Its phase III trials were blocked by the FDA in 1994 in the face of both scientific controversy and skepticism. It also faced opposition from AIDS activists. Additional support comes from the experiences of the Vaxgen vaccine. Its FDA approval in the summer of 1998 was met with perhaps even greater scientific controversy and skepticism than was the gp120 vaccine. In both cases, critics and proponents alike acknowledged that even for the trials of these vaccines, the implementation process would be very difficult.

Indeed, today—twenty years after swine flu—when a far more benign viral threat, a "bird flu" from Asia, seemed imminent, a major study found that U.S. public health officials were no more ready to launch a broad vaccination program than they had been for that earlier flu.[3] This is the case despite the benefit of having twenty years to absorb those lessons and develop a set of strategies like those we advocate here. So here too, in the area of viral threats far less severe than AIDS, little progress has been made in preparing for these inevitable management challenges and acting in advance to ameliorate or circumvent them.

As our analysis throughout suggests, the central problem facing public health executives and managers is the failure to sufficiently anticipate management problems and conflicts. Thus, the management approaches proposed in Chapter 8 are predicated on the concept of executives acting in advance of management problems with strategic skepticism—the ability to anticipate and predict what will go wrong in the implementation process and be attuned to conflicting interests and their likelihood of delaying, and even resisting, implementation. This approach enables them to take advance ameliorative action before the environment and events overwhelm such programs.

Some specific remedies involve increasing the economic rewards for private actors to behave in socially desirable ways. We call this making public use of private interest. For example, we propose that public executives attempt to anticipate competing interests through "stakeholder mapping" and develop interest convergence among these stakeholders. Public use of private interest is often a critical and necessary maneuver, creating incentives and inducements for cooperation that seek to change weak or strong resistance into active support. And our proposal to consider indemnifying vaccine manufacturers against potential liability in advance and providing them with strong incentives to participate by removing uncertainty and costs also flows from such an approach.

Developing remedies now, in advance of the discovery of an AIDS vaccine, accomplishes these objectives: the acceleration of the development of an AIDS vaccine, especially by encouraging more entrants into the discovery race for such a vaccine, and assuring the smooth and universal vaccination of the entire population by facilitating the implementation process.

The chapters that follow provide the evidence and the lessons of more than forty years of public health management, which shape the methodology and approaches we propose to "tame the management beast." We are optimistic about the prospects for improving the role that proactive public executives, armed with strategy, tools, and insights, can play to meet the challenges of managing AIDS and myriad future public health threats.

As this book goes to press, the CDC has issued a sobering study that unfortunately provides additional support and urgency for our arguments and policy recommendations.[4] Insufficient attention to the complexity of managing public health responses and complacency can mean that good news is often bad news in public policy.

The CDC found that as drugs and wider access to treatment for HIV sufferers have greatly improved, the rates of decline in HIV infections and AIDS deaths have paradoxically slowed. This weakening of the relationship between improved treatment and health outcomes points to some sobering lessons that confirm our predictions. First, particular treatments often entail critical compliance challenges for patients that require vigilant management strategies and oversight. Second, there are problematic tensions between treatment and prevention approaches. Third, the availability of effective treatments often has perverse effects on prevention in general and on individual behavior in particular. And all these conditions mean that good news can also bring us bad news.

The CDC found that in 1998 the rate of HIV infection in the United States was no longer declining. Second, while the rate of AIDS deaths continues to fall, the rate of decline has slowed. In particular, nationwide AIDS deaths dropped 42 percent from 1996 to 1997 but only 20 percent from 1997 to 1998. The CDC concluded that even though the death rates were much lower than they were at their peak in the 1980s, the slowing rate of decline "indicates that more aggressive prevention efforts were needed." The necessity for prevention efforts was especially reflected in the disaggregated data that showed new HIV infections were "dangerously high" in some areas among young gay men and heterosexual women, particularly blacks and other minorities.

The likely explanations for these troubling trends strengthen the importance of our analysis and conclusions. Broadly stated, expensive combination treatment therapies require difficult and complex regimens that must be maintained very meticulously for many years, but compliance is weakening. Even with adherence to required protocols, these therapies do not work for everyone. Finally, when they do work, they are not likely to remain effective indefinitely. Even so, most patients probably will need them for a lifetime. Despite such problems, both these therapies and other factors have had sufficiently dramatic effects on reducing new HIV infections and AIDS deaths to create a perverse complacency effect. Complacency about HIV prevention is growing. Safe sex, prevention education programs, and vaccine development efforts do not have the urgency they once had, which seems to have led to the sad behavioral consequences that the CDC data indicate.

Combination drug therapies for HIV were expensive when first developed, and prices remain high, despite expectations. Cost limits the numbers who can take them and also negatively affects compliance. It limits those that will continue to take them, especially because they are needed for a long time—perhaps for a lifetime.[5]

Second, these combination therapies involve complex and difficult regimens with rigid schedules that makes compliance problematic. For example, protease requires up to twenty-one doses a day of a combination of three different drugs that need to be taken with meals. They have uncomfortable side effects. Moreover, to be effective, these drugs require meticulous compliance with protocols. Even motivated patients may find it very difficult to maintain them indefinitely.

Compliance weakens over time. As patients feel better and their lives approach pre-HIV status, the urgency may seem less immediate. For others, compliance weakens as weariness with these difficult regimens naturally begins to set in as time passes. Thus, compliance among a large number of combination therapy patients is declining. Sometimes policy bad news can have spiraling consequences as multiplier effects set in. The factors that are diminishing compliance can have compounding negative effects. Drug-resistant HIV strains seem to be developing,[6] and a major contributor to this development has been compromised compliance among patients taking these treatments. Indeed, we describe in Chapter 5 how similar effects occurred when drug-resistant strains of TB developed as compliance with complex combination therapies weakened.

Third, because these HIV therapies are expensive, they are often not covered by public insurance. They are difficult to live with, and not all infected people will or can take them. Indeed, physicians often refrain from prescribing such therapies for all eligible cases. Outreach may be approaching its saturation point, and fewer new patients may be taking these therapies as time goes on. Thus, we may be reaching a point of their diminishing marginal effectiveness over time.

Fourth, many drug treatments have a limited half-life with individual patients, even in the absence of drug-resistant strains. This factor can also contribute to the diminishing positive impacts.

Thus, many factors cumulatively create complacency. Patients and those at risk use less caution, and public officials direct their energies to competing threats. As we will discuss, when TB rates fell in the 1980s, ironically, public health resources were shifted to fighting the new threat of AIDS. Moreover, the "good news" of these breakthrough therapies did not lead to the "end of AIDS" that some activists and the media hyped in the early days of the therapies. Perversely, they have led to complacency about the entire prevention effort. The assumption is that the necessity and urgency of HIV is reduced because effective treatments now make AIDS controllable.

Upon releasing these data, the CDC's AIDS head worried that "in this era of better [treatment] therapies, it is clear that people are becoming complacent about prevention."[7] And with the population experiencing slower rates of decline in HIV infections and AIDS deaths, we may be facing the paradoxical "worst of both worlds." People are "feeling better" about AIDS but in reality are not doing as well as they were a few years ago or as well as they could be given the amazing recent scientific HIV breakthroughs. This paradox has been the thrust of CDC concerns as early as their 1998 study that concluded, "research suggests that some individuals may assume that HIV-positive individuals taking protease inhibitors are not infectious. As a result they may believe that there is no longer the need to avoid high-risk sex and drug use. CDC is concerned that people may be placing themselves at unnecessary risk because of these assumptions. Another concern is the transmission of resistant strains, which could undermine the benefits of treatment advances."

Most perversely, these developments may be reducing the pressure for the development of an AIDS vaccine, which already faces many hurdles: scientific obstacles, funding limitations, and controversy about the relative emphasis on treatment approaches in contrast to prevention. Continued vigilance, not complacency, is needed in these best and worst of times.

Throughout the book we have attempted to identify the significant management challenges that any large-scale public health initiative poses for public executives. To some degree, however, treatment approaches may provide unique challenges. Treatment regimes like those for TB or protease inhibitors for AIDS require complex protocols. Patient education and constant compliance requirements pose special management challenges.

It was just this issue of the necessity "to preclude the need for people to undergo complex treatment" that led a 1998 CDC report to conclude that "as researchers continue working to develop better treatments, we must continue to focus on preventing HIV infection, which precludes the need for people to undergo complex, costly treatment regimens. . . . [T]here must be a focus on developing and strengthening biomedical prevention interventions such as vaccines."[8] Vaccinations may be multiple and timing may matter, but vaccination programs confront most of their management challenges at the point of delivery. Managing long-term treatment for a chronic illness such as AIDS may strain the system even more.

To some, recent CDC data on AIDS probably seem a reason for pessimism about the near-term prospects for continuing accelerated decreases in HIV deaths and new infections. But to us, though sobering, the data do not lead to the pessimistic warnings of a Jeremiah. Instead, they confirm the potential optimism of our positive counsels of a Joseph—our proactive and anticipatory executive strategies. They underscore that all public health interventions—whether breakthrough discoveries like these combination therapies or prosaic implementation strategies like directly observed therapy (DOT)—are not sufficient in themselves. On the contrary, management matters. Indeed, effective management is the specific route to improving even prosaic but essential elements in this battle, be they daily compliance with treatment regimens, HIV education programs, or safe sex. In the chapters that follow, we analyze the typology of management challenges confronting public executives and the strategies likely to successfully surmount them.

1. Bowin Poole, "Data Link Dentist's Office with AIDS Virus in Three Patients," *Washington Post,* January 12, 1991.

2. John Szrezak, "Genetech's Biocine GP120 HIV Vaccine's Phase II Should Continue," *Pharma Pink Sheet* 56, no. 26 (June 27, 1999).

3. Lawrence K. Altman, "Bird Flu Reveals Gap in Plans for Possible Global Outbreaks," *New York Times,* January 6, 1998.

4. "Recent HIV/AIDS Treatment Advances and the Implications for Prevention," Centers for Disease Control and Prevention, July 1998.

5. Ibid.

6. Ibid.

7. "New Data Shows Continued Decline in AIDS Deaths," Centers for Disease Control and Prevention, August 31, 1999.

8. "Recent HIV/AIDS Treatment Advances and the Implications for Prevention."

Acknowledgments

Any effort of this magnitude involves the help and support of many individuals. Because the book developed from research on a large number of individual cases, most of which had never been analyzed from a management perspective before, the data collection relied on both primary and secondary sources and was supported by the able research assistance of a number of highly motivated and resourceful graduate students. In particular, we are indebted to Vince Greiber who as a student at the Milano Graduate School at the New School provided meticulous research on the swine flu case, continued his invaluable research assistance long after he had graduated and began his public policy career at the Department of Health and Human Services (HHS). He was thorough and tireless, sustaining his focus during periods of personal transition. Bonita Sowell, who proceeded him at Milano, provided able assistance on the New York City TB case, helping to track down recent and historic data from retentive city and federal agencies and to connect us to all the relevant public health players in the political and bureaucratic environments relevant to the New York City case.

Melissa Buis, now on the faculty of Wellesley College, as a graduate student in the political science department at Brandeis, provided an excellent literature review and early drafts on the polio immunization effort. As a Harvard law student, Russ Hanser, a law clerk for the United States Court of Appeals, wrote fine research memos on a variety of legal issues and an early draft of sections on legal remedies available to respond to indemnification issues. Unfortunately, space constrained us from using much of this thoughtful draft.

We owe a particular debt to Ruth Katz, currently a dean at the Yale Medical School, and her colleague Tim Westmoreland, now director of the Medicaid and Child Health Programs at HHS. As counsel to the House Subcommittee on Health and the Environment, Ruth provided us access to an abundance of legislative materials. She and her colleagues also spent countless hours providing

insight into legislative history and politics, especially on childhood immunization and the debates on indemnification. Her huge Rolodex and personal and professional credibility provided access to a wide community of critical actors and
scholars important in the drama of national and local health policy and politics.
Her leadership on legislative and policy successes central to our story was as
inspirational as it was edifying. Rebecca Donner provided invaluable editorial
assistance.

The Gordon Public Policy Center and the generous support it receives from
the Gordon Foundation provided an ideal home for research. Among colleagues
at the center who gave generous feedback and suggestions, Marc Landy's advice
was especially wise and his personal support was warm. The trustees of the Gordon Foundation of Chicago—John Adelsdorf, Sandy Blank, Burton Feldman,
Robert Green, and David Silberberg—deserve special thanks. Their faith in this
project, as well as the other endeavors of the Gordon Center, has been steadfast.

The University of California's Goldman School of Public Policy provided
lively formal and informal settings for this work during many visits there. Old
friends at the school—Gene Bardach, Mike O'Hare, and Lee Friedman—were
most generous with their insights. As editor of the *Journal of Policy Analysis and
Management,* Lee's substantive advice on Marty's presidential address and article, "The Day After an AIDS Vaccine is Discovered: Management Matters," was
quite important in shaping the early drafts.

Any author has special appreciation for the assistance of a wise and intelligent editor. Michael Briggs, the editor-in-chief at the University Press of Kansas
is an academic's dream. He was both substantively helpful and personally supportive. He was particularly helpful in navigating the occasional obstacles that
arise in any collaborative project. Rebecca Knight Giusti provided production
assistance that was timely and helpful.

Many friends helped to challenge our ideas and suggest alternative formula-
tions. Our friends from the public management community at the Association for
Public Policy Analysis and Management (APPAM) were particularly supportive,
and we have welcomed the opportunity to preview this work at the annual
research conference. Bob Behn, Paul Light, Karen Paget, Ellen Schall, and others were particularly supportive throughout the process. Their friendship, intellectual engagement, and sensitivity to the intersection of theory and practice have
broadened our thinking and enriched our education, all of which has made this a
better book. Arthur Klebanoff was always available as a friend and professional
to assist on publication issues. Since Bryna held an administrative job while
undertaking the research and writing of the manuscript, her investment sorely
strained the resources of the Milano Dean's Office. In particular we thank Jack
Krauskopf, whose support was essential. The friendship of colleagues David
Howell and Bob Beauregard and their commitment and interest made life bear-
able and helped Bryna maintain her optimism when obstacles blocked the way.
The Milano Graduate School and the New School have provided a home that has

respected and supported a diversified academic career. Bryna is grateful to have had an association with such a unique institution. Her opportunity for managerial leadership there has helped inform and illuminate our understanding of the managerial challenges facing public executives

Thomas P. Glynn III, an inspirational public manager at all levels of government, has been a supportive and helpful friend for many years. As a highly reflective practitioner who is at home in the worlds of ideas and action, he made many useful suggestions on early drafts, especially Chapter 7. Tom Burke, a good friend at Wellesley College, provided us with early drafts from his forthcoming book on adversarial legalism. He helped us sharpen our thinking on non-tort alternatives for Chapter 8.

In recent years the Gordon Center's luminosity has been immeasurably heightened by the intellectual and personal contribution of Steve Teles of Boston University. This and his strong friendship have had a major indirect impact on this work. His move to Brandeis is a fine addition.

For over twenty-five years the personal and intellectual generosity of Martin Shapiro of the University of California at Berkeley has been wise and warm. For this project, his advice on legal policy issues was only one of the ways he advanced our understanding of subtle issues throughout the manuscript.

Nia Lane Chester, dean of Pine Manor College, has been personally supportive and intellectually creative as she warmly persevered with this project. It would not have been completed without her.

We give special acknowledgment to Allen S. Kramer, who has been helpful in creating this work. Allen currently serves as senior research director of market analysis at MORPACE Pharma Group in Concord, Massachusetts, assisting international pharmaceutical and biotechnology companies. Allen has worked closely with Marty. His ideas and insights proved valuable to Chapters 1, 2, 3, and 8. He assisted in the writing of the Preface and Chapter 7. He provided able assistance to early conceptions of Chapter 6 and identified useful sources that significantly affected our thinking. Allen has coauthored a conference paper for APPAM with Marty on the impact of protease inhibitors on a future AIDS vaccine. We are grateful for his assistance and the book is better for having had it.

Finally, much of what we learned in doing this research derives from the efforts of those public executives who have undertaken what must seem like "impossible jobs in public management." Ultimately, our confidence and belief in the possibility of an excellent and highly professionalized public service to meet increasingly difficult challenges are what has motivated this book. We are always humbled by the magnitude and importance of the jobs they take and the roles they play in a highly complex and rapidly changing policy and political environment. This book is dedicated to them.

While writing a book of this sort is a highly professional effort, it affects one's personal life in direct and tangible ways. Bryna's daughters, Margot and Meredith, and her husband, Harry Katz, have been her greatest boosters. They make any endeavor feel as if it's worth doing, and they provide support even when it's not. Without them, little could have been accomplished.

Throughout the years of writing this book, Marty's daughters, Becca and Jesse, gave him much comfort and joy, especially as he has seen their personal and professional happiness.

To all these people we are very grateful. For all their efforts we are truly indebted. We accept responsibility for any remaining errors or omissions.

1

Taming the Management Beast: Approaching Management with Strategic Skepticism

INTRODUCTION

Alarming stories about emerging disease and the limits of medical science fill the headlines and the best-seller lists. As new and mysterious threats—such as the Ebola and Hanta viruses and mad cow disease—frighten the public, medical researchers struggle to identify and cure, or at the very least contain, an increasing number of these baffling diseases. Even diseases for which safe and effective cures have long been known continue to perplex: as the form and severity of tuberculosis (TB), malaria, and a variety of venereal diseases continue to evolve, they have begun to resist standard treatments. Fears of emerging drug-resistant bacteria, long under control with standard antibiotics, further challenge medical researchers and threaten health care institutions.[1]

However unsettling the limits and abilities of medical science to keep pace with these developing threats are, more pervasive and endemic is the incapacity of public health institutions and leadership to mobilize and manage organized programmatic responses to them. The growth in new and increasingly frightening public health crises has highlighted the weakness of managerial preparedness and institutional arrangements. Even when safe and effective treatments are available for diseases whose etiology is well understood, efforts to control them are often insufficient and success is uneven. As we will demonstrate through analyses of public health responses to serious threats from a wide range of disease over many decades, *the discovery is not the cure.*

Indeed, witness over the past forty years the continued battle to control TB, the world's most widespread killer. Although the cure was heralded over forty years ago, the disease remains widespread throughout the world. After years of declining rates of infection in the United States, it began to reappear in inner cities in the 1980s in a more dangerous multidrug-resistant form. Conventional

1

therapies were no longer effective in treating it. Soon, however, new multiple antibiotic drug therapies were developed. But the day after their development, a new and more effective delivery system was also required.

To find and treat infected individuals and ensure that they continued to take the full course of drug therapy (a necessity to avoid the proliferation of drug-resistant strains) required strategic management initiatives by focused and aggressive public health executives. TB is a good example of a disease that eluded control, in part through lack of public health vigilance about the effects of changing social conditions and the public health needs of mobile populations. But in New York City, a creative and effective commissioner of public health built a new management system to identify, treat, and manage infected individuals, which even included requiring that treatments be conducted through a well-managed delivery system of directly observed therapy (DOT). These strategies reversed a deadly rise in serious infection.

Gaining control of TB depended first on the discovery of effective new combination drug therapies. Where there was effective management, as in New York City, TB declined. But where management was ineffective, it did not—for example, in Washington, D.C., where the incidence continued to climb.

The reemergence of TB also reflects a failure of management and the capacities of the public health infrastructure. The increasing connection between the biological, social, and political realms in managing public health reinforces the conclusion that there is no magic bullet.[2] Managing large-scale public health crises will remain an enduring challenge regardless of the state of scientific knowledge. Given the history of both the success and failure of previous efforts in the United States, it is regrettable how little has been learned and how rarely the significant management lessons of earlier initiatives inform current efforts.[3]

DISCOVERY IS NOT ENOUGH: SILVER BULLETS NEED BETTER DELIVERY SYSTEMS

Medical science continues to be assaulted by new viral and bacterial agents that public health authorities strain to identify, prevent, cure, or contain. And while the media often frighten the public and distort the nature of the dangers we face, many recent outbreaks have posed serious public health threats. With the increasing mobility of populations and organisms worldwide and the extreme disruptions to stable ecological systems brought about by expanding development, serious and continuing public health threats are certain to emerge.[4]

Even so, we have some certainties, and sometimes they are positive. First, science is likely to continue to respond to these threats, even as they challenge our knowledge and resource base.

Second, scientific progress will continue, but implementation and management problems will cause some of those treatable diseases to resist complete eradication. Safe and effective treatments and vaccines have long been known for TB, many childhood diseases, and a variety of venereal diseases. But these treatments and preventive therapies are never self-implementing. Their success depends on the management of their administration to multiple and diverse populations in complex political and social environments. Further, even the effective implementation of treatment may not suffice since diseases change, often mutating and in the process providing new medical and public health challenges.

Third, even critical scientific breakthroughs such as those against AIDS may be incomplete. For example, AIDS developments are likely to come more slowly than expected ten years ago and in a less ideal form. Effective treatments may supersede a vaccine. And whatever their form, medical developments may be less effective than we had hoped for. It is quite possible, for instance, that the best AIDS vaccine available, unlike most vaccines for childhood diseases, may be less than 100 percent effective. Indeed, this has been the case with several widely used vaccines, such as that for hepatitis B, which has an effectiveness closer to 65 percent.

Eradication is an increasingly unrealistic prospect. The need for continued public health vigilance remains high. Even safe and effective treatments and vaccines do not in themselves ensure the elimination of disease, because they are not self-implementing. But better delivery systems can make a difference—they can help silver bullets better hit their target. We must create and effectively manage better delivery systems both for breakthrough discoveries and for more prosaic but essential treatments and preventions such as DOT, condoms, bleach for needles, and safe sex education. The missing link in disease control is management.

AIDS: THE OCCASION FOR
CONFRONTING MANAGEMENT CHALLENGES

When AIDS was first acknowledged as a distinct disease in 1982, it was primarily a killer of gay men. This fact generated enormous fear and relief: fear that a disease so deadly could suddenly stymie modern medicine; relief that the risk of infection appeared relatively concentrated in a defined and somewhat limited subpopulation. Political and scientific controversy have confounded public health officials and buffeted the management of AIDS ever since its emergence. In the history of public health leadership, early management of the AIDS crisis represents a conspicuous low point: efforts to discover the nature of the disease and how it spreads were attenuated and poorly financed, and responses to reduce infection and fear were tentative. Clearly, the knowledge base was weak; AIDS represented a new and unknown threat. Calling attention to and mobilizing resources for a "gay disease" appeared politically risky to most political actors, and the increasing politicization of the advocates reinforced the hazards of such actions.

In addition to difficult politics, institutional processes and regulations confronted a fragmented public health infrastructure that appeared poorly suited to respond quickly and decisively to the crisis. Most early cases were identified in a few urban areas, such as San Francisco and New York, and a full two years transpired before Assistant Secretary of Health and Human Services Edward Brandt proposed that the disease should be designated a national priority. Early development, testing, and distribution of promising treatments were stalled and impeded by inappropriate regulations, inadequate funding, and failure to develop coordination between a myriad of agencies at all levels of government. Further, the potential opportunities to collaborate with private research firms were unappreciated. The combination of these factors resulted in a failure to contain the disease through prevention or the mobilization of aggressive support inside and outside of government.

While the complex etiology of the disease is vexing in many ways, the recent failures in the scientific and public health communities emanate as much from the ineptitude of local and national leadership as from insurmountable scientific challenges. Indeed, even if few scientific breakthroughs were made over this fifteen-year period, much success could have been realized in reduced rates of infection and an improved climate for investment in research and development. Policy and management success in public education and prevention could have dramatically diminished the domestic human and economic costs of AIDS.

Thankfully, after fifteen years there are good developments in treatment alternatives. But even with currently promising treatments, which may change AIDS from an acute to a chronic illness, the future is uncertain. New protease inhibitors are very successful, but their long-term effects are unknown, and the extraordinary cost will limit their use. The profound difficulty that many victims experience in managing their drug treatment protocols is already raising serious questions about the appropriateness of protease inhibitors for many cases.[5] Mistrust and suspicion in underserved communities—in which the highest infection rates are increasingly represented—often discourage this population from seeking appropriate treatment and complying with protocols when they are prescribed.[6]

Mutating viruses and the speed with which they replicate may ultimately render current "cocktails" ineffective. If failure to strictly comply with treatment protocols results in increasing drug resistance, protease inhibitors may soon be dangerous for use among these victims, since they risk spreading a drug-resistant strain to others. Further, if symptoms abate, victims and their partners may relax critical preventive behavior. Thus, even effective treatment is no insurance of control, a recognition that has plagued public health gains for many dangerous and communicable diseases.

Prevention is likely to remain an increasingly attractive option. Even so, progress on an AIDS vaccine has been needlessly stalled and underfunded, largely because of intense political struggles. All indications suggest that even if a vaccine were discovered, the ability of the public health infrastructure to manage its production, distribution, and use would be poor.

Managing a large-scale public health initiative is always challenging. Politics and scientific controversy influence the social construction of the disease, which influences the public perception of its victims. These factors, in turn, influence public health policies and the commitment of economic, institutional, and managerial resources. The AIDS case is an eloquent summary of these dynamics; in fact, the power of politics and controversy have had an unprecedented effect on public policy choices and public management performance.

In some respects, AIDS is unique: the complex and enigmatic biology of the virus (confounding treatment and vaccine development), the intense stigma experienced by its victims, and the politicization of high-risk groups. But while the initial response to the AIDS epidemic revealed an extraordinary level of indifference—and later, gridlock—acrimonious politics and real and pervasive obstacles threaten the management of even relatively prosaic public health threats. Indeed, the chapters that follow demonstrate that large-scale public health initiatives typically confront predictable types of management obstacles. Although various areas of uncertainty ensure that judgments for public health policy are always more or less probabilistic, public executives seldom approach the management of public health crises with anticipatory readiness or resilience [7] for even the most common sources of difficulty. Further, they seldom manage uncertainty with contingency plans or alternative scenarios, and when reasonable but faulty assumptions are ultimately exposed, most public executives find themselves scrambling to recover.

Large-scale vaccination and treatment programs always confront the boundaries between private actors and the public interest, including the behavior and incentives of private medicine, pharmaceutical manufacturers, insurance companies, and the civil liberties of individuals. Further, these programs provoke difficult and controversial decisions about the most fundamental questions of a democratic society: How should scarce treatments be rationed? Who should receive priority? Who should pay? These fundamental questions of distributional equity are difficult enough to resolve in an environment in which the incidence of disease is widespread and the chances of becoming a victim appear random. But when victims' behavior is regarded as intentional, or the deleterious consequences of their behavior are viewed as deserved, serious stigmatization develops, and questions of societal responsibilities are more difficult to resolve. When complex interactions between cultural, social, and biological forces exist, managing a public health initiative with political support and dispatch is formidable indeed.

The AIDS crisis may represent a relatively extreme case, but in most respects it confronts public health institutions with many of the same challenges they have previously faced in other large-scale public health threats. It is curious, however, how little has been learned over the last forty years, and how seemingly ill-prepared the national public health infrastructure is for what we argue are the common and predictable demands of disease management.

In this chapter we provide an overview of the dimensions of management that all large-scale public health initiatives inevitably confront. The AIDS crisis is the current occasion that underscores the need to develop a more enduring management framework for addressing public health challenges. Our broad exploration of a range of contemporary and historical cases demonstrates that when public health executives and institutions fail to recognize the need for anticipatory and preventive actions, the prospects for success in managing emerging public health threats are discouraging.

First we review the typical dimensions of issues raised by all large-scale public health threats and then summarize the particular lessons that our studies of polio, swine flu, childhood diseases, reemergent TB, and AIDS have provided. Our goal is to illuminate the respective problems and propose a framework for anticipating and responding to the predictable management challenges presented by most public health threats.

DIMENSIONS OF PUBLIC HEALTH MANAGEMENT CHALLENGES

Market Failures

Public health crises highlight the limits of markets and the critical role government plays in a market economy. Although a number of federal agencies — including the National Institutes of Health (NIH), the Centers for Disease Control (CDC), and the Food and Drug Administration (FDA) — conduct, regulate, or review research and development of new drugs and treatments, most of these activities are undertaken by private drug companies and nonprofit academic institutions.[8] Most health care and treatment services in the United States are delivered by private and nonprofit health care providers regardless of how these services are financed; indeed, private financing represents 56 percent of all national health expenditures.[9] Whatever its regulatory role in ensuring the nation's health, our government is entirely dependent on the ability and willingness of myriad private actors to carry out some of the most essential public health functions.

In a crisis, when speed and effective performance are paramount, the most critical role for government will always be setting policy and designing an implementable programmatic response. But the success of public health policy and programmatic design, as we have mentioned, will ultimately depend upon ensuring the cooperation and coordination of private actors with government mandates once a course of action has been defined. The dependence on private markets to carry out essential public purposes is common in broad areas of government functions, but nowhere is it more essential than in public health.

Markets, however, have a logic of their own, and this logic may not extend to important public purposes — like immunizing all young children against childhood diseases or developing new treatments or vaccines to meet emerging health threats. For reasons that we explore in later chapters, market forces often conflict with pressing social goals. Drug companies, for example, do not internalize the full social benefits, the positive externalities, that accrue to society when they develop and market a new vaccine. As a result, they often stand to profit far more by developing and marketing drugs that treat common, chronic conditions, which are used daily by millions over many years. Although these drugs, too, may be socially valuable, their increased profitability may produce incentives that reduce investments in preventive drugs that have equal or even greater social value.

Vaccines, for example, are usually administered only a few times over a lifetime to a huge population. The largest markets for vaccines are in developing countries, however, where the ability and willingness to pay market prices are limited. With little hope of recouping their costs, private companies may therefore be unwilling to make necessary R and D investments. Further, any vaccine administered to hundreds of millions of people inevitably carries inherent risks for which the courts may allow redress and compensation if a manufacturer is found to be responsible for any resulting harm. Since liability risks for drug producers are often unknown and without limit, private firms may face costly insurance premiums; some insurers may be unwilling to cover a producer at any cost.

Threats of lawsuits affect the economics of the drug industry, altering the market incentives for manufacturers to make certain kinds of R and D investments. These private market decisions have a profound impact on the important public purposes of government. Inducing private firms to behave in ways that maximize the public interest is often a central concern for a government charged with ensuring public health. Nevertheless, private firms have a right—and a responsibility to shareholders—to profit from their activities. Every major public health crisis we examine in this book indicates that the role and behavior of private actors and their relationships with government figure critically in the success or failure of major public health efforts. Managing these relationships and anticipating the economic protections that private firms may require to undertake the research and marketing of potentially valuable drugs are important functions of a government's management of public health.

Nevertheless, as we will demonstrate, rarely do public managers anticipate the kinds of difficulties that inevitably arise. As a result, initiatives undermine the potential to harness the public use of private interest. Few institutional or policy vehicles have been developed that provide enduring solutions for resolving the inherent tensions impeding public reliance on existing markets in times of great public need. The swine flu initiative, for example, was virtually derailed by liability concerns among private producers when private insurers were unwilling to provide them with coverage. Providing indemnity, therefore, may be a necessary anticipatory role for federal authorities to induce manufactures to invest in vaccine development and to meet vital public production goals.

Accordingly, public executives designing and managing effective and responsive public health initiatives frequently confront problems like liability that undermine the ability and willingness of producers and private health care providers to cooperate. Sometimes private companies simply refuse to enter the market, and enormous public demand for drugs and treatment services cannot be met. If they do enter the market, the government may face intense criticism resulting from perceptions of these private actors profiteering while they carry out a needed public health function. Or health care providers' timidity in the face of extreme uncertainty may cause needless delay, frustrating effective delivery. Finally, government performance targets may require unprecedented speed and output levels to respond to a dangerous threat, which may compromise private capacity. Oversight of production and distribution is critical in ensuring quality control and accountability, a management function that represents a formidable challenge for public executives.

In a market economy, government will always face risks in managing private partners. Indeed, the cases presented in the following chapters all represent historic examples in which the limits of private markets to meet the public's needs figured prominently. Again, the success or failure of large-scale public health initiatives will always depend on how public executives manage private markets, ensuring both their viability and that the public interest is served. This challenge can be anticipated, and public executives can act in advance to develop mechanisms that promote private participation. To a great degree, this challenge involves seeking the means to bring about interest conversion between private interests and public purposes. Subsequent chapters outline the ways in which private markets affected public health outcomes and how public officials can better manage them.

Managing Scientific Controversy

Even before a public policy is selected to meet a disease threat, public executives must rely on expert knowledge to advise them of the benefits and costs of various treatment or prevention options. While political and policy concerns are always important, scientific knowledge is often critical in decisions of this magnitude. Although many of the nation's most eminent scientists and physicians work in government, at the NIH or the CDC, for example, the scientific community of researchers and medical practitioners is often widely dispersed in academia or private health care institutions. Public health policies depend upon eliciting the best and broadest expert opinion of various members of this community. Consensus, however, on complex scientific issues that interact with social, cultural, and behavioral dynamics is seldom reached; the culture and values of science itself encourage controversy. Indeed, the very test of significance requires researchers to demonstrate that their findings are not random: they must demonstrate that they can reject the null hypothesis.

Significant scientific advance relies on overturning existing paradigms and challenging dearly held assumptions. Scientists, through their training, seek controversy and alternative explanations, and their quest for professional distinction encourages them to challenge conventional ideas. It should not be surprising, then, that in even relatively established areas of knowledge, dissenters—both inside and outside government, in official and unofficial roles—are vocal and often quite bold. Even after considerable momentum had been generated to pursue Jonas Salk's plan to immunize the nation against polio using killed virus vaccine, Albert Sabin, an outspoken rival, sought to sabotage and derail the effort on the grounds that only live virus vaccine would produce adequate levels of effectiveness. This controversy produced confusion and mistrust and nearly threatened the entire effort.

When public authorities are charged with ensuring the well-being of large populations, they are often highly conservative and cautious. Reaching consensus on the safety and effectiveness of various public health strategies is both difficult and politically charged; all decisions are probabilistic and subject to some level of risk. Given the proprietary nature of scientific knowledge and the inability of ordinary citizens and decision-makers to assess the relative merits of scientific controversy, dependence on the assessments of experts is great. Controversy, however, often frustrates swift and decisive action.

Some controversy derives from personal and institutional biases and rivalries of competing institutions: the NIH is composed of academic scientists with a bias toward basic research; the staff of the CDC is oriented toward applied research and is more likely to be comprised of medical practitioners. Each have different constituencies, and their chief executives may have competing personal agendas. Thus, conflicting and competing strategies may be championed by members of different scientific communities.

Some recent critics of academic scientists who failed to support human trials of a bioengineered AIDS vaccine point to the inherent conflicts between the theorists of academic science and the empiricists of applied research.[10] They characterize an empiricist as one who applies "existing knowledge to seek pragmatic answers to urgent public policy problems." A theorist, on the other hand, is described as one who pursues "new knowledge to build models to explain the complexity of nature and perhaps offer elegant solutions." This characterization exemplifies a more long-term orientation, since the practical application of the theorist's particular research may remain unknown. Empiricists and theorists, therefore, inevitably conflict when circumstances demand urgent decision-making; indeed, efforts to develop and test the polio vaccine, which we explore in Chapter 2, were frustrated by this incongruence.

The NIH's academic culture and the CDC's practical and applied orientation render these institutions incompatible in their outlook, short-term purposes, and public health assessments.[11] There are often additional conflicts between other complementary agencies like the FDA and specific institutes at the NIH like the National Institutes of Allergy and Infectious Diseases (NIAID).[12] Effective management depends upon recognizing the differences in orientation of these agencies and developing ways to reconcile inherent controversies. The challenge in such a strategy is allowing a forum for all responsible points of view without inducing a paralysis of action or inciting media hysteria, which undermines the support necessary to implement any strategy.

In Chapter 3 we examine how CDC Director David Sencer's preventive health agenda dominated the more cautious approaches embraced by scientists from competing agencies in the initial interagency task force charged with responding to the threat of a swine flu epidemic. In evaluating the necessity of a nationwide immunization effort, Sencer's preventive medicine agenda shaped the design of a response. Further, he influenced its evaluation: to ensure the elimination of controversy, dissidents were simply removed from the panel of "experts" who were responsible for briefing President Gerald Ford on the epidemic and making recommendations for an appropriate response. Ford was therefore uninformed about more cautious alternatives. In contrast, the conflict and competition inherent in early efforts to respond to the AIDS crisis simply paralyzed action. Both stifled dissent and unbridled conflict are likely to result in suboptimal decision-making environments. Nevertheless, both scenarios represent risks facing all executives who seek to manage large-scale public health enterprises.

It is crucial to develop appropriate forums capable of airing a full range of views while providing a mechanism for closure and decision-making. Competing views that are inadequately evaluated or aired often serve to undermine outcomes: first, by increasing the chance that the decision chosen is wrong or has failed to consider important factors; and second, by providing great incentives for dissidents to have their hearing inappropriately aired in the press. Using the media to expose policy debates at the decision-making level threatens public and political support as well as the credibility of the enterprise.[13]

The Politics of Scientific Research

Scientific controversy is endemic to public health policy-making as responsible leaders seek to integrate the best scientific knowledge with appropriate policy. But the generation of scientific knowledge itself is influenced by the way politics and public actions determine what research agendas are pursued.[14] Controversy can be engineered; "the persistence of controversy is often not the natural consequence of imperfect knowledge but a political consequence of conflicting interests and structural apathies."[15] An appropriate focus of investigation is what does and does not get studied, something that has been dubbed the "social construction of ignorance."[16]

Public funding is a critical determinant of research investments, and politics influences public support for the level and distribution of government resource allocations. AIDS policy is widely viewed as both the victim of public unease reflected in the level of resources committed and the captive of organized interests in the allocation of scarce research funds. Indeed, the increasing resources have flowed more toward basic research for treatment than toward applied research on vaccines for prevention, reflecting the preferences of organized interests. Overall funding levels were generally viewed as inadequate for many years; although resources have since increased, recent figures indicate that only 10 percent of the AIDS research budget is allocated to vaccine research.[17]

Many endorse the view that the social construction of a disease—how the characteristics of the disease and its victims are framed in a social context—is chiefly responsible for suppressing overall levels of public investment and shaping the character of the resulting budget allocations. Indeed, the very state of knowledge is influenced by social categories, political preferences, and scientific biases of dominant agencies.[18] These factors ultimately shape both what is *known* and what is *done*.[19] Illness attracts the most powerful social and political meanings and represents the result of a process by which biology and culture interact.[20] The important role that a public executive could play in creating alternative coordinating mechanisms and administrative structures to help shape these perceptions has been unappreciated and its potential impact unmeasured. Indeed, developing the means to promote more collaboration among potentially adversarial agents could be a powerful vehicle.

Interagency Conflict

Controversy may be inherent to scientific advance, but it is also endemic to the institutional arrangements with regard to the function and mission of the agencies under the U.S. Public Health Service. As discussed earlier, the NIH is staffed by academic scientists whose work is largely related to the funding of academic research. The CDC, in contrast, is largely staffed by medical doctors who disperse public health resources and provide technical assistance and federal guidelines to state and local public health agencies. The CDC has its own laboratories and scientists for identification and disease tracking, but its mandate is practical and highly applied. The CDC sits between the NIH, with its highly academic basic research orientation, and state and local public health agencies. Although their needs are for resources and technical assistance, local agencies seek to protect their autonomy and independence and are often loath to accept federal mandates. With less prestige than the NIH and weak authority in the states, the CDC's role at the center of crisis policy is difficult to navigate. Their professional scientists, with an emphasis on action and implementable responses, are often at odds with NIH researchers.

Federalism

Federal authority is strictly limited in many areas of public health, but even when federal directives prevail, administrative oversight is often inadequate, and coordination and cooperation among public health institutions are more the exception than the rule. Public health authority is highly fragmented because of significant state and local autonomy and a diversity of practices and preferences, which reflect the culture and politics of local jurisdictions. Thus, service delivery and infrastructure vary profoundly within and between states. All the cases we review in the following chapters illustrate the difficulties that federal policy-makers face in ensuring a uniform level of effort and compliance with federal mandates or guidelines by states and local governments.

Some of the most important preventive action for AIDS remains at the discretion of state and local public health officials. Closing bathhouses in New York City and San Francisco, free needle exchange, sex education, condom distribution, and other such policies might have prevented an extraordinary level of infection in the early days of the epidemic. Nevertheless, local discretion often meant that official timidity and short-term politics dominated local policy-making, foiling decisive action that might have saved thousands of lives.

Federal agencies depend almost entirely on the behavior and performance of local public health agencies to ensure that a policy is implemented, but local leadership capacity varies. As Chapter 5 illustrates, federal efforts to respond to the threat of reemergent and drug resistant TB depended in large part on the leadership at the local level, even as the CDC increased resources and assistance to state and local governments. The infrastructure available to identify and treat TB, however, varied greatly from jurisdiction to jurisdiction. Further, high-risk groups like the homeless, prisoners, and immigrants are differentially distributed within and between states. Thus, leadership means different things in different places. In New York City, where the health commissioner designated TB as a key citywide priority, the response was exceptional, resulting in considerable success. In Washington, D.C., where leadership was far weaker and community resistance more prevalent, control was more elusive.[21]

While leadership is always scarce, resources, expertise, and effort also vary from state to state. The state and local public health agencies are sources of considerable progress and innovation, though they can also impede the achievement of national public health goals. The efforts of New York City and Washington, D.C., to combat reemergent TB illustrate this dichotomy: each city had great discretion and flexibility in meeting federal guidelines and directives, but performance and results varied greatly.

The federal public health infrastructure more often than not depends on fiscal mechanisms to encourage local participation in federally designed and initiated policy. Thus the Vaccines for Children program analyzed in Chapter 4 used the availability of federally purchased low-cost vaccine as an inducement for states to provide free vaccine to health care providers to dispense to the poor. Nevertheless, considerable discretion still resides with the states on the design and implementation of their programs for early childhood immunizations, and coverage still varies enormously. Further, rather than acting as an incentive to increase immunizations, some states simply used the low-cost vaccine to offset existing state funding for vaccine purchase, freeing up resources for other uses.

Free vaccine was provided during the swine flu effort; however, federal executives failed to educate and mobilize local actors about the importance of the effort or incorporate incentives or sanctions for compliance in the program design. Consequently, the program, which sought to immunize 200 million people in just a few months, was initially hamstrung by unevenness in state capacity and unwillingness to undertake a large-scale program.

Limited state cooperation with federal policy goals, due to limited local capacity or weak commitment, serves to undermine national efforts of control. Indeed, poor management of intergovernmental relations is a frequent explanation for policy and program failure. However, there is often considerable policy and management conflict between states and their localities as well. Competition for funds and conflicting strategies are as troublesome within states as they are between states and the federal government. The state of New York, for example, has profoundly different public health needs and risks in rural upstate areas than it does in New York City. State health officials were slow to respond to the increases in multidrug-resistant TB cases when they emerged in New York City, perhaps because they believed that the problem was local and would be more appropriately financed by the city. The state of New York increased its commitment, however, when new cases were identified among prison guards in upstate correctional facilities.[22]

Federalism therefore imposes costs and constraints on efforts to respond to large-scale public health threats. Because local circumstances differ, national policies and programs must be designed to accommodate variations in local needs, capacity, and preferences. No federal initiative can be implemented nationwide and hope to achieve a similar impact in all states without the cooperation and coordination of many different local agents. Nevertheless, the development of institutional and political coordinating mechanisms is seldom regarded at the federal level as central to public health management, even in a crisis. In the swine flu case, neither state nor local representatives were even consulted in the planning and design of the universal immunization strategy—a failure that, not surprisingly, resulted in very uneven rates of immunization from state to state in the initial stages of the program. Indeed, skeptical local actors easily resisted the federal initiative by simply stalling.

In fact, our analysis in subsequent chapters reveals few examples of good federal management models designed proactively to ensure that local actors would be willing and able to support federal initiatives. Notable failures of state participation in the Clinton administration's Vaccines for Children program were the result of weak accountability mechanisms, which left federal initiatives open to abuse, circumvention, or inaction at the state level. A principal management challenge for federal executives is building program support at the local level while assisting and adapting program design to meet local needs. An additional challenge is ensuring accountability for important public goals while providing local program flexibility.

Coordination

Although cooperation is critical, when multiple actors play different but indispensable roles in program design and implementation within and between governments, coordination is also central to program success. Coordination is necessary among federal agencies under the U.S. Public Health Service to provide for integrated policy activities. As already discussed, the history of the Public Health Service leaves a legacy of multiple agencies, each of which has carved out a different function, culture, and source of ambition. Their goals may differ, and the agendas of each agency chief often contribute to this interagency competition and conflict.

Media as Public Educators

No large-scale public health initiative can be successful without a public education component. Citizens need to be informed about the nature of any threat, the risk of infection, and the behavioral and social factors that influence the risk and severity of disease. Once a threat is well established and a systematic response is designed, an equal effort is necessary to inform the public about the need for and availability of immunization and/or treatment. The CDC, the surgeon general, and other senior public health executives have a powerful platform for educating the public, and their success in doing so may be the critical element in preventing or controlling disease:

> In principle, education of the public and health professionals is the most pervasively powerful intervention. Appropriately instructed and motivated, individuals can often eliminate hazards and reduce risk. They can learn, for example, how to prepare food to avoid salmonella poisoning and how to avoid or remove the tick that transmits Lyme disease. In the AIDS epidemic, education provided an alternative to aggressive case finding, which raised concerns of privacy, discrimination, and reduced cooperation.[23]

Whether or not such an education component is well designed by public agencies, the media always play a critical role in disseminating disease information, defining its significance, and shaping public opinion. Threats of epidemics or exotic infections and diseases are news; so are reports of program failure or treatment errors. If their cause or responses are not well established or widely accepted, their newsworthiness grows. In particular, sensation and controversy, as well as official incompetence or malfeasance, are characteristics ripe for press and television coverage.

An astute policy observer notes that the press is interested in four kinds of health and science stories: "fire alarms," breakthroughs, controversies, and human interest.[24] To this list we would add official managerial incompetence or malfeasance. Sensational articles about the threat of drug-resistant TB in New York City were front-page news, even though some were filled with misinformation; these articles could be considered "fire alarms." Breakthrough stories about the "miracle" of protease inhibitors appeared on the covers of all the popular news magazines in early 1997. Widespread news reports detailing the controversies about the safety and effectiveness of the killed virus polio vaccine ultimately threatened the entire immunization effort, resulting in a moratorium that was later lifted.

Similar controversial stories accompanied debates on recommended mammography protocols for women under fifty. Human interest stories—like those about AIDS patients unable or unwilling to fulfill the protease inhibitor drug protocol—also proliferated. The media, on the heels of a General Accounting Office report, exposed the costly mismanagement of efforts to implement the Vaccines for Children program by federal administrators who sought to assign state vaccine stockpiling and distribution to the General Services Administration, an agency with no experience managing such activities. Seeking to expose incompetence, the stories unleashed serious criticism against the Clinton administration's new program, resulting in delay and embarrassment.

Because of the need for timely, interest-grabbing stories, the media are often poorly suited to explain and describe complex scientific ideas or to permit a balanced assessment of the risks and merits of various treatment or prevention approaches. Except for sophisticated career science reporters, most journalists are poorly prepared to assess the credibility of various scientific judgments or health-risk reporting.[25] All judgments on emerging threats are more or less probabilistic, and the media are not well positioned to take a responsible leadership role in public health education. Nevertheless, they often play this role with very mixed results, needlessly generating fear and anxiety and undermining responsible efforts to provide sober and informed public health education. Indeed, reporters often seek controversy or even create it to sell newspapers or increase ratings.

Facts about disease, such as causation and risk, are often subject to controversy and judgment.[26] More complex phenomena often defy simple and easy explanations, which are most suitable for sound bites on the evening news. Although disease may be the result of a simple bacterium or virus, the factors related to the risk of infection, serious illness, and/or death may be related to complex behavioral, social, and genetic factors. This information, while crucial to public education—particularly when large-scale organizational cooperation and citizen compliance are needed for program success—is difficult to disseminate. Failure to provide accurate and dispassionate information, whether the facts lead to diminishing concern or heightened vigilance, inevitably weakens public confidence in the government's ability to manage crisis. And lack of public confidence and support threatens the efficacy of even the most well-designed initiative.

Once there is general understanding about the disease and the public program designed to respond to the threat, the media often seize upon any controversy regarding the safety and effectiveness of a treatment or vaccine. This proclivity is also quite common in product safety disputes when media coverage of litigation and individual circumstances can often establish a consensus of public opinion, even where professional and scientific evidence are inconclusive or contrary.[27] This effect has been well documented in the case of silicone breast implants: most credible scientific evidence finds no relationship between silicone and disease, but the FDA nonetheless has virtually banned the implants in response to intense public concern.[28]

Once an immunization effort is under way, the media typically seize upon rare cases of side effects or cases in which the disease itself is caused by the vaccine. This was the case in both the polio and the swine flu immunization programs. In the polio immunization initiative, tainted vaccine produced by the Cutter Company was sensationalized in the press and threatened the future of the effort—even though the risk was limited to a few Cutter batches and official response was swift and effective. Sometimes the reporting can damage a program through unintentional misinformation. In the early days of the AIDS epidemic, CBS news reports about contaminated blood product factor inaccurately identified the product but caused panic among hemophiliacs using the factor.[29]

Whatever the motivation, however, program executives need plans and briefing channels developed well in advance to deal quickly and responsively with unanticipated problems and to provide timely and accurate information. These strategies include efforts to reinforce continued confidence in the program and demonstrate the responsiveness and credibility of program management. Preparation for such risks is simply prudent management and represents an anticipatory approach to inevitable management obstacles. The risk of media sensationalism and misinformation is not remote; it was a common experience in all the cases we have studied. Nevertheless, program executives were, in general, ill prepared to respond to media misinformation because they had developed few systematic and institutionalized channels to educate the press and respond to damaging reports. Indeed, few, if any, executives were found to be proactive, even though "nothing takes the wind out of the sails of aggressive investigative reporters more than being scooped by the responsible agency."[30]

The media can be powerful partners in dissemination if a media strategy is well designed;[31] if it is not, the relationship is often adversarial. But the media have biases as commercial entities, and market needs can conflict with public health needs. This conflict is particularly problematic when existing knowledge is partial or contradictory, as was the case for both AIDS and swine flu in the early period of their discovery.

Clearly, federal and local public health agencies should pay a great deal of attention to public education. In the early stages of a disease threat or epidemic, when information is partial, the mass media most often have the leading role in informing the public. How media outlets break the story, present the facts, and discuss expert opinion can often be the determining event in the course of public health outcomes. In the chapters that follow, we examine the media's role in shaping the outcomes of public health efforts. In all cases—the swine flu initiative, the polio immunization program, childhood immunization, the reemergence of TB, and the early response to the AIDS crisis—the media played a leading role in undermining or supporting public health efforts.

Nevertheless, as history dramatically illustrates, public executives' failure to develop a well-designed public education campaign, including a well-managed media strategy, more often than not impedes progress in implementing large-scale public health initiatives. As New York City's success in controlling TB demonstrates, an important management strategy in any effort is educating the public and especially the media.[32] Had federal officials initially been less fearful of the political cost of focusing managerial resources and financial commitment on the AIDS crisis, they clearly would have saved thousands of lives. Instead, they relinquished their responsibilities and witnessed the policy debate as it was framed in the press.[33]

Distributional Equity

Rationing. Nowhere is the market less suited to arbitrate between competitive beneficiaries than in the area of public health. Public health has significant externalities; the actions of one individual affect others. Individuals who fail to seek treatment for TB risk infecting their classmates or cellmates. Unvaccinated children are not only at risk of serious disease themselves, but they can spread childhood diseases to adults, risking death, birth defects, and serious harm to pregnant women. Thus, relying on individual behavior through a market mechanism to ensure public health is bound to compromise important public policy objectives.

Virtually every large-scale public health crisis faces a limited time line and constraints on available resources. If the crisis is a contagious disease, prevention is critical, and access to preventive information or therapies affects both the large-scale impact of the crisis and the distribution of risk. When the availability of vaccine dosages is limited by production constraints, or treatments are restricted because of cost, public health decisions about who has priority access to protection or treatment are necessary. Such decisions are difficult and controversial. Americans and their political representatives are decidedly uncomfortable with explicit rationing of health care, even though all areas of health care are implicitly rationed.[34] When the consequence of rationing may be life or death, as in the case of organs for transplant, there are moral and political imperatives to develop a careful and well-documented basis for doing so.[35] Indeed, the perception of political motivations in rationing policy can undermine the legitimacy of the larger enterprise and threaten its credibility. The determination about who should get what, when, and at what cost is an important implementation decision.

In the early years of TB drug development, promising therapies were promptly sensationalized in the press even before their safety and effectiveness could be well documented. Thousands of desperate petitioners, including dying victims of TB or their family members, sought the limited supplies of newly developed but often costly antibiotics. Ultimately, a federal committee empowered Corwin Hinshaw at the Mayo Clinic to review requests and make difficult allocation decisions. Such decisions raise complex ethical dilemmas; perceptions about the influence of power or money over such decisions taint the enterprise. For example, recent claims suggest that although Mickey Mantle's personal behavior would have rendered him a poor risk for a liver transplant, he received the organ because of his popularity. These conjectures raise serious concerns about the process of distributing scarce organs.

Most large-scale programs have limited resources to provide equal access at all times. Rationing policies are often needed in advance but are seldom anticipated. When swine flu vaccine field trials on children became problematic, indicating that dosages for this population were excessive, program managers failed to develop a responsive plan, even though production targets at the outset were generally considered questionable. If an AIDS vaccine became available, such rationing decisions would inevitably present themselves. Selecting appropriate candidates with HIV and AIDS for the distribution of expensive and complex protease inhibitor treatment has already provoked controversy.[36] Anticipating such issues and developing standards for action before implementation would preempt delays, establish credibility, and reduce the inevitable controversy, which generally accompanies hasty and ill-considered policy.[37]

Distribution of treatment and prevention—even if resources are adequate for universal coverage—is rarely uniform for all groups. Ensuring equal access and behavior requires assessing the constraints, information, values, and preferences of various groups. Although early childhood vaccines are presumably available to all families, vaccination rates vary dramatically by income, social class, ethnic group, and area. Some groups are harder to reach through conventional vehicles. The lifestyle of the homeless, for example, is chaotic, and they often have difficulty taking their TB antibiotics regularly. But failure to do so promotes the development of multidrug resistance, as stronger bacteria tend to survive if a longer course of treatment is not sustained. The homeless therefore represent a significant challenge for public health workers. Other groups, such as the uninsured or the very poor, may be less likely to have or seek sources of care. They may have higher levels of skepticism about the safety of various interventions, or family or work demands may force constraints on when or where they can receive care. A well-designed strategy must anticipate uneven responses to similar educational outreach and service delivery and thus develop different approaches to ensure the protection of hard-to-reach groups.[38]

Financing. Finally, questions of distributional equity always require a consideration of who pays and who benefits. Program financing can often represent a highly public and controversial element of program design. Considerable debate accompanied the Clinton administration's original proposal of the Vaccines for Children program, which sought to provide universal free vaccine to all young children. An expensive middle-class entitlement, the program was ultimately rejected in its original form and was reshaped to target free vaccines for the poor and the uninsured. Continual debates about costly AIDS treatments such as protease inhibitors focus attention on both who is deserving and who should pay. When the threat of victimization or disease is random and does not involve intentional behavior, issues of who should pay most likely involve questions of ability to pay and incentives for compliance. When the threat is limited to a narrower demographic group or is geographically localized, decisions about program financing often hinge on arguments about fiscal federalism and politics. If the threat is associated with high-risk or voluntary behavior, it becomes a "moral hazard," and as a result, financing for prevention or treatment becomes particularly politicized. Indeed, there are those who oppose the free distribution of protease inhibitors because of their view that successful treatment will induce increases in high-risk behavior.

Distributional questions raised by a public health initiative are important to resolve in advance. Controversy about priorities and costs can stall program progress and derail a swift and certain implementation. Values, politics, and economics inevitably collide in an effort to shape practical and defensible program decisions. Failure to develop both the mechanisms and the means to confront these factors too often result in serious program obstacles.

Postmodern Politics and the Decline of Public Trust

The recent debate about the state of civil society appears in academic outlets and popular journals of public affairs and is discussed by scholars and political observers from a variety of disciplines and fields.[39] There is abundant evidence that documents the increasing decline in public trust and confidence in government: citizens question the ethics and motivations of public officials and the competence and beneficence of public managers.[40] In short, citizens are more mistrusting, more cynical, and less willing to accept the judgments of experts or the authority of the state.[41] While mistrust of government decreases as economic conditions and the political environment improve, in the currently robust economy only 37 percent of those interviewed in a 1998 Roper Survey said they trusted the federal government, a number too small to depend upon when a crisis occurs and large-scale participation is essential.[42]

Thus, however well prepared public executives are for the management of public health crises, learning to anticipate the likely obstacles characteristic of previous initiatives, the state of civil society has introduced a new and independent wrinkle in the environment for public leadership. Public action is increasingly difficult and the politics more complex. The standards to which leaders are held are ever higher, while the judgments about their performance are increasingly negative. In this environment, tolerance for errors is low and performance standards are increasing; public executives need to be better just to maintain the status quo.

When doubts were raised about the safety and effectiveness of the polio immunization program, which surface in any large-scale initiative of this type, Jonas Salk allayed public fears when he appeared on national television, a maneuver that literally saved the program. As a national figure esteemed by millions for his heroic fight against a deadly killer, Salk's personal imprimatur went a long way toward compensating for management failures otherwise evident in program planning and implementation. In 1976, when the swine flu program attempted universal vaccination, the revelations of Watergate, the Vietnam War, and the public's disappointment with the War on Poverty had irrevocably shaken public confidence in government action, which just twenty years earlier had skyrocketed due to the success of the polio initiative. No one figure or action could easily repair the breach, and subsequent initiatives faced increasing cynicism and doubt.

The environment for initiating these kinds of programs has dramatically changed, and as a result it is even harder to be successful. The economics of drug development are unfavorable, production and distribution are more complex, consumer attitudes and behaviors are less hospitable to state-sponsored programs, and a more complex environment governs relationships between important institutions and politically organized constituents. Current public health programs face a postmodern political climate that is characterized by extreme skepticism and is decidedly antiauthority and antiscience.

Thus, the challenges facing public executives now are even more daunting than those faced by the implementers of the Salk vaccine immunization program. Nevertheless, a study of more recent efforts reveals that a host of management obstacles are predictable and inevitable. The key to success for executives lies in understanding, anticipating, and planning for these predictable and inevitable problems that can or will emerge.

Declining public trust is not easily addressed by public executives charged with responding to public demands, and it increases their odds of failure and the scope of the challenges they face. Clearly competent, open, and professionally managed and evaluated operations help establish the credibility of any public effort. Anticipating the scope of those challenges and developing — in advance — a series of contingency plans to address them appears the most promising and practical approach in the face of both scientific uncertainty and political and behavioral minefields.

SCENARIO BUILDING: METHODS FOR MANAGERS

Initiating programs of the scope and complexity analyzed in the chapters that follow requires planning and a strategy for management. But bounded rationality prevents even extraordinary executives from understanding and predicting all the likely problems that may emerge following the announcement of a new initiative. Myriad factors may sabotage efforts to respond quickly and effectively to large-scale public health threats; uncertainty accompanies even quite prosaic public health efforts. Public confidence is difficult to harness under the best of circumstances, but when public managers grope from crisis to crisis in the face of unpredictable events, cooperation and trust, so essential for success, are impossible to sustain. Reducing uncertainty is the optimal approach but clearly has its limits.[43] Public executives, therefore, must find approaches that better prepare them to consider, in advance, the range of possible outcomes they might confront. Armed with contingency plans, they are more likely to circumvent the obstacles that delay and derail program implementation and management.

Implementation literature is a virtual catalog of the failure of public programs, highlighting in descriptive detail the range of obstacles—political, organizational, bureaucratic, institutional, and social—that frustrate public policy success.[44] Public health programs face additional obstacles, for example, unknown or unanticipated scientific factors, such as changing disease strains or risk patterns, which can change the conditions and the appropriateness of even well-formulated and managed approaches. Contextual and environmental factors can converge in ways that are idiosyncratic and anomalous. Public health programs are unusually dependent on actors and institutions outside government, further complicating the implementation challenge. Thus, even strategically directed planning has its limits.

Application of the implementation literature implicitly leads to a prescription that compromises policy goals in light of implementation realities,[45] seeking tamperproof legal imperatives to ensure clarity of goals and strong authority that can resist subversion.[46] While no single implementation perspective emerges from the literature, most scholars identify governmental organizations as endogenous political actors. As such, public executives need to mobilize their resources to anticipate the conditions (such as contract disputes, lack of or misdirected incentives, weak relationships, and ineffective communication) most likely to undermine program success.

Effective management of a vaccine program or large-scale treatment program therefore demands an implementation and management design that realistically confronts the *most likely* saboteurs. Identifying likely culprits requires recognizing the categories of important and predictable obstacles and the organizations, institutions, and actors who are or could be affected by any initiative and its design. Further, federal executives must identify those who have, or perceive they have, a legitimate stake in any initiative and systematically anticipate their likely positions and/or reactions to program elements. If a federal immunization initiative depends critically on the cooperation of local public health agencies, as was the case with the swine flu program, federal executives need to understand their stake and their likely positions. Program management and design can then build in elements that either address those concerns or provide incentives or sanctions for particular performance. The critical problem is in anticipating all the existing or potential stakeholders, their likely positions, and the nature of the obstacles that they might pose. One approach to full and systematic consideration of the level of difficulty inherent in program implementation is stakeholder mapping.[47]

At some level, every new effort involves considerable risk and uncertainty; minimizing these factors and developing contingency plans may be the keys to success. Managing crisis is principally an approach to dealing with complex systems with a high degree of interaction and uncertainty when time is limited. Planning for and dealing with natural and environmental disasters, such as those managed by the Federal Emergency Management Agency, involves many of the same challenges observed here.[48]

All effective executives need to be flexible and adaptive, but they should also face the program implementation process with "strategic skepticism." This means anticipating and predicting possible or likely risks to formal plans and being attuned to conflicting interests and their likelihood of delaying and even resisting implementation. A strategically skeptical implementer, we argue, would have anticipated the likely implementation difficulties of the swine flu vaccination program. Using historical insight and scenario writing, program executives can develop strategies in advance: walking through the program, they can try to anticipate what will (or could) happen and what will go wrong. Writing an implementation scenario is an attempt to invent plausible stories that might highlight the more obvious, and thus predictable, flaws of a program, or where under differing assumptions it might be vulnerable. From plausible stories can emerge important insights that help shape strategies.[49] Such an approach will be critical in planning for the potential implementation of an AIDS vaccine program. Implementers who embrace strategic skepticism and use historical insights can anticipate the following critical obstacles: scientific controversy over safety and effectiveness; manufacturers' requests for indemnification and threats of lawsuits; professional and institutional timidity and conflict; and media sensationalism. Further, they can develop plans in advance to respond to these potential obstacles.

This chapter has laid out a typology for characterizing the challenges for designing and implementing public health initiatives, which are likely to vary for different diseases and in different political, economic, institutional, and social environments. Anticipating and evaluating the level of difficulty inherent in program management depend on correctly characterizing these environments and predicting how key players are likely to behave. In subsequent chapters, we will suggest several specific strategies to assist in this process. Anticipating competing interests through stakeholder mapping and developing a means to find interest convergence among them are activities central to any effective strategy. Making public use of private interests is often a critical and necessary maneuver; creating incentives and inducements for cooperation can change weak or strong resistance into active support. Indemnifying needed vaccine manufacturers against potential liability in advance and providing them with strong incentives to participate by removing uncertainty and costs constitute one such strategy.

Many management challenges are typical and predictable, so they can be anticipated, neutralized, and even prevented by preemptive actions. But because uncertainty will always be high, preparing for the unexpected is essential. Effective managers must approach the program implementation process with "strategic skepticism," which involves diagnosing the environment and inventing likely scenarios. In the chapters that follow, we will provide a road map of five actual cases. The management insights that can be gleaned from our analysis of the common and idiosyncratic features of these cases provide a methodology for diagnosis and a foundation for scenario building that is based on historic insights. The AIDS crisis is the case that gives this book its most compelling argument; in our systematic review of the public management lessons in these cases, we will suggest how they may be applied to the management of AIDS and to other future large-scale public health threats.

In many ways, we will argue that the AIDS epidemic represents a particularly extreme example on all the relevant dimensions, although any large-scale public health initiative poses similar challenges. Indeed, some would argue that the job of a public health official facing the AIDS crisis is an impossible job of public management.[50] The range and complexity of competitive political, social, institutional, and professional interests pose profound impediments to effective consensual policy. Nevertheless, the public management lessons gleaned from our analysis of other large-scale public health efforts suggest that although significant difficulties are more often typical and predictable, current public management responses are rarely informed by them. Our analysis here, however, provides the lessons of management success and leads us to craft positive and optimistic counsel for proactive and anticipatory executives. The rest of the chapter summarizes the organization of the chapters that follow and the major themes they seek to address.

CHAPTER 2: THE POLIO IMMUNIZATION PROGRAM: AN AMERICAN SUCCESS STORY

Success in mobilizing a relatively swift and large-scale response to the polio epidemic benefited from a social construction of the disease, reflecting society's deepest social, cultural, and moral values—which in this case made its victims sympathetic and deserving.[51] Although victims were not stigmatized or regarded as responsible for their own fates—a view that can significantly restrain the political and institutional responses to an epidemic—contextual factors such as an underdeveloped federal public health infrastructure, powerful provider and producer interests, and weak political support for a governmental role impeded efforts to respond to the public health crisis. These factors were exacerbated by scientific controversy, media sensationalism, and a relative absence of managerial oversight and responsibility for production and service delivery. Such conditions affect the response to all major public health initiatives, including, we will demonstrate, AIDS.

The success of the polio immunization effort despite these implementation difficulties was generated by the widespread public support it enjoyed even before it was initiated. Basil O'Connor, executive director of the National Foundation for Infantile Paralysis (NFIP), developed over many years a carefully orchestrated public relations effort, the core of which was specific activities to make individuals feel personally invested in the polio fight. Although a brilliant manager involved in the research, development, and implementation effort, the establishment of the March of Dimes was perhaps his most important initiative. Year after year he aggressively courted the emotional and financial support of the American public through a wide range of grassroots activities using a core of volunteers from all walks of life.

Dimes were solicited from the public anywhere people gathered and collectively generated millions for the NFIP for polio patient care and research. But even more important, the breadth and depth of the efforts connected all Americans to the cause. Even in the face of serious implementation difficulties and weak federal leadership, the Salk vaccine initiative survived and succeeded through a preemptive management strategy focused on building public trust.

In many ways, the polio immunization program illustrates the threats to implementation and the complex management needs for large-scale cooperation and coordination among diverse interests, institutions, and constituencies. If these management lapses had also been accompanied by forces that seriously questioned the legitimacy of experts, the safety and effectiveness of the vaccine, or the worthiness of victims, implementation and management would have been greatly impeded. The polio epidemic and the response to it illustrate the fundamental challenges of the management of all disease control and suggest the critical problems that can be predictably anticipated and for which management strategies can be developed in advance.

CHAPTER 3: THE SWINE FLU DEBACLE

The case of the swine flu debacle demonstrates the significant role that organizational interests and scientific uncertainty play in defining the existence of a serious public health crisis and in managing its response. This chapter analyzes the series of events that led to a hasty and ill-considered effort to immunize all Americans against a disease whose threat was inadequately assessed. Implementation obstacles were never investigated, nor were critical constituencies consulted about their abilities and willingness to meet performance requirements necessary to immunize 200 million Americans. The failure to consider predictable implementation obstacles and plan for various contingencies resulted in a rigid plan with no room for adaptation to changing circumstances or new information.

Problems of production capacity, liability, side effects, and service delivery capacities crippled and derailed a program with unrealistic goals and ill-conceived implementation plans. Key actors were never consulted, and methods to mobilize a highly decentralized state delivery system were ignored. Although the fundamental errors derived from scientific judgments (about which considerable disagreement persists), the blundered response to these judgments demonstrates the need to ask the right questions, consider the impacts of alternative outcomes, and plan for predictable contingencies.

We conclude the chapter with the observation that scientific judgments about the seriousness of potential threats are always more or less probabilistic. Even though vaccinating millions needlessly may be better than failing to protect the population against what turns out to be a real pandemic, weighing these choices explicitly and planning for the myriad possibilities of error are central to effective management. Finally, we summarize the areas in which anticipatory actions and contingency planning appear most crucial.

CHAPTER 4: CHILDHOOD IMMUNIZATION AND THE BIAS AGAINST MANAGEMENT

Managing public health initiatives is critical to successful implementation, but public officials often have a bias against management. Indeed, policy solutions are preferred to management solutions, even when there is little indication that a change in policy is actually indicated. Political goals favor policy pronouncements when policy goals often demand attention to executive management and service delivery efforts.

When President Clinton entered office, his administration selected a problem of significant political value for its first health care effort: low rates of immunization against childhood diseases among very young children. The Clinton administration seized on this issue as a key policy target, and in doing so enunciated a policy agenda and laid out a political blueprint for a broader health care agenda. President Clinton's policy prescription lowered the cost of immunization to all children by reducing the cost of vaccine. Nevertheless, the reasons for low rates of immunization were more the result of serious and pervasive impediments to service delivery than of income constraints. Although the costs of vaccine had risen, low-income children were eligible for free community health clinic immunizations; those eligible for Medicaid could seek free care in private physicians' offices as well. Indeed, evidence suggests that income inadequacy was a small, if not unimportant, part of the problem. Nevertheless, the Vaccines for Children program, an expensive and difficult program to administer, was selected as the policy prescription.

Efforts to coordinate fragmented actors in the public health arena around discreet program delivery activities often have the greatest potential to improve public health. Policy solutions provide greater political rewards and opportunities for important symbolic victories among targeted constituencies. Management solutions are often invisible and nonpartisan, involving difficult and complicated strategies to gain the cooperation of unaccustomed allies. Moreover, problems with system management are rarely identified as the source of public health problems, largely due to natural political and institutional biases that encourage political actors to select policy solutions even when management solutions are clearly indicated. This tendency represents a serious and pervasive constraint on public health successes.

CHAPTER 5: REEMERGENT TB: SUCCESSFUL MANAGEMENT OF AN IMPOSSIBLE JOB

National rates of TB infection have declined continuously over the century, first as a result of improved standards of living and public health and later because of the discovery of effective antibiotic treatments. Although the route to discovery was impeded by scientific controversy, professional competition, and "smart" bacteria that continually mutated, effective triple antibiotic therapy made TB a treatable disease.

Since 1980, however, TB infection has been on the rise. Most observers attribute this increase to reduced public health vigilance and treatment and to a dismantlement of the public health infrastructure during the 1970s, when the number of new cases was declining. In addition, social conditions such as crowded hospitals, increases in the homeless and prison populations and in drug addiction, and a surge in immigration from areas of high incidence created environments that were hospitable to TB contagion.

By the mid-1980s, a new and far more serious form of the disease presented itself. Multiple-drug-resistant (MDR) strains of TB threatened the most vulnerable populations: the poor, the drug-addicted, the homeless, and prisoners. Conventional therapies and protocols were no longer effective, and a significant new public health service delivery approach was required.

In this chapter we explain how MDR-TB emerged, and why the initial public health response was so stalled and ineffective. Further, we explore the public management success of New York City's commissioner of health in launching an effective, coordinated, and cooperative interagency strategy to address the threat. She built a new management system to identify, treat, and track infected individuals throughout the system. This even required some treatments to be directly observed. These strategies reversed a deadly rise in serious infection, a result not achieved in cities where management of disease control was poor. Finally, we conclude with a model for public executives to apply in evaluating how difficult a programmatic response will be and for designing appropriate implementation strategies. We also elaborate general lessons of public health management and strategies for overcoming typical and predictable impediments.

CHAPTER 6: PREDICTING THE FUTURE FROM THE PRESENT: EARLY MANAGEMENT OF THE AIDS CRISIS AS A CASE OF PUBLIC MISMANAGEMENT

In this chapter we argue that there is ample evidence to indicate that our scenario is not far-fetched; indeed, it may even underestimate the difficulties that lie ahead. Historical insight and stakeholder analysis provide the basis for our conclusion that AIDS prevention and treatment policy is already characterized by typical patterns of management and political conflict and official timidity. Mismanagement and failure to anticipate predictable obstacles have needlessly undermined most of the early efforts to respond to the crisis. An analysis of federal and local activities in the early 1980s, when the AIDS crisis presented itself, demonstrates how poorly we were prepared for the political resistance that undermined policies to reduce infection, such as closing bathhouses in New York and San Francisco and needle exchanges among drug users. Further, our analysis of FDA drug review and development policy and of protease inhibitor distribution policies will show that the "cure" has been needlessly stalled by a failure to understand the public use of private interest and the limits of institutional cultures.

The social construction of AIDS has made the politics of public health exceptionally difficult, but public mismanagement has exacerbated the problematic crisis. Early AIDS policy suffered from the typical and predictable obstacles that public health officials faced in earlier crises. Success depends on even greater levels of skills, however, and few public executives appear up to the task. We believe they can do better than what our scenario plausibly predicts, which is political and managerial defeat. Using strategic skepticism and our framework to first diagnose and anticipate the probable management obstacles and to then respond in advance to circumvent or minimize them holds promise for the future.

CHAPTER 7: SCENARIO BUILDING: THE DAY AFTER AN AIDS VACCINE IS DISCOVERED

Scenario building allows executives to develop alternative visions of likely implementation events. It requires hypothesizing what can go wrong and thus provides a basis for plans to overcome likely or potential obstacles. Planning for contingencies and acting in advance to prevent predictable impediments to program implementation are critical public management tools. In this chapter we develop a probabilistic scenario of what would happen if an AIDS vaccine were discovered. The scenario develops, illustrating the predictable obstacles and suggesting the series of events likely to stall and derail any program effort maneuvering from discovery to wide-scale immunization. The scenario highlights the probable scientific, political, and economic impediments to full implementation over a one-year period, beginning with the announcement of the vaccine discovery, by hypothesizing the following activities: securing support for federal funding, planning for production and distribution, and assessing safety and effectiveness through field testing. The scenario illustrates themes that emerge in earlier chapters about the determinants of successful public health initiatives.

CHAPTER 8: CURING THE DISEASE: PROSPECTS FOR IMPROVING THE MANAGEMENT OF PUBLIC HEALTH INITIATIVES

In the final chapter, we explicate a series of principles for managing large-scale initiatives. Using the lessons from previous chapters, we identify the key features that will impede success in implementing an AIDS vaccine and derive general lessons of how energetic executives can improve the prospects for success. First, we review the methodology for the kind of scenario building we propose and identify a framework for predicting how hard it will be to develop consensus on the character of a response. To this we add general findings from our cases of the management impediments found in all large-scale initiatives to control serious diseases. In each area we suggest how preemptive action can forestall and even prevent serious resistance to consensual and cooperative action. Building interest convergence, anticipating private interests and the need for public-private partnerships in production and distribution, managing the media and public opinion by developing a strong knowledge base, and increasing incentives for intergovernmental and interagency cooperation are all necessary elements in managerial effectiveness. Second, we apply the framework to launching an AIDS vaccine program implementation strategy and review how our scenario might change under alternative actions of vigilant executives. Finally, we propose a set of generalized insights and management lessons applicable to all future public health initiatives. Our ultimate goal is to contribute enduring insights about the methods and prospects for management reform and the conditions under which it is most likely to emerge.

2

The Successful Management of Polio

INTRODUCTION

With the exception of the rare photograph of Franklin Roosevelt's leg braces, we are seldom reminded of the disease that once terrified a generation of American parents. Polio, long associated with the poor and with immigrants living in slums,[1] reached national prominence when it struck the popular patrician politician in 1921, at once changing the meaning and significance of the disease. Prior to public knowledge of Roosevelt's affliction, polio was considered a disease of the marginal, largely removed from the consciousness of most middle-class Americans even as recurring epidemics struck in the early part of the century. Like AIDS, the social construction of the disease shaped the political and scientific responses to it: by the 1950s, polio's elevated image stimulated aggressive financial investment in the development of a vaccine and the initiation of the largest immunization program in history.

Americans made a national hero of Jonas Salk, the scientist who developed the vaccine and saved thousands of children and adults from death or debilitating paralysis. Everywhere, Americans celebrated the end of polio; one commentator likened the event to the end of World War I: "Now, as in November 1918, church bells and, in many cities, trolley bells and factory sirens hailed the development, the testing, and the licensing of the Salk vaccine as the great step forward for humankind that it was."[2] While this view characterizes the public perception of a seamless flow from discovery to cure, the historical truth, as we will illustrate, is quite different. Discovery, testing, licensing, and delivery of a vaccine to millions certainly do not constitute a single event, and although the polio vaccination initiative was viewed almost universally as an unqualified success, it faced significant and typical design, implementation, and management challenges that provide important lessons for future public managers.

Specifically, the vaccine initiative was threatened by the following impediments that typify any public health enterprise: genuine scientific controversy over the safety and effectiveness of the vaccine; professional competition between scientists that compromised coordinated action; production problems and supply shortages; distribution problems that threatened the established plans for initial vaccination of high-priority groups; intergovernmental competition from conflicting strategies; misinformation spread by the media; disputes over cost issues; and low immunization rates among the poor and nonschool-age population.

The polio case was likewise unique in many ways. First, the principal player launching the effort to eradicate the disease was a private organization, the National Foundation for Infantile Paralysis (NFIP). Second, the vaccination program suffered from a primitive federal public health infrastructure and weak leadership resulting from a virtual absence of previous federal experience with public health programming. The polio immunization effort probably would not have withstood these bumps in its implementation path if it did not have widespread public support even before it was initiated. But this support was not some Hegelian "will" spontaneously developing on its own. Rather, it was carefully orchestrated over many years by the NFIP and its executive director, Basil O'Connor, whose highly specific efforts made people feel invested in the polio fight.

O'Connor's management skills were instrumental in the research, development, and implementation success of the polio vaccine. The NFIP developed a highly effective public relations effort and from the 1930s through the 1950s aggressively courted not only the financial but also the emotional support of the American public.

Perhaps NFIP's and O'Connor's most important initiative for vaccine research was the establishment of the March of Dimes fund-raising campaigns. Year after year, the March of Dimes actively sought emotional and financial support from the American public for the polio cause by developing a wide range of grassroots activities based on the efforts of a core of volunteers from all walks of life. The strategy included collecting at movie theaters, enlisting the assistance of the movie and radio industries for high-profile spokespeople, utilizing reserves of women volunteers, and generally bombarding the public with requests to contribute dimes at the movies, in train stations, during parades, and anywhere people gathered.

Those dimes added up to millions of dollars that enabled the NFIP to fund polio patient care and research. But even more important, the breadth and depth of these efforts made Americans feel connected to the process. They then came to see the March of Dimes and the NFIP as unique enough to warrant their special support, both emotionally and financially. Thus, in the face of its many implementation difficulties in the mid-1950s, the Salk vaccine was able to survive and succeed because of the public trust generated by this management strategy and despite the rather primitive public health infrastructure available at the time to guide a national vaccination program. The polio case is singular for the extraordinary public support and confidence that the vaccination program created, a public trust difficult to imagine in any modern setting.

The case of polio is both unique and instructive for future vaccinations campaigns of its scale. Although the case is more than forty years old, it remains germane. The polio vaccination initiative was the first and largest effort of its kind, almost universally viewed as an unqualified success. Even so, under the most favorable conditions of public support, the initiative faced significant and typical design, implementation, and management challenges.

Today, polio is a disease unknown to an entire generation of American children, a substantial achievement in public health policy. And although public support, carefully cultivated over several years by the National Foundation for Infantile Paralysis (NFIP), eased the difficulties encountered by the polio case, there were still significant impediments to overcome. Thus, the history of our country's first nationwide immunization effort has much to teach current students of public management. The lessons of the successes and blunders of the polio case will help construct the framework necessary to build useful scenarios that suggest the appropriate contingencies from which to design flexible policy and responsive management for future public health efforts.

THE HISTORY

One of the most striking elements of the polio case from a public policy perspective is the critical role played by the NFIP, a private organization. Prior to his presidency, Roosevelt invested two-thirds of his personal fortune into Warm Springs, Georgia, with the intention of developing it as a healing vacation spa for polio victims and their families.[3] A predecessor of the NFIP, the Warm Springs Foundation resembled a joint public-private enterprise. Roosevelt maintained an active role in publicity and used his presidential prestige to raise money for the organization: the first annual President's Birthday Ball in 1934 amassed over $1 million in donations.[4] The Birthday Balls conscripted the postmasters as organizers, and although pressing civil service employees into outside fund-raising activities is now illegal, at the time it reinforced the quasi-public nature of the foundation and added to its early financial success.[5] When Roosevelt's political fortunes declined in 1935, he announced the establishment of the NFIP as distinct from his Warm Springs Foundation.[6]

The NFIP represented philanthropy and scientific research on a large scale. Under the leadership of its president, Basil O'Connor, the NFIP developed into a highly successful venture, at first devoting its resources to assisting families with medical care expenses, then, as the foundation grew, concentrating on financing important preventive research. By 1945, its assets had grown from $3 million to $20 million, in part due to aggressive fund-raising that included a close relationship with Hollywood.[7]

By the mid-1950s, the NFIP had become a large and well-established organization. Once a vaccine was developed, the foundation carried the burden of the polio fight through costly research and extensive field trials. In addition, it supported programs for the care and rehabilitation of crippled victims of polio and training programs for orthopedists, nurses, physical therapists, and social workers. The NFIP also participated in polio education, including the funding of new textbooks for medical students and five separate international conferences that enabled American and European researchers to share information.[8]

A public health problem for more than forty years, polio grabbed serious public attention in 1952, a year when three thousand Americans died. Even more frightening, however, was the number of paralytic cases that year: 57,872.[9] While the number of its victims was relatively small compared to influenza or even the current AIDS epidemic, polio's public impact was profound. Parents worried about polio contagion from almost all forms of summer recreation: camps, lakes, swimming pools, baseball parks, and movie theaters.[10] Ironically, it was wealthy children, isolated at summer cottages away from urban areas, who became most susceptible to new epidemics, since exposure to the polio virus built lifelong immunity.[11] The social impact of polio was enduring: because the disease did not respect socioeconomic boundaries, its course appeared random, its victims tended to be young children, and the aftereffects on survivors—crippling paralysis—were heartbreakingly visible.

Polio prompted a public relations campaign of unprecedented proportions. As John Paul, a prominent polio scientist, explains in *History of Poliomyelitis:* "The effective use of propaganda techniques [by the NFIP created] public interest in poliomyelitis research as a holy quest. The image of the disease as an evil thing that must be conquered and banished forevermore took hold."[12] By the time of the national field trials of the Salk vaccine in 1954, the NFIP had developed an extensive network of volunteers through their annual March of Dimes fund-raiser. Year after year, the March of Dimes aggressively courted the emotional and financial support of the American public for the polio cause, enlisting the assistance of high-profile Hollywood spokespeople, utilizing reserves of women volunteers, and collecting at movie theaters, train stations, and parades, effectively bombarding the public with requests for dimes anywhere people gathered.[13] The dimes added up to millions of dollars that not only provided the NFIP with the resources to fund polio patient care and research but also made Americans feel invested in the polio fight.

Neither past nor present research has ever quite captured the imagination of the American public in the same way. The National Tuberculosis Association targeted a single disease and was supported by private philanthropy, much like the NFIP, but it was smaller than the foundation and lacked the vision and commanding presence of NFIP president Basil O'Connor.[14] Funding for AIDS research has likewise suffered from a lack of public support and still labors under the weight of social construction that views the disease as one caused by morally corrupt behavior, not one that strikes innocent victims.

Indeed, public support would prove to be an invaluable asset to the NFIP, especially as the foundation became embroiled in the ensuing scientific controversies. Competitive rivalries and disagreements in the scientific community, fueled in part by the NFIP's connection to media and public relations channels, would prove to be almost intractable problems throughout the discovery, testing, and mass inoculation of a vaccine.

SCIENTIFIC CONTROVERSY

One of the most bothersome problems faced by public (or private) managers of any vaccine program is the inevitable scientific controversy resulting from a new discovery and the dissemination of that discovery to the public.

Research and development of the polio vaccine was directed by the Immunization Committee, a purely nongovernmental organization of NFIP-funded scientists. The committee was characterized by deep divisions, personal competitions, discrimination, and professional norms that impeded vaccine development. The medical director, Dr. Don Gudakunst, described the group's deficiencies in a 1944 report to Basil O'Connor: "The vision of poliomyelitis research workers is sharply limited. For the most part they have narrow backgrounds . . . are self-satisfied . . . [and] jealous of prerogative."[15]

Development of a vaccine was initially constrained by the live-virus versus killed-virus debate. Jonas Salk, after working with inactivated influenza virus vaccines with senior colleague Thomas Francis Jr., believed in the safety and long-term effectiveness of a killed-virus polio vaccine, a view adamantly disputed by other virologists. For example, prominent researcher John Enders feared that a killed-virus vaccine would result in a population more, not less, vulnerable to polio; another well-respected scientist, Tom Rivers, believed a killed-virus vaccine would cause allergic reactions, even cancer; and Albert Sabin, Salk's major competitor, objected to resources being diverted to what he considered a temporary vaccine, asserting that only a live-virus vaccine would ultimately protect against polio.[16] The divisions between the NFIP and the live-virus advocates continued until at least 1966, and the debate over the effectiveness of the Salk and Sabin vaccines is ongoing.[17]

Sabin proved to be the most ardent and vocal opponent of the killed-virus vaccine, and often his professional rivalry with Salk seemed to border on personal animosity. Sabin did not keep his contentions confined to NFIP committee meetings. In fact, he often took his complaints about Salk to the wider medical community, which threatened respect for the enterprise and the positive publicity that the NFIP took years to develop. As a speaker at the 1953 annual convention of the American Medical Association, Sabin warned the audience to dismiss the rumors of Salk's progress.[18] Sabin's criticism was unceasing, as Richard Carter describes in *Breakthrough: The Saga of Jonas Salk:*

So intense were his [Sabin's] energies that he not only could attend to his own scientific tasks but also had time to become ubiquitous public analyst of Salk's problems, many of which he seemed to consider insoluble. During the difficult years of 1953 and 1954, when meaningful national field trials of the Salk vaccine depended on public confidence in the merits of the undertaking, the National Foundation found it necessary to establish a kind of intelligence network to keep itself posted on Sabin's negative utterances at medical meetings and press conferences.[19]

Sabin, of course, was developing his own vaccine and was undoubtedly concerned that the field trials were premature. However, his speculations about failures in mass production of the vaccine caused further delay by creating pressure on government officials and generating significant public skepticism.

In addition to widespread discrimination against Salk in the scientific community because of his Jewish heritage,[20] he suffered from charges that he sought glory and fame; there was some quiet satisfaction when the 1954 Nobel Prize committee for medicine announced not Salk's name but those of his scientific predecessors.[21] Salk was well aware of his reputation as an opportunist. In a conversation with Basil O'Connor, he argued: "It embarrasses me with my colleagues to have it called 'Salk Vaccine.' I'm not entitled to that kind of credit and everyone knows it . . . they think me a self-seeker."[22] Nevertheless, Salk did not need to seek publicity, even if he desired it: the NFIP frequently requested his presence for publicity events, newspapers and magazines sought interviews, and television solicited special appearances. Many believe that NFIP's cultivation of the media, so important in sustaining public support, had the unanticipated consequence of injuring Salk's standing in the scientific community. One historian described the competitive behavior of scientists as smacking of the "arena rather than the scientific laboratory."[23]

Today, disagreements still persist in the scientific community about the merit of Salk's work. The Salk vaccine requires more doses than the Sabin vaccine (which results in predictable risk of paralysis), and although many countries have eradicated polio with the Salk vaccine, its effectiveness is still disputed. Nevertheless, controversy and competition are integral and inevitable parts of any scientific endeavor, characterizing the long fight to find a cure for tuberculosis and just as alive in the current environment to develop a vaccine for HIV.[24] Fortunately, the scientific controversy over the polio vaccine, although highly contentious, did not ultimately derail vaccine development or significantly undermine public confidence, both real and possible outcomes in any major public health crisis.

PRODUCTION PROBLEMS AND SUPPLY SHORTAGES

Circumstances vary for any widespread vaccination campaign, but production problems and supply shortages are predictable when huge supplies of a carefully produced product are needed quickly. Rarely are program designers or managers in control of the means of production or the production process. Indeed, public dependence on the performance and cooperation of private industry represents a critical challenge for a mass immunization program. The challenges are significant for a number of reasons, namely: duplicating tightly controlled laboratory procedures for large-scale manufacturing requires extensive, complicated protocols, quality checks, and uniformity of timing and measurement that are difficult to maintain as the scope of production enlarges; demand almost invariably will exceed short-term supply; and short-term supply shortages (especially for diseases with a "season") create pressure on manufacturers to accelerate production, which exacerbates the already complicated transition from laboratory to large-scale production. These dynamics invariably result in production and supply problems.

Although production and supply difficulties temporarily derailed the polio vaccination program, it should be remembered that such difficulties do not necessarily result in the failure of a widespread vaccination campaign. Distribution measures can anticipate production setbacks, supply shortages, and other logistical complications endemic to vaccine production. In the polio case, the NFIP had presided over a smaller initial program in the field trials, which positioned the foundation as an ideal adviser to a wider mass vaccination program. Unfortunately, the federal government did not recognize this valuable resource and in fact failed to recognize the need for a coordinating entity as vaccine production and distribution moved to a massive scale. The limited federal efforts suffered as a result.

Prior to licensing of the vaccine for widespread distribution, statistical requirements to determine the vaccine's safety and effectiveness demanded large numbers of vaccinated and control children.[25] The massive field trial conducted by the NFIP involved 1.8 million children between the ages of six and nine and created a tremendous logistical burden for planners. The NFIP's difficulties in launching human trials were the result of inexperience with a project of such dimension, which among other considerations demanded highly orchestrated coordination in its administration: "Organizing the logistical details of the Salk vaccine field trials was like teaching a large troupe of elephants to do the mambo. . . . The Salk vaccine field trial would not only test a new vaccine, but also invent a new way to conduct those tests."[26]

In addition to scientific conflicts over the proper control groups, the NFIP faced further challenges. The difficulty in establishing and assuring uniform vaccination procedures (for instance, how many doses, at what dosages, and at what intervals) and the problem of recruiting a qualified, respected virologist willing to make the significant time commitment required to monitor and evaluate the trial results quickly consumed the NFIP scientific leadership after they announced their intention to conduct field trials. After insisting on a number of conditions, Dr. Thomas Francis, a well-respected virologist, agreed to conduct the evaluation of field trials and established a vaccine evaluation center at the University of Michigan.[27]

The project was complicated further by the burdens imposed by federalism, creating for the NFIP and Dr. Francis the overwhelming task of coordinating with school districts, local health officials, and city governments across forty-four states.[28] Dr. Francis experienced great difficulty in getting much of the paperwork to the evaluation center after the vaccines had been administered:

> [The reports] traveled a slow route from volunteer clerks at each of several field-trial clinics, to volunteer district coordinators, to overworked and sometimes unenthusiastic state and local health departments, to individual doctors and hospitals charged with the extra task of reporting on their patients while also caring for them, to research laboratories asked to master new and difficult techniques of virus analysis for a temporary project guaranteed to bring them no credit whatsoever.[29]

Later, when a vaccine was licensed, the fragmented nature of the public health infrastructure, centered around counties and small districts, would significantly impact vaccine distribution. Federal policymakers' failure to understand the necessity for a central coordinating mechanism to manage the highly decentralized medical delivery system (a result of both the federalist tradition and the unique local development of public health institutions) initially resulted in low vaccination rates and large variations in the availability and costs of vaccine among districts.

Despite manufacturing experience during field trials, supply shortages plagued the vaccination efforts throughout 1956 and 1957. In a letter to House Speaker Sam Rayburn on January 19, 1956, Secretary of Health, Education, and Welfare (HEW) M. B. Folsom asserted that the progress of the federal vaccine program rested on two factors: approval of state plans (only one state lacked a HEW-approved plan) and the rate of vaccine production. By February 1956, Folsom estimated that only "one-fourth of the total vaccine supply required for implementation of the federally aided vaccine programs" would be available for distribution.[30] In other words, even the limited federal resources given as grants to states to purchase the vaccine for public distribution exceeded supply of the vaccine.

NFIP Director O'Connor anticipated the future supply shortage during the field trials and took steps to mitigate the problem months before it was known whether the Salk vaccine was effective. He gambled that the vaccine would be both safe and effective and would create tremendous demand. Wanting to vaccinate as many children as possible once the vaccine was licensed, O'Connor ensured that there would be a ready supply after the field trials by committing $9 million of March of Dimes funds to the six vaccine manufacturers for continued production of the vaccine during the trials, guaranteeing revenue whether or not the vaccine was ever licensed.[31] In other words, O'Connor and the NFIP eliminated the risk to manufacturers who continued to produce vaccine in excess of what was needed for the field trials. His gamble paid off: the

Salk vaccine was licensed, allowing the NFIP to vaccinate millions of first and second graders, most importantly those who had received placebos during the field trials[32] before the vaccine went into general distribution. This success was clearly the result of a proactive executive willing to assume risks of significant proportions.

At least three lessons emerge from the experience of polio vaccine production. First, for any vaccine, production is complicated by the transition of environments, from a well-controlled and heavily monitored laboratory to large-scale production. Opportunities for dangerous and costly errors increase as manufacturers produce at an elevated rate to meet high demand. Second, a complicated production process coupled with high demand results in supply shortages. The Salk vaccine supply remained low for years after licensing. Finally, the inevitability of both production problems and supply shortages for any long-awaited vaccine that promises to save lives requires a centralized monitoring and coordinating mechanism at the federal level. These lessons are as applicable today to a future AIDS vaccine or a new flu vaccine as they were in the polio case forty years ago.

The polio case further teaches that the efforts and vision of one man and one private organization are inadequate to fully address the production and supply issues. Despite O'Connor's prescient and bold precautions to ensure a vaccine supply immediately available to the most vulnerable population of first and second graders, total eradication of polio required a much wider vaccination process and a much greater supply. Inoculation of the entire population required production of a magnitude that could be met by producers only several years after discovery of the vaccine.

Current parallels can be found in a similar need to overcome private market disincentives to production of an AIDS vaccine. Bold leadership, like that exhibited by O'Connor, is required to negotiate with manufacturers reluctant to make significant investments and undertake considerable risk in the discovery process for an AIDS vaccine. The proliferation of costly liability claims in recent years poses further disincentives to manufacturers and stifles risk-taking despite the potential for an enormous social good. Manufacturers may need some form of indemnification now, before discovery, in order to ensure their willingness to begin production immediately upon licensing.

THE CUTTER INCIDENT

Supply shortages were exacerbated by a breakdown in production techniques by Cutter Laboratories, a manufacturer that was not involved in the field trials. The Cutter vaccine resulted in the sudden paralysis of several children after inoculation, illustrating not only the problems of managing production but also the need for federal leadership for oversight, planning, and regulation of vaccine production and distribution. Furthermore, the Cutter incident, as this calamity came to be called, provides important lessons for crisis management.

After the field trials were successfully completed—vaccinating almost two million schoolchildren in 217 health districts across forty-four states—private manufacturers began producing the vaccine for public distribution using somewhat different production techniques than those used for the original field trials. As a result, one manufacturer, Cutter, inadvertently released a batch of vaccine containing live activated virus. During the field trials, the vaccine lots underwent three separate safety tests by three separate laboratories; however, the federal government did not ensure similarly rigid safety tests for mass production.[33]

By examining several of Cutter Laboratory's protocols, Salk determined that "some of the tests of the inactivation rate had been omitted at the plant."[34] But this determination was not made before twenty-six cases of paralytic polio occurred in children inoculated with the vaccine by April 30, 1955. In the end, "204 cases of poliomyelitis associated with Cutter vaccine [were] reported in the summer of 1955. Seventy-nine of these cases were vaccinated children, 105 their family contacts, and twenty what are called community contacts—primarily playmates of the vaccinated children. Three quarters of these people were paralyzed. Eleven died."[35] The Cutter incident provided the catalyst to push the federal government into action.

Dr. Alexander Langmuir and staff at the Centers for Disease Control (CDC) alerted public officials about the new polio cases. When it was determined that the victims had all received Cutter-manufactured vaccine, Surgeon General Leonard Scheele called for the immediate withdrawal of all Cutter vaccine but publicly stood behind Cutter Laboratories. When Scheele's appointed Technical Advisory Committee determined that Cutter had released vaccine with live virus, Scheele suspended the distribution program while insisting that the vaccine was safe.[36] These conflicting messages prompted general confusion and uneasiness in the public about the vaccine in May and June 1955.[37] To his credit, Scheele succeeded in establishing a Polio Surveillance Unit and implemented stricter testing requirements.[38] In the meantime, vaccine distribution halted, public confidence was shaken, and most of the 204 vaccinated children and their contacts suffered irreparable harm. Forty suits for damages were later settled in the California courts.[39]

The Cutter incident illustrates the necessity for comprehensive planning of vaccine production and distribution before the implementation program begins. With proper federal leadership and regulation, the Cutter incident could have been avoided.[40] Furthermore, supply problems, a function of vaccine production, were exacerbated by the increasing pressures to immunize everyone quickly. Strong demand in the face of supply shortages inevitably led to improper procedures and insufficient supervision of the production process, resulting in a contaminated vaccine supply that forced more delay and shortages. The risk of such a result is typical and predictable in programs of this scale.

FEDERAL MISMANAGEMENT: THE EXECUTIVE ROLE
IN PROGRAM IMPLEMENTATION

The federal government's mismanagement of the polio vaccine initiative is particularly instructive. In essence, there was no initial attempt to construct a preemptive plan of action despite evidence and testimony by Basil O'Connor about the need for an implementation strategy. Furthermore, the Eisenhower administration neglected to view polio as a national public health issue. Despite broad expansion of the scope of programs and activities of the federal government during the New Deal and World War II that emphasized planning and central coordination, few administration officials seemed to imagine an expanded and comprehensive federal role in public health matters. This was true even though Eisenhower had created the Department of Health, Education, and Welfare (HEW) in 1953, the first national health agency.[41]

Prior to the Cutter incident, HEW Secretary Oveta Culp Hobby maintained a hands-off approach to the polio vaccine and efforts at mass vaccination. With the support of both the American Medical Association and the American Drug Manufacturing Association and the political cover of Barry Goldwater, Hobby stressed that federal control of the vaccine would result in socialized medicine "by the back door."[42] Although she accepted responsibility for licensing the vaccine, her reputation as a staunch conservative explains her unwillingness to take a more proactive role in aggressively regulating production and managing distribution.

The Licensing Committee authorized use of the Salk vaccine during Dr. Francis's jubilant announcement of the field trial's positive results. But no one had planned for the crucial step when the vaccine moved from the controlled experimental stage into the "hurly-burly of the market place."[43] No systematic attention was given to questions of vaccine inspection or quality control; neither was there a plan for national distribution, allocation, or supervision. Since the program was to be voluntary, no initial efforts were designed to deal with issues of outreach using advertising or marketing.

Ironically, Hobby's consultant for medical affairs, Dr. Chester Keefer, was a well-respected professor previously involved in the national allocation of other lifesaving drugs initially in limited supply (for example, penicillin, streptomycin cortisone, and gamma globulin). However, no efforts were made to prepare a rationing strategy for allocation of scarce polio vaccine. Hobby's behavior threatened to imperil the entire program and seemed to be motivated more by the politics of a conservative administration than a result of ignorance: she did not support government allocation and indeed believed distribution was best handled by the private sector as a routine matter of manufacture and commerce.[44]

Although Dr. Martha M. Eliot, chief of the Children's Bureau of the Social Security Administration, approached Hobby about designing a federal plan to manage the tremendous demand for the vaccine once it proved safe and effective, she was told that "it would be best to see how the Francis report looked before trying to plan anything."[45] Reflecting the states' historic domination of public health programs, Hobby advised President Eisenhower even after licensing of the vaccine that it was best to "wait and see what the states set up, then fill in the gaps" rather than committing the federal government to spend $50 million for poor families.[46] Her neglect and ignorance of the distribution problems of a limited supply of a long-awaited, much-sought vaccine just prior to polio season constituted a managerial fiasco.

Some public commentators and journalists criticized the inaction of Hobby and the Eisenhower administration with comparisons to successful Danish and Canadian vaccination programs. Gerald Johnson's sarcastic comments in a July 1955 issue of the *New Republic* is illustrative: "Danish children who would have been doomed will not die of polio this year; but Denmark is afflicted with more or less socialized medicine, which some Americans seem to regard as a worse calamity than the deaths of a few children."[47] Another article in *U.S. News and World Report* outlined the planning and implementation success of Canada, whose officials had confronted the limitations of their own federalist system to coordinate a successful vaccination program.[48] In fact, the Canadian provincial and federal authorities had agreed to a distribution plan months before the Salk vaccine was approved and had instructed mass production of the vaccine with purchase guarantees, which facilitated immediate implementation of the plan with a significant supply when the vaccine was licensed.[49]

Insufficient federal leadership contributed to the Cutter incident through lack of oversight and had the additional effect of undermining public confidence. A Gallup poll conducted the week of June 7, 1955, revealed that only 36 percent of the people interviewed planned to be vaccinated when supplies became available.[50] Additionally, in 1958 a few manufacturers stopped production of the Salk vaccine due to what they termed "public apathy."[51] While the precise legacy of the Cutter incident and the role of federal leadership are difficult to assess, the persistence of low immunization rates suggests that public confidence suffered during the confusion of the early years after the discovery of the vaccine.

Although some commentators have blamed the Cutter incident on the NFIP's role in accelerating scientific research and generating publicity around polio and the Salk vaccine, their claims seem largely unfounded.[52] The field trials were conducted in an exemplary manner with the backing and scrutiny of respected virologists. The conclusions of the respected Dr. Francis that the vaccine used in the field trials was both safe and effective have not been seriously questioned.[53]

Shortly after the Cutter incident Hobby resigned from her job. Testifying before Congress on May 19, 1955, she admitted, "No one could have foreseen the public demand for the Salk vaccine."[54] Her wait-and-see approach to vaccination management provides a stunning example of federal mismanagement that need not be repeated. Hobby's belief and trust in the superiority of the private sector's invisible hand, coupled with her lack of appreciation for the problems and demands of vaccine management, were responsible for her inappropriate reactive posture that prevented swift implementation of a vaccine program. Despite Eisenhower's cabinet meeting clashes with Hobby and his rhetoric that no child should be denied the vaccine due to lack of resources, he ultimately stood by his HEW secretary.[55] Since it became clear that Hobby did not seem to think that there were *any* national health issues, Eisenhower's stance must be viewed as a major leadership and managerial failure.

There may be reason to judge Scheele's handling of the Cutter incident less harshly. He inherited a situation that was exacerbated by initial lack of leadership. In fact, Scheele's refusal to designate the vaccination program a disaster and blame either Cutter Laboratories or the Eisenhower administration preserved the credibility of the effort and may have saved the Salk vaccine.[56] Nonetheless, he resigned from his job a year after Hobby's resignation.

The Cutter incident reveals how the rigid protection of a political ideology can impede the swift eradication of a disease. Hobby's failure to view polio primarily as a national public health concern, instead framing the issue in ideological terms, contributed to the debacle and the resultant public mistrust and initial low inoculation rates. A similar tendency can be seen in the AIDS debate, when political ideology supersedes public health concerns and confounds federal management decisions. The Cutter incident demonstrates the potential costs of the lack of federal leadership and further serves as a stark reminder of the powerful role the media plays in any large-scale national public health program.

THE MEDIA'S ROLE

Public health, unlike most areas of public policy, depends on expert judgments of a scientific nature often inaccessible to the general public. In the face of inevitable scientific controversy, individual citizens rely heavily on external sources of knowledge and interpretation to define their views, and the media plays a critical role in shaping them.

Due to the sophisticated publicity and fund-raising efforts of the NFIP, public perception of the polio vaccine effort was initially quite favorable. Enamored of Jonas Salk and the fight to eliminate polio, public support and trust for the effort were strong. The media's attention to the effort helped generate public demand and support for the licensed vaccine.

However, the case of polio is further instructive in highlighting the potential opportunities and risks that the media poses for the management of public health programs. News coverage prior to the field trials of the Salk vaccine revealed the media's capacity and, indeed, tendency for sensationalism. The media's role in aiding and impeding the progress of polio immunization suggests that skilled actors must anticipate media interests and incentives and need to have a strategy for media management clearly in place when program implementation is planned.

The NFIP's cultivation of the media was criticized heavily by researchers both during and after the development of the Salk vaccine.[57] In addition to drawing attention and distinction to Jonas Salk, the media's participation and handling of the release of the Francis Report on the results of the field trials evoked special vehemence from scientists. As Dr. Thomas Rivers, head of the NFIP's Virus Research Committee, describes: "The newspaper people and photographers created a madhouse. I don't know when I have seen such wild people. Talk about putting frosting on the cake, these boys and girls put Christmas trees on with the frosting."[58] The media's attention to the development of the polio vaccine was, however, essential to the NFIP for fund-raising purposes to heighten awareness about the importance of polio. This publicity was carefully managed as early as the 1930s, when the media facilitated Roosevelt's personal crusade by redefining the nature and importance of the disease. Furthermore, the cultivation of the media by the NFIP was crucial later for handling its subsequent attacks on the vaccine program.

The capacity of the media to damage public health initiatives was demonstrated most dramatically by the popular commentator Walter Winchell, who attacked the Salk vaccine and the NFIP just prior to the commencement of widespread field trials of the vaccine. Paul de Kruif, a disgruntled former NFIP scientist, had begun spreading rumors that Salk's vaccine was lethal. Kruif took his claims to Walter Winchell, and on April 4, 1954, just weeks before the field trial was scheduled to begin, Winchell called the vaccine a killer on broadcast news. He also published his accusations in a syndicated newspaper column. One week later, Winchell went on to accuse the NFIP of "stockpiling little white coffins in depots around the country" for the children who would die in the field trials.[59]

Although it is difficult to measure precisely the impact of Winchell's comments, negative publicity can partially explain the withdrawal of eighteen thousand children from the field trials.[60] Nevertheless, public fear of the disease, coupled with trust in the NFIP and faith in Jonas Salk, kept most participants committed to the field trials throughout the crucial three months. The NFIP had labored to build public confidence and had invested the American people in the polio cause and Jonas Salk. The NFIP emphasized the historic role played by the children participating in the field trials, dubbing them "Polio Pioneers," while Salk was touted as a scientific Horatio Alger who constituted "an inspiring example of a poor immigrant's son who had made good."[61] After the success of the field trials, Salk's popularity reached an unprecedented level for a scientific researcher. Thus, a calculated investment in public relations and media management at the outset created an environment able to withstand an attack even by a popular journalist that, in other circumstances, might have resulted in panic and program failure.

Despite high levels of public confidence in Salk, however, the Cutter incident provided a much more difficult challenge to NFIP publicists since reports of polio contraction from the vaccine proved to be true. Surgeon General Scheele sought to mitigate media sensationalism during the Cutter incident with repeated assurances that the vaccine was safe. However, it is unclear whether this assuaged the public or only confused the issue, since he was suspending all inoculations while testifying to the vaccine's safety. There were many critics of Scheele's handling of the entire Cutter incident, including the *New York Times*: "The result of all the confusion has been twofold. First, the nation is now badly scared. Never before have reports of the number of polio cases been so widely publicized and so carefully studied. Millions of parents fear that if their children don't get the vaccine they may get polio, but if they do get the vaccine, it might give them polio."[62] Senator Estes Kefauver called the vaccination program "one of the worst bungled programs" he had ever seen.[63] A May 13, 1955, article in *U.S. News and World Report* began: "The truth is turning out to be that Americans expected too much from the Salk vaccine against polio."[64] Numerous newspaper and magazine articles during the summer of 1955 questioned the Salk vaccine's safety. Clearly, the public was confused.

A converse argument could be made, however, that if more of the vaccine had been tainted with live virus because of widespread but improper production techniques, Scheele would have been celebrated for shutting down the program entirely and protecting public health. Certainly, his actions were exemplary, if only because he assumed responsibility and took control of an adverse situation, which no one else in government seemed willing to do.

Still, Scheele's shutting down of the vaccination program halted production, which increased supply problems. When initial CDC reports surfaced that some people had contracted polio from the vaccine, manufacturers who were initially unaware that Cutter was using different techniques to inactivate the virus worried that they too were producing a defective vaccine.[65] Doctors who were administering polio shots to friends and family in addition to small children telephoned manufacturers in a panic.[66] It was several days before the CDC traced all of the polio cases to one manufacturer, Cutter Laboratories, and still longer for Salk to examine their procedures to determine the problem. The federal government was equally implicated for failing to monitor the vaccine lots properly.

The media certainly provides important information and education, often performing a public service. Throughout the development of the vaccine and Cutter incident there was much responsible reporting that sought to clarify issues and inform the public. Although public confidence was damaged by both the Winchell attack and the Cutter incident, the NFIP had consciously built a great deal of public trust and support that served to mitigate the negative effects of the media. The public's disillusionment and confusion during the Cutter controversy may have been unavoidable, but the lessons are instructive for future endeavors. The media must be educated throughout any extensive and complicated vaccine program about the nature of both the virus and the vaccine to avoid unnecessary sensationalism. Effective management of the media requires an understanding of their role, a consistent and well-managed strategy for media relations, and systematic attention to accommodating their needs for timely and accurate information. Such management served New York City well as it confronted the crisis of reemergent tuberculosis in 1992 (see Chapter 5).

VACCINE DISTRIBUTION DIFFICULTIES

Determining what groups should be given priority for immediate inoculation was not difficult in the case of polio: young children were the disproportionate victims of the paralyzing and life-threatening disease. But, as the NFIP and local governments learned, merely setting that priority, even in a climate of consensus, would not translate into adherence to the priority system.

In an effort to inoculate as many children as possible, the NFIP established a priority system for vaccine distribution. The twenty-seven million doses were earmarked first for the Polio Pioneers who were given placebos in the field trials; second, for all other Polio Pioneers as booster shots; and third, for all first and second graders.[67] Distribution problems started, however, before the NFIP received their vaccine doses. Again, the lack of federal control or supervision resulted in the misdistribution of thousands of doses of vaccine intended for children, the most vulnerable population.

The siphoning off of valuable and limited vaccine supplies could have been predicted. Without any federal enforcement, priority systems were easily violated. In fact, "although the National Foundation was still without enough vaccine for its own program among the schoolchildren, hundreds of thousands of vials of the stuff were turning up in peculiar places. More than half a million doses went into commercial or other inappropriate channels before the Foundation got what it had contracted for."[68] In addition to reports of physicians inoculating adult friends and family members, stockholders from Cutter Laboratories received coupons for free immunizations, while Cuba received two thousand doses of Parke-Davis vaccine.[69]

Despite these problems, the NFIP did an extraordinary job of providing free vaccines and vaccinating millions of children, all with privately donated money. The foundation's success could have been used as a template for a larger national effort to completely eradicate polio. Unfortunately, O'Connor's plan for "centralized purchase of large amounts of vaccine at a reasonable price, rapid distribution of the vaccine for free inoculation on a mass scale, and first service to those most susceptible to paralysis"[70] did not serve as a model for a federal program.

The Eisenhower administration did not begin discussions about any vaccine program until April 14, 1955, when the president directed HEW Secretary Oveta Hobby to report to him on the best means of assuring equitable distribution of the vaccine.[71] Manufacturers voluntarily agreed to establish a system of allocation among the states based on the number of children in each state.[72] In contrast to Hobby's ideological rigidity, President Eisenhower showed room for flexibility on the issue, calling the threat of polio an emergency that required immediate action.[73]

Still, the administration seemed to have no sense of the potential abuses of an unmonitored distribution system, perhaps because of inadequate briefings by program executives. A product in such great demand is ripe for violations of a priority system, even when the priority population is young children. Furthermore, once the federal government assumed a role in the eradication of polio, the issues of who would pay and how much came to the forefront.

COST

Paying for the polio vaccine pitted conservatives against liberals, medical societies against public health services, providers against distributors. With no significant public precedent for universal free access, Secretary Hobby had to confront issues of how much the vaccine should cost and who should bear the expense. The NFIP's program of inoculating first and second graders provided one model. O'Connor provided the vaccine free and refused to allow physicians to charge for inoculations despite objections from some medical societies.[74] Richard Carter estimates that "it would have cost Washington less than $100 million to provide the National Foundation with enough vaccine for all elementary school children not already covered by the Foundation program."[75]

However, the affordability of a vaccination program to eliminate polio was not the primary issue according to members of the Eisenhower administration. Hobby, conservatives within the Republican Party, and local medical societies viewed government involvement in the vaccination program as a step toward socialized medicine.[76] The question was not whether government *could* afford to provide free vaccinations to all citizens, but if it *should* preempt the private health care market. In the end, the Eisenhower administration and Congress agreed that the federal government should intervene on the behalf of the poor. On May 27, 1955, the Eighty-fourth Congress passed the Poliomyelitis Vaccination Assistance Act, which provided grants to "assist States in assuring that no child is deprived of an opportunity for immunization against poliomyelitis because of inability to pay the costs of vaccination."[77]

The purpose of the legislation clearly was not to facilitate eradication of polio but to ensure that poor children would not be deprived of the opportunity for vaccination. In other words, the Poliomyelitis Vaccination Assistance Act framed the issue as one of fairness and equality of opportunity, not of public health. Unfortunately, neither Congress nor the administration examined the cost of treating polio as a public health threat or organized public efforts for mass inoculation; in the end, the legislation's stated goals were not achieved.

Continued debate over the financing of protease inhibitors for HIV and AIDS cases in the states reflects similar tensions: while policy advocates may focus the debate around cost/benefit ratios, the real objection may actually involve a judgment about the appropriateness of government intervention. It should be no surprise when a similar phenomenon occurs with the development of an AIDS vaccine. The rhetoric may focus on costly government programs or the inherent fairness or unfairness of distributing costs across all taxpayers, but the underlying issue will be determining the proper role of government and private medicine.

Again, the polio case proves instructive for future vaccination program managers, as issues of cost are often intricately bound up with disagreements on the proper role of government. Opponents of a "costly" federal program did not apply a cost-benefit analysis to governmental action. If the benefits of eliminating polio had been compared to costs of providing free mass immunizations, administrators and legislators may have made a very different decision and supported mass inoculation. Instead, the debate over cost was framed around the issues of government intervention and threats of socialized medicine.

OUTREACH

Typically, the poor and marginalized in society are the least likely consumers of preventive health care, which to this day remains a pressing problem in ensuring full immunizations against childhood diseases. Polio immunization was no exception. The goal of mass immunization in the swiftest possible manner was never explicitly pursued: the Poliomyelitis Vaccination Assistance Act did not provide the means to ensure that every child would have an opportunity for immunization, as it stated, regardless of economic status. Although the federal government provided grants to states to purchase the vaccine, no provisions were made for doctor or administration fees.[78]

Manufacturers set a retail price of $6 for three shots of the polio vaccine. Even with this cost underwritten by the federal program, nothing precluded doctors from demanding and collecting fees for their services. Furthermore, though private physicians could obtain three shots of the vaccine from the manufacturer for only $3.50, county medical societies made it clear that the patient would nevertheless pay $2 for each shot plus the regular fee for an office visit, which typically averaged $5. The total price of immunization would therefore average $21 per child,[79] which represented a sizable expense at the time, especially for low-income families.

Even in states that established public clinics, equal access was often illusory. According to the 1960 census, the majority of the poor in the United States were dispersed across rural areas, and since public clinics were often located in central—in other words, urban—locations, the rural poor confronted significant barriers of cost and inconvenience.[80]

Despite the tremendous public demand, vaccine supplies were limited, and immunization rates remained low throughout the late 1950s, particularly among nonschool-age children and adults ages twenty to forty.[81] This fact was terribly troubling and mystifying to those who had spent tremendous energy combating polio: "For the scientists, doctors, and fund-raisers who had spent their careers helping polio victims and searching for ways to conquer the disease, the most frustrating adjustment to the post-vaccine era was the realization that people were neglecting to get their shots of Salk vaccine, now that it was available."[82]

Federal efforts did not create equal opportunity for the poor, but even more important, the emphasis on *opportunity* in the Poliomyelitis Vaccination Assistance Act seems especially misplaced. The language essentially dictates that providing the opportunity for access to the vaccine was sufficient—with no further mandate on outreach. If the federal government and the states had adopted the goal of inoculating as many children as possible instead of merely providing opportunities for inoculation, outreach necessarily would have played a much greater role in vaccination programs.

The polio immunization effort demonstrates the importance of program management and design in ensuring an optimal transition from the discovery to the cure. Providing opportunity by subsidizing the cost of a vaccine is only the first step. The crucial next step is outreach, which must be an integrated goal of any vaccination program, ensuring that at-risk segments of the population, like younger than school-age poor children, receive the vaccine. Effective outreach requires a service delivery system that is accessible, adequately staffed, and designed to be responsive to the special needs of the multiple populations being served. The controllable barriers to vaccination are access and cost. Any directed effort at mass vaccination not only must reduce these barriers in the passive sense of providing equal opportunity for rich and poor but also educate, encourage, and promote widescale participation even among traditionally reluctant populations through a well-managed service delivery effort. Current advocates of the Clinton administration's Vaccines for Children program continue to debate the relative merits of these elements of program implementation and management (see Chapter 4).

PROGRAM SUCCESS

Despite considerable impediments, mass immunization was ultimately achieved, which ensured universal protection from polio in the United States. Some of the hindrances were the result of ideological disputes within the Eisenhower administration about the proper role of public intervention; inexperience, inadequate management, and implementation planning posed additional challenges. Executive discretion was clearly constrained by prevailing public values and political ideology: Hobby erred in part as a result of her political views on the limitations of the government's role, an ideology that was widely shared at the time. Whatever the correct distribution of blame, the uneven and problematic vaccination program ultimately resulted in severe public criticism of government performance and a change in the view of government's role in regulating the production of biomedical products. Nevertheless, the success of the NFIP's efforts encouraged the growth of national health and research efforts in the 1960s.

The management lessons from the polio case are clear. Indeed, virtually all the line decisions required to implement the polio vaccine program also confronted federal executives responsible for the swine flu vaccination program; however, in contrast to the swine flu immunization initiative, directors of the polio immunization initiative learned and adapted by confronting a near catastrophe with the Cutter incident. Those who are ultimately in charge of implementing an AIDS vaccine program will have much to learn from the lessons of history. Even so, the obstacles they are bound to confront will be more recalcitrant and numerous,[83] and systematic management planning will be even more critical to program success.

CONCLUSION: THE LESSONS OF POLIO

The polio vaccination program, as it developed at both the federal and state levels, is rich in lessons for public managers of future public health initiatives, especially an AIDS vaccine program. The experience of polio and, as will be discussed later, a number of other large-scale vaccine and treatment programs demonstrate the importance of anticipating and planning for a common set of management obstacles, any one of which is capable of seriously undermining success. Public health managers should expect to confront the following:

- inevitable controversy and competition within the scientific community;
- production problems and supply shortages;
- the threat of media sensationalism and misinformation;
- distribution and rationing problems;
- financing issues and debates on the appropriate role of government and the private market; and
- the necessity for public education and active outreach to diverse populations.

If future public managers fail to anticipate and plan for these and other typical and predictable problems in program implementation (for example, the establishment of a priority system during limited supplies and the need for aggressive outreach), they will needlessly compromise public health and program effectiveness.

Complicated political and operational issues posed by attempting new but potentially lifesaving interventions obviously have unpredictable elements. Knowing whether a scientific discovery will prove ultimately effective, safe, and justified in cost is only partially answered by even the best and well-managed research protocols. Certainly, risk and uncertainty are important operating elements in any new human endeavor; being entirely averse to risk, however, is one of the surest obstacles to success.

The key recognition, as Gordon Chase so wisely reminds us, is predicting risks and knowing the level of difficulty inherent in achieving success.[84] One method of identifying probable obstacles is through the use of a framework for predicting these obstacles from previous efforts; the polio experience is one such case (the swine flu vaccine program, the childhood immunization program, and the current efforts to eliminate tuberculosis are additional cases we will consider). A final vehicle for prediction is scenario writing, which provides a strong basis for anticipating the level of difficulty in achieving success and suggests some set of remedies for anticipated obstacles that could be taken prophylactically. Thus, the management lessons from polio form the first, generalized list of common obstacles that will be discussed in the chapters that follow.

3

The Swine Flu Immunization Program

INTRODUCTION

The polio effort's extraordinary success created a profound public respect for the potential of organized science and medicine to reduce human suffering and engage in socially important activities. Despite the missteps and obstacles resulting from inexperience and lack of federal leadership, the program remains part of a great American success story. With polio as a still recent memory and the subsequent development of a highly capable federal public infrastructure, the Ford administration's swine flu debacle represents a particularly illustrative case of a failure of management. Clearly, much had changed over the ensuing twenty years; numerous perceived failures of public policy and authority—the War on Poverty, the Vietnam War, and the Watergate scandal—undermined public trust in the competency and legitimacy of public enterprises. But the federal public health system was in the hands of sophisticated executives supported by a well-developed infrastructure, a fact that provided considerable promise for a preventive health agenda. It is all the more curious, then, that the swine flu immunization program stands even today as a prototype for policy errors and management failure.

In 1976, when four soldiers at Fort Dix, New Jersey, were found to be infected by a new and potentially dangerous strain of flu, the aggressive response was firmly in the hands of a complex and capable federal public health infrastructure with a mandated policy of preventive medicine.[1] The ability of this new and modern public health infrastructure was tested, and most observers expected a sound and effective result. Indeed, it was the assumed competence and capacity of the federal public health system that drove the decision to undertake an ambitious preventive medicine approach to the anticipated epidemic.

Even a large and well-financed public health infrastructure, however, proved more of an obstacle than an asset, given multiple directives and an unforgiving timetable. As such, the swine flu case reveals, to some extent, the gap between the goals of public health and the limited capacity of its management. For this reason, it continues to serve as a classic example in the history of public policy-making and management for the rich lessons it provides about the opportunities and limitations of public administration.[2]

In hindsight, the swine flu immunization program can still boast a significant success: forty million people were immunized in less than ten weeks.[3] This success, however, is overshadowed by a dubious legacy of controversy, hype, and mismanagement. Ironically, the credibility of the public health system was saved by the failure of any real threat to materialize: not a single related case of swine flu virus ever appeared in the population. Even so, the costly and ill-conceived implementation plan ultimately compromised the Ford administration's reputation.

The following significant challenges characterized the swine flu case: the limitations of federalism underlying the existing public health infrastructure; production and distribution problems caused by public dependence on private markets; manufacturers' concerns about liability and indemnification; the media's role as public educator; public mistrust; and the culture and politics of science.

In many respects, these challenges parallel, even replicate, those faced by the polio program, such as production and distribution problems, supply shortages, and a complex intergovernmental system of public health delivery. Other challenges, such as liability and indemnification, exaggerated goals, and media management, are unique to the swine flu case but have continued relevance to the AIDS crisis and other emerging disease threats. In light of today's public health concerns, particularly those surrounding an effective response to the AIDS crisis, such challenges are likely to reemerge. A successful response will depend ultimately on the ability of program managers to anticipate and identify key challenges and develop responsive contingency plans.

BACKGROUND: 1918 PANDEMIC INFLUENCES 1976 DECISIONS

Epidemiological evidence and hypotheses about swine flu existed long before the discovery of the infected Fort Dix soldiers. In 1918, a worldwide pandemic of the most virulent strain of influenza ever recorded (antigenically related to swine flu) contributed to the deaths of twenty million people, over half a million in the United States alone. Although bacterial pneumonia was responsible for a great many of these deaths, an unknown number succumbed to the flu itself.[4] The pandemic was characterized by a relatively mild wave in the spring, proceeded by a more virulent second wave, followed by a less severe third wave in the spring of 1919. Whereas mortality rates in the first wave were concentrated in children and the elderly, victims in the second wave were between eighteen and forty years old, the strongest and healthiest age group. And while as many as 40 percent of those afflicted were under thirty-five years old, only 10 percent of seventy-year-olds showed clinical infection, suggesting immunity through previous exposure.[5]

Scientists have used these data, in addition to further information gathered in the outbreaks of 1946, 1957, and 1968, to hypothesize occurrences and effects of influenza pandemics, to clarify the significance of antigenic shift (a natural occurrence that slightly alters the strain periodically and confounds immunization strategies), and to promote a cyclical theory of influenza outbreaks approximately every eleven to twelve years.[6] In 1975, one of these scientists, Dr. Edwin D. Kilbourne, published *The Influenza Viruses and Influenza,* which predicted an upcoming outbreak of a new strain of influenza in the late 1970s. According to one researcher, Kilbourne's speculation was widely known in virologic and public health circles and was taken very seriously in 1976, since it not only seemed to explain the appearance of influenza over the previous thirty years but also seemed to fit with the most recent information on the biology of the influenza virus.[7] In addition, since many survivors of the 1918 outbreak were still living, firsthand accounts of widespread sickness and death contributed to the body of knowledge about swine flu.

Thus, when an investigation into the death of one of the Fort Dix soldiers confirmed the presence of the swine flu virus, the Centers for Disease Control (CDC) quickly instructed the HEW Advisory Committee on Immunization Practices (ACIP), a panel of government and private experts in immunology, to make recommendations on vaccines for the upcoming flu season. Among these experts was Dr. Kilbourne, whose reported assessment was, interestingly, that the new virus was "an unlikely candidate for the next influenza pandemic."[8] Although the ACIP determined that the odds of a serious threat were between 2 and 20 percent and recommended vaccine production and an administration plan, the committee did not state whether persons should actually be immunized.[9] The committee's apparent lack of interest in program strategies could be regarded as a cautious wait-and-see posture at this early stage.

SWINE FLU PROGRAM SOLD ON PREVENTIVE MEDICINE PHILOSOPHY

In contrast to the ACIP's cautious speculations, Dr. David Sencer, director of the CDC in Atlanta, expected a much more virulent outbreak. Sencer presented a memorandum in an emergency session with HEW Secretary David Mathews and Assistant Secretary Theodore Cooper, which recommended a national immunization program and outlined the ensuing responsibilities of the CDC, an agency under HEW. Mathews was highly impressed by the report and further exaggerated the necessity and feasibility of a federal swine flu response in his recommendations to President Ford. When Sencer conducted a telephone poll of ACIP committee members concerning the memorandum, most of the members abandoned their initial caution and expressed support for the mass immunization program.[10] Sencer found further advocates for his position when he handpicked a blue-ribbon panel of his supporters to meet with President Ford and discuss the government's response to the possibility of a national epidemic.

There was near unanimous support among the committee members for the implementation of a universal immunization program, and for the first time, the CDC believed it had the time and resources to provide a lifesaving preventive health service to the nation. Because the mission of the CDC was preventive health services, Sencer believed that swine flu vaccination was the challenge to which the CDC, and indeed the federal public health infrastructure, must respond. At the briefing, Ford's blue-ribbon panel recommended *without dissent* that the government undertake a massive program to inoculate the citizenry against swine flu. Although opposing opinions could be found in both science and government, Sencer excluded them from the discussion.[11]

Ford's decision, then, was influenced by the blue-ribbon panel's belief in the threat of an epidemic on a scale similar to 1918 and was reinforced by the conviction that the federal government not only *should* respond but also *could* respond with a nationwide immunization program. His decision was further informed by election-year politics: as the incumbent president, bold action in the public's interest would be an asset to his waning reelection campaign. Ford's televised announcement of a national swine flu immunization program occurred the day after Reagan's surprise victory in the North Carolina primaries.

Sencer, Mathews, and Cooper communicated a sense of urgency and an optimism about the plausibility of a federal response, which magnified Ford's interest in a full-blown swine flu immunization effort and provided an unrealistic impression of what the federal government could hope to accomplish. Ford was clearly ill advised and was not briefed on the predictable serious side effects inherent in any immunization program. Neither was he properly informed in advance about other challenges he was likely to face, such as liability insurance and especially opposing expert opinion. Consequently, Ford's credibility suffered throughout the rest of the campaign.

Earlier in the program design, however, Sencer had considered similar challenges in a memorandum to Cooper and Mathews. The memorandum proposed four possible strategies: no action; a minimum response consisting of "a limited federal role with primary reliance on delivery systems now in place and on spontaneous, non-governmental action"; a program based on "virtually total government responsibility for the nationwide immunization program"; and a combined approach that would "take advantage of the strengths and resources of both the public and private sectors."[12] Sencer's recommendation, supported by Cooper, was the combined approach, and he anticipated only two disadvantages to this strategy: the required federal expenditure of $134 million and the "greatest possibility of some people being needlessly re-immunized."[13]

Sencer implied reasons for the rejection of the three other alternatives in listing their disadvantages:

> There is little assurance that vaccine manufacturers will undertake the massive production effort that would be required. . . . There would be no control over the distribution of vaccines to the extent that they are available; the poor, the near poor, and the aging usually get left out. . . . Breakdowns would occur because the program is beyond the scope of official [government] agencies . . . [and] a totally "public" program is contrary to the spirit and custom of health care delivery in this country.[14]

He therefore promoted a one-sided case for the public/private immunization program by stressing its comparative lack of serious disadvantages, which, as we will discuss, emerged nonetheless.

VULNERABLE PROGRAM BEGINS LATE IN FLU SEASON

According to the Sencer memorandum, program implementation involved a collaborative approach from both public and private health officials and a narrow schedule that discouraged hesitation or adaptation of the program design. At the federal level, Sencer and the CDC were joined by Dr. John Seal, scientific director of the National Institute for Allergy and Infectious Diseases (NIAID) under the National Institutes of Health (NIH) and the Public Health Service (PHS), and Dr. Harry Meyer Jr., director of the Bureau of Biologics (BoB) under the Food and Drug Administration (FDA). Parke-Davis, Merck Sharp & Dohme, Wyeth, and Merrell National were responsible for manufacture and distribution of the vaccine as well as the provision of supplies and equipment, voluntary assistance, and liability insurance coverage.

If immunization was to begin before the next flu season in September and conclude before winter, there were only five months to manufacture,[15] test, and deliver the first of 200 million doses of the vaccine.[16] According to HEW targets, production and distribution called for 8 million doses by July, 120 million by September, and the full 200 million by the end of October.[17] Since it took at least two weeks for the vaccination to produce adequate antibodies to an injected antigen, it was imperative that manufacturers adhered to the strict schedule to ensure protection before the onset of the flu season. A further complicating factor concerned the nature of the swine flu virus: unlike the polio, measles, or smallpox vaccines, variety and shifts among flu virus antigens reduce vaccine shelf life. Thus, neither manufacturers nor distributors ever want to stock large amounts of flu vaccine, and as a result they plan their production schedules carefully.

The CDC established a PERT (Program Evaluation Review Technique, originally used for weapons systems) system that charted relations among critical steps in the program implementation process to avoid bottlenecks. However, not long after Ford's announcement of a 100 percent goal (with 95 percent acceptable), the CDC discovered that vaccine manufacturers could not possibly supply the 200 million doses required before the flu season began.[18]

Roughly six months passed between Ford's announcement and the beginning of the mass immunization program on October 1, 1976. The program design was changed three times: first to conform to delays in vaccine manufacturing, then to retest results of field trials to include a second dose for children (who had painful reactions to the single dose during the field trials), and finally to override indemnification and consent problems through legislation. Ten days after program implementation, in which over one million adults were immunized, three elderly residents of Pittsburgh died after receiving immunizations at the same clinic.[19] The next day, the Allegheny County Health Department, responsible for the Pittsburgh region, suspended flu shots; nine states followed. For the first time since commencement, CDC officials publicly detailed the vaccination risks: ten to twelve deaths per 100,000 in the elderly population were expected daily.[20] To discourage further suspensions, the first family received televised flu shots.[21]

In the third week of November, the seventh week of the program, an observant physician in Minnesota reported a case of ascending paralysis associated with the swine flu vaccination to the state immunization program officer. Reports from other states soon followed; ultimately, one thousand cases were reported. Although little was known about the paralysis, Guillain-Barré syndrome, the statistical relationship to swine flu immunization[22] was sufficient to suspend the program at the federal level nine months after Ford's announcement.[23]

In January 1977, the Carter administration moved into the White House, and appointments were transferred at all federal departments. The new HEW director, Joseph Califano, declared a halt in further production of the swine flu vaccine and announced the replacement of David Sencer as the director of the CDC. The swine flu immunization program officially ended after only immunizing roughly 22 percent of the population.[24]

The cessation of the program was the result of multiple management and implementation difficulties. Compounding policy-makers' failure to consider various implementation problems was their additional failure to plan for diverse contingencies. No effort was made to consider how they might modify the program should certain obstacles—such as production and distribution delays or side effects, such as Guillain-Barré syndrome—foil the initial strategy. Although policy-makers in the Pentagon and Federal Emergency Management Agency routinely plan for a host of contingencies, policy-makers involved in the swine flu immunization initiative produced a rigid plan with no room for adaptation to changing circumstances or new information. The explicit sense of urgency that characterized the early stages of program development discouraged a more thorough, cautious approach; according to Cooper, "the flu season would have come and gone" had planners devoted more time to the program design.[25] Hence, critical and typical problems emerged, and anticipatory actions were ignored.

LACK OF INTERAGENCY COORDINATION

The failure to include significant representatives from agencies and offices whose participation and support would be critical to the program's success was a fundamental weakness in federal management. The delegation of responsibilities among various agencies in an integrated federal public health system to ensure a comprehensive response mechanism depends on informed participation of all relevant agencies. Nevertheless, of the seven scientists and government officials responsible for briefing President Ford, the entire federal public health system was represented solely by the HEW Department and its component, the CDC, both of which actively promoted a single agenda. Curiously absent were representatives from the Office of General Counsel, the Office of Management and Budget, and Congress, all of whom would later be called upon for key decisions.[26]

Although the bulk of program responsibilities fell to the CDC's discretion, its activities were limited by strategies adopted by HEW, the FDA, and state and local health offices. Considerable confusion accompanied the assignment of management responsibilities. For example, Sencer appointed Donald Millar, CDC director of the Bureau of State Services, to the position of program manager, while Cooper conferred the same title on Dr. Delano Meriwhether, special assistant to the assistant secretary for health at HEW.[27]

Responsibilities overlapped among the BoB, the NIAID, and the CDC. The NIAID, an HEW subsidiary, was in charge of expanding the scope of influenza research.[28] However, funds were instead channeled into a computerized surveillance system at the CDC that monitored disease indicators around the clock. The BoB, under the FDA, was responsible for testing the vaccine prior to its release, including laboratory analysis and clinical trials to ascertain the appropriate dose of vaccine and to document vaccine potency, safety, purity, and effectiveness. The overlapping chain of command must have been frustrating to program officials as well as outside observers, especially as accountability became an issue.

Intergovernmental competition and conflicting strategies among agencies exposed weaknesses in management, especially in the failure to enlist the support and cooperation of public health authorities at the state and local levels. In contrast to the uniformity that contributed to the polio vaccination program's success, swine flu initiatives varied dramatically by state and locality, exacerbated by the fragmentation of responsibilities among federal agencies. Further, federal officials in the chain of command acted independently of other agencies' efforts, and as a result issues concerning direct implementation were easily considered someone else's responsibility. In the event of an AIDS vaccine, the lack of unified leadership at the highest levels would surely create similar fragmentation among both government providers and state and local delivery systems.

FRAGMENTATION AT STATE AND LOCAL LEVELS

Varied responses from state and local health agencies threatened, and eventually undermined, the success of the swine flu program. Delays in delivery and low levels of support from private medicine, other health care providers, and volunteers discouraged state and local health structures from fully implementing federal program strategies.

Sencer required state and local health offices to submit immunization plans that would be financed by federal grants.[29] Some plans were statewide, while others were county by county; some called for injection guns for a few roving teams, while others sought supplies for many; some relied on public health facilities, schools, and hospitals, while others implemented corporate support. Although state and local providers required discretion to design plans responsive to local conditions, they lacked clear guidelines that would have connected each response to the federal program. Since state and local planners interpreted program goals as they perceived them, subsequent federal evaluation was almost impossible.

Among state and local project directors who submitted immunization plans to the CDC and received project grants to assist in implementation, some "clearly evidenced a lack of serious intent to conduct mass immunization programs."[30] Several directors underestimated or openly rejected the anticipated threat of a swine flu epidemic. As one director instructed local health officers: "Let's not encourage people to get shots, [we] can't really say [the shots are] . . . absolutely necessary, and you don't need more work than CDC will generate for you. But, must push to inform [the] public that they will have reactions and may even get the flu in spite of [the] campaign."[31]

Although forty million vaccinations were administered nationwide, immunization efforts varied widely from state to state, and high success rates were only achieved where local leadership was strong and supportive of federal goals. If there indeed had been a genuine threat of a swine flu epidemic, the widely varying success rates would have been a major policy failing of the program. Such was precisely the result of more than a century of smallpox vaccination efforts that relied almost entirely on the varying commitment and implementation skills of local and state departments of health.[32] Future federal programs that rely on states for implementation must be designed to anticipate widely varying levels of support and include proper incentives or sanctions for compliance. Moreover, each design must conform to specific guidelines that allow evaluators to assess effectiveness according to common standards.[33]

POOR MOBILIZATION OF PRIVATE
PHYSICIANS AND DELIVERY AGENTS

Program officials consciously disregarded the importance of enlisting the support of the private medical community in attacking the swine flu epidemic. Although federal authorities issued directives to this group, they provided little additional support in implementing the immunization program. Kilbourne urged Sencer to disseminate weekly publications to every private doctor, but the medical community was never sufficiently informed about program implementation. Private physicians accounted for only 15 percent of all inoculations, which suggests that the lack of informed local-level physicians resulted in disappointing vaccination rates. The failure to develop plans for enlisting the support of the private medical community in the face of an expected epidemic reveals an important lapse in management that was foreseen yet overlooked by program officials.[34]

HEW and state plans anticipated the support and cooperation of nursing and retirement homes in addition to private physicians. Such cooperation was undermined, however, due to emerging concerns about liability, vaccine safety, supply shortages, and confusion about appropriate doses. Delays caused by concerns over field trials and production limitations adversely affected demand, and by the time expected deliveries arrived, program support had waned. For example, one private industry conducting workplace vaccinations for its employees was offered only six thousand of the twenty thousand doses requested, and the supplies were consequently rejected.[35]

Misguided state and local programs suffered from staffing issues in addition to weakened commitments from institutions. Local health departments relied on temporary employees and volunteers to supplement key positions. Because of delays in production, however, recruitment for these positions was postponed to avoid exhausting grant funds before implementation. Nevertheless, at least twelve project directors received supplemental grant funds totaling roughly $184,000 for local staffing, and another project obtained about $2,800 in direct personnel assistance from the CDC.[36] In addition, program directors developed plans that incorporated volunteer assistance in all phases of their programs, yet uncertainties concerning vaccine delivery led to a loss of trained volunteers and disenchantment of large volunteer organizations such as the Red Cross.[37]

The lack of volunteers forced many program directors to eliminate weekend and holiday clinics from their original designs. Even then, volunteer support was in such demand that jet injectors were idle while people waiting to be vaccinated stood in line; in one county, two volunteers were pulled from the ranks of those awaiting vaccination.[38] Future programs that rely either on increased temporary staff or volunteers have much to learn from this example. If direct service providers are dependent on temporary or voluntary personnel, additional measures at the federal level should ensure that local officials utilize this support.

CHILDREN'S DOSAGES THREATEN LIMITED SUPPLIES

The CDC recommended a one-person, one-dose vaccination program before field tests had even been conducted. The incidence and severity of adverse reactions among children and young adults in the June 21 field trials, however, led to conclusions that a single-dose vaccine was unacceptable for children younger than eighteen years old and not recommended for the eighteen to twenty-four age range.[39]

Almost one month before field trials began, scientists raised the issue of a two-dose test of split vaccine at a March 25 BoB meeting, but the NIAID planners were unresponsive.[40] After the disappointing results of the single-dose vaccine in the June 21 field trials, NIAID Scientific Director John Seal reported: "It would have been no trouble to bring back the volunteers in the right age groups for a second shot of split vaccine. . . . We just didn't think of it."[41] Finally, in November, the ACIP released recommendations for two doses of the split vaccine for children younger than eighteen and two doses of monovalent vaccine for the eighteen to twenty-four age range.[42] However, there were only eight million doses of the split vaccine left in stock, so just four million of the estimated *57 million* children under eighteen years old could be vaccinated, scarcely a reassuring figure in a possible emergency.[43] One could argue that although two doses had been anticipated, the idea was rejected in the program design because program directors were aware of the limited egg supplies and restricted themselves based on that assumption.[44]

LIABILITY ISSUES: MANUFACTURER DELAYS
FORCE MODIFICATION

One of the most formidable obstacles faced by program managers derived from a failure to anticipate potential liability issues, which frustrated efforts to achieve timely production goals. This critical oversight resulted in needless and avoidable delays and further serves to illustrate the extent to which large-scale federal programs are vulnerable to private interests.

Before commencement of the program, the Congressional Budget Office projected that only $2.58 million in liability payments and litigation costs would be recovered from third-party program participants; since these costs would come from manufacturers' self-insurance funds, insurance companies stood to gain at least $8.65 million in profits, and even more as acceptance rates declined.[45] Since negotiations with insurers began after the program started, government bargaining power was weak.

Health care providers suffered the repercussions of liability issues as well. Local service delivery agents, who varied from state to state to ensure adaptability to local needs and capacities, were vulnerable to possible claims and therefore hesitant to participate in the immunization program. Health clinics, it could be argued, were under federal jurisdiction and therefore covered by federal liability legislation. Private physicians, on the other hand, were understandably more cautious.

Nine days prior to Ford's announcement, the secretary of agriculture addressed mounting concerns over egg supplies, assuring that "the roosters of America are ready to do their duty."[46] In March, HEW officials established October 29 as the deadline for the production and distribution of 200 million doses. When manufacturers submitted their first formal proposals for vaccine production and delivery in June, however, they estimated that only about 80 million doses would be available by October 1 and only 146.7 million by December 1. Manufacturers significantly reduced their estimates in revised proposals submitted in August and September: only 20 million doses would be available by October 1 and 113 million doses by December 1.[47]

If manufacturers had been consulted earlier, the October 29 deadline for 200 million doses would have been deemed unrealistic. Likewise, planners could have addressed manufacturers' indemnification issues, which compounded production difficulties: on May 24, Merck ceased production after its primary insurer refused coverage for swine flu, followed by Parke-Davis's announcement that its coverage would expire on June 30. Wyeth and Merrell National also delayed plans to bottle vaccines.

HEW officials responded to manufacturers' insistence on indemnification and drafted an indemnification bill that went to Congress on June 16. Congress modeled the Swine Flu Tort Claims Bill (P.L. 94-380) after the Tort Claims Act, which determined that claims would be filed against the federal government while reserving the government's right to sue for compensation from other participants.[48] The congressional action freed manufacturers and insurers from liability, and production resumed.

Remarkably, HEW made no attempt to communicate with insurance companies prior to June. According to Mathews, "The insurance companies are parties to the manufacturers, not us. We are not in direct negotiations with them except through the manufacturers."[49] However, HEW officials had raised indemnification issues early in the program: in January 1976, Sencer sent a draft proposal prepared by CDC Assistant Program Director Bruce Dull to Cooper and Mathews urging federal indemnification whenever there was federal sponsorship for immunization.[50] Cooper lamented that he had not consulted with the American Insurance Association and the individual insurance companies in the decision-making period, an error that resulted in needless production delay and bad press.

Although states could waive tort liability under the doctrine of sovereign immunity,[51] local government employees, private physicians, and other health professionals who administered the vaccine in publicly run clinics could be sued by the federal government for negligence in administering the vaccine, failing to warn about vaccine risks, and improper storage and handling of the vaccine. When the CDC conducted an analysis of state liability protection, only ten states provided adequate liability protection for all participants, while fourteen states offered liability protection for none.[52] Only one state purchased insurance protection against the government, which suggests that if future government programs intend to use local delivery services, consideration of possible litigation should include all relevant actors.

Had the CDC anticipated the unwillingness of insurance companies to cover legal risks, another significant obstacle to program implementation would have been avoided. This negligence occurred in spite of the serious and well-known liability problems in the polio vaccination program that took years to resolve and resulted in costly judgments.[53]

LEGISLATION CONFRONTS INFORMED CONSENT

The Swine Flu Tort Claims Bill required HEW to consult with the National Commission for the Protection of Human Subjects of Biomedical and Behavioral Research on the content of the consent forms. However, the CDC had already drafted, printed, and distributed over eighty-three million consent forms. When the commission met with the CDC in late August, they suggested that the CDC staple an additional page to the original form concerning adverse effects. A month later, the commission sent a letter to Sencer specifying the weaknesses in the consent form that required correction, including contradictory statements concerning vaccine safety during pregnancy, possible confusion concerning the purpose of the introduction, and incomplete information on who individuals should contact in case of an adverse reaction.[54] When the immunization program was halted in December, however, the recommended changes still had not been made.[55]

None of the clinics evaluated adhered to HEW's eight minimum requirements of informed consent. HEW's own clinic, which served its employees, failed to meet these requirements as well: the clinic did not have available the introductory page that outlined adverse effects of the vaccine, and 13 percent of those vaccinated had not signed informed consent forms.[56] These examples demonstrate the significant potential for mishaps in delivery and federal liability protection.

POORLY PLANNED MEDIA RELATIONS

The CDC's publicity campaign relied heavily on the media to disseminate information to the public and encourage immunization. Program designers, in fact, included a fundamental role for the media in their proposed design, anticipating that public support would be critical to the program's success. However, despite numerous press releases from officials such as Sencer and Cooper, poor communication and uncultivated relationships with the media resulted in declining support from television and newspapers as deadlines passed, manufacturers balked, and hypothesized success rates dropped. Reporters responded by seeking others whose opposing opinions were more accessible,[57] and major network correspondents featured dissenters within the ranks of the CDC and medical experts critical of the public health establishment.[58]

The CDC assumed a largely responsive posture, starting a publicity campaign three days *after* the immunization program had begun. Instead of engaging in an effort to build public support through education, almost immediately the CDC publicity campaign focused on "responding to media inquiries concerning crises that arose, such as deaths associated with the immunization program."[59] As a reactive policy, the chief function of the publicity campaign was to curb the effects of negative publicity, resulting in the CDC's weakened ability to support state and local immunization campaigns.

Perhaps inadvertently, the media exposed gaps in the external management of the program. The CDC had no contingency plan to inform the public in the event that obstacles altered the program design; rather, they sought to resolve the issue of disseminating information internally before immunization began. Thus, when negative test results required the exclusion of those younger than eighteen years old, it was the media, not official press releases from program directors, that informed the public. When dosage recommendations were finalized two months into the program, the public was still unsure whether children would need a booster.[60] This failure to maintain consistent and credible channels of information between program officials and local service delivery was a serious weakness in the program design that undermined vaccination efforts. If the swine flu threat had been real, many children would have been left insufficiently protected or worse.

In addition to informing the public about actual shortcomings in the immunization program, the media also misconstrued important facts and compensated for information gaps with conjecture. The media regularly associated the program with the 1918–1919 pandemic, consistently citing the twenty million mortality statistic without noting that bacterial pneumonia caused a large number of the deaths. Although only four of the five hundred ill soldiers were discovered with the swine flu virus, a *Washington Post* article reported that "the Fort Dix outbreak . . . may have infected as many as 500 recruits."[61] Reporting on the congressional debate surrounding appropriations legislation, in which several congressmen voiced their concerns over poor immunization rates for other viruses, several articles erroneously suggested that the swine flu vaccine would be combined with polio and measles vaccines.[62]

As media support declined, reports expressed doubts concerning the threat, evidenced by such headlines as "The Swine Flu Virus: Not So Lethal" and "Swine Flu Program Is Dying." Early in the summer, the press was already speculating on the likelihood of political motivations, adding that "the epidemic is unlikely to occur next year, but if it does it will not be serious."[63] A study conducted for the British medical journal *Lancet* even found its way into the editorial pages along with the criticism: "With the passage of time there has been

increasing incongruity between the panic measures advocated by President Ford
. . . and the reality that not a single natural case of this supposedly deadly disease
has been observed."[64] When field tests concluded, Martin Goldfield, the associate commissioner and chief epidemiologist of New Jersey's Department of Public Health, was equally critical: "The results are very mediocre in terms of
immunological protection."[65] Finally, Bruce Dull, Sencer's assistant director for
programs, announced at an emergency forum on swine flu in June that "there is
no reason to believe that the new swine flu virus will be similar to the 1918–19
pandemic, nor any more deadly than other strains of influenza in recent years."[66]

In addition to promoting the doubts of both the existence of the swine flu
threat and the efficacy of the program's response, the media also fostered fears.
For example, on the day that liability issues were debated on the floors of Congress, twenty-three people died of mysterious respiratory ailments in Philadelphia. The press drew connections to swine flu, adding that health officials could
start mass immunization within days if they could get the vaccine. The same day,
a related article claimed that 100 million doses of the swine flu vaccine were
ready for administration.[67] Although Legionnaire's disease, not swine flu, was
the discovered cause of these deaths, the *Washington Post* placed the news alongside articles detailing the swine flu vaccination liability hearings. The media,
however inadvertently, generated support for the Swine Flu Tort Claims Act by
reporting on the deaths from Legionnaire's disease, which occurred simultaneously with the bill's presentation in Congress.

Ten days after the commencement of the immunization program, the media
reported three deaths caused by the swine flu vaccine in Pittsburgh. As the death
toll reached twenty-four, the press began reporting what officials had known all
along: some of the deaths, however small in number, were an inevitable consequence of vaccination. The ensuing volley of articles, linking the deaths to the
vaccine and then denying any connection, would continue unchecked throughout
the rest of the program.[68]

MISINFORMATION SPREADS QUICKER THAN FACTS

The media, which was eventually quite hostile to the swine flu program, might
have served a better purpose had President Ford not made such a quick decision.
If he and HEW had educated and cultivated the media prior to his announcement,
reporters would have been better informed, helping to disseminate accurate and
timely public information. They also might have raised the valid objections of
dissenters and the attendant implementation difficulties. Open debate could have
produced an improved decision-making process and perhaps induced plans to
manage several potential contingencies.

Reporters were forced instead into a reactive position by Ford's preemptive
announcement. By ignoring the media's professional interests in investigative

reporting, the federal government missed an opportunity, handing the media an adversarial role from the beginning that ultimately undermined the entire enterprise. Throughout the program, misinformation was left unchecked, and very little positive and timely public information was released to offset negative press. In other words, program officials made little effort to plan for or alleviate concerns fueled by the press.

Media relations can be cited as one of the major shortcomings of the external management of the swine flu program and a fundamental lesson to future public health initiatives. According to Neustadt and Fineburg, planning for media responses had been discussed from time to time at higher levels but was discounted "on the grounds that information spreads, and to alert the public might reduce the numbers willing to be immunized."[69] If program officials had considered the fact that negative information spreads even more rapidly, perhaps they would have given greater attention to media relations, especially in cultivating positive relations with timely information about negative side effects.

STATE AND LOCAL PROJECTS HINDERED BY FEDERAL-LEVEL PUBLICITY

Because of the immediate need to respond at a national level to adverse and conflicting publicity, material prepared for state and local projects was not disseminated until two months after these projects had begun.[70] Although many project directors had initiated their publicity campaigns when the vaccine became available, some began their campaigns more slowly due to concerns about demand overwhelming limited supplies of the vaccine.[71] Nevertheless, limited supplies throughout the program caused many dates and locations to be rescheduled, thus defeating the purpose of the publicity campaigns to create demand and encourage immunization.

Such delays also raised program costs, and the CDC had to make additional grant funds available to states to launch or alter their publicity campaigns. Some states received these funds in November and December—too late to achieve the desired results, since the program was suspended on December 16.[72] The absence of a strong relationship with publicity professionals prior to the implementation of the program affected the government's ability to promote vaccination as well as quickly recover from negative publicity.

TARGETING MARGINALIZED GROUPS: OUTREACH AND EDUCATION

Government reliance on local delivery exposed additional shortcomings of the manipulated market. For example, among states that opted to use public health clinics for immunization, success rates were higher than when they used private clinics. Clinics operating in high traffic areas on weekends were particularly effective, a fact that demonstrates the success of strategies that are "customer-sensitive" and designed to target hard-to-access groups. One major city vaccinated 16,500 persons in one weekend and 18,000 in a follow-up clinic; another state vaccinated half as many persons on one Saturday as it had during the entire first six weeks of the program.

Although state publicity campaigns were budgeted in project grants, the CDC intended to conduct an additional nationwide campaign aimed at increasing public awareness and promoting demand for the vaccine. Due to delays in production, however, public awareness activities were delayed, in some cases until after immunization had begun. The consequences of poorly planned information campaigns prevented full commitment at the distribution level, which in turn decreased demand and hindered immunization rates.

In addition, greater attention to external elements such as press relations and public awareness could have improved immunization rates among underrepresented populations. Throughout the program, however, little attention was given to targeting marginalized groups through education and outreach. According to Neustadt and Fineburg, ghetto acceptance rates were lower than suburban rates.[73] In addition to lack of access to immunization centers and health care in general, simple fear was a possible contributing factor to these lowered rates. This conclusion is reflected in the results of two simultaneous polls conducted by Dr. Pascal Imperato, first deputy health commissioner and director of the inoculation program in New York City, which revealed that residents of inner-city neighborhoods were more afraid of the shots than persons from more affluent sections.[74]

Although such issues extend beyond any single public health initiative, efforts to reach these groups could have been facilitated by program officials in charge of overseeing local operations and by more population-specific advertising. For example, there was no effort to enlist an active role for more appropriate agencies in PHS; the mandate of the Health Resources and Services Administration (HRSA) emphasizes underserved populations, and the public information staff at PHS was considered one of the department's best.[75] However, Cooper's decision to assume responsibility effectively ignored these valuable resources. The failure to mobilize this talent illustrates a central weakness in the program's overall design, which focused on internal aspects of the effort without addressing the challenge of public awareness. Ironically, program officials understood that outreach and education were fundamental to the program's success.

MANAGING DISTRIBUTIONAL EQUITY

When President Ford announced an immunization program for every man, woman, and child in the United States, little consideration was given to rationing limited vaccine supplies or allocating scarce delivery resources. Unlike the polio case, which immunized children first, there was no hierarchy of vaccination in the swine flu effort that prioritized high-risk groups.

Although the program immunization goals included children, the elderly, and those with chronic heart and respiratory ailments, there was no special consideration given to these vulnerable populations. Some states included a two-phase design that targeted the elderly and chronically ill in the first phase, although these decisions were made locally and were not informed by federal policy. In fact, the only federal acknowledgment of a distributional hierarchy in the early stages of planning was the decision to reserve thirty million bivalent doses of swine flu Victoria A vaccine for the elderly.[76]

The program designers' failure to establish a hierarchy of vaccination was clearly shortsighted: there was no contingency plan to distribute the vaccine supply when egg supplies proved limited and production targets fell short during liability delays. Had the epidemic materialized, the most vulnerable might have been at serious risk.

RATIONING AND PRIORITIZING VACCINE DISTRIBUTION

With implicit CDC approval, most state and local immunization plans called for a two-phase procedure that targeted high-risk groups in mid-July and the remaining population in September. These plans dictated that private physicians, nursing homes, retirement homes, special clinics for the aged, and public health departments would implement the first phase. However, because of children's adverse reactions in the field trials, plans either eliminated or postponed their inoculation, leaving the aged as the group at highest risk.

The decision to designate the elderly as the highest priority group demonstrated a disregard for well-documented evidence that they benefited from previous immunity, and that the age group comprising twenty- to thirty-year-olds was most afflicted in the 1918–1919 pandemic. Further, a strategy that targeted a traditionally vulnerable group seemed suspiciously like an effort to win greater public support. The prioritizing of the elderly was arguably a policy in which politics took precedence over an understanding of historical effects.

The elderly was also the group most vulnerable to negative side effects, including death. Indeed, the first deaths in Pittsburgh were elderly patients with medical conditions, and public knowledge of the tragedy negatively affected overall immunization rates. Program officials should have focused their inoculation efforts on the stronger, healthier general populace to promote success rates.

DECLINING PUBLIC TRUST AND CIVIC DISENGAGEMENT

Much of the success enjoyed by directors of the polio immunization program was a function of the public trust and widespread support generated by an effective public relations campaign. Public confidence in the government's ability to enact and regulate public policies, however, declined significantly in the period between the polio and the swine flu programs, eroded by the perceived ineffectiveness of the War on Poverty and the blunders of the Vietnam War and Watergate. Indeed, the day after Ford announced the swine flu program, a congressional oversight committee accused nine federal agencies of "lack of public concern and closeness to industry's 'special interests.'"[77] Whereas the polio eradication efforts were supported by a chief executive afflicted by the disease, the swine flu immunization program was initiated by a chief executive who assumed the office through the disgraceful resignation of his predecessor.[78]

Federal policy-makers, including those in charge of public health campaigns, misunderstood the public mistrust reflected in newspaper headlines. As one reporter noted:

> Even before the swine flu experience, the public shied away from some aspects of preventive medicine. Immunization against polio, diphtheria, measles, and other infections are reported at dangerously low levels. Preventive medicine experts contend that the success of immunizations is partially responsible for making the public apathetic about diseases younger Americans have never known.[79]

Even after Ford's announcement, articles related to the swine flu program repeatedly questioned the political motivations behind the nationwide effort.

Although forty million Americans were immunized in the first ten weeks, program officials failed to maintain this initial high level of public support throughout the program. With no new reported cases of the swine flu virus, the initial sense of urgency that program officials hoped would impel people to get immunized was difficult to maintain.[80] As deaths and paralysis were sensationalized in connection with the swine flu vaccine, CDC officials finally began to address the issue of expected deaths associated with any immunization program. As anticipated, success rates did decrease as more information was released. From mid-October on, polls showed a downward drift of persons who intended to be immunized: by mid-October, 2.4 million people were immunized, despite the deaths in Pittsburgh; by mid-November 6.4 million were immunized, decreasing to 2.3 million by mid-December.[81]

One *New York Times* editorial suggested that the government had created the scare propaganda used originally to expedite legislation for the swine flu program through Congress.[82] Another *New York Times* editorial, published just two weeks later, suggested that the politically charged atmosphere of the presidential election year and the dependence of most medical researchers on federal funding explained the relative paucity of plain-speaking expert voices in this country.[83]

The media exposed conflicting estimates and dissenting opinion and reported the slow initiation of local programs and their directors' indifference or incertitude about the threat of an epidemic. Even prior to the commencement of the program, the press reported that local efforts would make the vaccine available to anyone who wanted it, although as one *Washington Post* article stated, "it was unlikely that everyone would want to be inoculated or could be."[84]

The swine flu immunization program occurred at a time of great social change in America, best exemplified by the shift in the notion of informed consent from a moral responsibility to a legal one. In addition, because of the public's eroding confidence in government's ability to protect its citizens, the public perception of the government's image was one of suspect political agendas and ineptitude. Consideration and understanding of the environment are fundamental to public policy initiatives, especially for proposed health programs that critically depend on fostering public acceptance and trust. Program officials responsible for implementing the swine flu program failed to accurately judge the decline in public trust or the difficulty in cultivating a public commitment to the effort. Further, they did not appreciate that advancing their program depended on educating the public on both the merits and the dangers of immunization.

THE CULTURE OF SCIENCE

Despite the scientific controversy that threatened the polio immunization effort at critical points, the management of dissenting opinion allowed an unprecedented initiative to proceed. In contrast, the swine flu initiative seized a perceived public health threat and transformed it into a highly organized political vehicle by excluding controversy from both scientists and administrators in agencies at the federal and local levels. As the initiative based on a "state of emergency" moved forward, critics within government were threatened or fired, and no process was available to reconsider previous judgments when new information developed.[85] Ironically, this approach created a camp of opposition willing to talk to the media that served to increase public skepticism and prevent a face-saving option, such as stockpiling the vaccine when questions about the decreasing probability of an epidemic surfaced.

Critical scientific judgments were necessary to determine first, the likelihood of the threat of an epidemic; second, the public health consequences of alternative vaccine program designs; and third, the safety and effectiveness of a new vaccine at different potencies for various groups. Certain members of the scientific community urged caution, recommended stockpiling the vaccine supplies until more concrete evidence emerged, and opposed the introduction of foreign substances, even vaccines, into the body without greater certainty that the threat was real.

HEW officials estimated that the swine flu vaccine would adequately protect 70 to 90 percent of those vaccinated, basing their judgment on information about the efficacy of past vaccines and the results of the swine flu clinical trials. Scientific estimates of past flu vaccines, however, ranged from 20 to 90 percent.[86] In addition, the duration of protection is difficult to predict; although estimates expect vaccines to last one year, such estimation varies with age and physical health, children being the most vulnerable. Even the delayed vaccine recommendations for the population under twenty-four years of age were based on limited data.[87] Finally, the ability of a vaccine to adequately protect against influenza viruses is difficult to determine. Over the past twenty-five years, flu vaccines have been only 67 to 90 percent effective because of antigenic shift, and the lead time for vaccine production is too great to keep up with the spread of flu. Thus, a great deal of the information about the vaccine was based on conjecture, warranting both caution and full disclosure to the public. Many scientists contended that based on the failure of past flu vaccines to appreciably affect the course of epidemics, the degree of effectiveness was questionable.[88]

The swine flu program executives expressed few concerns about potential side effects from vaccination. HEW officials countered scientific opposition concerning the safety and effectiveness of the vaccine with the observation that killed-virus flu vaccines had rarely been associated with adverse reactions or permanent disability and were considered medically safe and quite suitable for wide-scale community use.[89]

When there were unanticipated adverse side effects that could be traced to the vaccine, such as a thousand cases of Guillain-Barré syndrome, program executives found themselves with no response or formal plan to publicly manage the crisis. An already hostile media responded with unrelenting skepticism about the entire enterprise. Policy-makers' failure to manage a process that included a full range of scientific opinion and anticipate potential side effects, as well as their poor management and education of the media, made the crisis the undoing of the policy initiative.

EMERGENCY NEVER MATERIALIZED

With the exception of the four cases infecting the Fort Dix soldiers, the swine flu virus did not emerge, and the threat of an epidemic never materialized. Nevertheless, officials continued a red-alert campaign throughout the program in an effort to increase immunization rates and justify its existence. At no time after April 15, when Ford signed the special appropriations bill into law (which provided federal financing through July), were any additional cases of swine flu reported anywhere in the world despite increased surveillance.[90] The fact that epidemics were always preceded by several outbreaks fueled opposition to a full-scale immunization program. A British study, which concluded that the Fort Dix strain was milder than other human flu viruses and that its attribution to a single death could be disputed, further reinforced the notion that the threat of an epidemic was remote.[91]

HEW's decision to proceed with the program was based on the assumption that most of the population was susceptible to the new virus, and that the excess deaths and costs of the Asian and Hong Kong flu epidemics of 1957 and 1968–1969 could have been avoided if the vaccine had been administered earlier.[92] Although such arguments might have merited increased surveillance, production, and distribution, the leap from stockpiling to full-scale immunization went against the better judgment of many scientists and policy-makers. HEW officials maintained that major antigenic shifts in flu viruses always led to pandemics and opposed stockpiling because distribution and administration of the vaccine could not be accomplished in time to allow for the vaccine to achieve maximum effect.

The outbreak of Legionnaire's disease and its attribution to swine flu created additional unnecessary panic, yet immunization rates did not significantly increase. In this instance, the exercise of greater restraint in policies that expose limited knowledge and shifting circumstances might have prevented the accusations of misinformation that were leveled against the government once the scare proved unjustified.

CONCLUSION

Public health policy choices ultimately require considerable dependence on a wide range of scientific evidence and judgment. Policy-makers' initial decision to treat the reports of a swine flu virus as indicative of a possible epidemic rested primarily on their interpretation of the nature of the particular health threat, the likelihood of its emergence, and the anticipated severity of the resulting condition (given the probability of disease risk). Because the influenza pandemic of 1918 was one of the most devastating in history, fears of its return in 1976 weighed heavily on scientists and policy-makers.[93]

Although most agree that the public policy response to these revelations was fraught with error and avoidable implementation blunders, considerable disagreement accompanies how much scientific judgments could or should have been responsible for the many policy failures.[94] Nevertheless, policy-makers failed to ask the scientists the right questions, failed to develop an implementation strategy that would consider the possibility that predictions might be wrong, and thus failed to conceive of alternative scenarios as contingencies.

Viruses are very slippery phenomena: they mutate so quickly that each flu season scientists must develop new vaccines based on their best estimation of what surface proteins will determine the nature of the next season's strain. From a public health perspective, the key is determining the new strain in advance of the flu season so that producers can develop the correct vaccine in sufficient quantities for wide-scale distribution; the conditions of next winter's flu season, for example, must be known by February.

The speed with which the flu virus evolves has been the basis on which scientists determine its likely new mutation. Typically, scientists subject a current strain to another strain that leads to a rapid proliferation; the plentiful viruses are then attenuated for next year's flu season.[95] The well-known problem is that scientists run a significant risk of error in judging which virus will cause the next year's illness; some estimate that the probability is as high as 50 percent.

When scientists at the CDC determined that a swine flu epidemic was a clear and serious threat with the potential severity of the 1918 outbreak, they concluded that mutations in the previous year's strain must have led to major changes in viral surface antigens—changes that are quite rare, occurring only three times this century. Sequence analysis on the virus genome would have provided better evidence on whether there was a new antigen shift capable of causing an epidemic, but the technology was not available at the time.

Judgments on all of these matters are more or less probabilistic, and the certainty with which policy can proceed on these bases depends on the state of scientific knowledge. While it may indeed be better to needlessly vaccinate millions than to risk endangering the population in what turns out to be a real epidemic, weighing these choices explicitly and planning for the possibility of being mistaken are critical to effective executive management. Whatever the course of action, federal executives should be unrelentingly skeptical about the assumptions informing their decision.

The possibility of error in the numerous assumptions on which policy action is based can seriously affect the policy, how the outcomes are perceived, and the credibility of the enterprise. Sound executive management depends precisely on anticipating what can go wrong and planning for contingencies; in other words, policy-makers must exercise relentless skepticism in assessing the possibility of error and impediments, what their impact may be, and how responsive plans can be created in advance.

There are clearly cognitive limits to anticipating all possible direct and indirect outcomes of alternative actions. Further, even if many obstacles can be identified beforehand, the solutions may not always be obvious, nor is immediate implementation always possible. Managing press relations is a crucial managerial function, yet even vigilant and sophisticated executives may not always be successful. Again, good management requires anticipating as many contingencies as possible and remaining flexible and responsive to unexpected events. Adaptation to crises and opportunities is the mark of an effective and successful executive.

Several clear lapses occurred in the swine flu debacle that were unnecessary and preventable. The most egregious have been amply explored: failure to include, consider, and manage dissenting scientific judgments; failure to consider, include, and design program operations to accommodate the needs and views of state and local actors, including those of private medical practitioners who are important constituents for program operations; inadequate considerations of the needs and capacities of producers in the private sector; poor planning for public and media education; and, finally, reactive and inadequate media relations.

The contrast with the polio immunization program is stark. Although profound improvements in the federal public health infrastructure might have facilitated program management of the swine flu effort, poor contingency planning and low levels of public trust exacerbated the failures as each obstacle hindered program operations.

4

The Clinton Administration's Childhood Immunization Policy

INTRODUCTION

The fate of the swine flu immunization effort provides a vivid case of avoidable program failure. Politics and policy goals drove decision-making to the virtual exclusion of sound management planning. If a real epidemic had occurred, the failure to anticipate predictable obstacles to program management would have proved disastrous. Although federal competence and prestige suffered blows in the aftermath of the debacle, only luck saved the nation from the more serious effects of a potentially deadly public health crisis.

The tendency of public executives in American political life to treat management as secondary to policy is widespread. For example, when a policy goal is articulated, initial consideration of how the goal will be achieved—the implementation and management of the program—is frequently absent, even though effective management often determines policy success. Further, when a public problem is identified, such as rising disease rates or increasing poverty, the management of existing programs rarely is investigated as the source of the problem. Indeed, both elected and appointed public executives maintain a bias against management solutions, limiting the range of choices they consider and the criteria they use to assess them. This bias has an independent impact on the success of public enterprise, especially on large-scale public health initiatives.

A preference for policy solutions rather than management solutions exerts a distorting influence on public executives. Vaccines for Children (VFC), the Clinton administration's childhood immunization initiative, is a particularly illustrative case. We analyze it here to explain how institutional and political realities constrain public executives, who thereby fail to define critical public problems as managerial in nature and to allocate resources for their solution. These constraints will underscore the inherent difficulties faced by public executives in pursuing a management agenda and will suggest a limited set of vehicles for developing a constituency for management.

POLICY VERSUS MANAGEMENT

The Clinton administration entered office with a broad policy agenda. But while policy may capture the public imagination, fueling a demand for change, it is overemphasized and overused as a vehicle to improve the performance of governmental organizations. Much of the disappointing outcome of public activities derives as much from an absence of adequate attention to issues of program management and service delivery as it does from misguided public policy choices. Indeed, public policy more often than not develops at the implementation stage, when field conditions can shape or subvert initial policy designs developed in advance.[1] Further, American culture, institutions, and politics impose a strong bias against viewing public problems as cases of public management or implementation failure and consistently discourage building a case for management.

Policy choices are fundamental. As we will argue, a policy choice is a point decision "that involves a self-effectuating choice among competing alternatives; a line decision is one that requires the coordination by plans of action of many people over a substantial period of time."[2] Point decisions are shaped by ideas; by contrast, line decisions are mostly shaped by organizational or situational resources and how they are assembled. Assemblage, the process following the formulation and adoption of an initial policy mandate, is the essence of a line decision and the chief difficulty facing public executives.

We are distinguishing between policy and management—between point and line, between policy goals and the means to realize them. Although in practice the temporal sequence may not be as clear as we suggest (since policy is often developed through the program implementation process), there is an important analytical distinction here between enunciating a new policy as a solution to a problem and diagnosing and treating the problem as one of failed management. Further, even when policy solutions are indicated, they need to be followed by a carefully engineered process of program assembly, which is an interactive process. We argue that both the failure to recognize the problem of low immunization rates among young children as a management and service delivery issue and the related failure to attend to the centrality of management after the policy was designed are more generalized problems of American governance. Indeed, we have seen the phenomenon in the swine flu initiative (see Chapter 3), when the principal architects overlooked or ignored critical management and service delivery challenges, many of which were understood just two decades earlier after the polio immunization experience.

VFC was a dramatic and ambitious *policy* response to what we will show is a case of significant *management* and implementation failure. The aggressive and targeted policy response to low rates of early childhood immunization ultimately diverted attention away from significant evidence of fundamental problems of service delivery, infrastructure, and parental knowledge and behavior. The analysis that follows seeks to evaluate the underlying reasons for the poor fit between diagnosing the problem of existing childhood immunization policy and the Clinton adminstration's policy prescription, which relied almost exclusively on reducing the price of vaccines.[3]

An abundance of research demonstrates the small role that vaccine prices play in explaining disappointing rates of vaccination among young children despite the more than ample supply of free vaccine that is currently available. Increasing federal vaccine expenditures have not resulted in significant improvements in immunization rates. Indeed, the problem of inadequate vaccinations among young children is not due to high-priced vaccines, but rather a result of a poorly designed and funded infrastructure to deliver existing supplies to hard-to-serve populations.

SEIZING CHILDHOOD IMMUNIZATION

Early in the administration, President and Mrs. Clinton focused widespread attention on the low rates of immunization among preschool-age children. Pointing to increasing incidence and deaths from preventable diseases such as measles,[4] the president blamed greedy pharmaceutical companies for price gouging and profiteering. The most recent data from the Centers for Disease Control estimate that between 28 and 44 percent of selected categories of preschool children in the United States between the ages of nineteen and thirty-six months have not received all the immunizations recommended by public health officials and the medical establishment. The varying rates of immunization depend on the income, race, and residences of the children; low-income children have the lowest rates, as do children who live in rural areas.[5] Overall, 67.1 percent of three-year-olds receive the combined series of four doses of DPT (for diphtheria, pertussis, and tetanus), three doses of polio vaccine, and one dose of MMR (for measles, mumps, and rubella).[6] The immunization rate jumps to 97 percent among school-age children, since all states require immunization prior to school registration.

This difference between 67.1 and 97 percent is of crucial significance, since children between the ages of two and five are particularly vulnerable, and disease rates have been increasing (before age two, natural antibodies may offer some protection). Young children also may spread a potentially serious disease to younger siblings and playmates as well as to unprotected adults.

Significantly, national data on childhood immunization rates have not been systematically collected since 1985, when the CDC discontinued the *Annual United States Immunization Survey* for budgetary reasons. A letter from the U.S. General Accounting Office (GAO) to the House Committee on Energy and

Commerce explains that after 1985, data obtained by special surveys or through the states are not nationally representative, current, or age-specific and therefore do not provide an adequate basis to assess national immunization levels. Thus, all rates are estimates.[7]

Indeed, three administrations representing both parties have ignored the essential requirements for management of an important public policy objective by abandoning these surveys. As a result, an accurate evaluation of the impact of efforts to improve the management of immunization policy is all but impossible. The macro-policy significance, which is the focus of this chapter, is that the abandonment of these evaluation efforts strikingly indicates of how little value three administrations placed on management for improving public policy outcomes.[8]

The increasing incidence of preventable childhood diseases and the subsequent rise in deaths and birth defects stand in stark contrast to rising immunization rates in comparable Western industrialized countries, even in some developing countries. Indeed, sixteen countries had higher immunization rates than the United States in 1988 and 1989.[9] In response, Clinton proposed the Comprehensive Child Immunization Act of 1993, sweeping legislation that would have guaranteed free vaccine to all children in a program of universal immunization. Expensive and controversial in a period of budget contraction, Clinton's proposal met resistance and ultimately faced compromise, passing in a more modest version in June 1993 (P.L. 103-66).

The existence of a public health crisis and the Clinton administration's response—a strategy of blaming the drug companies and proposing expensive legislation—reveal important weaknesses in the capacity or willingness of elected officials to respond to fundamental problems of management and service delivery. In the analysis that follows, we will examine the bias of public executives toward policy prescriptions instead of public management solutions.

In this chapter we will first discuss the history of childhood immunization policy, which will be followed by an examination of the current policy-making environment and an analysis of the evidence that childhood immunization rates constitute a public health crisis. Next, we will explore the ways in which program management and service delivery affect immunization rates. We will illustrate the poor fit between Clinton's legislative solutions and the immunization problem and propose an explanation for why managerial problems are often neglected or redefined as policy problems. Finally, we will offer a series of prescriptive reforms and suggest the limited vehicles for developing a constituency for management.

BACKGROUND: HISTORY OF CHILDHOOD IMMUNIZATION POLICY

As discussed in Chapter 2, the passage of the Poliomyelitis Vaccination Assistance Act of 1955 was the first federal initiative that approached the notion of universal immunization of children. Prior to this legislation, the federal government's role was limited to preventing the introduction of contagious and infectious disease into the United States, controlling international and interstate quarantine, licensing vaccine manufacturers, and regulating vaccine production.[10] The goal of the Eisenhower administration was to ensure universal vaccination of children, and the legislation provided states with grants to fund free vaccination services to children and pregnant women without regard to ability to pay. However, there continued to be many unvaccinated children, particularly among the poor, and in 1960 Congress appropriated an additional $1 million for the purchase of vaccines to control epidemics.

Throughout the 1960s, vaccine legislation that provided funding in the form of categorical grants increased for polio and other childhood diseases such as measles, pertussis, diphtheria, and tetanus. In 1966, under section 314 of the Public Health Service Act, categorical grants were replaced by block grants, which continued to fund vaccination programs until the legislation's expiration in 1968. Despite the program design's flexibility in responding to a range of health problems in different areas, within several years it became clear that these efforts were ineffective in ensuring the immunization of children against communicable diseases.

Increasing incidence of childhood diseases and low immunization rates provoked a series of federal legislative efforts over the following decades that sought to reverse this troubling trend; throughout the 1970s, section 314 of the Public Health Service Act was continually reauthorized. Although these diseases were not eliminated, disease rates were down until 1983.

Significantly, increased federal funding for free vaccine and vaccine-related activities had limited impact on early childhood immunization rates. Federal funding for a range of public health activities, including immunization, increased from $31.4 million in 1979 to $1.44 billion in 1991. Early childhood vaccination rates, however, were still well below federal goals. Further, these figures do not include Medicaid funds, which financed at least 50 percent of vaccines and immunization administration costs in state programs.[11]

Both federal supplies and state purchases increased from 1983 to 1986, even though the per dose cost rose from $12.35 to $21.87. Nevertheless, the number of doses administered did not rise at a comparable rate. Indeed, public sector dosages to children increased by only two million during this period of considerable growth in expenditure and supply, suggesting that factors other than availability and vaccine cost must have impeded increases in immunizations.[12]

The legislative history of childhood immunization demonstrates an increase in bipartisan support for improving immunization rates and increasing levels of funding. However, the number of doses dispensed and the rate of immunization among young children have decreased. Thus, greater expenditures and an increased supply of free vaccine have not resulted in significant improvement in the rate of full immunization of children with recommended vaccines before their second birthday. The Clinton administration, therefore, faced a federal policy with decreasing effectiveness in achieving a policy goal that enjoyed significant and widespread support.

DEFINING THE PROBLEM: WHY ARE EARLY CHILDHOOD IMMUNIZATION RATES SO LOW?

President Clinton's original legislative proposal in 1992 and the legislative compromise in 1993 rely heavily on a particular analysis of low immunization rates that identifies the primary problem as one of economics and implicates manufacturers that over the decade have increased vaccine cost by six times the rate of inflation.[13] Critics like the Children's Defense Fund have also pointed to increased levels of poverty and inadequate access to health care. But another body of analysis focuses on other factors that explain why early childhood immunization rates lag so significantly even as the number and effectiveness of vaccines against childhood diseases grow.

The American Academy of Pediatrics and the CDC currently recommend five vaccines for all young children.[14] Their provision requires a fixed schedule of physician or health center visits over a period of several years, thus necessitating an available and accessible health care provider. The policy debate focuses on three primary factors that explain the declining proportion of fully immunized preschool children: vaccine costs that impede parents' ability to immunize their children; parental compliance with suggested protocols; and the public health infrastructure. The fundamental policy problem is to distinguish between the relative importance of the cost of vaccine, inadequate health care access, lack of knowledge among parents about the need for and benefits of early childhood vaccines, and provider and parental behavior.

THE ROLE OF VACCINE PRICES

The Clinton administration's legislative compromise was passed as part of the 1993 budget bill and placed considerable importance on the role of vaccine prices in declining immunization rates. VFC mandates that all vaccines purchased by the federal government for children's immunization be available at discount capped prices.[15] The federal government is responsible for the delivery of the vaccines to the states, which are in turn responsible for distribution to public clinics and participating private physicians. Participating physicians must provide the vaccine at no cost to eligible children (such as those who are on Medicaid, who are Indian, who lack health insurance, or who are seeking immunization at federally qualified health clinics because their health insurance does not cover immunizations). States are eligible to benefit from low-cost federal supplies if they purchase the vaccine with their own resources, and they are permitted to distribute the vaccine free of charge so that they may immunize all children regardless of family income.[16]

Original estimates of VFC's annual cost were as high as $585 million; however, a 1996 estimate by HHS placed the figure at $410 million.[17] Further, original plans indicated that the implementation of the program was far more ambitious than originally anticipated, resulting in federal purchases that might exceed the estimated need by as much as 40 percent. Original plans also relegated warehousing and distribution responsibilities to the General Services Administration (GSA), which involved purchasing what manufacturers claimed was 80 percent of the nation's privately produced vaccine supply.[18]

The cost of fully immunizing a child younger than two years old with all the recommended vaccines has clearly increased over the past decade. Vaccine costs alone for recommended immunizations are now estimated to be $188.19 compared with $20.17 in 1982. In constant dollars this represents a sixfold increase in a single decade. Two factors must be considered, however, in the accurate computation of cost increases since 1982. First, 12.5 percent of the current price represents a federal excise tax for the Vaccine Injury Compensation Fund, mandated by Congress in 1986 to provide no-fault compensation to victims demonstrated to have been injured by the vaccine. Second, the more recent inclusion of hepatitis B and bacterial meningitis in children's vaccine recommendations has added to the total cost of immunizations. Additionally, while vaccine prices for MMR and DPT have experienced significant increases, costs of the polio vaccine have remained relatively stable. When these factors are considered, a more accurate estimate of the annual cost increase is 13.5 percent, a threefold increase over the last decade. Thus, the Clinton administration's alleged evidence of price-gouging and profiteering by manufacturers is considerably weaker than initial impressions may suggest.

Manufacturers claim that increasing R and D costs as well as the additional costs associated with manufacturing protection explain most of these increases. Nevertheless, when private physician charges are added (far more significant than the cost of vaccine itself),[19] the cost of full immunization can reach $525. A critical policy concern is how significant these cost increases are, whatever their justification, in explaining declining levels of early childhood immunization. An accompanying issue is whether they suggest the need for a change in policy or in program management and delivery.

Most evidence suggests that a range of factors is responsible for variations in immunization rates, and that increased vaccine prices carry extremely modest, if any, impact.[20] In states where vaccines are publicly financed and distributed, the immunization rate is 66 percent, or 9 percent higher than states that do not provide free vaccines.[21] Analysis demonstrates, however, that states providing free vaccines differ in their outreach and in other institutional factors. Medicaid-eligible children have access to free vaccines in community and rural health centers and in private physicians' offices. Nevertheless, these populations, particularly the inner-city poor, often experience the lowest rates of immunization.[22]

A recent audit of total vaccine purchases indicates that enough vaccine is purchased to ensure vaccination of 110 percent of the four million children born annually in the United States. Prior to Clinton's initiative, the CDC purchased and distributed free vaccines, mainly to public health clinics, to serve 25 percent of this population. A recent study estimated that only 500,000 lack access because they are uninsured, a number too small to explain the current rates.

PHYSICIAN COSTS AND ADMINISTRATION

Recent research examining alternative explanations for declining immunization rates identifies increasing physician costs as a potential factor in discouraging uninsured, non–Medicaid-eligible children from receiving recommended immunizations. A study by the Children's Defense Fund and a recent GAO report indicate that declining rates of private physician participation in Medicaid are due to low reimbursement rates, which forces larger caseloads on public providers.[23] Further, while the costs of vaccines affect a small but important segment of the target population, physician fees for immunizations have risen at a more significant rate than vaccine costs, currently representing nearly 64 percent of the total cost of immunizing a child ineligible for free immunization.

Although vaccine may be generally available at no cost to those unable to afford it, availability does not ensure that it will be administered or used. A range of factors have been shown to affect immunization rates,[24] the most important causes originating in our system of vaccine administration. Currently, about 50 percent of immunizations take place in the offices of private physicians, the other 50 percent in public facilities including city or county health departments, community health centers, and public hospital clinics. These immunizations may be administered with other preventive health services, provider visits, or as an independent categorical service.[25]

Half of all public sector costs for vaccines are federally financed, while half are borne by the state and local governments. Nevertheless, federal direction for vaccine programs is poorly coordinated with both local and private sector delivery efforts. Overall, the past decade has seen fewer and fewer federal dollars allocated for service delivery and infrastructural improvements. Further, there has been no investment in central record-keeping or tracking at either the federal or local levels. Three administrations failed to see systematic monitoring of national immunization rates as a key managerial prerequisite to ensuring ultimate policy outcomes.

RESTRICTED ACCESS: A SIGNIFICANT BARRIER

In addition to cost constraints, restricted access is often responsible for the lack of a regular source of primary care among poor families with young children.[26]

Although a recent study demonstrates that 82 percent of poor children and 80 percent of black children have a regular source of care, those who lack regular providers often use hospital emergency rooms as their primary care provider. Since regular preventive care depends on a provider who monitors a child's ongoing health status and immunization schedule, families who lack such consistent care and regular follow-up often will be unaware of the need for and timing of regular immunizations. Families who are not in a regular system of care and do not have acute medical conditions that bring them to a provider lack any systematic way to be identified as needing required preventive care. Further, emergency room and other hospital visits often result in missed opportunities for immunization because immunization status is seldom evaluated in these acute care settings.

Solutions to the problem of restricted access could best be developed at the first point of medical intervention, the child's birth. Aggressive outreach and community education can also assist in overcoming this encumbrance. Immigrant populations may have language barriers, different cultural views about preventive health services, or, if their status is illegal, a fear of revealing their identity at public facilities. Some parents are misinformed about the need for or timing of immunizations, or they fear dangerous side effects, the rare cases of which have been highly publicized.[27] The media bears some responsibility for the problem, but a coordinated program management strategy might involve the media and public relations in expanded outreach and community education.

Access is also seriously constrained by inadequacies in public and poverty health clinics where free vaccine is already available. Understaffing of personnel, such as public health nurses who administer vaccines, and limited clinic schedules that do not offer working parents weekend or after-work hours act as significant barriers. Administrative requirements, identified in a CDC survey of program managers in fifty-four of the fifty-seven largest public immunization projects in the country, serve to further restrict vaccine administration to eligible children.[28] For example, most reported that appointments were necessary to receive immunizations, a physician must conduct a physical exam prior to immunization, physician referrals were necessary, and vaccine administration fees were required. In clinics, therefore, eligible infants often miss opportunities to be immunized when they are visiting for other conditions, or physicians and/or nurses miss opportunities to administer multiple immunizations. A Los Angeles study of clinic care found that one-third of the 254 children studied had not been vaccinated at the first available opportunity. Another study found that 82 percent of infants from birth to thirty-six months had missed at least one vaccination, and that there was a mean of 7.2 missed opportunities. Minor illness explained most of the missed opportunities in the first study; in the second, contraindications were not a factor in most cases, but emergency visits accounted for 18 percent of missed opportunities.[29]

Further, providers do not uniformly know or understand protocols for when immunizations are contraindicated. Thus, children miss opportunities when they have colds or ear infections without fever, even though these factors are not con-traindicated.[30] These administrative impediments, in addition to the limited clinic hours, insufficient clinic personnel, and shortage of clinic locations, would potentially undermine the efforts of even motivated and well-informed parents to get their children immunized.

Public providers clearly lack significant infrastructure to provide an optimal service delivery system. Federal program funding is not specifically allocated to ensure increased spending for improved service delivery capacity or access and delivery; instead, funds come in the form of state grants, which allow consider-able flexibility in how they meet their local immunization needs.

An additional barrier to low-income people who use multiple and irregular providers is the current infrastructure, which depends almost exclusively "on parents, pieces of paper, and/or memory to know the status of a child's vaccina-tions."[31] The absence of centralized record-keeping impedes surveillance, moni-toring, and parental notification necessary to ensure compliance. A central tracking system with specific information about a child's vaccination dosages and dates would inform a health care provider at any point of intervention about that child's immunization and risk status and could integrate immunization records of both public and private providers. Such a system would then facilitate individual notification when immunizations were due as well as track national progress on immunization. The system could further be integrated with a national child health preventive system.[32] At present, the development of this system is in its infancy.

Finally, public programs or publicly regulated programs that have access to the relevant population do not ensure that recipients are immunized. In four cen-tral city sites experiencing measles outbreaks, an estimated 86 percent of non-immunized children were enrolled in AFDC and 61 percent in WIC. These are federal programs for the poor where regular contact is maintained with partici-pating families, and thus there is opportunity to ensure that current recipients are fully immunized, perhaps as a condition for receiving benefits. In contrast, since as many as two-thirds of all children in day care are supervised in unlicensed set-tings, these are missed opportunities to reach the target population.[33] Ensuring that children are fully immunized in these settings would require changes in reg-ulations regarding licensing of the bulk of existing day care providers. Clearly, there is significant opportunity to achieve well-defined policy goals through improved management of the existing service delivery system.

PARENTAL MOTIVATION AND BEHAVIORAL FACTORS

The previous section identified significant service delivery and implementation failures that affect access to free vaccine among even motivated parents. Although vaccine cost may contribute to the problems of low-income parents, even the availability of free immunizations from public providers does not ensure that parents will comply with suggested immunization schedules. The lack of parental motivation is another factor that some analysts add to constraints such as program management and service delivery impediments.[34] Gallup poll results support the notion that parents place immunizations lower on their list of priorities than access to and provision of necessities such as housing, food, and employment. Since the location, hours, and administrative requirements at public facilities often compete with these other necessities, parents may fail to meet immunization schedules. Parental education about the need for vaccines has been demonstrated to be unsystematic, so knowledge is often partial or faulty. The Gallup poll found that 47 percent of those interviewed did not know that a second measles immunization was necessary, and many more were unaware of the new recommended Hib immunization.[35] However, as previously mentioned, when parents are *required* to obtain immunizations before their children enroll in school, compliance levels reach 97 percent. Indeed, some have used this figure to demonstrate the potential of parental coercion to solve the immunization crisis.

If parents are aware of the recommended vaccines, some do not see any real threat of disease. Others are regarded as simply "disorganized or irresponsible." Multiple studies of immunization reminder systems demonstrate the modest but important impact of simply reminding a parent to bring his or her child in for a scheduled vaccination.[36] Further, while low-income families and those dependent on public sources of care have lower immunization rates, middle-class children and those using private physicians or living in suburban communities have also been found to have unacceptably low levels of immunization.

To some degree, the debate over coercive versus facilitating solutions to the immunization crisis is fundamentally ideological. How much burden should reasonably be placed on parents to access available services, given the well-documented service delivery problems? Some have even argued that the barriers to service delivery are simply parental rationalizations that have been redefined as institutional failures. In fact, 90 percent of all children under the age of one *do* have a regular source of health care; the high degree to which parents seek out private physicians provides additional support for the argument that when parents value the service, they allocate their personal resources (that is, effort and time) accordingly. Yet full immunization falls much below this level, and critics argue that parental behavior is responsible.

There is controversy, often along political lines, about the value of defining the problem as one of access and service delivery capacity or of citizen behavior; critics offer very different remedies and kinds of investments. Those who define the problem primarily as one of service delivery believe the solution lies in investment, improvements in clinic availability and capacity (the size and training of clinic staff), outreach, and education. These are solutions that require changes in program management, not policy. The Clinton administration's program provides no direct funds for outreach and surveillance. Indeed, other than vaccine purchases, the program provides states with increased resources only by allowing them to free up existing allocations under other titles.

States experience a windfall resulting from the replacement of their Medicaid funds, currently financing most vaccine purchases, with federal funds. However, states will have no obligation to use the dollars freed up under Medicaid for any immunization or health-related activities. In fact, they will be quite free to use those funds to finance *other* nonhealth-related state activities.

Those who consider parental responsibility as central to the issue of low vaccination rates stress mandatory parental requirements for complete immunization of children by age two. Some have even attempted legislative actions to require sanctions for noncompliance and elements for enforcement.[37]

Nevertheless, neither definition identifies universal access to free vaccine as the most significant or cost-effective means for addressing low vaccination rates. Indeed, the cost of the vaccine would appear to be a very small part of the problem. In the next section we will compare the Clinton initiative with competing legislative proposals and examine VFC, the final legislative compromise.

THE LEGISLATIVE DEBATE

President Clinton's original childhood immunization proposal called for universal access to free vaccine, which the federal government would purchase from private companies at a negotiated price. The original cost estimates were roughly $1.1 billion. The legislation also called for state grants for surveillance, outreach, and the development by 1996 of an immunization registry.

In hearings on the legislation, HHS Secretary Donna Shalala argued the philosophy of "universal entitlement" in the proposal: "Proper immunization should be a basic right for every child in America—rich or poor—just like in most other industrialized countries. We don't 'means-test' the right to public education, to clean air or clean water. Nor should we make access to the most basic form of disease prevention a matter of family income."[38]

In addition to universal purchase and distribution, the original proposal provided state grants for the development of a registry that would monitor and assist with surveillance and outreach. Resistance was great; the proposal received virtually no support from Republicans, while Democratic support was lukewarm at best. Two major criticisms were voiced during congressional hearings: first and most pressing was the significant expense during a period of needed budget reductions; a second, related concern was the fact that free vaccine would be given to middle-class families with insurance and/or the means to pay for it. Legislators also expressed fears that federal funding of vaccines provides incentives for insurance companies who now pay for vaccinations to cease doing so, resulting in a perverse cost shifting from the private to the public sector.[39] Republicans argued that drug companies would suffer from artificially low negotiated rates, thus threatening research and development, and their incentive to invest in the market at a time when new and improved vaccine development is needed for both domestic and international markets would be reduced.

Most Republican and Democratic legislators supported efforts for outreach, parental education, surveillance, and monitoring. However, they also viewed the primary policy vehicle of Clinton's proposal, universal purchase and access, as a needless middle-class expense unresponsive to the nature of the problem, and fears of establishing a new, costly, and unjustifiable middle-class entitlement were widespread.

Several Republicans and Democrats raised issues of parental responsibility, arguing that reducing vaccine prices would not meaningfully affect immunization rates. Further, they argued that the initiative was a costly and ineffective vehicle to improve access, knowledge, and compliance. Conservative legislators supported competing bills that sought to punish public assistance recipients who failed to immunize their children by withholding some portion of their monthly welfare grant, thus holding parents of the highest risk group accountable for seeking and receiving immunizations.[40]

VFC, the final compromise, modified Clinton's proposal significantly. The childhood immunization provisions of the Budget Reconciliation Act of 1993 provide access to free government-provided vaccine to children who are Native American, who are eligible for the Medicaid program, and who are uninsured or underinsured and whose families seek services in federally qualified health centers. Participating private physicians may receive free vaccine from the state for the purpose of treating eligible children, and states may purchase additional vaccine at the federal price to distribute to noneligible children regardless of income. Further, states may use existing federal funds for childhood immunization programs already in place to improve the infrastructure for vaccine delivery, such as longer clinic hours, more outreach workers, parental education, innovative community-based activities, and improved physician fees. Thus, the final compromise embraces income testing, scorned by Clinton's original proposal. No new funds were authorized for outreach and tracking. In contrast, the CDC recently spent $11 million for computers just to monitor the *distribution* of vaccine.

The legislative compromise only indirectly addressed service delivery: states were allowed to improve local service delivery by using resources already allocated in the form of grants for federal immunization efforts. The legislation met few of the Clinton administration's political objectives and provided a very modest response to a problem for which ample evidence documented that a different approach was necessary.

Indeed, the appropriate approach involves management solutions, not a new policy prescription. Administrative constraints, ignorance among providers, and inadequate service capacity often discourage vaccination attempts. Further, not all those eligible for free vaccine are educated about the necessity for childhood inoculations or know where to seek public health centers or participating private physicians. Some critics have argued that parental noncompliance requires greater use of incentives, sanctions, or efforts to change the culture around immunizations. Although the cost of vaccine has increased significantly, the evidence is very weak that cost is an important determinant of vaccinations. Much more convincing evidence exists that institutional inadequacies and parental noncompliance are central to low participation in vaccination programs, factors that responsive program management could successfully address.

Why, then, did the Clinton administration so rigidly embrace a significant *policy* initiative in light of the overwhelming evidence that a failure of *program management* is responsible for the problem? The answer lies in the fact that political objectives and institutional constraints made a bold policy assertion most attractive. The particular political motivations in this case may be idiosyncratic, but the institutional disincentives for choosing management solutions in preference to policy initiatives are more universal and fundamental.[41] In examining a number of cases of administrative failure in the Social Security Administration, Martha Derthick reminds us of the inherent constraints on administrative success in the American system: "The institutional features of American government uncertainty and problems of timing related to legislative deliberation make planning for implementation and management difficult, if not impossible. These factors are further complicated by calls for action (sometimes with a false urgency) that may cause executives to sponsor bold departures of policy that inevitably create administrative risks."[42]

These disincentives plague political executives and impose an often perverse bias for choosing a bold and attractive policy solution when public management approaches are called for. In many respects, the decision to move ahead quickly with a universal swine flu immunization program suffered from these kinds of political motivations (see Chapter 3). In the next section we will review the political and institutional factors influencing the Clinton initiative for childhood immunization and explore the ways in which incentives can be increased for improved management that solves public problems.

POLITICAL INCENTIVES FOR POLICY OVER MANAGEMENT

The original legislation proposed by President Clinton introduced a series of important symbolic policy and political arguments that were a means to assert a set of principles about the policy agenda and values of a new administration. Some have argued that these same values would be used later in the centerpiece of the Clinton administration's legislative agenda—health care reform—thus providing continuity and thematic coherence to its mission: to generate broad public support for its policy goals. Indeed, universal vaccine entitlement (later dubbed by cynics as "middle-class entitlement") was good politics and a good middle-class issue.

The Clintons had a strong and visible relationship with Marian Wright Edelman and the Children's Defense Fund (CDF). The CDF is an aggressive advocate for a set of social welfare objectives that include national health insurance, a guaranteed minimum income, and government-sponsored programs to improve the health and economic well-being of children and families. In early 1992, the CDF published a study that identified increasing child poverty and high vaccine costs as major determinants of falling immunization rates and increases in illness and death.

The Clinton administration seized the issue, embracing CDF's analysis because it met political objectives. First, the initiative identified a popular villain—greedy, price-gouging drug companies—and a sympathetic victim—young, defenseless children. Second, by aligning itself with a strong children's advocacy group whose progressive philosophy set a tone for its own agenda, the administration thought it would solidify its liberal constituency. Third, Clinton positioned himself as a bold and aggressive policy actor early in his tenure, in stark contrast to his Republican predecessors. Finally, focusing on price as the problem and government purchase as the solution provided an appealing approach that was clear and easily understood; infrastructural or behavioral factors, on the other hand, are much more complex. Thus, in an effort to find an easily understood, powerful symbol that could galvanize the middle class and provide a trial run for overall health care reform, the administration seized the vaccine initiative.

The Clinton administration pressed the initiative to meet a misguided political strategy, and although much of the initial interest appeared to be driven by an attraction to powerful symbols and dramatic pronouncements, the initiative ultimately did not enjoy political support. Some critics have interpreted the effort as simply a miscalculation. Instead of pursuing a traditional liberal agenda, the administration's approach to the childhood immunization crisis (for which there was firm evidence that its causes were both infrastructural and behavioral) should have more directly and equitably balanced rights *and* responsibilities. This approach would have set a more centrist tone capable of galvanizing both Republicans and Democrats.

Whatever its weakness in assessing the political landscape, however, the Clinton administration clearly pursued a political—*not* a management—strategy with its childhood immunization policy. In the next section we will explore why a management strategy has so little appeal to ambitious public executives.

A BIAS AGAINST MANAGEMENT

The Clinton administration had a highly political agenda when it chose childhood immunization as a policy target and universal access to free vaccine as its vehicle. Indeed, there are few incentives for executives to become involved in implementation, although management, as we demonstrate throughout this book, is central to success even when a new policy is justified.

When public executives choose their investments, they seek to distinguish themselves: to associate themselves with new and important accomplishments and to further their own reputations. Although policy initiatives—whether legislative or regulatory, successful or insignificant—provide the appearance of action and innovation, management initiatives seem elusive and undramatic to ordinary citizens. Management agendas, therefore, rarely receive much media coverage and public attention. The media often look for novelty or for stories that grab the public's imagination; their incentives are similar to those of public officials. Since building a portfolio on which to run for reelection is a primary motivator for an elected official to take action, he or she is generally less attracted to investments in management.

In addition, as elected or appointed officials, public executives have a short time frame, as defined by the next election, in which to make their mark. Changing the management of an institution or an operation, which is most often characterized by bureaucratic rules and relationships, is correctly viewed as difficult and time-consuming.[43] Thus, adjusting the cost of immunization may appear easier and faster than changing the way in which current immunization services are provided.

But while there is much truth in the assessment of the difficulties of pursuing a management agenda, there is considerable misunderstanding about the ease with which new *policies* are effectuated.[44] Indeed, recent reports on the problems involved in launching the administration's modest program to reduce vaccine costs to the poor is a stark reminder of the critical role of management in policy implementation.

Management challenges such as buying, distributing, and tracking government-purchased vaccine are a major determinant of policy success[45] and are critical to the success of the Clinton strategy. Legislative debate, however, seldom considers these critical factors when evaluating a new policy initiative.[46] Early assessment of the capacity and experience of the CDC and the GSA to manage these aspects of the initiative suggests that effective implementation of the plan may be compromised. As we will discuss in the epilogue, VFC's initial management crisis raises serious questions about whether the development of an implementation plan or a design for program management was ever a central concern in policy development.

Management is a difficult focus for a public executive. It is especially difficult in substantive areas where authority is fragmented among a number of federal agencies and among multiple levels of government, all of whom have competing interests. Program performance in both the polio and swine flu immunization initiatives, for example, depended critically on the behavior of thousands of state and local governments. Because the federal government's role is largely concerned with policy coordination, research, and funding, immunization authority rests primarily with the states.[47] Even within states, operational authority usually resides within localities in county or city public health authorities. Thus, managing the service delivery process from the federal level is an inherently difficult enterprise, as is often the case in our federal system of policy-making, which disperses both political and policy authority to the subfederal level. The difficulties inherent in federalism have been well illustrated in all the public health initiatives we have examined in this book.

In addition to the problems of intergovernmental relations, multiple actors and competing interests among private and nonprofit interest groups pose additional impediments. In the public health arena, drug companies, child advocates, organized disease constituents, health providers, organized labor groups, and other actors can—and often do—organize to undermine efforts to change how immunization or any public health services are delivered.

Management in government involves a difficult and complex process of assemblage, coordination, and bargaining. It is seldom possible to anticipate in advance the myriad problems and pitfalls involved in changing how services are rendered (Will citizens respond to outreach? Will providers sabotage new procedures? Will fearful parents resist mandates?). Rather than assuming in advance how all elements of a delivery plan will perform, executive success more often depends on the development of a vision that sets specific goals while providing local operatives with considerable flexibility in how they meet them. The vigilant oversight of a focused executive should allow adaptation of initial programmatic design to accommodate field-based conditions.

Designs incorporating field-based learning are more realistic and successful than fixed designs, which assume an ability to anticipate all local conditions. But success depends on a strong, focused executive capable of making multiple line decisions about myriad operational matters over an extended period of time.[48] The supervision and assessment of management performance are crucial, which is why the federal government's abandonment of a reliable and systematic national immunization survey in 1986 (and the failure of the Clinton administration to rectify the problem) is so striking. The decision ignores the centrality of management by preventing even a motivated executive from having any management information to evaluate and ensure the improvement of policy outcomes.

As previously mentioned, an additional disincentive to assuming a management approach is the time-consuming nature of such a solution, which is even more significant given the time constraints imposed by terms of office. It is not surprising, then, that critics and official bodies charged with looking for opportunities to "reinvent government" continue to seek ways that have broader time horizons, like increasing terms of office, to institutionalize a public service.[49]

Broadening the time horizons of career executives is a recommendation often associated with efforts to reform public performance. Many argue that broader time horizons would reduce dependence on quick fixes in favor of more fundamental management changes. However, even career executives depend on elected officials for their mandates, and therefore even longer time horizons cannot protect them from the pressures that elected officials impose on their performance. The tension between the need for a responsive and accountable elected government, and the need for more long-term professional management who can consider the larger picture without immediate political risk is an enduring theme in American governance.

With no institutional incentives and few political rewards, how can attention to management be promoted? What political and institutional initiatives will counter the extreme bias of public executives toward policy when management is required? The next section explores the possibilities and constraints for changing the incentives and shifting the preferences.

USING CRISES TO BUILD A MANAGEMENT CONSTITUENCY

In spite of the significant disincentives involved, successful management has been shown to generate tremendous payoffs; management really does *matter*.[50] If we examine the conditions under which attention to management approaches—rather than policy initiatives—prevails, we can suggest a situational model that explores the optimal timing and circumstances for a management approach.

Are we dependent on crises to generate management solutions that improve public performance? In our study of highly successful executives,[51] we identified a number of them who used crises as an opportunity to change their management and/or policy strategies. These bureaucratic entrepreneurs then effectively institutionalized the changes under their management.

Recognizing and making use of a crisis is clearly one approach. Another is providing a credible and abundant case record of inspirational management success stories. These stories, like those depicted in the book *In Search of Excellence,* serve to sensitize public executives to the centrality of management and the sometimes handsome payoffs that result.[52]

More than a decade of continual budget crises at all levels of government has inspired informal and formal movements to reinvent or reengineer government. An extended period of economic restructuring, reduced levels of economic growth, and profound shifts in the distribution of income in the 1980s inspired the search for new ways to produce public outputs, reflecting, in part, a public sector facing increasing demand for more limited resources.

These pressures encouraged the recognition that historic patterns of public production must be altered. At the federal level, Vice President Al Gore's National Performance Review represents an effort to emphasize new management practices.[53] Similarly, the National Commission on the State and Local Public Service explored choices for addressing subnational performance.[54] Cities such as Philadelphia and New York are attempting significant management changes in distribution of services and the way in which they are provided.

The outcomes of these efforts are difficult to determine at this point. They have certainly produced profound changes in the relationships between the sectors, and the definitions of appropriate sectoral roles are undergoing radical readjustment.[55] Some efforts rely on naive and simplistic assumptions about, for example, the value of private sector techniques and providers in doing the public's business. The crisis of fiscal capacity and public confidence, however, has inspired executives to look more closely at management solutions.

The more important recognition is that a perceived or actual crisis can provide one of the few opportunities to focus on management. Exploiting the appearance, if not the reality, of crisis can induce management solutions for which there would be little interest at other times. Mayor Rudolph Giuliani, for example, successfully redefined New York City's fiscal and "quality of life" environment as crises when he was elected and was therefore able to institute many executive initiatives that would have been impossible at other times. Public perceptions of the success of Giuliani's strategies have provided further license for continued change.

Crisis fuels action and quiets the natural opponents, providing the political and organizational support necessary to change old management patterns. In addition, a crisis can provide an opportunity for exceptional executives to exercise their considerable talents. The following chapter, for example, examines how New York City Health Commissioner Margaret Hamburg galvanized multiple public and private agencies by effectively convincing them of the seriousness of the city's tuberculosis crisis. Fiscal crisis, in particular, can motivate a pattern of responses that emphasize a management-focused approach over a policy agenda because of the perception that better management produces greater expected cost savings.[56]

Executives often cleverly redefine ordinary problems as crises to galvanize an otherwise recalcitrant public service. Newly elected officials are often able to use an impending budgetary crisis, hidden by a predecessor, to promote a new agenda. By exaggerating the budgetary problems with which they are initially faced, executives can more freely innovate, unshackled by political opposition, and claim themselves "successful" when they "solve" the fiscal crisis. At such times, it is possible to build a political constituency for managerial change— especially when it can be shown to reduce costs.

A crisis does not, however, alter the inherent disincentives against management approaches. Crises may be used opportunistically by a clever executive when they exist but inventing them poses a risky dilemma. Such strategies are subject to abuse and thereby threaten democratic accountability. Therefore, using crises offers only a situational recommendation to shift the bias toward management.

In the following section we will describe the most recent VFC implementation debacle and the lessons it teaches. Our discussion suggests a set of conditions under which even an uninterested executive can be induced to focus on management.

EPILOGUE: IMPENDING MANAGEMENT CRISES
PROVOKE A MANAGEMENT RESPONSE

The VFC initiative failed to interpret falling immunization rates as a public health crisis capable of galvanizing support for profound management changes, though such an approach could have been possible in the kind of well-designed strategy that we suggest. Indeed, attention to management only became apparent with the impending threat of a management crisis provoked by the poorly designed implementation plan for VFC.

At the end of the first congressional session, legislative amendments to the original VFC program received considerable attention. Earlier, legislators had in fact requested and received a GAO report on the critical issues in design and implementation of the program.[57] In addition, a number of such reports were requested after the first year of implementation.[58] Although no agreement on critical program management issues was reached before the session's end, the negative and highly public nature of the discussion focused attention on important program implementation flaws. Thus, the epilogue to this case is still being written.

Our last section will review the management issues that threatened to derail the initiative and the debated congressional amendments. We will demonstrate the consequences of inattention to the management of policy implementation; even a misguided *policy* response to a *management* problem requires appropriate program management strategies.

PROGRAM DESIGN AND IMPLEMENTATION FLAWS

Intense public criticism of the plan forced the Clinton administration to focus greater attention on important implementation issues. Indeed, public criticism led HHS Secretary Shalala and GSA Administrator Roger Johnson to abandon the original plan for GSA to warehouse and distribute vaccine to the states.[59] Responsibility for distribution was ultimately shifted to the private sector: vaccine manufacturers now operate under separate distribution contracts, while the CDC consolidates state orders and ensures the federally capped price.

VFC was censured for several basic implementation issues.[60] In particular, initial plans for GSA distribution generated significant criticism. The plan's allocation of 30 percent of the vaccine supply to a GSA warehouse in New Jersey, for example, was regarded as an astounding oversight, since the warehouse also stored flammable paints and solvents. Some critics argued that GSA did not have the managerial expertise and infrastructure to move hundreds of millions of fragile and highly sensitive products on a tight schedule in accordance with FDA requirements.[61] More recent reports suggest that HHS relegated warehousing and distribution responsibility to GSA because drug companies, which would have operated more cheaply, efficiently, and safely, had their margins cut so low by the federal price controls that there was nothing left to fund distribution.

Effective storage, packaging, and shipping are critical to ensure vaccine efficacy. However, no plans to evaluate these factors were incorporated in the implementation schedule, and no other distribution options (public or private) were seriously considered. Since GSA had no previous experience in vaccine distribution, this represents a serious oversight.

Critical delays in implementation were also problematic. As late as July 1994, only four of the fifteen vaccine manufacturing contracts under negotiation were awarded. In addition, providers other than federally qualified health centers were not yet enrolled, and participation levels were unknown. Because private providers must justify fees based on administration costs, there were problems associated with costs exceeding the allowable Medicaid administration fee; in fifteen states, the proposed administration fees exceeded the allowable limit by as much as ten dollars. Further, software and hardware that would be used for order processing assumed an implementation schedule with no margin for error, even though states were unfamiliar with the new technology and workers had not yet been trained. More recent evaluation finds the software itself inadequate for most states.[62]

Accountability remains a significant problem. The lack of accountability mechanisms for ensuring states' proper use of federally purchased vaccines suggests a potential for fraud or misuse, according to the GAO. No special enforcement authorities are legislated, so efforts to ensure accountability depend on existing enforcement authorities such as the inspector general.

Finally, and perhaps most significantly, the CDC has no evaluation plan to assess the cost and effectiveness of VFC in comparison with current policies. Although few federal programs initially build evaluation into their plans, VFC, which sets specific goals and deadlines for meeting them, appears to require such an effort. Without the ability to monitor the dosages administered to children in private providers' offices, for example, evaluation of particular aspects of VFC is impossible (such as whether immunization rates have increased among the neediest, or whether federally financed vaccines have simply been used to underwrite the costs of children who would have been immunized anyway).[63]

Again, the absence of evaluation mechanisms illustrates the Clinton administration's failure to consider the role of management in improving policy outcomes. Since one of the explicit goals of VFC is to remove the burden on the public infrastructure by making free vaccine available to participating private physicians, an inability to determine the number and characteristics of children receiving free vaccines from private physicians impairs the evaluation of whether program goals are being achieved.

The dangers of unintended consequences are significant. For instance, some states have purchased bulk amounts of the vaccine at the federally capped price to resell at a profit to private physicians.[64] Private physicians profit from such transactions as well, since the costs are well below market prices. These practices are clearly a distortion of legislative intent and further serve—and without any good public policy reason—to undermine the industry. At least one state has "induced" insurance companies to donate to a state trust fund for the purpose of buying vaccine at the discounted price. Converting private dollars to public dollars is a perversion of the legislative intent that allows states to purchase discounted vaccine with state dollars. Some argue that these examples illustrate mismanagement and poor implementation of VFC. More cynical observers might regard these abuses as efforts of an ideologically and politically motivated administration to subvert legislative intents to promote its original goal of universal access. Recent immunization figures from the CDC do not demonstrate dramatic improvements but are close to attaining annual goals.[65]

CONCLUSION

The threat of management failure and reports of an impending policy and political disaster did induce the Clinton administration to reconsider how the program could be most effectively implemented and managed. There will be continual scrutiny of program performance, and failures may further embarrass the administration. As we have argued in this chapter, crisis is one of the few ways to stimulate attention to program management. One year after implementation, however, criticism of program focus and implementation remained.[66]

Even if impending management disasters, as we have argued, have had an ameliorative effect, building a constituency for management remains very difficult. Further, we are not optimistic for a correction to the policy-management bias. Waiting around for crises and disasters, even creating them, may make situational sense, but given the inherent dilemmas of democratic accountability, such strategies are insufficient. We need to raise the consciousness of executives and a cynical electorate about the payoffs of managerial solutions by promulgating examples of their previous success. Further, we need to warn the foolhardy about the limitations of policy solutions when management is neglected.

Management can provide a particularly good example of a win-win solution.[67] When management solutions serve widely supported goals like universal protection against costly childhood disease, they address the values of diverse political constituencies. Improved management achieves both conservative goals by reducing cost and liberal goals by expanding access. Altering the bias against management involves the challenge of refocusing the perceived political and substantive payoffs for selecting management solutions.

The next chapter examines the policy and management challenges that confronted New York City public executives in their response to a virulent form of reemergent tuberculosis. An exploration of the scientific and policy history of tuberculosis reveals many commonalities with the other infectious diseases we have analyzed in previous chapters. While Chapter 4 identifies significant barriers to pursuing a public management agenda, Chapter 5 determines the conditions under which such a strategy is possible and the odds of success are greatest.

5

Controlling Reemergent TB: Successful Management of an Impossible Job

INTRODUCTION

Safe and effective therapies to treat tuberculosis (TB) have been available for four decades, but ensuring their administration has historically been a formidable management challenge. Public executives are often the critical actors in directing public health initiatives like TB control, but as we have discussed in previous chapters, they often have a bias against management. Many political and institutional constraints militate against focusing on the management of disease control, even when it is clear that managerial solutions are indicated. Like other public health crises we have analyzed, efforts to eradicate reemergent TB in the United States have been frustrated by these and other challenges. In this chapter, we will describe a successful effort early in the decade by the commissioner of health in New York City to launch and manage a comprehensive program to control reemergent TB. Given the obstacles she faced, her success represents a particularly instructive case of managerial vision that has broad application to new and emerging public health threats.

To a considerable degree, the crisis resulted from the unfortunate convergence of a number of worsening health and social conditions that are hospitable to TB contagion, such as increasing numbers of individuals with HIV or AIDS,[1] homelessness, crowded prison environments, growth in drug-addicted populations, and immigration from countries with high levels of TB. These social factors coincided with a shifting set of public health funding priorities that dismantled a historic local and federal infrastructure because the disease appeared to be in decline. A growing number of TB cases with mutant strains resistant to conventional therapies soon emerged, in part due to this increase in marginal populations; with limited access to regular health care, these poor and vulnerable groups were often unable or unwilling to comply with appropriate treatment protocols. And since drug-resistant cases require very aggressive therapies over long periods of time and at great expense, the public health consequences for failing to identify, isolate, and ensure completion of treatment of these cases were dire. Thus, current TB prevention, treatment, and management efforts pose somewhat different and more complex public management challenges than in previous decades.[2]

As we have seen, some obstacles to public health success are known and predictable. Others derive from competing interests and political choices. Still others develop through the peculiar and often surprising nature of natural phenomena. Mutating bacteria and viruses, for example, demand continual vigilance from public health officials in their surveillance of disease incidence. The New York City TB case is a cautionary tale, reminding us that failing to learn from the history of this virulent killer has meant that we often seem bound to repeat the mistakes of the past.[3]

This chapter has several goals: first, to briefly review the history of public health efforts to control and eliminate TB; second, to illustrate how the application of even effective and safe therapies was deflected by complex social, political, and organizational factors in predictable and typical ways; and finally, to evaluate a successful public management response to a dramatic crisis of reemergence in New York City over the last decade. Our goal will be to reveal a set of common obstacles and identify appropriate responses that might apply to the management of a wide range of public health and public policy initiatives.

The New York City case reveals lessons similar to those we gleaned from our discussion of public health responses to polio, swine flu, and childhood diseases—that *disease control requires management.* This case will also demonstrate that in facilitating cooperation among a diverse set of institutional actors and engaging resources, the commissioner of health's strategic management approach represented a successful response to key obstacles common to all large-scale public health initiatives.

APPROACH

In his classic article on the implementation of human service programs, Gordon Chase provides a framework for assessing in advance the probable obstacles for implementing service delivery programs.[4] Three categories of the sources of obstacles that are particularly powerful are explored: the operational demands required by a program concept; the nature and availability of resources needed to run the program; and the need to share authority or retain support from other bureaucratic and political actors. Within these categories he identifies for consideration fifteen areas and forty-four factors that, when systematically considered, he demonstrates are powerful predictors of the obstacles to implementation for three New York City health services initiatives. Although Chase's emphasis is on using the framework to help improve programmatic choices and design decisions, we will emphasize learning to anticipate obstacles and to identify actions and strategies to respond to them proactively.

Our principal case for analysis is federal and local policy response to reemergent TB. However, our previous case analysis of the polio vaccine initiative, the swine flu program, and the childhood immunization program suggests that a management framework is both useful and widely applicable for understanding the success and failure of a public response to any large-scale public health threats. Further, any future effort to launch a wide-scale AIDS or HIV vaccine or treatment program could benefit from these lessons.

The New York City case is significant in a number of ways. First, the crisis that ensued was predictable and preventable, arising in part because of management failure and inattention. Second, it posed many management obstacles typical of large-scale public health efforts and thus, provides generalizable lessons. New York City's effort to control reemergent TB, however, is still a work in progress. As we will demonstrate, systematic and organized management approaches were used to develop coordinated responses that involved a complex set of activities by myriad city agencies. Early multiyear declines in the number of TB cases, increases in the proportion of active cases who complete drug therapy, and increases in the number of case contacts that can be located and tested represent good indicators of success. Nevertheless, as we will show, attention to management and service delivery, maintenance of effort, extreme vigilance about changing correlates of disease, and sustained resource commitments will be necessary over a long period of time to ensure ultimate success.

Before we examine that effort, we will look back even farther to the roots of the recent TB epidemic. The history of scientific and public health efforts to develop a treatment or cure for TB provides valuable insights into the enduring challenges facing any new public health threat. The recent challenges posed by the AIDS crisis—in discovering treatments and managing their application— have much in common with those historically faced by TB. Although our focus in this chapter is on the management of a disease with a known cause and treatment, identifying the myriad obstacles to discovery[5] as well as the process by which discoveries are deployed will reinforce the complexity of managing a public health crisis. After this brief historical analysis of the obstacles to the ultimate development of a safe and effective chemotherapy (which depends significantly on the excellent recent work of Paul Ryan, *The Forgotten Plague*), we will describe the federal public health role in implementation. Finally, we will present the New York City case, provide an analysis of its significant management lessons, and propose a framework for public executives facing the initiation of a major public health program.

BACKGROUND

Tuberculosis, a potentially deadly disease if untreated, is caused by a bacterium called mycobacteria tuberculosis, isolated and identified by the German scientist

Robert Koch in 1882. Koch emphasized the significance of the disease in reporting his findings to the Physiological Society: "If the importance of a disease for
mankind is measured by the number of fatalities it causes, then tuberculosis must
be considered much more important than those feared infectious diseases,
plague, cholera and the like. One in seven of all human beings dies of tuberculosis. If one only considers the productive middle-age groups, tuberculosis carries away one third and often more of these."[6] While the threat of TB was great
in the late nineteenth century, evidence of its existence from examination of
mummies and bones extends as far back as ancient Egypt and even earlier.[7]

The fear of contracting TB and the organized effort to combat it greatly
increased after its causes were known. Indeed, prior to Koch's discovery, TB was
so prevalent and the incidence so high in certain families that the view prevailed
that the disease was hereditary and noncontagious; contracting it was understood
to be "an act of providence."[8] As a result, TB did not become a focus for public
policy, nor did it concern public health officials of the day.

Tuberculosis is usually spread through airborne droplets from an actively
infected individual who is coughing or breathing.[9] Although many people are
exposed to TB and even carry the infection, the bacteria are often latent or slow-
growing in individuals with a normal immune response. Under conditions in
which health and nutrition are compromised, individuals are more likely to contract active TB after close exposure to an actively infected carrier.[10] It is estimated that 1.7 billion people worldwide test positive for TB, a third of the
world's population.

Often, the first infection is fought off by the body, and the abscesses are
walled off from the rest of the lung by a fibrous shell. Much like HIV, TB
remains alive and can erupt full force at any time, particularly when an individual's mental or physical defenses are low. Roughly 10 percent of TB cases
progress to high fevers, night sweats, and the coughing up of blood—a slow,
wasting away of the body that, if untreated, results in death. Nonpulmonary TB
is found in about 10 percent of active cases, attacking the spine, the bowel, the
brain, and other internal organs, with abscesses often erupting through the skin.

The incidence and course of TB through history was so prevalent, virulent,
and random that the disease, formerly known as "consumption," became imbued
with cultural significance, finding its way into major artistic works by Puccini,
Verdi, and Dickens, among others. Some of the leading artists, musicians, poets,
and intellectuals of previous centuries were among TB's victims, including
Chopin, Paganini, Schiller, Keats, Poe, Eugene O'Neill, Sir Walter Scott,
Chekhov, Emily Brontë, and Vivian Leigh. Even Eleanor Roosevelt was
unspared, whose autopsy in 1962 revealed blood-borne TB as the cause of death.[11]

Prior to the discovery and widespread use of antibiotics and other effective
drug therapies in the 1940s and 1950s, TB was treated by "The Cure." Patients
were isolated, provided nutritious food, and given bedrest in sanatoriums, often
sequestered in the mountains. Rest and fresh air were occasionally supplemented

by surgical removal of the infected areas. Surprisingly, absent any real under-standing of the etiology of the disease, these treatments sometimes aided in recovery, bolstering the immune system through rest and improved nutrition and isolating those who might spread the disease. Pasteurization and treatment of infected animals mitigated the milk-borne spread of the disease. By 1930, how-ever, ninety thousand people still died annually of TB in the United States.[12]

SCIENTIFIC COMPETITION AND CONTROVERSY

The race to identify the bacteria and discover a safe and effective cure resembles in many ways the current scientific competition to develop a treatment or vac-cine for HIV and AIDS. During a period when national governments rarely financed or assumed responsibility for scientific research, a worldwide scientific research program was dependent upon university labs and pharmaceutical com-panies.[13] After twenty-five years of aggressive worldwide research, frustrated by the tenacity of the tuberculosis bacillus to mutate and develop drug-resistant strains, an effective and safe chemotherapy was finally discovered. And while each individual therapy initially proved promising, the ultimate battle was won only when all three were put together; such is the tenacity of the tuberculosis bacillus to mutate and develop resistant strains to each drug.

The capacity for mutation of the HIV virus poses similar challenges for developing a treatment or effective vaccine for AIDS. The discovery of various remedies that promised but ultimately failed to treat TB had a depressing effect on the scientific community and public confidence. This climate of disenchant-ment echoes current public attitudes generated by failed efforts to develop an effective vaccine for AIDS, fueling skepticism about the possibility of finding a prevention or cure.[14]

In 1945, a graduate student at Rutgers, Albert Schatz, isolated a promising microbe known as actimyces, which produced a potent antibiotic known as strep-tomycin. Clinical tests confirmed its apparently effective attack on TB bacillus. Around the same time, Jorgen Lehmann, a Danish scientist working in Sweden, developed para-aminosalicylic acid (PAS) that appeared in initial trials to be as effective as streptomycin. To fight negative publicity and extreme scientific skepticism in Sweden, private fund-raising was undertaken to subsidize clinical trials that proved the effectiveness of the new drug, although early claims were overstated. Even though patients initially improved dramatically, many devel-oped resistant strains. In 1948, the British Medical Council's study revealed that patients receiving both PAS and streptomycin had a greatly reduced risk of developing resistant strains.[15]

Derivatives of a new class of compounds called thiosemicarbazones pro-duced a third effective anti-TB agent called isoniazid, which proved to be as effective a treatment as PAS and streptomycin together. Nevertheless, patients also developed drug resistance to isoniazid. While PAS and streptomycin were costly and in short supply—requiring $3,500 for a full course of treatment—isoniazid, derived from simple coal tar, cost only $100 for a full course of treatment.

SKEPTICISM AND MEDIA SENSATIONALISM

Early researchers suffered from an extreme scientific bias against drugs; some scientists believed that immunotherapy and vaccination were the only legitimate methods to cure disease. Indeed, when Prontosil was discovered to be effective against dozens of infections from scarlet fever to rheumatic fever, doctors around the world rejected the discovery and questioned its validity.

The media exaggerated initial claims and distorted risks about many of these discoveries, profoundly affecting research and the likelihood of ultimate clinical acceptance. Competing scientists often discredited legitimate research findings and undermined the funding potential for new research through professional jealousy, intellectual bias, and simple disbelief. Similar to early promising research findings on new AIDS drugs, excessive claims led to widespread clamoring for TB drugs during the research phase, raising serious ethical dilemmas about human trials and the distribution of limited and often expensive experimental drugs. Initial recommendations on appropriate dosages, length of treatment, and other protocols for humans were often arbitrary; only through successive trials was the methodology refined. Further, no one drug ultimately constituted a safe and effective cure: streptomycin, for example, caused intestinal problems and often resulted in deafness.

SMART ORGANISMS

The TB bacillus, like the HIV virus, is smart, with an amazing ability to mutate and develop drug-resistant strains. After initial dramatic results, apparently recovered patients relapsed, and often the second treatment proved ineffective. Most of the earliest patients treated with streptomycin showed clearing of TB on chest X rays, while only 8 percent of those administered conventional therapy showed any improvement. In 1948, a British trial of fifty-five cases of acute pulmonary TB showed early promising results: in six months, fourteen of those treated at the sanitorium were dead, while only four patients treated with streptomycin died. When another group of doctors analyzed those same patients five years later, the results were disturbing: thirty-two of the original fifty-five patients treated with streptomycin had died.[16]

This experience contributed to the media's sensationalism. The deaths following treatment with streptomycin almost certainly were due to the bacteria becoming drug-resistant. Thus, in addition to the side effects evident in a small minority of patients who experienced dizziness, ringing in the ears, and deafness, the relatively high degree of ultimate bacterial resistance defined the limits of streptomycin as a "miracle cure."

Early work on the effectiveness of thiosemicarbazones as an antibacterial agent was also initially rejected because of the serious side effects caused by overly large and incorrect dosages. Later work revealed its critical importance in what became isoniazid. In 1951, three pharmaceutical companies had independently discovered the same wonder drug: Bayer in Germany and Squibb and Hoffman La Roche in the United States. But its original synthesis by chemists was discovered to have occurred in Prague more than three decades earlier with no anticipated application to TB, and thus a potential conflict for patent rights ended with no financial gains to the companies involved.[17]

PHARMACEUTICAL COMPANIES

Much like trials of promising AIDS treatments, problems of allocating and rationing accompanied the first supplies of these drugs, since demand was so high and production levels were inadequate. When the media reported early successful trials, doctors, health care institutions, and pharmaceutical companies fielded desperate requests for drugs from patients and their families. Early supplies of streptomycin, however, were extremely limited. Directors of the clinical trials at the Mayo Clinic attempted to keep their activities confidential, but dramatically positive results made publicity unavoidable. H. Corwin Hinshaw at the Mayo Clinic reportedly stated that he "didn't want to create a demand for drugs that was unattainable."[18] But the early results were so sensational that within weeks of the first responsible articles, the drug was not simply a promising treatment but, as Paul Ryan recognized, *a miracle cure.*

Responding to the overwhelming volume of requests for the drug around the world was impossible. Hinshaw was ultimately empowered by a committee set up by the federal government to review all requests and make the difficult allocation decisions. These decisions, while based as much as possible on reasonable criteria, were ultimately arbitrary by necessity, thus posing wrenching moral dilemmas since they often were a matter of life and death.[19]

Ultimately, scientists engaged in these major TB drug efforts needed to collaborate with pharmaceutical companies in the discovery and development processes. These relationships were often tense, even as the company's involvement often facilitated drug discovery and its effective operational use. Sometimes the tensions were caused by resource allocation questions: Domagk at Bayer fought to sustain the family's commitment to the enterprise even when its commercial potential appeared questionable. Like Bayer in Germany, a family company that ultimately had the discretion to put aside exclusively commercial interests in favor of more humanitarian goals, some companies furthered development by purely charitable acts: Merck, for example, relinquished the patent rights on strepto-mycin in the United States.[20] When doubting physicians questioned the curative value of PAS, the Swedish company Ferrosan refused to supply any more free of charge for further trials. Indeed, the researchers themselves, Lehmann, Sievers, and Vallentin, "were compelled to approach every possible charitable source for money to keep the research on its course of expansion."[21]

The incentives, timetables, and goals of pure researchers are different from those of a pharmaceutical company that must balance the risks of investment in research and development with considerations of profit and accountability to shareholders. Thus, the tensions between research goals and commercial inter-ests are fundamental: with no formal mechanism or set of public policies to mediate these competing interests, public health has often suffered.[22] During these years of intense scientific competition, medical skepticism, and profes-sional and commercial timidity, the struggle to find a cure was often needlessly attenuated, and the speed at which promising products entered the market was ultimately compromised.

Nevertheless, early experience with the control of TB and the lessons of sci-entific research provided sobering insights into the management of the disease itself and the significant social factors related to its spread. Most significant is the fact that even today far larger numbers of individuals can test positive for TB than have or will ever have any active infection. Indeed, the fact that the bacillus can remain dormant and controlled under one set of circumstances and then quickly erupt into active infection in a hospitable social and physical environment means that until the disease is entirely eradicated, the seeds of the next epidemic will continue as a threat. Vigilant public health officials are thus always aware of the possibilities of reemergence as social and environmental conditions change.

Further, changing strains of the disease continue to challenge science by confronting the limitations of current drugs and drug regimens. Also critical is the management of public health service delivery, since disease management in changing social, political, and physical environments is the principal determinant of disease control.[23]

TB IN A POSTANTIBIOTIC WORLD: DECADES OF PROGRESS AND REEMERGENT THREAT

Although the TB threat was a worldwide phenomena for thousands of years, the last forty years have witnessed a significant decline in new cases worldwide, especially in advanced Western economies. Improved living standards—better nutrition and general health—contributed to reducing the numbers vulnerable to active disease. Further, greater access to specialized treatment facilities (TB hos-pitals), where appropriate drug therapy could be provided and monitored for an appropriate period of time, meant that active cases could be cured. The United

States saw a continual decline in the rate of cases (per 100,000) from 53 in 1953 to 8.7 in 1995.

From 1970 to 1980, U.S. federal investment in TB control saw a decline from $20.3 million in 1969 to a virtual cessation when federal financing shifted to block grants in 1972. These disinvestments reflected the view that the disease was waning. TB project grants were not resumed until 1982 and even then at very low levels. By the early 1980s, when federal public health officials became refocused on the emerging AIDS epidemic, they were ironically ignorant of the seeds of the dual epidemic.

As early as the 1970s, federal efforts waned, and the CDC had abandoned most federal research efforts for TB. From 1970 to 1982, when budget pressures worsened and the AIDS epidemic was recognized, shifts in federal funding and research priorities resulted in inadequate federal support for local TB efforts.[24] By 1985, when national case rates began to increase, virtually all federal public health attention focused on AIDS, and TB was virtually abandoned as a federal priority. Ironically, the connection between HIV and TB was missed or underappreciated. Not until 1988, when the seriousness of the case rate increase was acknowledged, did the CDC coordinate the "Strategic Plan for the Elimination of TB in the United States." Testifying at hearings in 1990, senior CDC official Alan Hinman claimed that TB could be completely eliminated in the United States for an annual appropriation of $36 million. In 1992, the Public Health Service revised its estimates of the cost of eliminating TB to $515 million a year, reflecting the profoundly changing environment of the disease with an expanding number of multiple-drug-resistant TB (MDR-TB) cases.[25] The significant increase in expense estimates was due in part to twenty years of the virtual dismantling of the existing TB infrastructure around the country and the increased cost associated with treating MDR-TB cases. Garden-variety TB was estimated to cost $10,000–$15,000 per case at the time, while MDR-TB cost as much as $250,000 per case, with many dying anyway.

CDC funding did not return to the nominal 1969 levels until 1989, and the crisis was already quite serious before funding levels began to reflect its public health importance, increasing almost twofold from 1991 to 1992 and again from 1992 to 1993. In the late 1980s, TB research and development funds from NIH and its National Institute of Health and Allergy and Infectious Disease also began to increase, from $3.8 million in 1989 to $53 million in 1996. Most important was the increase in federal funds provided by Medicaid, which since 1994 has matched state funding for TB and thus provides funds to support state programs for directly observed therapy (DOT).[26] This Medicaid funding increased from $50 million in 1993 to $140 million in 1996, an almost threefold increase.

Federal efforts and funding priorities, however, *followed* rather than *anticipated* the increasing acuteness and proliferation of new cases. Further, levels of funding remained very low even when federal officials alerted Congress about the impending crisis, a shocking lapse in management oversight.[27] Thus, reemergent

TB resulted in part from federal neglect, disinvestment, and distraction, and a centuries-old disease for which modern science had developed a cure progressed unabated.

AN UNANTICIPATED CRISIS: THE RISKS OF COMPLACENCY

The history of TB clearly confronts public health officials with the enduring lessons of the remarkable tenacity of the TB bacillus and the serious risks of complacency. In the early 1990s, the crisis of increasing cases of MDR-TB in New York City was treated with alarm and an aggressive public health response, one from which important public management lessons emerge. New York City's successful TB control initiative resulted from a focused executive who developed a strategic management approach to overcome the obstacles to coordination and cooperation among diverse agencies and actors. Dr. Margaret Hamburg, the commissioner of health, generated a clear mission for which she mobilized widespread support. Further, she seized a mechanism for identifying and addressing the operational obstacles facing critical actors between and within agencies.

Specialized chest clinics and sanatoriums in the fifties and sixties coupled with systematic screening and increased living standards had reduced the rate of incidence from 98 per 100,000 in 1950 to 17.2 in 1978. So successful was the reduction in risk that the public health infrastructure for TB monitoring, treatment, and surveillance at both the federal and local levels was reduced and shifted to other activities. During the 1960s and into the fiscal crisis of the 1970s, New York City closed facilities and reduced inpatient beds with no resource commitment to ensuring their substitution with outpatient services.

In 1967, when New York City had four thousand cases of active TB, there were still more than one thousand hospital beds in municipal hospitals specifically designed for TB patients; by 1992, however, more than a decade after TB cases were on the increase in New York, there were fewer than seventy-five beds. In 1967, the city had an inventory of twenty-two full-time chest clinics, but by 1992, only nine remained. During this period of complacency about the continued threat of TB, the quality of remaining services was severely eroded. Staff were inadequate and poorly trained, and hundreds of existing budget lines for health department workers were simply left unfilled.[28] Clinics lacked modern diagnostic tools, and the city's limited capacity was sorely strained by overcrowded and dilapidated facilities that discouraged and undermined active cases from seeking and continuing appropriate treatment. The city, while monitoring the annual increase in cases, did little to respond over the decade, as it too became refocused on the growing increase in HIV and AIDS cases. Indeed, the Department of Health had little will and no money to focus on TB, although reported cases grew by 100 percent in the decade.[29] Ironically, it was the increase in the number of HIV and AIDS cases that exacerbated the already growing incidence of MDR-TB, since immunosuppressed individuals exposed to TB are unable to contain it and are more likely to become active and spread it before they are diagnosed.[30] Further, the presentation of TB in HIV and AIDS patients differs from typical patients, and thus for a long time the identification of TB in these cases was misdiagnosed or failed to be diagnosed at all.[31]

In some ways, TB control was the victim of its own success. While public health services have always remained a largely local function,[32] federal funds to support research and locally generated efforts were important in leveraging these activities and in directing local public health institutions to appropriate standards of care.

For example, in 1979 a $75,000 cooperative program grant from the CDC allowed New York City to test directly observed therapy (DOT), a new kind of service delivery to TB patients. Used in other parts of the world and supported by the World Health Organization, DOT sends health care workers to communities to oversee and ensure that active and known TB patients who cannot or do not appear regularly at health care facilities take their proper course of drug therapy. The danger of nontreatment or inadequate length of treatment (a function of patient compliance) is that drug-resistant strains will proliferate and that patients will relapse or become sicker and more dangerously contagious.

Unsupervised therapy is one of the most serious problems of ensuring a TB cure in patients not monitored in an inpatient facility. MDR-TB can be life-threatening if it cannot be controlled by standard therapies. Resistant strains require aggressive drug therapy, a far more expensive and longer course of treatment (during which infected patients are contagious for longer periods of time) that poses many potentially undesirable side effects. In 1992, standard treatment required six to nine months of drug therapy costing about $353, while drug-resistant TB could require eighteen months to two years of therapy with many different drugs and cost upwards of $8,700. With an annual increase of 12 percent a year, 1999 drug costs are that much higher.[33]

The development of drug-resistant TB can occur in one of two ways. A garden-variety TB patient can develop drug-resistant strains by failing to comply with a standard treatment regimen, thereby allowing the drug-resistant strains to proliferate. Once there are large numbers of drug-resistant cases, however, those infected can more easily spread the new strains to previously uninfected victims. If these victims are in poor health and otherwise immunosuppressed, they can easily develop active MDR-TB.

Failure to treat can result in death, particularly in vulnerable populations. Although the threat of multiple-drug-resistant strains was not a serious concern in 1979, the increasing numbers of garden-variety TB cases were. The CDC's program grant provided a good test of the DOT approach and clearly demonstrated the potential success of this treatment modality.[34]

Thus, the growing AIDS epidemic, along with increasing poverty, third world immigration, drug addiction, and expanding immunosuppressed populations living in congregate facilities significantly increased the incidence of TB in the New York City population by the mid-1980s. But it was the growing incidence of MDR-TB that finally signaled the seriousness of the crisis. Fear of contagion and the threat of ineffective drugs ultimately provoked public outcry and a political response.

CHANGING SOCIAL CONDITIONS

Between 1980 and 1990, New York City saw an increase in social and environmental conditions hospitable to TB following a period of significant dismantling of the public health infrastructure.[35] Poverty rates grew 25 percent over the period,[36] as did the incidence of homelessness, drug addiction, and populations living in congregate facilities.[37] The average daily inmate population grew by more than 330 percent over the decade, homeless individuals seeking shelter increased by more than 200 percent from 1985 to 1991, and immigration from countries with a high incidence of TB including Asia, Africa, and Latin America continued unabated.[38]

These conditions, coupled with a decades-old dismantling of the TB infrastructure, made the reemergence of garden-variety TB predictable and inevitable. The increasing growth in multiple conditions hospitable to active TB should have provided obvious clues to its resurgence, but what also emerged was the more serious, less understood MDR-TB. It was not until 1991, however, when several newsworthy cases of TB erupted in upstate prisons and several New York City hospitals[39] among prisoners, patients, and (more significant politically) prison guards and health care workers that city officials appreciated the seriousness of the crisis they were facing.

At the time, at the end of the Koch administration, Health Commissioner Steven Joseph devoted all his time to the AIDS crisis. He assumed a high-profile role in the media as a crusader drawing attention to the seriousness of the AIDS situation and acting as an outspoken advocate for resources from the state and federal government. Joseph championed highly controversial policy initiatives like the distribution of hypodermic needles to IV drug users and was described by the New York Times as "New York City's own surgeon general."[40] Ironically, while the city focused its attention on the AIDS epidemic, it ignored the increasing incidence of TB and the increasing seriousness of the threat of MDR-TB compounded by the growth in HIV and AIDS. Joseph was so unaware of the emerging threat of a TB crisis that the director of the health department's Bureau of Tuberculosis Control was budgeted as a part-time position.[41] With no resources, inadequate treatment facilities, poor information systems, and a late start in recognizing the seriousness of what they were confronting, "the DOH found itself in the middle of an epidemic with little ability to act."[42]

The new city administration under Mayor David Dinkins, provoked in part by the publicity accompanying TB outbreaks among guards in an upstate prison and several New York City hospitals,[43] began to take the situation seriously. Further, the tabloid press reported on the dangers of contagion, suggesting that even subway riders might be at risk. Although distorted and often sensational, the press provided a needed lens for a new administration about the risk of continuing to neglect the growing TB threat.

The new administration with Dr. Margaret Hamburg as the commissioner of health responded to the crisis with considerable dispatch. Defining TB control as a city priority, she recognized the significance of the 143 percent increase in cases since 1980, representing 15 percent of cases nationally or an incidence five times the national average. In very low-income neighborhoods like Bedford Stuyvesant, Harlem, and Mott Haven, the rates were ten times the national average. Twenty-five percent of the cases were homeless, 33 percent were chemically dependent, and 27 percent were HIV- or AIDS-infected. In all, blacks and Hispanics composed 82 percent of the 1991 cases, and 33 percent of the city's cases manifested drug resistance to standard TB treatment.[44] Indeed, the epidemic reflected high incidence among those living in TB-hospitable environments.

CRITICAL CHALLENGES: COOPERATION AND COORDINATION

A number of profound challenges faced the new administration in responding to the crisis. First, Dinkins came into office facing a potential budget gap of more than a billion dollars.[45] Thus, a TB control program would need to compete with other critical public services, many of which had been experiencing budget cuts.[46] Second and perhaps most important, while resources were critical to rebuild the health department's infrastructure of both personnel and facilities, the department could not be successful without the coordination and cooperation of myriad city agencies, all of which would have to provide resources and energy. The MDR-TB outbreak in upstate prisons in the fall of 1991, for example, prompted a lawsuit by the Legal Aid Society to ensure protection of inmates in the city's prison system. This development ultimately required the planning and building of state-of-the-art communicable disease isolation units to protect prisoners and prison staff from infectious diseases.

Thus, any systematic effort to identify all active cases, ensure diagnosis and treatment, and monitor therapy would have to involve a large number of city agencies and private and nonprofit providers most likely to have contact with at-risk populations. For example, the Human Resources Administration (HRA) manages homeless shelters, the Department of Corrections manages the city prisons, the Health and Hospital Corporation (HHC) manages the public health care system including eleven public hospitals and numerous ambulatory care facilities, and EMS manages emergency transportation to hospitals.

The Department of Health could not institute and manage an effective program of surveillance, treatment, tracking and monitoring, detention (when necessary) training, and education without the commitment of effort and resources from a wide range of city agencies. All of these agencies have direct contact with the populations primarily affected, who were least likely to have regular sources of health care. Further, most were poor, and many were homeless, transient, or living marginal lives, often in congregate settings like shelters or prisons. Thus, they posed threats to others and were least likely to comply with strict drug therapy protocols, even if they could be identified by the agencies with which they came in contact. There existed a real danger that an active case leaving an HRA homeless shelter, for example, would be lost without any assurance that the infection was cured, posing continued harm to himself or herself as well as to others in settings where he or she might later be found, such as the prison population. Because tracking of cases was critical and many city agencies had contact with the same clients, there was a vital need for agencies to communicate, share case information, and coordinate their procedures. The nature of the disease necessitated a well-focused and coordinated approach, but cooperative activities have rarely characterized these agencies' relationships.

Thus, the health department was convinced that while their facilities, infrastructure, and resources were inadequate to deal with the scope of the problem, even rebuilding their public health infrastructure would not sufficiently ensure success without a comparable commitment from a myriad of other agencies. TB could be reduced through two principal means: increasing treatment completion and infection control—and Commissioner Hamburg was certain that she had no choice but to make this goal her highest priority. She understood that her responsibility was a clear-cut public health function, but she was dependent for success on exercising leadership over a vast set of institutions without any history or experience of working cooperatively. Perversely, the budget process itself traditionally functions to encourage agencies to overstate their needs and rewards those who make the most compelling case. Thus, city agencies were typically turf-oriented, territorial, and protective over their limited resources; their relationship was inherently competitive. Further, although each agency faced the risk of contagion among their populations and dangers to their workers from uncontrolled TB, with the exception of the Department and Health and HHC, few city agencies saw TB control as central to their missions.[47] They feared being responsible for a set of activities without being provided with the necessary resources to manage them.[48]

PLANNING A COORDINATED STRATEGY

Provoked to action by the well-documented scope of the resurgent TB,[49] a committed and activist commissioner, and a media promoting in a sensational way the risks facing the city, the mayor and his deputy mayor for human services, Ceasar Parales, gave Hamburg their blessing and encouraged her to take leadership in developing a coordinated response to the crisis. Thomas Frieden, M.D., a former CDC epidemiology intelligence officer who had demonstrated in his original research the incidence and nature of MDR at several city hospitals, was appointed full-time director of the health department's Bureau of Tuberculosis Control.[50] Viewing the problem strictly in public health terms, the department team regarded the crisis as a "front burner issue" and had support from the mayor to take leadership and establish a set of priorities. But they needed a focused interagency effort that would involve all the relevant stakeholders, educate them about the extent and seriousness of the crisis, and identify the steps that each agency would need to take to realize the program goals. While Hamburg felt strongly that her department had the expertise and was the appropriate agency to establish the program goals to respond to the crisis, she was dependent on cooperation and commitment from multiple city agencies and other important actors.

It was at this point that the Department of Health drafted a preliminary blueprint with goals and objectives that laid out a series of recommendations: to increase drug completion rate, which was responsible for the proliferation of cases and especially MDR cases; to prevent the spread of TB in congregate settings; and to prevent future cases through screening and prevention.[51] While these were simple public health goals, they involved a significant investment of city resources during a period of intense budgetary contraction[52] and necessitated considerable interagency cooperation. While the Office of Management and Budget was sympathetic to department needs and agreed that the TB crisis required immediate attention, they also questioned their ability to evaluate the relative priorities from a public health perspective of budget requests from various agencies seeking funds for TB.[53]

Thus, the mayor's office assigned responsibility to Hamburg to evaluate the requests of all agencies, to establish programmatic priorities, and to present a consolidated TB budget for consideration. This consolidated budget request was significant in a number of ways: it distinguished the TB effort from other common city programs; it established Hamburg as the leader of the effort and the department as the repository of expert knowledge; and it recognized the necessity of pursuing a single, cooperative, and interagency agenda. Hamburg and Frieden, her director of tuberculosis control, regarded the necessary action as fairly straightforward, representing a return to traditional public health activities that had been allowed to lapse, such as increased surveillance and prevention activities that would ensure that cases were reported and tracked, increased outreach to high-risk groups, increased and improved clinic treatment and follow-up services, and improved public and clinical education. Risks to prison guards and hospital and social service workers were perhaps the most salient aspect of the crisis; apparently, the necessity of joint action among city agencies to ensure that labor and occupational safety codes were upheld was most urgently realized when TB threatened their own personnel.

Mary McCormick, president of the Fund for the City of New York, a foundation providing management assistance to city government, proposed to Hamburg that she engage in a new kind of strategic planning process that could be organized quickly to facilitate change. Using a method known as "Real Time Strategic Change,"[54] the Fund helped coordinate an interactive planning process with the Mayor's Office of Operations and the Department of Health that would produce goals, implementation plans, and operational activities integrating multiple agencies, divisions, and actors. Convinced that policy planning could not be divorced from implementation and operations, McCormick helped provide a new technology incorporating all three aspects that could be organized quickly to facilitate change.

The Fund organized a steering committee with high-level executives from all the relevant agencies and mayoral offices (including Budget and Operations) and a design committee, which helped plan the central vehicle for problem solving and implementation. This vehicle, called a "large-scale event," took place over a three-day period and involved four hundred people from multiple agencies and all levels of responsibility, from commissioners to frontline workers, as well as outside stakeholders. Its purpose was to mobilize a citywide effort to implement a coordinated TB control program. While the general goals were laid out in Hamburg's blueprint, the large-scale event was designed to collectively identify the critical organizational and political obstacles within and between agencies. Further, it was designed to build bridges for communication and coordination; according to McCormick, this process "broke down traditional hierarchies and constructively put them back together again."[55]

Following the event, each agency and the mayor's Office of Operations created continuous working groups to sustain progress on the development of agency-specific plans and to ensure oversight, monitoring, and follow-up of clearly identified tasks on a monthly basis. Operational assignments and timetables for implementation with specific measurable goals were established, and the interagency steering committee monitored ongoing progress.

Although follow-up was clearly evident and early goals were generally met, agency commitment and investment were uneven, and skepticism persisted.[56] Frieden, for example, regarded the entire challenge as a relatively straightforward set of operational problems that were obvious and uncontroversial. He identified the key ingredients of success as managerial and largely within the control of the Department of Health, given aggressive and affirmative budgetary support from the Office of Management and Budget. The central challenge, according to Frieden, was providing proper resources, treatment, and support to a patient with active TB. Although he acknowledged the highly unusual role that the budget office played and its critical importance to the effort, he attributed the department's success to Hamburg's widespread respect and a well-orchestrated series of internal management steps, including the building of a surveillance and tracking system, the hiring and training of personnel for treatment and directly observed therapy, and a series of critical purchasing initiatives. He further emphasized the importance of the department's "post-audit status," issued by the budget office and the Department of Personnel, which released previously frozen city and federal funds for staffing expansion.[57]

Despite skepticism about the importance of the large-scale event, most participants acknowledged that the process produced a rationalized program that was disciplined, integrated, and operational and was critical to the commitment of city resources. Further, some agreed that the event, with its somewhat unorthodox approach, provided the planning process with a signal and an energy that had enormous symbolic value. Many at the mayoral level had never seen an interagency effort launched with this level of speed or effectiveness; like "elephants all moving in the same direction" the effort built relationships and miraculously mobilized a diverse group who recognized and committed to their respective responsibilities.[58]

THE TB CONTROL PROGRAM: WHAT WAS ACCOMPLISHED?

A series of court-ordered activities accompanied the planning process that mandated huge capital expenditures for the city as a result of litigation on behalf of inmates at Rikers Island Prison in 1991.[59] Fearful of the growing epidemic and uncertain about the future need to protect inmates and prison personnel, the city relied on physicians to determine whether isolation units were necessary for newly admitted inmates until they could be deemed noninfectious. In addition, a consent decree required the prison to build an isolation infirmary to service inmates and to construct CDUs, or communicable disease isolation units. The $60 million city expenditure resulted in 140 state-of-the-art units on Rikers Island. In retrospect, most observers have deemed the effort unnecessarily ambitious and costly, representing an inappropriate allocation of scarce city resources.

Nevertheless, despite the questionable CDU expense, the majority of the public health activities were appropriate, well-focused, and coordinated, undertaken in record time with impressive results.[60] In 1989, less than 50 percent of patients who began treatment were cured. Drug resistance among untreated patients had grown from 10 percent in 1983 to 23 percent in 1991. By 1992, nearly one in five TB patients in New York City was suffering from MDR-TB, more than a 100 percent increase over a seven-year period and an astounding 61 percent of the country's total MDR-TB cases. In 1993, the city's aggressive response resulted in a substantial decline in TB cases for the first time in fifteen years,[61] constituting 42 percent of the nation's decline in new cases that year.[62]

Emerging cases of MDR-TB were largely the result of the failure to ensure completed treatment. As we have already discussed, resistance increases the likelihood of treatment failure and relapse and greatly complicates the control of the disease.[63] Since high-risk groups in congregate settings posed the greatest threat to themselves and others, a multiagency approach was critical in ensuring the testing, treatment, and follow-up of these groups.

Recent studies and city audits have documented a 44 percent reduction of new cases among children and a 30 percent reduction among adults ages twenty to forty. High-risk groups experienced dramatic decreases in a two-year period: among persons with documented HIV infection, cases were down 24 percent; among blacks, 24 percent; and among Hispanics, 21 percent. The number of MDR cases had decreased 44 percent.

The TB program's success can be attributed to a number of specific activities undertaken by the city, such as DOT, infection control in congregate facilities (especially in hospitals), and improved treatment protocols. These programmatic improvements depended on Hamburg's leadership as well as the actions galvanized by the planning process, including increased budget allocations and investments in the TB infrastructure; increased capacity in treatment facilities and dramatic increases in trained DOT personnel; improved identification and surveillance within city agencies (including upgrading city laboratories and updating and improving interagency access to the city's TB registry); improved preventive services such as tracking, testing, and treating infectious patients and their contacts; worker protection procedures; and improved hospital infection control.

During the six-year period from 1988 to 1994, the budget of the Bureau of Tuberculosis Control increased from $4 to $40 million. The augmented budget included initial increased allocations from the city's own sources and, more recently, significant federal CDC grants and state allocations, permitting a dramatic growth in bureau staff from 144 to 600.

Most vital, perhaps, was the significant investment in DOT, which can be directly attributed to the dramatic decrease in the number of new cases and the proportion of treated cases completing therapy.[64] Since 1994, TB spending has continually increased; in 1996, TB investment was $48.2 million.[65] More than twelve hundred patients were being treated with DOT in 1994—compared with fewer than fifty in 1988—with 90 percent successfully completing treatment. This is a significant increase since 1989, when the DOT completion rate was less than 50 percent. Also responsible for the dramatic decline in new cases were the increase in intensive case management and the continued use of detention orders for infectious patients for whom all other treatment options failed. Since progression from infection to active TB in HIV-infected individuals is approximately 30 percent (compared with 3–5 percent in non-HIV-infected individuals), the bureau estimates that DOT alone is responsible for preventing four thousand cases of TB infections and eight hundred active cases by keeping patients from becoming or remaining infectious.[66]

The planning process and direct actions by the Department of Health also improved knowledge, regulation, and implementation of infection control procedures in city and voluntary hospitals, which reduced the spread of drug-resistant TB.[67] In 1994, there were fewer than 30 cases of nosocomial transmission, a decline from the 115 cases documented in 1991. An unpublished 1991 study by the bureau reported that at least 4 percent of all TB cases in New York City were associated with a hospital stay, concluding that improved infection control is likely to have substantially decreased the number of TB cases.[68]

A factor that reinforced efforts to reduce opportunities for TB exposure was the city's decision in the early 1990s to eliminate or phase out large congregate shelters for homeless men. At the same time, noncongregate housing for homeless patients with AIDS was becoming available. The bureau reported that the number of patients on the computerized registry of the shelter system fell from 748 in 1991 to 293 in 1994. Thus, there was an unintentional but fortuitous consequence of the city's change in homeless housing policy that reinforced the TB control efforts.

Improved practices for screening, isolation, and follow-up of incarcerated individuals were also responsible for the reduction in TB infection. Each year, more than 120,000 people move through the city's correctional system, representing some of the poorest and sickest of the city's populations. Further, they have a disproportionately high incidence of HIV and AIDS infection as well as drug and alcohol abuse, all markers for a greater risk of TB infection.[69] Until the court-ordered construction of CDUs at Rikers Island, there was no facility that isolated infectious prisoners. In 1992, all confirmed or suspected TB patients were enrolled in a program of DOT. Incentives and outreach followed prisoners after they were released, resulting in increased compliance from less than 20 percent to 92 percent.[70]

Also significant in infection control was the health department's modifications in recommended antibiotic treatment regimens and preventive therapies with high-risk groups. Further, the department developed better laboratory methods for diagnosis and drug susceptibility testing and a higher index of suspicion for the disease.[71] These activities, in addition to a slight decrease in HIV-infected individuals, clearly contributed to the reduction of new cases, and most significantly to new drug-resistant cases.

Although DOT is simply an altered form of service delivery—a prosaic profundity—it is worth emphasizing that the development of a service delivery system appropriate for high-risk clients and the management of its implementation was a key component of the health department's success. The detention of unrooperative patients in inpatient facilities, if necessary, further reinforced DOT's efficacy; *managing* the treatment was as much a determinant of success as the treatment itself.

THE UNFINISHED JOB OF TB ELIMINATION

The resurgence of tuberculosis resulted largely from neglect, complaisance, and distraction. Originally, the increase in new TB cases resulted from reactivation of an earlier infection.[72] In an environment of HIV and AIDS, however, at least 30 percent of current cases may result from recent transmission. Mobilizing extra-ordinary managerial energy and resources is clearly much easier when the threat of disease is widespread and life-threatening. Nevertheless, TB control requires the consistent implementation of rather commonplace public health activities: surveillance, diagnosis, and case-managed treatment.[73] Indeed, the most important factor in reducing the new cases of MDR-TB was *management* of the delivery of treatment through DOT.

As recently as 1994, there were still 2,995 reported cases in New York City. Although this represents a drop of 21.4 percent since 1992, the number of TB cases in New York City is still more than four times the national average. An increasing proportion of new cases are occurring among foreign-born patients, most often from Latin America, the Caribbean, and Asia, where the incidence of infection is high and often the leading cause of death from a single infectious agent. Controlling active disease in these high-risk groups will depend more on preventive therapy, that is, allocating public health resources to those who do not know that they are sick and for whom preventive therapy may be a low priority.[74] Also critical are the quality and availability of local treatment services, complete case reporting, rapid and accurate diagnosis, appropriate prescription and provision of treatment, sustained follow-up, and education of health professionals and patients concerning the disease and its treatment.[75]

The New York City Department of Health demonstrated significant success over a short period of time in managing these critical elements. However, the cases that remain represent the most difficult to reach and treat. There is extensive evidence about the effectiveness and cost savings of TB control activities;[76] low-profile, continuous cost activities during periods of extreme budget contraction and a diminishing disease threat depend on intensive managerial focus and oversight. Such activities also depend on engaging and sustaining the commitment of new administrations that may not see tuberculosis control as central to their mission.[77]

PREDICTING PUBLIC MANAGEMENT CHALLENGES AND ACTING IN ADVANCE

Relative agreement exists on appropriate methods of TB control, treatment, and case management.[78] The principal obstacles that remain are public management obstacles, and as we have illustrated in the preceding chapters, it is a predicament common to many public health challenges.[79] Even in relatively simple matters of public health, anticipating and responding to likely obstacles are generally critical components in program success.

In this section, we will briefly describe the relationship between Gordon Chase's framework and the TB control initiative in New York City and suggest its usefulness in understanding the remedies that Hamburg employed. In our final section, we will attempt to draw some implications for public management of other public health initiatives—specifically, planning for a future AIDS vaccination program.

Chase identifies the three main sources of obstacles to program implementation: the operational demands of the program concept, the nature and availability of the resources required, and the need to share authority with or retain support of other bureaucratic actors in the implementation process.[80]

The operational demands implied by the TB program were extraordinary given the virtual elimination of all previously existing infrastructure. The development of practically all of the subsystems required substantial effort: expanding the health department's chest clinics; redesigning screening initiatives for high-risk and often transient populations; increasing isolation facilities and redesigning HHC hospitals, city jails, and homeless shelters; hiring and training hundreds of public health field-workers to provide DOT; employee screening, prevention, and environmental control (often involving engineering changes in facilities as well as investment in safety equipment) at HHC, HRA, and department facilities; and upgrading lab facilities for TB testing.

During a citywide period of budgetary contraction when intergovernmental funds were virtually absent, the implementation of a TB control program required a significant increase in resources to meet the minimal first year needs. Further, TB control depended upon a large number of bureaucratic actors with whom the Department of Health had no historic working relationship or formal authority.

Chase identifies additional obstacles that are highly relevant to the TB initiative. The largely transient population targeted by the TB initiative was difficult to screen and follow, and its use of conventional health care facilities was sporadic, frustrating treatment compliance. The cooperation of nongovernmental providers and institutions, such as voluntary hospitals, was essential. Compliance with Department of Health regulations for patient and employee protection required expensive changes in infrastructure and procedures. Special interest groups, including client advocates, unions, and medical rights activists, imposed legal constraints on policy and program choices. Finally, management and education of the press were critical to ensure accurate reporting of the crisis for public education.[81]

Chase suggests a few possible remedies to the obstacles identified. One such remedy, to design a program that limits the involvement of other players, was not considered by Dr. Hamburg. Since other agencies often had the first point of contact with victims, and since identification of infectious patients to ensure treatment and follow-up was critical to program success, involving other players was at the very core of Hamburg's initiative. Similar interagency and multisector collaboration would be at the center of any future AIDS immunization effort.

Chase also emphasizes the importance of winning strong support from the chief executive, which was the sine qua non of Hamburg's strategy. Her ability to mobilize the planning strategy—from the blueprint to the consolidated budget, the large-scale event, and the final action plans—rested principally on the mayor's endorsement. Hamburg successfully focused executive attention on the magnitude of the TB crisis and the need for an extraordinary level of cooperation. The support of the mayor and overhead agencies inevitably assisted in relationships with outside actors, such as unions, special interests, and advocates.

A final solution Chase proposes is behaving as though key players will be noncooperative. This approach was central to Hamburg's strategy. She understood that program success depended on cooperation, which was difficult to ensure, so she pursued what she acknowledged was a high-risk strategy. Hamburg's unprecedented approach to the budget eschewed the usual turf-specific process of budget construction while maintaining the leadership and the legitimacy of the Department of Health in establishing public health priorities. Further, she embarked on a complicated and innovative large-scale planning effort, developed and sustained largely by players outside her agency. Hamburg's bold and aggressive approach exposed her to possible public failure, since so many of the determinants of success were beyond her control.

Thus, Hamburg's strategy was designed to build interagency understanding and trust, which was essential for cooperation. The nonhierarchical emphasis in the large-scale event engaged all relevant groups in problem solving, galvanizing them into action with an understanding of the importance of their work.[82] Her focused strategic management constituted the principal solution to a complex set of operational challenges.

In a recent article, Robert Behn suggests the big questions that scholars of public management should attempt to answer in their research in order to contribute to improving public performance.[83] How can public managers diminish the distrust that appears to be inherent in the relationship between different units of government? How can public managers help clarify how legislators, political executives, and career civil servants should share responsibilities for policy-making and implementation? How can public managers define and develop an entrepreneurial approach to public management that is not only necessary but legitimate and ethical? How can public managers motivate public employees (and citizens too) to pursue important public purposes with intelligence and energy?

The next section attempts to elicit some insights from the New York City case, with particular emphasis on their value to future public health management practices. Further, we seek to assess the relevance of the insights to the literature of public management and address how well our analysis of this case informs the larger questions surrounding management issues.

PROPHYLACTIC REMEDIES

We have the technical capacity to eradicate tuberculosis, and thus, it is a wholly achievable goal. The story of its reemergence in a more virulent form and the serious challenge that faced New York City challenges our practice of public management more than our level of scientific knowledge. The public health challenge of eradicating HIV and AIDS, however, poses all the present-day TB management challenges in addition to those that faced the heroic TB researchers in the early part of the century. The scientific challenges surrounding AIDS are indeed formidable: scientific controversy and competition, private sector incentives and public priorities, media sensationalism and intense political controversy about the worthiness of the victims. Even so, the case of reemergent TB is instructive for identifying the difficult public management challenges that inevitably follow any meaningful scientific breakthrough. Further, it suggests that even successful crisis management, illustrated by New York City's response, faces an underdeveloped public infrastructure for confronting interagency and intergovernmental elements of public health management.

Behn's model of the big micromanagement questions—how to diminish distrust between different units of government, how public managers can share responsibilities for policy-making and implementation, and how they can develop entrepreneurial approaches that are legitimate and ethical—are illuminated by Hamburg's strategy. In addition, the New York City case also contributes a model of how to answer the "motivation question," which eschews a purely command-and-control approach.[84] Hamburg selected a means to motivate diverse actors to pursue an important public purpose with intelligence and energy. She recognized that while the ultimate goals of TB control may be relatively well defined and understood, many people within and outside public agencies have much to contribute, not only in achieving such goals but also in deciding the best approach.[85]

The Department of Health was skillful in conducting a systematic campaign of public, professional, and elite education to establish the necessary commitment among diverse actors including private citizens, private physicians, and government bureaucrats.[86] But the strategy most critical to program success was establishing a compelling mission, elaborating a set of explicit and measurable goals, and developing a mechanism to secure the commitment of diverse interagency actors who would play discrete roles for which they would be held accountable.

Virtually all institutional actors involved in the planning process, even the skeptics, were impressed by the unprecedented level of interagency cooperation in this collective mission. Although state and federal support followed rather than preceded the city's efforts, the focused interagency planning process represented a significant accomplishment that mobilized resources.

The New York City TB initiative suggests the necessary, if not sufficient, elements for managing complex public health programming. Strategic management that defied agency and sectoral boundaries generated a formal institutional vehicle for mobilizing economic, managerial, and staff resources. The initiative's success owed much to a commissioner with bold leadership and a high degree of credibility who gained the unequivocal support of her chief executive. Also essential was a vehicle that brought diverse actors together, provided them with a clear understanding of the challenges facing them, addressed problems, and suggested solutions.

Eradicating tuberculosis is still a distant goal. Crisis provides managers with an impetus of unprecedented license.[87] The signs of complacency as new TB case rates continue to fall have already been evident. The new administration has abandoned the consolidated TB budget, and progress reports on the action plans have ceased. This change reflects, in part, the lower priority with which a new mayor holds the initiative.[88] The weakening of support also points to the fragile nature of interagency alliances and the difficulty of sustaining priorities under shifting fiscal and political pressures. Nevertheless, the need to build consensus on public health missions, construct a delivery system, mobilize cooperation of myriad agencies and levels of government, and ensure accountability and performance is crucial for all large-scale public health initiatives.

If a treatment or vaccine for AIDS is developed, it seems certain that the obstacles to swift and appropriate service delivery would be formidable. Public health executives will need to plan boldly, in advance, for the kinds of institutional arrangements likely to allow consensus building, foster interagency cooperation and coordination, and ensure service delivery management and accountability. These are clearly the activities necessary to ensure success, but few prototypes currently exist for these kinds of arrangements. The New York City case provides a good model for how some obstacles can be prevented and further elucidates one public executive's solutions to some important public management problems.[89]

Finally, the history of the reemergence of TB is a sobering reminder of the ever-fluctuating history of infectious disease: even the discovery of safe and effective cures or vaccines cannot guarantee eradication. Viruses and bacteria are intelligent, and, as we have discussed, active infection can quickly erupt in a hospitable social and physical environment. TB has existed for thousands of years, and despite the promise of a cure over forty years ago, it has infected a staggering one-third of the world's population. In this chapter we have attempted to identify the critical and independent role of management in disease control: without strenuous efforts and extreme managerial vigilance, the threat of another epidemic is ever present. In a world faced with AIDS, the dangers of complacency are pervasive, and the lessons gleaned from the history of TB merit attention: it can happen again.

6

Predicting the Future from the Past:
The Early Mismanagement of the AIDS Crisis

INTRODUCTION

The early public health response to serious epidemics has common elements. Whatever the threat, public health officials are equally engaged in a scientific, social, and political endeavor. They look to scientific evidence on the etiology of the disease, on epidemiological factors influencing incidence, and on treatment and prevention choices and their relative effectiveness. Scientific understanding of the HIV virus, to be sure, was initially weak and over time increasingly confounding as the complexity of its function and adaptation were learned. But, as we have discussed, the speed and resolve with which official agents engage in aggressive public health response depend on a wide variety of factors outside the purely scientific realm and the state of medical knowledge. Even in the early days of the AIDS epidemic when science was weak, knowledge of prevention—the use of condoms and chlorine bleach—was widely known. Yet no massive public education campaign was launched nor were resources devoted to the dissemination of life-saving information.

The previous chapters have documented how a variety of factors in addition to scientific and medical knowledge has significant effects on the timing and character of public responses to disease. These factors have had a profound effect on the historic response to the AIDS epidemic. One that has a powerful role in shaping the collective public support for action is disease definition—the cultural construction of disease. Early views of polio victims and current images of MDR-TB victims remind us of the importance of these social constructions, the ways in which they influence public support, public health responses, and the insidious ways in which science and social phenomena are linked.[1] For a new phenomenon—like AIDS—where the course of the disease is certain death, negative public perceptions of the victims had a powerful impact on the behavior and performance of public authorities. A weak scientific knowledge base coupled with a societal framing of its meaning contributed to an irresolute institutional response.

> [AIDS] . . . reminds us of the way society has always framed illness finding reasons to exempt and reassure its agreed upon etiology. But it also reminds us that biological mechanisms define and constrain social response. Only the sophisticated tools of modern virology and immunology have allowed it to be defined as a clinical entity; yet its presumed mode of transmission and extraordinary transmission levels have mobilized deeply felt social attitudes that relate only tangentially to the virologist's understanding of the syndrome. . . . The social response to AIDS also reminds us that we live in a fragmented society. To a substantial minority of Americans, the meaning of AIDS is reflected in, but transcends, its assumed mode of transmission. It was, that is, a deserved punishment for the sexual transgressor; the unchecked growth of deviance was a symptom of a more fundamental social disorder. . . . The meaning lies in behavior uncontrolled. When an epidemiologist notes the incidence of AIDS correlates with numbers of sexual contacts, he may be speaking in terms of likelihoods; to many of his fellow Americans he is speaking of guilt and deserved punishments.[2]

The social construction of AIDS had a lot to do with the emerging politics that resulted in a highly organized, radical, and vocal disease constituency; organized opposition by a radical and organized religious right; and considerable controversy among members of the medical and scientific community. This was a lethal combination capable of paralyzing and reinforcing the timidity of legitimate public actors, from elected officials to appointed agency heads. Further, the legitimate scientific complexity and uncertainty of developing safe and effective treatments and preventive agents exacerbated the impediments to purposeful action.

The tremendous costs of research and treatment contributed to the difficulties of motivating decisive public action. Bitter debates were provoked about the role of the private sector: how much dependence should there be on private sector research and development, and how much should the private sector benefit from subsequent research and drug treatment development? What should the public investment be, and how should the distribution of very costly treatment alternatives be determined? Questions of public financing and distributional equity have been central to most of the public health efforts that we have studied. But AIDS represents a particularly extreme case due to the extraordinary costs of both research and treatment and the public ambivalence about the worthiness of the victims.

In a number of cases that we have reviewed, dependence on the private sector has been key to managing the public's response. Nevertheless, the public looks with suspicion on the motives and behavior of unchecked private actors benefiting too much from a public health crisis. Fears of profiteering or denial of access to lifesaving treatments based on ability to pay reflect the public's discomfort with the private market role in public health, even while support for public financing remains mixed. Nevertheless, for AIDS research as well as for all the diseases we have studied, the reality is that public authorities depend significantly on private partners in confronting large-scale public health crises. Private roles may extend to research and development or production and distribution, but rarely can public authorities undertake all of these functions independently. How to balance the needs of private enterprise for fair compensation and protection against risk (especially against unlimited liability) with the legitimate fears of private market exploitation of vulnerable populations is an important role for public management. Even so, as we have already discussed, the politics of cooperation is often difficult to manage.

The cases described in brief in this chapter do not seek to be exhaustive, but instead suggest specific examples of ways in which the history of the response to the early epidemic illustrates the presence of powerful social, economic, and political dynamics that made the initial management of the AIDS crisis so poor. They also illustrate the problems of managing intergovernmental relations and organizational cooperation. Some of the examples illustrate creative and managerially sophisticated ways that public executives found to surmount significant obstacles to programmatic success. Such was the case of Anthony Fauci of NIAID and his efforts to improve the FDA drug approval process for promising treatments. But most of the examples illustrate how public authorities squandered opportunities to improve the well-being, and often to save the lives, of innocent victims.

While AIDS is in many ways a unique public health problem, public response in the early days of the crisis could have been managed better.[3] In this chapter we provide some historic evidence of the weakness of that early response in an attempt to imagine how future efforts at large-scale vaccine development and distribution might fare. The "social construction" of AIDS probably contributed to the weakness of the public health response, but here we emphasize the broad and generic nature of the unpreparedness.

In Chapters 2–5 we described how typical this response is in the initial stages of public health threats such as swine flu, TB, and the polio vaccine. For strategic purposes, it may behoove AIDS activists to stress the significance of the social aspects of AIDS. But we will show that the public health infrastructure's incapacity to handle large-scale public health crises and infectious diseases like AIDS is generic.

The general organizational failure to anticipate in advance emergencies and unanticipated events was compounded in the case of AIDS by the convergence of difficult science and downsized government in the 1980s Reagan era. However, our analysis of the public health response to the diseases examined in Chapters 2–5 suggests that if a new infectious disease were to break out in the United States tomorrow that did not bear any "social burden," such as a new strain of chicken pox or smallpox, the public health response most likely would be equally unprepared and unable to anticipate necessary actions.

Indeed, a recent report found that the U.S. public health infrastructure was not prepared for a "bird flu" pandemic likely to strike the United States from Asia without warning. The lessons of the swine flu debacle have apparently been forgotten. But one need not develop hypothetical cases or cite government predictions of current unpreparedness if a crisis should occur. Within the arena of AIDS, lessons of just a few years earlier seem to go unheeded. The lessons of distributional equity and individual compliance generated in efforts to deliver AZT in the early 1990s did not help to anticipate similar challenges in managing the delivery of and patient compliance with the protocols demanded by protease inhibitors in the late 1990s.

In the following chapter we build a scenario based in part on these historic lessons. Our scenario is designed to be both analytically derived and to provide a realistic blueprint of the events likely to be associated with the development of an AIDS vaccine. But the future is not yet written, and so our goal is to illuminate and provoke. We hope to enlighten the complaisant leadership about the consequences of a failure to invent new scenarios as well as provoke anticipatory managerial actions capable of a shaping a different future. As we have argued throughout, management matters.

CASE 1: SAN FRANCISCO BATHHOUSE CLOSURES

The difficulty of managing the public health response to a disease that was initially afflicting an oppressed—but politically influential—minority was nowhere more acute than in San Francisco's handling of gay bathhouses and sexual establishments in the early eighties. The shaping of public health efforts through the power of highly organized disease constituents has many illustrations in the early AIDS epidemic. The dilemma of the city's public health officials, and how they handled it, would reverberate throughout the country and down the years of the epidemic as individual rights and the public's health wavered in an uneasy balance. The solutions reached at the time did not completely satisfy anyone, but in retrospect they highlight difficult politics and uneasy solutions that are applicable even today. They illustrate the potential effectiveness of forging cooperation among affected communities, political leaders, and public health officials to craft workable regulations that preserve rights and protect the public health. Unfortunately, the initial timidity and inaction by responsible public executives was very costly to public health early in the epidemic.

In the earliest years of the AIDS epidemic, San Francisco's gay newspapers, largely dependent upon the advertising revenues of bathhouses, bars, and other sexual services, played down the growing epidemic lest they anger or alienate their customers and revenue base. A lead story in the *Sentinel*, purporting to be an investigation into the safety of bathhouses and sex clubs, turned out to be about their lack of fire safety precautions rather than the sexual activity that went on there. Rodger Streitmatter notes in his history of the American gay press that at the *Bay Area Reporter*, the city's other gay weekly, "rather than attacking the unrestrained promiscuity of the bathhouses [editor Paul] Lorch set his sights on AIDS patients and activists." Streitmatter says that Lorch actually "denounced patients as freeloaders and activists as fanatics."[4]

In 1983, *San Francisco Chronicle* reporter Randy Shilts began to focus on the city's gay bathhouses in his own drive to get gay men to change their sexual behavior in a less promiscuous, more responsible way. In a May 27, 1983, article, Shilts quoted the city's public health director, Mervyn Silverman, as saying, "There has been some pressure on me to close the bathhouses." The approach of San Francisco's annual Gay Freedom Day Parade and the expected flood of gay people into the city for the massive celebration raised concerns that those from smaller towns and other places where AIDS had not yet appeared were likely to fill the extraordinarily popular baths and receive an unanticipated souvenir of their trip to the gay mecca—and contribute to the spread of the epidemic outside the "epicenter cities," one of which was San Francisco. Surprisingly, Silverman eschewed efforts to regulate the bathhouses or to close them down as threats to public health and left it entirely to gay men to monitor their own behavior, trusting that out-of-town visitors "will realize they can't do the kinds of things they might do at home" because of the epidemic under way in San Francisco.[5] He did, however, require the bathhouses to post warning notices about AIDS.

Gay activists battled with one another over "sexual freedom" and the bathhouses. They viewed any restrictions on the sexual establishments as tantamount to impingements on their civil rights. Meanwhile, other gay men were apparently heeding the warnings about AIDS: Sal Accardi, the owner of a large bathhouse in San Jose, estimated that attendance at the baths in San Francisco had dropped by 65 percent in 1983.[6] Six of the city's twenty bathhouses closed. The owner of the Hothouse said he closed the bathhouse because his business had been cut in half by the fear of AIDS.[7]

In February 1984, Jim Curran, director of the Centers for Disease Control's AIDS program, said: "I wish the gay community would officially express concern over the bathhouses. I'd like to see all bathhouses go out of business. I've told bathhouse owners they should diversify and go into something healthy—like become gymnasiums. Gay men need to know that if they're going to have promiscuous sex, they'll have the life expectancy of people in the developing world." Openly gay city supervisor Harry Britt announced plans to meet with doctors and AIDS researchers to organize a campaign to inform gay men that "sexual activity in places like baths or sex clubs should no longer be associated with pleasure—it should be associated with death."[8]

The following month, veteran gay activist Larry Littlejohn announced that he would propose placing a measure on a citywide ballot to prohibit sexual activity in the baths. Many believed the measure would pass. Feeling pressured to act against the baths but still hoping the gay community would take action on its own, Mervyn Silverman on April 9, 1984, proposed a ban on sexual activity in the baths rather than an outright closure, as some were hoping. Looking back, Silverman said in an interview that he continued to hope the gay community itself would take responsibility for dealing with the issue of sex in the bathhouses. "I felt that since it was a situation having to do with sex," he said, "the government never dealt well with those issues." He also might have feared the political retribution of an important constituency. The gay community had dealt effectively with other gay-owned establishments that were in violation of city health or safety codes, and Silverman believed they would do so again. When some gay bars had only one exit, making them a fire hazard, gay people set up pickets and information tables outside. Said Silverman, "It didn't take long for the facilities to change." Pursuing gay activists, Silverman urged, "Why don't you all do what you did with fire hazards? Get out there and really do something to get them to clean up their act."[9]

San Francisco mayor Dianne Feinstein resisted taking action of her own to close down the bathhouses lest such a move be seen as a political rather than public health decision. Instead, she pressured Silverman to do it. But part of Silverman's reluctance was a fear that closing the baths in San Francisco would be viewed nationally as a move against gay people in the most liberal American city. As he put it, "If San Francisco, as a bastion of liberalism, closed down the baths, what impact would that have on other communities?" No one could be sure, given the general hysteria over AIDS at the time, whether closing down the baths might be the first step to closing down gay bars or passing or enforcing antisodomy laws. As Silverman and others grappled with these volatile issues, groups of gay men, clad in towels, demonstrated at one of the health director's press conferences, carrying placards stating, "Today the tubs, tomorrow your bedrooms" and "Out of the Baths, Into the Ovens." Although the tension between individual rights and public health was clearly evident, in their reluctance to intervene the major elected and appointed officials may have been more politically self-serving than champions of civil rights.

Jim Ferels, head of the Kaposi's Sarcoma/AIDS Foundation, proposed imposing a "safe sex code" on all gay sex venues. The plan, which Ferels had worked out with the city's gay political clubs, would mandate that the baths and sex clubs give space to posters, literature, condoms, lubricants, public service announcements, minimum lighting standards, and educators from AIDS information groups.[10]

But just before the foundation was to publicly announce its plan, Silverman finally took action and closed down the city's remaining bathhouses and sex clubs. Speaking more forcefully than he had earlier, Silverman announced at an October 9, 1984, press conference that he had ordered the closure of the city's remaining fourteen bathhouses that "promote and profit from the spread of AIDS." He was blunt: "Make no mistake about it. These fourteen establishments are not fostering gay liberation. They are fostering disease and death."[11] The bathhouses reopened within hours, forcing the city to take the matter to court. Seven weeks later, the state superior court ruled that the baths could remain open, but only if they no longer provided private rooms and had monitors present to prevent high-risk sex.

In other cities, there were similar debates over bathhouses, often with the same kind of rancor and resistance from the gay community—and also with more outright political rather than public health justification. New York City and Los Angeles closed down their bathhouses within a year of San Francisco. In November 1985 New York health authorities closed down the Mine Shaft, the bar famous for its raunchy, no-holds-barred sex scene. In Miami, Randy Shilts reported that Club Baths owner Jack Campbell "brushed off questions about the baths' role in the epidemic by insisting that most of Florida's AIDS cases were Haitians, and it wasn't a problem for gays."[12]

And in Chicago, Howard Brown Memorial Health Center cofounder and physician David Ostrow left the gay clinic because of the hands-off way it was dealing with the bathhouse issue—largely attributable to the fact that the clinic's leaders were associates of Chuck Renslow, owner of the city's largest bathhouse and several bars. "I thought it was inappropriate for the head of the baths to have so much control over the clinic," said Ostrow. Although he believes the baths should be allowed to stay open and can be effective venues in which to provide prevention education, Ostrow is adamant about the role the bathhouses played in "amplifying" HIV among gay men in America and Western Europe. "Normally," he explained, "people have sex within a social network of a certain race, age, and economic status. In the bathhouses, you had sex with anybody you wanted to have sex with, and they went on to have sex with others. So not only do you spread it rapidly in that bathhouse, but you spread it into all sectors of the community that are in that bathhouse, and they go out and spread it."[13]

Clearly, the sexual promiscuity facilitated by the bathhouses had a major role in the spread of HIV among gay men. Equally clearly, the issue of bathhouses and other "public sex" venues was a difficult one for public health officials to manage because of the sensitive political and individual rights issues it raised. In San Francisco, workable solutions were ultimately reached, the result of a gay-friendly mayor and public health director and a gay community that initially refused to yield one whit of what it saw as gay men's "right" to have public sex. Whether these positions represented responsible and moral public health policy or cynical political judgments about the feasibility of public action in a unique political environment, certainly many lives were lost due to inaction in the early stages of the epidemic.

Delay ultimately permitted the city to negotiate a balance among political interests with minimal bad feeling and fairly exemplary cooperation among all concerned. "How to Have Sex in an Epidemic," the title of an early gay community safe-sex brochure, was a confusing matter, and it can't be surprising to anyone that finding answers required difficult and emotional arguments and sometimes even grudging compromises. Clearly, the interests of potential victims were balanced against the political costs of unpopular and unilateral moves against individual rights. Public executives took few risks to protect early victims and their efforts to shape compromises more expeditiously were quite modest. Their approach stands in contrast to the means employed by Commissioner Hamburg to stem the tide of MDR-TB in New York but illustrates the enduring political constraints on managerial effectiveness in public health. The role of a public health commissioner during the early days of the emerging AIDS epidemic may be seen by some as "an impossible job in public management,"[14] but more aggressive and creative efforts to balance individual rights and public health are necessary and possible when the consequences of public executives' timidity carry such heavy public and private costs.

CASE 2: FDA DRUG DEVELOPMENT

Since its 1927 creation, the Food and Drug Administration (FDA) has overseen the licensing, research, and regulation of foods, drugs, cosmetics, and medical devices in the United States. The 1938 Food, Drug, and Cosmetic Act made it illegal to market a drug in the United States until it is proved safe. In 1962, Congress extended the FDA's mandate, requiring not only safety but also proof that a drug's claims of efficacy are legitimate. New drugs can be approved by the FDA only after careful testing in a three-phase clinical trials process. The trials are intended to show scientists whether and how a drug works, the dosage at which it is most effective, and its potential side effects. Typically, the trials involve homogeneous populations, those of the same age range and sex with similar medical histories.

Phase one trials focus on safety and generally take less than a year. Phase two trials usually take about two years, involve fewer than two hundred patients, and are intended to test a drug's efficacy and dosage. Most trials are controlled and randomized, meaning that one group of patients is actually given the drug being tested, while a second group is given a placebo. In a blind study, the patient does not know which category he or she is in, and a double-blind study is one in which neither patient nor researcher knows what the patient is taking. Phase three trials confirm the information gathered in the first two phases by testing the drug in a large number of people over one to three years.

Adherence to FDA regulations and protocols for ensuring the safety and efficacy of drugs comes under severe scrutiny when testing is undertaken for promising new therapies, especially for life-threatening illnesses. This is particularly the case when no or few effective alternatives are available, and when a lack of treatment results in serious illness or death. Early experiences during the drug development stage for TB (described in Chapter 5), even before the founding of the FDA or the development of its protocols, illustrate the severe pressure placed on researchers and physicians to respond to the demands of desperate victims and their families for access to drugs that promise any hope of recovery, however unverified. Efforts to balance legitimate needs for conclusive research and determination of drug safety and effectiveness with the desperate pleas for help constitute a critical public management strategy. Lessons from the early struggles to assist AIDS victims while maintaining the integrity of the drug review process suggest that speed and access can be improved through creative and humane strategies by public executives.

The process by which AZT (azidothymidine) became the first federally approved drug treatment for HIV illustrates the way in which public and private interests can be balanced. The pharmaceutical industry was initially reluctant to get involved in researching treatments for HIV because of the risks of working with live virus and the view that there were no profits to be made despite the considerable expenses that would be incurred. Samuel Broder, director of the National Cancer Institute (NCI), in 1984 approached pharmaceutical companies trying to generate interest in developing and marketing HIV drugs. Given its success with acyclovir, the first effective treatment for the herpes virus, Broder believed that Burroughs Wellcome was ideally suited for involvement in AIDS research. Brokering public-private partnerships is one strategy creative public executives can use to foster the public use of private interest.

Originally developed and then put aside in the 1960s as an ineffective treatment for cancer, AZT had remained in the public domain. German researchers in the 1970s found AZT to be effective against retro viruses in mice, and further studies in the eighties reported its retro viral benefits in animals. Burroughs Wellcome had tested AZT for veterinary uses but decided not to develop it, in large part because retro viruses rarely caused disease in humans. But in early 1985, NCI scientists found that AZT (then code-named "Compound S") showed activity against HIV in the test tube. Scientists hoped the drug would prevent viral replication and, therefore, further damage to the immune system of an HIV-infected individual. In June 1985, Burroughs applied to the FDA for approval to test the drug in humans, submitting an IND (investigational new drug) application to the FDA. AZT was first given to a Boston furniture salesman on July 3, 1985. After early, encouraging results, the speeded-up approval process of AZT was to become a cautionary tale of the risks of cutting corners and an example of the influence of informed and savvy activists.

When the FDA approved AZT in March 1987, "the world of clinical research was turned upside down," as the National Academy of Sciences put it.[15] Not only was there now at least one promising and approved treatment, but the very process by which the FDA tested and approved new drug therapies was shaken up. The FDA's relatively swift approval of AZT was a radical departure from the agency's traditional three-phase drug testing procedure. After passing the bare minimum first phase of the clinical trials process, AZT was deemed "safe" even though it had been tested in only nineteen AIDS patients. Next was the phase two trial, to determine the correct dosage. A 1986 study of 282 patients with AIDS and a milder form of the illness then called AIDS-Related Complex, found that those given AZT lived longer and had fewer of the opportunistic infections associated with AIDS.[16]

The FDA monitoring board overseeing the development of AZT recognized that the drug was having what seemed to be dramatic effects in the early trials. When the "blind" was taken off the study, in September 1986, patients who were being given the placebo were offered AZT. Burroughs Wellcome, the pharmaceutical company that held the patent on AZT, provided the drug, free of charge, to some 4,500 people with AIDS between September 1986 and March 1987. The FDA waived phase three of the clinical trials and allowed Burroughs Wellcome to submit new drug application paperwork requesting approval of AZT. Despite reservations over the limited knowledge about the drug, its hasty six-month phase two trial, and the lack of a phase three trial, the FDA approved AZT on March 19, 1987. The symbolic importance of having even one drug to treat AIDS was tremendous, although in the years ahead AZT's value as a "mono-therapy" would be challenged after longer and larger clinical trials were finally conducted.[17]

In March 1987, the FDA also announced a plan to make promising but unapproved drugs available under its new "Treatment IND [Investigational New Drug]" policy, which allowed designated drugs for life-threatening illness to be sold after the phase one trial so long as research on the drugs continued. To be designated as INDs, there had to be evidence that the drugs were not clearly ineffective or dangerous. The FDA had used a similar approach in making other drugs (such as those for cancer) available to patients even before they were approved. AIDS advocates praised the new policy for demonstrating flexibility in the face of a deadly disease. Vice President George Bush, chair of the Presidential Task Force on Regulatory Relief, also praised the policy as proof that the FDA's stiff regulations, viewed by the pharmaceutical industry as impediments to its profits, had been loosened. Others, however, criticized the Treatment IND policy because they feared it would invite fraud and risk. Representative Ted Weiss (D-N.Y.), chair of the House Government Operations Subcommittee on Intergovernmental Relations and Human Resources, said, "The proliferation, in uncontrolled settings, of inadequately evaluated, potentially dangerous experimental drugs is a prescription for the premature deaths and needless suffering of large numbers of people."[18]

Despite the flexibility that the FDA showed in its willingness to speed up the testing and approval of AZT, activists were outraged at the $10,000 annual price tag that Burroughs Wellcome had attached to the drug, making it one of the most expensive drugs in history. Since its creation and demonstrated ineffectiveness against cancer in the sixties, AZT had languished with other failed treatments. Although scientists from the National Cancer Institute and National Institute of Allergy and Infectious Diseases (NIAID) had participated heavily in the development of AZT,[19] Burroughs Wellcome officially was awarded the patent on the drug. After the FDA approved AZT for treating AIDS, Burroughs stood to make a huge profit. Despite its limited contribution to early research on AZT, the company earned more than $1 billion on the drug by 1991, when the second AIDS drug was finally approved. And despite protestations by government scientists, Burroughs Wellcome claimed to have discovered AZT singlehandedly.[20]

In response to a speech by New York writer Larry Kramer on March 10, 1987, hundreds of people banded together to form the leaderless protest group ACT UP (AIDS Coalition to Unleash Power) to get "drugs into bodies." ACT UP's first action, on March 24, 1987, was a demonstration on Wall Street against the high price of AZT. The group handed out copies of a *New York Times* op-ed article by Larry Kramer that had run the previous day. "There is no question on the part of anyone fighting AIDS," wrote Kramer, "that the FDA constitutes the single most incomprehensible bottleneck in American bureaucratic history." He continued: "Double-blind studies were not created with terminal illnesses in mind," calling for the FDA to make experimental AIDS drugs available on a "compassionate usage" basis.[21] By the end of 1987, pressure from ACT UP had prompted Burroughs Wellcome to reduce the annualized cost of AZT by 20 percent to $8,000.

Meanwhile, activists sought to take matters into their own hands. Groups in New York and San Francisco in 1987 started what they called "buyers' clubs" to make available drugs that were not FDA-approved but attainable outside the United States as well as to import and offer cheaply drugs that were purchasable in the United States at higher cost. Taking advantage of an FDA regulation that allows individuals with life-threatening diseases to import for personal use drugs approved elsewhere, the buyers' clubs brought such drugs into the country in bulk and made them available to people with AIDS. Michael Callen, a founder of the PWA Health Group, a buyers' club in New York, said, "If a substance cannot hurt and may help, we will make every effort to see that those PWAs [people with AIDS] who desire to obtain a substance may do so."[22]

In 1987, the PWA Health Group began importing a food substance manufactured in Israel from egg whites, called AL-721, believed to have some effect against HIV based on test tube studies. Like so many other substances and drugs that raised and then dashed hopes, AL-721 turned out to be essentially useless. In 1988, a Japanese drug called Dextran Sulfate was the rage. In 1989, the PWA Health Group imported two drugs from England that did indeed prove effective—and eventually win FDA approval as treatments for HIV-related infections. Fluconazole was brought in because it appeared to be useful in treating cryptococcal meningitis, an inflammation of the lining of the brain affecting 10 to 15 percent of AIDS patients. Aerosol pentamidine, used to prevent *pneumocystis carinii* pneumonia, was already available in the United States but was very expensive. Although the drug typically cost $125 to $175 per dose in the United States, the PWA Health Group imported it and made it available for only $40.

At the July 1988 national gay and lesbian health conference in Boston, FDA Commissioner Frank Young announced that the agency would allow individuals to import small quantities of unapproved drugs for personal use in trying to treat AIDS. The new policy codified the FDA's long-standing compassionate usage policy, essentially approving what the buyers' clubs had already been doing for a year at that point. ACT UP was not satisfied, however, and on October 11, 1988, the group virtually closed down the FDA's headquarters in Rockville, Maryland, with its largest protest to that point. The group shrewdly played to the news media in its efforts to pressure the FDA.

Among ACT UP's demands were its insistence that the FDA shorten its drug approval process to "ensure immediate free access to drugs proven safe and theoretically effective," eliminate double-blind placebo trials and instead measure new drugs against other approved or experimental drugs, and "include people from all affected populations at all stages of HIV infection in clinical trials." ACT UP contended that when it comes to a new disease like AIDS, the testing of new drugs itself is a form of health care, and that everyone should have the right to access to health care.[23] Eight days after the demonstration, the FDA announced new regulations to speed up drug approval, making formal the expeditious process used the previous year in moving AZT quickly through the pipeline to the market.

Traditionally, the testing of new drug treatments has been conducted in university hospitals, underscoring the "academic" orientation of the research. Research on drugs and the care of patients were seen as mutually exclusive. A January 1988 report from NIAID—foremost of the federal scientific institutes conducting research on HIV and AIDS—underscored this point in saying that "the primary intent of [NIAID's clinical trials program] is not the delivery of medical care to AIDS patients, although providing excellent medical care is a component of every good clinical trial."[24] But NIAID's congressional overseers would not accept this assessment. "In the context of AIDS and other life-threatening conditions," noted the House Committee on Government Operations, "clinical trials cannot be considered solely scientific experiments. Access to clinical trials becomes access to therapy, access to quality health care, and for many, access to hope."[25]

As they had done with the buyers' clubs, AIDS activists took matters into their own hands by setting up community-level research programs in which drug treatments would be tested in HIV/AIDS patients right in their own doctors' offices. San Francisco's County–Community Consortium (CCC) and New York's Community Research Initiative (CRI) tested aerosol pentamidine as a prophylaxis for *pneumocystis carinii* pneumonia, the main killer of people with AIDS. CRI cofounder and AIDS activist Michael Callen described CRI's mission as conducting "rigorous scientific research on promising AIDS therapies in a community-based setting faster and more cheaply than traditional systems do."[26]

In 1989, Lyphomed, the drug company that held the patent on pentamidine, presented data from the CCC and CRI studies to the FDA on May 1. Physician-researchers from the CCC in San Francisco spoke at the FDA committee hearing on the drug about the effectiveness of inhaled pentamidine, while speakers from New York's CRI offered additional information about the drug's safety. The FDA committee voted unanimously to approve aerosol pentamidine to prevent *pneumocystis carinii* pneumonia, the first time a drug had ever been approved based on research conducted at the community level. Looking back, Ellen Cooper, who at the time was director of the FDA Antiviral Drug Division, said, "I guess the lesson is, first, that important information can come from rather primitive trials as long as certain key elements are followed," including randomization, two "arms" of the study that are different enough to detect whether one was superior over the other, and reasonable "endpoints," in this case the development of PCP.[27]

The Presidential Commission on the HIV Epidemic mentioned the CRI in its June 1988 report, urging the federal government to fund similar community-based AIDS research. Following the commission's recommendation, Congress in the fall of 1988 approved a $6 million pilot program to conduct clinical trials in local hospitals, health centers, doctors' offices and clinics, and drug treatment facilities around the country, to be managed by NIAID. Advocates interpreted the new support for community-based research as an acknowledgment of what they had been criticizing as a flawed clinical trials process. By reducing the cost of research on prospective AIDS drugs and providing access to promising treatments directly through physicians who were caring for AIDS patients, the advocates felt community-level research would streamline the three-phase drug development process traditionally required by the FDA.

NIAID Director Anthony Fauci recognized that government-sponsored clinical trials would be in trouble if they were unable to get enough people with HIV/AIDS to participate in them. After a behind-the-scenes meeting with Larry Kramer in June 1989, Fauci announced that month that NIAID was going to implement what he called a "parallel track" program for AIDS drug development. One track of the program would allow patients to get promising experimental drugs from their personal physicians (as in the CRI and CCC studies) if they did not qualify for the formal scientific studies. The other track would be the more traditional closely monitored clinical trials. Said Fauci, "I thought we could kill two birds with one stone—the two birds were compliance with the clinical trial and sensitivity to people who have no options."[28]

"Parallel track" made Fauci a hero to AIDS activists—even his former critic Larry Kramer said that Fauci "has indeed become the 'hero' George Bush once named him."[29] The FDA was not quite so pleased, however, seeing NIAID's new policy of expanded access as usurping its own Treatment IND. FDA's Ellen Cooper had, in fact, met with AIDS activists not long before Fauci's announcement to discuss how they could get ddI, a drug similar to AZT, to AIDS patients even before it was approved.[30] James Mason, head of the Public Health Service, which encompasses both the FDA and NIAID, was said to be angry that Fauci had not consulted anyone above him about the new program. To stop the bickering between the two agencies, however, Mason endorsed the parallel track policy, effectively decreeing that the Public Health Service should speak with one voice.[31]

Fauci's innovations did not stop with the parallel track policy. By mid-1990, he announced that activists would have representation in all of NIAID's committees and its AIDS Clinical Treatment Group (ACTG), where he established the Community Constituency Group (CCG) to give them formal involvement with the ACTG.[32] Fauci explained: "Once they got our attention and they began to understand the issues, and we understood their issues more, they made a decision that it would be best, and they could work better, by actually being part of the process. That's why they're on the advisory committees and ad hoc groups."[33]

Members of ACT UP/New York's Treatment and Data Committee broke off from the protest group in 1992 and formed the Treatment Action Group (TAG) to "analyze and watchdog our nation's public and private AIDS research efforts and advocate for greater efficiencies and resources," as a leaflet for the group described it. TAG spokesman Spencer Cox said, "We tend to want to function within the system. Our feeling is you should cooperate with people who are actually doing the research."[34] TAG members were invited to join prominent federal policy review committees including the executive committee of NIAID's ACTG, the Office of AIDS Research's AIDS Research Program Evaluation Working Group (the Levine Committee), and the National Task Force on AIDS Drug Development. The group's 1992 report, *AIDS Research at the NIH: A Critical Review,* suggested reforms that were actually incorporated into the NIH Revitalization Act of 1993.

Largely because of Fauci's savvy political and administrative management, the relationship between scientists and activists developed in mutually beneficial ways. Robert M. Wachter describes this relationship as a "fragile coalition" in his book of that name.[35] As fragile a coalition as it may be, however, all the concerned parties view it as vitally important to advancing their own agendas. Scientists gain credibility and access to communities whose cooperation they need to conduct their research, and activists are able to offer input in the selection of drugs to test and the design of clinical trials. Larry Kramer described the new relationships between scientists and activists in his 1992 play *The Destiny of Me:* "When we were on the outside," he wrote, "fighting to get in, it was easier to call everyone names. But they were smart. They invited us inside. And we saw they looked human. And that makes hate harder."[36]

These early experiences with efforts to evaluate promising treatments for AIDS patients illustrate the difficulties and the possibilities that can emerge when skilled public executives are willing to consider innovative strategies and engage the interests of competing institutions, actors, and values. This case is an inspiring example of creative public management where compelling and competitive interests were successfully balanced and political risks were taken to further broad social objectives. Anthony Fauci confronted interagency competition and values; public and private interests; and the role of disease constituents in contributing to public health progress. Public health and politics may be inextricably bound, but effective public managers look outside the envelope for strategies that promote platforms for action. Recognizing the legitimate interests of the AIDS lobby and their powerful potential to improve the climate for public health turned adversaries into supporters and began a partnership and collaboration. This was a highly effective use of stakeholder mapping, similar to that used successfully to mobilize unlikely bedfellows for New York's TB initiative.

CASE 3: NEEDLE EXCHANGE

Since the start of the AIDS epidemic, the sharing of syringes and needles among drug users has been a major mode of HIV transmission. One-quarter of all U.S. AIDS cases—some 168,008 of the 665,357 AIDS cases reported to the Centers for Disease Control as of June 30, 1998—have been attributed to injecting drug use alone.[37] Two-thirds of all AIDS cases among women are linked to injection drug use or sex with a partner who injects drugs, and the infections of more than half of all children born with HIV are due to a parent's drug use.[38] Besides the poverty typically characteristic of injecting drug users (IDUs), particularly those who are people of color, the practice of needle sharing among them is mainly due to a shortage of sterile needles and syringes that results from state prescription and drug paraphernalia laws restricting syringe sales and possession.[39]

Despite the correlation between restrictions on access to sterile drug equipment and HIV transmission, heated battles have raged over the "morality" of allowing IDUs access to clean needles. On one side are those who insist that providing access to clean needles "encourages" the use of illegal drugs. This side views abstinence from drug use as the only "acceptable" form of HIV prevention for IDUs. On the other side are those advocating "harm reduction," a view that considers HIV prevention as preeminent and advocates treatment for addiction even while reducing potential harm (HIV infection) to actively using IDUs.[40] The tensions between these positions, as in debates over the use of public funds for preventing the sexual transmission of HIV, have polarized individuals, local communities, states, and even the federal government.

Needle exchange programs, whether operating as state-funded pilot projects or even illegally, have circumvented drug paraphernalia laws in the interest of preventing HIV transmission among IDUs. In addition to collecting and disposing of used drug injection equipment, exchange programs typically provide condoms, safe-sex counseling, and referral to HIV testing and addiction treatment programs.[41] More than a decade after the first needle exchange program in the United States—in Tacoma, Washington, in 1988—there are 113 programs in thirty states, exchanging 17.5 million needles and syringes annually, according to a survey by the CDC. About half the programs operate legally, 16 are illegal but tolerated by their local governments, and the rest operate "underground."[42]

Since 1988, federal funding has been prohibited for needle exchanges because of concern that such programs would encourage injection drug use. The federal law banning funding for the programs, however, contained a proviso saying the ban could be lifted if the surgeon general certified that "such programs are effective in preventing the spread of HIV and do not encourage the use of illegal drugs."[43]

In 1993, researchers at the University of California–San Francisco's Center for AIDS Prevention Studies reported in a CDC-sponsored study that there was no evidence that clean-needle programs exacerbated the use of illegal drugs. The researchers updated their report in 1998, noting that the combination of needle exchange programs, efforts to increase syringe availability by modifying restrictive laws and regulations, and outreach to increase the involvement of pharmacists in syringe sales "continues to hold promise for reducing the toll of HIV infection on drug users, their sex partners, and their offspring."[44] In 1995, a congressionally ordered study by the National Academy of Sciences reported, "There is no credible evidence to date that drug use is increased among participants [in needle exchange programs] as a result of programs that provide legal access to sterile equipment."[45] The report confirmed the findings and recommendations of the General Accounting Office and the CDC: that needle exchange programs reduce HIV infection without contributing to increased drug use.

In a January 1996 letter to Health and Human Services Secretary Donna Shalala, a group of thirty-two researchers asserted that the criteria for lifting the ban on federal funding for needle exchange programs had more than been met. In fact, they said, "What is most notable about research in needle exchange is the astonishing unanimity among researchers who have looked at this issue in detail."[46] And in 1997, the American Medical Association announced that it would work with members of Congress to revoke the 1988 ban on federal financing of needle exchange programs. "There is more and more evidence that the advantages of needle exchange outweigh the disadvantages," said Dr. Nancy Dickey, then chairperson of the AMA Board of Trustees and president-elect of the association. "We're addressing a public health epidemic."[47]

Although momentum was building toward repealing the federal government's 1988 ban on funding needle exchange programs, politics once again trumped public health in the nation's war against AIDS.[48] On April 20, 1998, President Clinton announced that needle exchange programs can indeed help curb the AIDS epidemic without fostering the use of illegal drugs, but he refused to allow federal money to be used for such programs. Although HHS Secretary Shalala had argued in a 1997 report to the Senate that needle exchange programs are an effective way to combat the spread of HIV,[49] the president yielded to political pressure not to appear "soft on drugs," a charge that his Republican adversaries were prepared to level against him if he allowed federal funding to be used for needle exchanges. In fact, leading Republicans in Congress blasted the president merely for endorsing the scientific evidence supporting needle exchange, claiming such programs condone drug use.[50]

Daniel Zingale, director of AIDS Action Council, the Washington-based lobbying organization representing AIDS service organizations nationwide, derided Clinton's decision. "It is like saying 'We acknowledge the world is not flat, but we are not going to give Columbus the money for the ships,'" he said.[51] The *New York Times* was even harsher, editorializing that "instead of making a principled decision, President Clinton is fecklessly trying to appease conservatives with a policy that will cost thousands of lives."[52] Dr. R. Scott Hitt, chair of the president's own HIV/AIDS council, said: "At best this is hypocrisy. At worst, it's a lie. And no matter what, it's immoral."[53]

Although Republican governors in New York, Connecticut, and Pennsylvania were using state money to pay for needle exchange programs, arguing that they save lives and spare taxpayers the high cost of HIV-related medical care, New Jersey was actually using sting operations to arrest AIDS advocates giving out clean needles. Governor Christine Todd Whitman asserted that needle exchanges send the wrong message to children, conveying the impression that illegal drug use is acceptable. "As a mother, I know that it sets a bad example," she told the *New York Times*, "'Do as I say, not as I do' is a lousy way to lead, whether you're running a family or running a state." So while New Jersey had 26,000 people with AIDS—including the nation's highest rate of HIV infection among women and children, and 9,100 orphans whose mothers had died from AIDS—Whitman rejected her own AIDS commission's proposal that the state's HIV prevention efforts include a needle exchange program. She wrote to the commission in the fall of 1998, saying she would never change her opposition to needle exchanges and that the commission should move on to more "productive" matters such as developing strategies to cut HIV infection rates among pregnant women and children. David W. Troast, director of the state's AIDS commission, said the group had already addressed those problems but arrived at the same conclusion: a small needle exchange program could cut the state's HIV infections (currently 2,100 new infections a year) by as much as 50 percent.[54]

Whether at the national or local level, politics reigned triumphant as HIV continued to spread. The personal views of politicians often had little if anything to do with scientific evidence and in fact seemed to grow more implacable as such evidence mounted. Then again, for two decades AIDS has been called "history's most politicized disease," a situation that was not likely to change anytime soon.

The failure of responsible politicians to embrace a program for which legitimate professional authorities and abundant public health research demonstrated effective prevention against HIV represents a particularly sobering example of the failure of public leadership in a highly charged political environment. Even the president could not (or would not) find a creative and politically palatable way to balance the symbolic need to articulate a policy that unequivocally supports getting tough on drugs while protecting hundreds of thousands of existing drug users from the risk of AIDS infection. Whether viewed as a political or a moral failure, the continued ban on federal financing of needle exchange programs provides considerable evidence about the limits of public health management and the need for more sophisticated strategies to engage competing stakeholders.

CASE 4: PROTEASE INHIBITORS

The scientists who gathered in Vancouver, Canada, in July 1996 for the Eleventh International Conference on AIDS were excited by reports of triple-combination drug "cocktails" that were reducing to undetectable levels the amount of HIV in many infected individuals, while rising CD4 (T-cell) counts seemed to indicate a rebounded immune system. "For the first time since the early days of the epidemic," noted the *New York Times,* "scientists seem actually to be gaining ground in treating a viral menace that has been largely incurable and almost invariably fatal."

But the good news about protease inhibitors and combination "cocktails" also had several caveats. First, there were potentially serious side effects such as kidney stones and nausea. It would be difficult for anyone to stick to the strict dosing regimen of more than fifteen pills a day, some taken with food and others on an empty stomach. If the regimen was not followed precisely, HIV might mutate and develop resistance to the drugs. Increasing the risk of spreading a mutated virus had even more serious implications, especially since access to these cocktails produced the apparent reduced fear and consequences of unprotected sex. Further, the drugs were not working for everyone or worked for a time and then stopped. And the drugs were extremely expensive, putting them out of reach for many of those who would need them. "But even after the caveats," said the *Times,* "it is hard to minimize the dramatic shift in thinking that has occurred."[55]

Even before the benefits of the new drugs could be measured, the exciting news continued to mount. In January 1997, New York City officials stunned the nation with their report of the first decline in AIDS deaths since the disease was recognized in 1981. Dr. Mary Ann Chiasson, the city's assistant commissioner for disease intervention research, reported that the number of people who died from AIDS in New York (the nation's hardest-hit state) fell 30 percent, from 7,046 in 1995 to 4,944 in 1996. Chiasson attributed the drop to the increased use of the new drugs (noting that the protease inhibitors were so new they were unlikely to have contributed significantly to the decline in 1996) and the increased availability of federal funding to pay for more and better AIDS care.[56]

As even more exciting reports of treatment successes emerged in 1997, AIDS researchers and activists cautioned against premature declarations of victory. "These new treatments are like hope with an asterisk," said Los Angeles doctor R. Scott Hitt, chairman of the Presidential Advisory Council on HIV/AIDS.[57] In addition to the caveats already noted, the "asterisk" might have referred to the fact that not everyone with HIV would have access to the drugs. The AIDS drug assistance programs in twenty-eight states did not yet cover protease inhibitors, while other states faced the prospect that a flood of requests for the drugs would threaten them with a funding crisis. Indiana and Missouri actually went so far as to organize lotteries to determine which patients would get the treatments. Veteran AIDS activist Larry Kramer described what he called a "good news/bad news AIDS joke" in the *New York Times Magazine.* "For the first time," wrote Kramer, "an awful lot of people who thought they were dying are saying, 'Maybe we'll live through this plague after all.' And an awful lot of people should be thinking, 'If I can afford it.'"[58]

As protease inhibitors became widely available in 1996, the natural history and associated cost of HIV disease were dramatically altered.[59] Clinical guidelines now recommend that most, if not all, HIV-infected patients be given combination therapy. But with the annual cost of combination drug therapy already well over $10,000 per patient, the additional treatments for associated toxicities—such as an indinavir-related kidney stone—can double the annual cost of treatment.[60] Given the costs of standard-of-care treatment, and given the fact that HIV is increasingly shifting from middle-class white gay men to poor women and adolescents of color, the question of "who will pay" becomes more pressing. Dr. David R. Haburchak, in an article titled "The Economics of AIDS in America," notes that "unless incidence is slowed in these groups, the prevalence of patients whose care falls on state resources will grow."[61]

Already, half of the people with HIV/AIDS in this country are enrolled in Medicaid, the federal/state program for Americans with few resources of their own. In fact, some twenty-seven federal nonresearch programs benefit people affected by HIV or AIDS, at an annual cost of more than $6 billion.[62] A 1997 study by the National Alliance of State and Territorial AIDS Directors and the AIDS Treatment Data Network for the Kaiser Family Foundation found that state-run AIDS drug assistance programs (ADAPs) were in the midst of financial crisis. A thousand new ADAP clients were seeking assistance in the first six months of 1996, and twenty-three states had imposed cost-containment regulations because of the growing need for the protease inhibitor cocktails currently in increasing demand.[63] The drugs were contributing significantly to declining inpatient costs as well as dramatic decreases in HIV-related morbidity and mortality.[64] But if rising costs for drug assistance were not met, expenses could become even greater if people were denied access to medication.[65]

Cost was not the only challenge to patients' benefiting from the drugs; at least as important was the issue of treatment adherence by those taking the drugs. Doctors have long been aware that patients typically do not complete their drug treatment regimens for the simplest of infections. Noncompliance with treatments has already been shown to represent the most significant cause of multiple-drug-resistant TB, a result that has significantly increased the risk of death from the disease. As medical writer Lawrence K. Altman pointed out in the *New York Times,* "In AIDS, skipping just a few doses can be fatal because it can allow drug-resistant strains of HIV to take over."[66] Despite continued good news about the salubrious effects of the drug cocktails, other news revealed how premature the victory celebrations really were. As many as half of those who had been "revived" by the drugs were failing.[67] A survey by New York's Gay Men's Health Crisis (GMHC) found that nearly three-quarters of its clients taking protease inhibitors had missed a dose in the previous three months—one in ten missed a dose on the very day they participated in the study.[68] And a telephone survey of 655 people revealed that 43 percent of them had not adhered to their drug treatment regimen.[69]

In some cases, doctors were withholding protease inhibitors from patients they deemed unable to follow their rigid dosing schedules. The *New York Times* reported that "the doctors maintain that poor compliance with the drug-taking regimen could not only spell disaster for an individual patient, but also create a potential public health risk through the spread of a virus resistant to many drugs."[70] Given their frequently chaotic lives, injecting drug users (who, after gay men, account for the largest number of AIDS and new HIV cases) have received protease inhibitors less often than other patients.[71]

But substance abuse is not the only reason that patients may not adhere to their treatment. Other issues affecting adherence, or compliance, include psychosocial factors (such as internal conflict, social stress, and stigma), the complex and inconvenient dosing schedules, and different worldviews and cultural influences of the patients; of course, substance use may also be accompanied by a lack of social support and tenuous living arrangements.[72] Clearly, interventions are needed that address these issues and bolster patients' adherence.

The experience of one Australian physician reveals the benefit of investing time in educating patients about their HIV medications and supporting their efforts. During their first visit with Dr. Cassy Workman of Sydney, Australia, patients spend two hours learning about the pathogenesis of HIV, the need for and benefits of treatment, and the importance of adherence. For her part, Dr. Workman learns about patients' lifestyles, including eating and sleeping habits, work, beliefs about health, travel, and "whether or not they wake up in a place other than where their medication is kept." She reviews treatment options and side effects and offers patients a choice of regimens that seem suited to their needs. According to Dr. Workman, patients need to be invested in treatment. She tries to help them understand why they need to adhere to their treatment schedules, how to do it, and to believe that they can do it. Using this strategy, Dr. Workman's patients—mostly gay males—have achieved an impressive adherence rate of approximately 90 percent.[73]

Questions about who has access to protease inhibitors and other emerging drug treatments for HIV and who pays for them raise all sorts of difficult ethical, moral, and public policy issues. There is the HIV-infected individual who must weigh choices about treatment against other quality-of-life issues. There is the dilemma of health care providers who feel ethically bound not to give protease inhibitors to patients they believe will not adhere to treatment and thereby risk worsening their own health and endangering others with drug-resistant strains of HIV. Finally, there is the double-edged choice for society and policy-makers:

who should pay for the drugs and who should get them? At this point, all these questions have created a state of flux wherein we know what needs to be done (those with HIV need the medications, and they need to adhere to their treatment), but public health officials have not developed programmatic innovations capable of ensuring drug compliance nor have they been successful in lobbying legislators for the funding necessary for universal access.

As a result, distribution depends more on the judgments of individual or institutional service providers and state Medicaid programs than on any explicit and equitable policy. Clearly, programs for directly observed therapy might be designed for patients with compliance problems, and explicit and defensible policies for allocation could be developed. Both political and fiscal challenges face efforts to allocate scarce medical resources, and as yet few public health leaders have been able to simultaneously reduce the costs of treatment and/or convince a reluctant public to allocate significantly greater resources to ensure universal access to treatment. Organs for transplant are scarce, but widely accepted policies and protocols for their distribution are practiced. Just as it is too soon to know how long protease inhibitors will continue to prove effective given the extreme instability of the HIV virus and its remarkable ability to mutate, it is also unclear whether political will and executive leadership are sufficient to successfully confront broader social, ethical, and economic solutions.

But perhaps most troubling is the public health infrastructure's unpreparedness to handle the implementation and compliance problems of protease inhibitors and the combination therapies. Their failure to learn and apply in an anticipatory manner the lessons from the implementation difficulties of AZT just a few years earlier is striking and disconcerting.

CONCLUSION

When compared to polio, TB, swine flu, or childhood diseases, experience with AIDS is quite recent, so much so that one might describe the public health response as a work in progress. Further, while in many ways AIDS is unique in its etiology, social construction, and politics, managing a large-scale, systematic, public health response confronts most of the same challenges that all large-scale public health efforts confront. The history of public health management in this century reveals a host of political, economic, social, and institutional hurdles. These were illustrated in a range of cases that have a common theme: management of complex systems in times of crisis is seldom routine. While all epidemic diseases present complicated management challenges, AIDS raises additional hurdles: the complex and enigmatic biology of the virus, the intense stigma experienced by its victims, and the extreme politicization of high-risk groups and their adversaries. But many of the difficulties we have observed to date might have been managed differently and more effectively if public executives had used their knowledge and understanding of the dimensions of managerial challenges outlined in Chapter 1 and had confronted the management enterprise with anticipatory readiness. If they had engaged in scenario building, they might have predicted and anticipated the nature of scientific controversy, the interagency competition, the media sensationalism, and the typical demands of accommodating private market interests with those of the public. The political challenges of shaping financing schemes that simultaneously balance distributional equity with fiscal responsibility might have been anticipated, and programmatic design might have reflected more suitable choices.

Protease inhibitors in particular raise special hope but also special problems. We just noted AIDS activist Larry Kramer's ironic observation that protease might be a "good news/bad news" AIDS joke "because of its cost." Unfortunatley, as protease inhibitors and combination "cocktails" have now been in use for several years, their good news/bad news quality seems much broader than the irony of the potentially prohibitive cost of living longer. Indeed, have these wonderful new therapies brought us the "best of times" or the "worst of times"? Are protease inhibitors the "end of AIDS," as some predicted, or do they pose management problems similar to TB, swine flu, and childhood immunizations redux? In most ways, these treatments have brought the best of times. Death rates from AIDS have dramatically fallen, and life expectancy has greatly improved. But protease inhibitors may also herald the worst of times—by generating complacency about prevention efforts.

The cases we have briefly presented illustrate that the early AIDS crisis shared many of the dimensions of management challenges that we described in greater depth in earlier chapters. But the AIDS crisis is still a work in progress. A safe and effective vaccine has yet to be developed even though early stages of research and testing have begun. Building a scenario now can be based on the skepticism that derives from historical analysis, contemporary experience, and a profound understanding of the institutional and economic, as well as political, currents that are important antecedents to immediate realities. Correctly characterizing the environment and how critical actors are likely to behave provides an opportunity to anticipate competing interests and the likely difficulty inherent in program management. Creating incentives and inducements for cooperation and building support can preempt resistance.

More often than not, we have seen that leadership is reactive rather than proactive, and events take on a life of their own without the careful stewardship of strategic and anticipatory executives. Scenario building, we shall see, provides an opportunity to imagine likely events, diagnose contemporary currents from historical insight, and in so doing inform preemptive management initiative. These brief cases of some early experiences in managing the AIDS crisis contribute further to our understanding and our ability, in the absence of anticipatory activity, to imagine the challenges public executives are likely to face if an AIDS vaccine became available for universal immunization. The chapter that follows is an effort to imagine that future absent active intervention. The final chapter will then suggest the means by which alternative futures might be created.

7

Scenario Building: The Day After
an AIDS Vaccine Is Discovered

With Allen S. Kamer

January 1. "AIDS vaccine approval likely soon!" proclaims *Washington Post* headline

The story focuses on a leaked memo from the National Institutes of Health's (NIH) National Institute of Allergy and Infectious Diseases (NIAID), which has reviewed preliminary Phase II data about the Biosci Company's AIDS vaccine candidate. The review found that preliminary results of Biosci's Phase II trial are very positive: "Some 2,000 patients have received this AIDS vaccine as part of a three-year clinical trial. At the halfway point of the trial, more than 90% of the subjects remain completely free of AIDS symptoms or HIV, the virus that causes AIDS." Though cautious, the NIH scientists are very positive about the preliminary trial results and recommend even more wide-scale testing in a Phase III trial. The memo, written by the deputy director of NIAID to her boss, concludes that following her review of the preliminary data about the vaccine candidate, she is impressed with the safety and apparent efficacy of Biosci's vaccine. Furthermore, she recommends that NIAID begin developing funding requests from Congress for future AIDS vaccine–related programs and policies.

January 2. Calling it number one weapon against AIDS, FDA commissioner predicts vaccine approval in six months if positive trials continue

"Our agency has committed itself to winning the war against AIDS. The only way to win this war that has claimed so many lives is to have an AIDS vaccine in our arsenal of weapons, and that could happen soon as long the data hold up," the FDA commissioner states. When questioned further about when this AIDS vaccine will likely be approved by the FDA, the commissioner said "possibly in six

months, though everything would have to work out perfectly, including cooperation from the biotech company, Biosci." However, the commissioner also urged
caution: "Jumping to the conclusion that this potentially viable AIDS vaccine is
both safe and effective before necessary scientific research has been conducted
and data have been collected is premature. Once we are convinced, though, we
will throw the weight of the agency behind the approval of an AIDS vaccine."

January 5. Washington Post hails NIH's findings as "the beginning of the
end of the AIDS epidemic"

Following up on their original "leaked memo" story, on Sunday the *Washington
Post* runs a long special report under the headline, "The AIDS Vaccine Discovery: The Beginning of the End of the AIDS Epidemic." It consists of interviews
with both enthusiastic AIDS activists and scientists at Biosci, who are hailed as
candidates for being the "next Jonas Salk." During the next week, this story is
picked by the media around the country. The following weekend several specials
featuring the Biosci team are aired on CNN, PBS, and National Public Radio.

January 6. President calls AIDS vaccine "a remarkable breakthrough" but
cautions more testing necessary

In a hastily called press conference yesterday afternoon with cabinet members
present, the president commended the scientific effort that has gone into developing the AIDS vaccine: "We are on the threshold of achieving a great scientific
breakthrough. . . . At this time, though, we must take the necessary steps to
ensure that this product is what we think it is and conduct the necessary tests to
protect the American people. The FDA and NIAID will continue to evaluate the
AIDS vaccine as a candidate for approval. Therefore, until the FDA grants its
approval, celebration is premature."

In a follow-up question, the secretary of HHS admits that she does not yet
know if the vaccine is completely safe or effective. Media reports focus on this
ambivalence.

January 7. Polls show public support for AIDS vaccine

The first polls are out, and the *New York Times*/CBS poll shows overwhelming
support for the development and use of an AIDS vaccine. Nearly 80 percent of
those surveyed said that they are planning to be immunized "within one year."
But 20 percent of the respondents voice concern over whether the government
will be able to make the vaccine available soon enough.

January 8. President forms AIDS vaccine commission to evaluate vaccine's safety and effectiveness, expedite delivery

The president holds a cabinet meeting including his top public health officials from HHS as well as heads of the FDA, NIH, and CDC to decide what to do about the AIDS vaccine. With the chief of staff pointing out that the latest polls show the public "wants the vaccine as soon as possible," the president decides to create the AIDS Vaccine Commission (AVC) to work on expediting the vaccine's delivery to the public. In a statement released to the press after the meeting, the president announces that he is forming the AVC "to expedite the delivery of the vaccine to save millions of lives and give the American people the ability to live a life free from AIDS." The president notes that the full committee is being formed immediately, and the vice president will represent it at the upcoming NIH and NIAID AIDS Research Advisory Committee meeting.

January 10. Scientific skepticism develops as researchers complain about media oversimplification and exaggerations

A leading university scientist who once headed the FDA congratulates the "marvelous work of the Biosci team," but she adds that the media has "oversimplified and permanently exaggerated the significance of their findings based on insufficient evidence." Arguing that currently there is insufficient evidence available on the AIDS vaccine to draw any conclusions, she adds that even if the vaccine turns out to be effective, it is premature to assess its safety. Without adequate testing, she maintains, a potential disaster could occur. Later that day, separate news conferences are held by infectious disease experts at the CDC in Atlanta and the National Academy of Science in Washington, D.C. Both groups of scientists hail the potential new AIDS vaccine yet caution the media over the benefit of such a product. A Nobel laureate from Johns Hopkins notes that "the media has not conveyed these promising findings with the proper respect for the associated risks common to any vaccine or medication."

January 11. Media focuses on possible side effects and the right stresses abstinence as "the best vaccine"

60 Minutes reveals that fifty-five people who subjected themselves to the vaccine during trials have become HIV-positive. But the coverage is vague about whether these people's HIV status is a direct consequence of the product or because the product was not successful in preventing the contraction of the virus from another HIV-positive individual. They also report that a group of religious conservatives oppose use of the government's AIDS vaccine and plan to protest at the meeting tomorrow. A leader of the religious right points out that "AIDS is a disease that already has a 100% safe and effective vaccine - it is called abstinence and is taken in the form of personal responsibility and proper sexual behavior."

January 12. Outside AVC meeting, opposing groups clash over issues while administration firmly backs vaccine

As group conflict raises its head from both sides, a tense and charged atmosphere exists at the National Institutes of Health campus in Bethesda, Maryland. Protesters for and against the AIDS vaccine are out in full force. Once inside the packed auditorium, opening comments are disrupted by hecklers in the audience. The religious right argues against the vaccine, while AIDS activists fight back in support, stressing that "this is another attack" on the vulnerable—gays, minorities, and women, and women are now the fastest growing HIV-positive group.

The vice president, who is chairing the committee, addresses the crowd and says that the administration is firmly behind the AIDS vaccine and will do all that it can to bring a safe and effective product to the market as quickly as possible.

January 13. After Biosci's early positive findings produce mixed results, AVC votes to withhold vaccine approval for three months

At a hastily convened AVC meeting, Biosci presents data from the halfway point of the Phase III trial, detailing the numerous subjects and seemingly beneficial effect of the vaccine. It does, however, confirm that fifty-five individuals out of two thousand have become HIV-positive since the clinical trial began, but the company points out that this figure is less than 3 percent of the trial's subjects.

The head of the AVC says that the overall news about the vaccine is encouraging, but at the same time, more definite data are needed before the product can be recommended for approval and nationwide use. She recommends meeting in three months to discuss updated data and progress of the trials. Another member of the committee disagrees vociferously, noting that "we have been waiting for this miracle vaccine for more than a decade, and any further delay will take even more lives." The scientist contends that waiting could mean the loss of thousands of lives. But the committee does not heed the objection and votes 7 to 2 to withhold approval of the vaccine for at least three months, noting the danger of introducing a potentially ineffective and unsafe vaccine too soon.

January 15. Intergovernmental competition pulls on reins with a cautionary note

Acknowledging that the trials reviewed by NIH are promising, the FDA commissioner adds a cautionary note: "While NIH is doing a good job carrying out its mission of scientific research, the FDA must— now more than ever—continue with its own mission of making scientific discoveries safe for humankind."

January 17. Cloudy postscript to early poll support

Critics of the early polls argue that the public has very little solid information on which to base their answers to the poll questions. Arguing that the media act as a filter through which the public and the government get their information about the vaccine, "A Second Look," a media watchdog group, alleges that "the media is shaping their portrayal of the search for a vaccine to meet their northeast, liberal agenda. After all, there are many complicated and compromising moral issues involved with this disease, and outside a few big cities, those suffering from it are a tiny and very unusual slice of our population."

January 19. Biosci lobbies widely for immediate approval of their vaccine

Seeking to seize the moment and prevent further setbacks, Biosci begins lobbying the administration, members of Congress, public health officials, and the AIDS activist community for quick approval of their vaccine. The company argues that the situation is urgent, and lives will be lost with a delay in approval from the FDA. When meeting privately with administration officials, the company stresses the potential for a great personal victory for the president if the vaccine, and ultimately a national AIDS vaccine inoculation program (NAVIP), is approved while he is in office. An unidentified source is quoted in the *Wall Street Journal* as saying that Biosci's CEO stated, "Just think how the world will remember the president who delivered the AIDS vaccine to the people and eradicated a horrible killer in the process." He contrasted this picture with what the public would think of a president who sat idly by and waited, afraid of limited political risks for broad social gain.

January 21. Support grows for AIDS vaccine and national vaccination program, especially in big cities

The mayors of New York and Los Angeles appear with leaders of a dozen civil rights groups to endorse the AIDS vaccine and call for a national vaccination program to begin immediately. The mayors also pledge cooperation and assistance within their cities and vow to use city facilities and personnel to vaccinate citizens when the vaccine is available for widespread distribution.

January 22. President orders emergency meeting to evaluate AIDS vaccine

The president calls a news conference to announce that after meeting with top scientific advisers and speaking with other world leaders over the weekend at Camp David, he is ordering the FDA and the NIH's AIDS Advisory Commission to meet within two days to evaluate the AIDS vaccine candidate and determine whether the product is ready to be widely distributed to the American people. To allow the scientists to properly review the scientific data and decide on the approval status of the vaccine, the president said that the meetings will be limited to those who receive an invitation from the FDA and selected media. The entire proceedings of the meetings, however, will be simulcast on C-SPAN.

January 24. After receiving responsibility to decide vaccine's fate, AVC meets with vice president

The president gives the AVC the responsibility to decide the fate of the proposed vaccine. The vice president convenes the first meeting of the AVC since the NIAID Advisory Committee meeting. The thirteen-member group, chaired by the vice president and composed of state and local public health agency directors and a small number of scientists, discusses strategy and reviews the scientific evidence surrounding the AIDS vaccine. The vice president stresses that the committee must also decide whether the government should commence an NAVIP as soon as possible.

January 26. Leading Republican senator predicts federal government will not authorize funding of national AIDS vaccine program

Senator James Morgan, Republican chairman of the Senate Finance Committee, on the Sunday morning talk show *Meet the Press* points out that for the upcoming fiscal year "all federal spending, with the exception of emergency disaster aid and discretionary military funding, has been determined. It is simply not feasible, after finally balancing the budget, for the country to jump right back into careless fiscal behavior."

January 28. Replying to conservative critics, first lady demands federal involvement and creation of national AIDS vaccine program

Appearing on all three major networks' morning programs, the first lady rebuts

Senator Morgan's assessment of the situation. She points out that AIDS is a grave public health epidemic that has plagued the nation for almost two decades: "Now that the ammunition is available to the medical community, it is time to act decisively with a national vaccine initiative in order to eradicate AIDS once and for all." She also reports that the president will immediately request funding for a national vaccination program.

January 29. Several at CDC criticize haste in rush for vaccine approval

Conflict and scientific controversy erupt within government. Amid charges of hastiness, several CDC researchers publicly criticize the administration's "overconfidence in this vaccine. The public could be in danger unless the vaccine is more thoroughly tested." Rushing to create and implement a national AIDS vaccine program could result in harm to citizens and a more resistant form of HIV, a result already evident in the use of antiviral medication.

January 30. Congress gets into the act, witnesses range from the positive AMA to critical deficit hawks

There is not only a broad and heterogeneous number of players, but there also is a diversity of views among them, as the Senate Finance Committee holds public hearings on funding an inoculation program. Members of the medical community praise the vaccine. But leaders of the liberal group United We Stand America and the Concord Coalition, a group concerned about the size of the deficit, also testify that the program may cause the deficit to balloon.

February 3. AVC to recommend national AIDS vaccine program to president but committee divisions revealed

Although science cannot reach a consensus, ABC's *Good Morning America* reports that White House sources have stated the president will announce at a press conference tomorrow that the AVC has decided the AIDS vaccine is safe and effective. The AVC report states that "[Biosci's] AIDS vaccine has thus far demonstrated a more than reasonable safety profile and it is the opinion of this committee that the benefits of commencing a National AIDS Vaccine Inoculation Program at this time outweigh the risks associated with this AIDS vaccine."

But later that day, *CBS Evening News* discloses that the AVC did not unanimously recommend the inoculation program. In fact, a leading scientist on the panel strongly opposed "giving this unproved vaccine to most of the public yet."

February 4. AVC recommends approval of AIDS vaccine and initiation of national vaccine inoculation program

The *Washington Post* reports that, according to a leaked memo, the thirteen-member AVC voted 9 to 4 to award immediate approval to Biosci's AIDS vaccine and 7 to 6 to initiate a national AIDS vaccine inoculation program.

February 6. President endorses inoculation program

In a Rose Garden ceremony, flanked by a tearful mother of a teenager who became HIV-positive after receiving a blood transfusion, the president endorses a national inoculation program. At a prime-time news conference, he hails the breakthrough as "one of the most beneficial discoveries that scientific research has given mankind. We have finally conquered, once and for all, this dreaded disease." He announces that the first lady will appear before Congress to request immediate funding for the program. The president then declares that April 15 will be the starting date for the AIDS inoculation program (NAVIP).

February 9. Congressional hearings include the ups and downs of optimism and public resistance

Congressional hearings allow many factions to air quite diverse opinions regarding the AIDS vaccine. Supporters are numerous, giving many examples of the potential benefits of the vaccine before a large national television audience. Scientists speak glowingly of conquering one of the worst plagues, assuming that there will be enough AIDS vaccine for everybody. Public health officials serving on the AVC describe ways to distribute the vaccine throughout the country and to all the people.

Other, differing opinions on the AIDS vaccine are also given, however, including those of the religious right and conservative groups. Not everyone shares the enthusiasm for the vaccine and the idea of an NAVIP. Perhaps one of the more poignant statements comes from the respected Parent Teacher Organization (PTO). Although supportive of the AIDS vaccine generally, the PTO has decided to oppose all efforts to inoculate children. "Children should not be exposed to this vaccine because the jury is still out on its safety," the PTO leader states. "If adults choose vaccination, that's their mature, if risky, choice. But forcing children to increase their risk of acquiring AIDS is unacceptable."

February 12. AVC scientist resigns, warns about vaccine's safety for children

Scientific controversy claims its first casualty as a prominent AIDS scientist who participated in the AVC resigns abruptly, citing "personal and moral" differences with the committee charged with reviewing the AIDS vaccine. ABC's *Nightline* topic that evening is "To Cure or to Harm." Interviewed there, this scientist says that she resigned because she believed the vaccine should be for adult use only. This vaccine "is not meant for children, especially before we know how well it works. As far as I'm concerned, the information that has been generated at this point looks good, but let me caution that this AIDS vaccine has not yet been tested adequately, and it has only been tested in adults. So exposing children to the vaccine at this stage is taking an extreme risk."

February 17. "AIDS vaccine is safe," declares vice president in renewed publicity campaign with special emphasis on teenage vaccination

The vice president begins a weeklong effort to convince the public of the vaccine's safety. In an appearance on MTV with members of the music industry, the vice president seeks to allay the fears of at-risk youth concerning the vaccine and announces that a series of public service announcements are being prepared to encourage vaccination among teenagers.

February 24. Large march for NAVIP is held in Washington

Pressing for NAVIP, a large rally and march is held in Washington, D.C. Police estimate that nearly 250,000 people came to the Capitol to urge the president to "save lives now and get the ball rolling so that the vaccine will get to the public as quickly as possible." Ryan White's mother notes that "at the beginning of this epidemic, people just waited for something to happen. Back then, people could say inaction may have been caused by policy-makers and health officials who did not know what they were dealing with. But now there just aren't any more excuses. Too much life has been lost by inaction. This time, we know there is a vaccine, we know it works, and something has to be done now to get the vaccine to the people and stop this deadly virus."

March 3. Media raises vaccine safety question by portraying vice president as uncertain about thoroughness of testing

As the vice president departs from New York to appear on a morning program, a reporter asks him if the vaccine has been thoroughly tested. He responds that he is unaware of any dangers posed by the vaccine. But the evening news sound bite makes his answer appear as if he is uncertain whether the vaccine has been thoroughly tested and therefore completely safe.

March 7. Media begins announcements of deaths among those awaiting vaccine

As the president's self-imposed April 15 deadline to launch an NAVIP approaches, ABC's *Nightline* discloses how many Americans—1,780—have become HIV-positive and how many—192—have died from AIDS during the past week while Congress debates NAVIP.

March 8. Criticizing promiscuity, the right questions government funding for vaccine for this "voluntary disease"

Traditional political cleavages are apparent at the debate's forefront as controversy arises over the significance of the AIDS vaccine and conservative leaders assail the use of government resources for this alleged health problem. They instead view AIDS as a "voluntary disease brought on by a behavioral problem that is best prevented by abstinence from promiscuous behavior and drug use." The Family First group argues that taxpayers should not be required to foot the bill for a problem primarily brought on by immoral behavior.

March 12. Liberals counter by demanding stronger leadership so that national vaccination program will promote positive role for government

At a press conference attended by leaders of the American Civil Liberties Union, National Organization for Women, Americans for Democratic Action, and Democratic members of the House, a prominent liberal author declares that the vaccination program will allow the president to show that government can be a force for good in society. "If he shows leadership on this issue instead of searching for the lowest common denominator with conservatives, he can prove that government programs can benefit the neediest in our society and reclaim the moral high ground."

March 13. Scientists and economists assail treatment approach to AIDS

Since prevention is not the only game in town, the range of solutions broadens. Respected AIDS researchers and Nobel Prize–winning economists criticize the attitude among many AIDS activists and some in Washington that drug treatments like protease inhibitors remain key in solving the AIDS crisis. In a released statement, the AIDS Physicians and Economists for Smart Policy argue that "while these drug treatments have made dramatic improvements, they are not a cure for AIDS or HIV infections. . . . And simply treating AIDS with drugs is complicated and has the potential to create an even more virulent strain of HIV, similar to TB." Furthermore, the group notes that the U.S. health care system may not be able to continue to pay for such expensive treatments while it fights an even larger—and more likely to ultimately be successful— war against AIDS on the prevention front.

March 14. Public shocked by sudden death of star beloved by millions

The public mourns when a famous movie star dies suddenly of AIDS-related diseases. Although he had been suffering from AIDS for several years, his condition had been withheld from the public. The actor, who had started his career as a pop singer, is mourned by broad elements of the public who had been fans of his mainstream movies, but particular public grief sets in among the nation's youth. A media blitz of stories about the star's fame, fortune, and premature death occurs. Commentators condemn Washington's slow pace in implementing the "new discovery."

March 17. Vaccine safety questioned by senator as side effect for trial participants acknowledged

At an Appropriations Committee hearing on funding a potential mational AIDS vaccine inoculation program, Biosci presents more recent data from their Phase III trials showing continuing positive results. Under intense questioning, however, the spokeswoman acknowledges that there were seventeen cases of apparent side effects from the vaccine. But she hastens to add that "these were only 17 cases—less than 2% of the total 2,000 subjects in the trials. . . . Furthermore, these are 'apparent' side effects. We are still trying to establish a firm link between the AIDS vaccine and all of the side effects, and on the whole we are dubious of such a connection. So we are being very responsible in trying to analyze these 17 cases."

March 22. Biosci works for indemnification against product liability lawsuits, cautions that without it they may refuse to launch vaccine

A headline in the *New York Times* announces that Biosci has been lobbying key congressional and administration members to establish permanent indemnification against product liability lawsuits. The article quotes an unnamed source who reports that the company decided to step up these lobbying efforts after recent news about potential litigation by an AIDS vaccine trial participant.

  The article adds that Biosci has spoken to congressional staffers about moving forward with a European launch of the AIDS vaccine prior to the U.S. release date if some sort of protection for the company cannot be arranged. The company explains that the public's perception of the vaccine's safety may become increasingly negative as the media publicizes apparent but inaccurate problems associated with the vaccine.

March 27. Key members of Congress criticize delays

Not all vaccine critics are from one "side." The views in Congress are no more predictable and consensual than anywhere else, and the divisions are not simply "bad guys vs. good guys." In fact, some of the critics of the administration want to go faster. Reflecting growing congressional divisiveness, two key Democrats and one Republican meet publicly with AIDS activists and leaders of the gay community to strongly support their demand for swift action on the vaccine.

April 2. President assures public that AIDS vaccine is safe but admits recommendation wasn't unanimous

The White House moves forward but not all scientists follow. Appearing before the nation at a prime-time press conference, the president assures the public that the AIDS vaccine is safe and that it should be widely distributed to all Americans as soon as possible. Proclaiming AIDS "the worst epidemic in the late 20th century," the president declares that the only way the murderous epidemic will finally be defeated is through a national AIDS vaccine inoculation program. "To remain on the sidelines and miss this window of opportunity created by the brilliant research accomplished by American science would contradict the entrepreneurial spirit that built this great nation."

But during questioning of the president, it is pointed out that the AVC scientists were not unanimous in their recommendation to initiate NAVIP. The president deflects this concern as being minor and a part of the democratic process. He notes that dissenting members of AVC do, however, wholeheartedly support continued development and testing of the AIDS vaccine. Finally, the president adds that if at any time the evidence suggests that the AIDS vaccine is either unsafe or ineffective, the national program would be halted immediately.

April 3. Vaccine safety questioned as trial participant says he is now HIV-positive

NBC Evening News carries the story of a twenty-one-year-old New York man who has tested HIV-positive after participating in Biosci's Phase III vaccine trial. He states emphatically that he is not homosexual or bisexual and has never had a blood transfusion or used IV drugs. Since the man was enrolled in the vaccine trial, the reporter thus speculates that the Biosci vaccine likely caused his HIV status.

The New Yorker also states that he is filing a $10 million lawsuit against the company. He vows to spend "his remaining days fighting against the approval of this vaccine."

April 4. Conservatives criticize White House universal vaccination plan

More ups and downs occur. A conservative senator from South Carolina denounces the administration's plans to initiate a national vaccination program because "it is time to rein in government, not create another bureaucratic nightmare in the form of a federally funded NAVIP." He also notes that not all of the evidence on the safety of the AIDS vaccine has been collected at this time, and any massive step like NAVIP is "jumping the gun and potentially harming many American children." The government's requirement that all citizens be vaccinated, the senator points out, would violate individual rights.

April 5. Fear of lawsuits leads insurance companies to deny coverage for vaccine manufacturers

Problems begin to multiply and broaden. At a Senate Finance Committee emergency hearing, convened to develop and finance the national AIDS vaccine inoculation program, the American Insurance Association declares that insurance companies will not insure vaccine manufacturers against liability for the AIDS vaccine. They cite the scientific controversy over vaccine safety and the probability of future lawsuits. After the hearing, the insurance association spokesperson points out that the media's sensationalistic treatment of the inevitable side effects associated with the vaccine will "create a very negative and litigious atmosphere that could likely bankrupt the very industry whose innovations are breaking the back of this scourge."

April 7. Media's focus on controversy in scientific community begins to erode public confidence

The network news programs report the continuing controversies within the scientific community over the vaccine's effectiveness and safety. ABC shows clips of a tearful researcher predicting dangerous side effects unless further and more complex trials are conducted. A CBS/*New York Times* poll finds that the percentage of Americans now willing to receive the vaccine has dropped from

80 percent to 50 percent in two weeks. Also, while 20 percent previously thought the government would not make the vaccine available quickly enough, 30 percent now feel that the government is not moving as cautiously as it should.

April 8. House Republican freshmen slam NAVIP as expensive and bureaucratic burden on their constituents

Declaring that they came to Washington to prevent massive federal programs from burdening their constituents, leaders of the House Republican freshmen caucus hold a press conference to announce their opposition to the president's NAVIP plans. Furthermore, they remind reporters that the scientific community is far from united on the safety of the vaccine.

April 9. Biosci seeks to alleviate safety questions and emphasizes concern for persons who have become HIV-positive from vaccinations

Responding to the media's depiction of the vaccine, Biosci states: "We stand behind our AIDS vaccine 100%. We believe that the use of the vaccine in Phase III trials has demonstrated that the vaccine is both safe and effective. Any purported harm attributed to the vaccine has yet to be substantiated by definitive scientific proof. Moreover, the company is concerned for the welfare of those who have contracted HIV since being vaccinated, and we will continue to do everything in our power to ensure the well-being of those individuals. But the company is exempt from financial liability for any harm putatively associated with the vaccine because these individuals signed the standard patient waiver that was given to all the AIDS vaccine trial participants. The individuals thus acknowledge the risk of enrolling in the trial, and this is standard procedure in all such vaccine trials. We deeply regret the unfortunate HIV status of this stricken individual, and we are offering help in the form of access to topflight medical care and counseling support as well as the necessary pharmaceutical products."

April 10. Many in poll doubt that taking vaccine is worth the risk

Complex considerations grow. *USA Today* cover story reports that in a recent CNN/*USA Today* poll, 72 percent of Americans believe that they are not at risk for becoming HIV-positive and therefore doubt that they will voluntarily take an AIDS vaccine.

April 11. Medical leaders support vaccine but question use for certain persons

AMA committees strongly endorse NAVIP but worry that it may not be safe for women of childbearing age. The doctors point out that most clinical trials of drugs and vaccines are not adequately tested on women. In addition, the clinical trials of the AIDS vaccine were predominantly conducted on gay men, a shrinking percentage of the newly HIV-infected population.

April 12. Blaming media sensationalism, Biosci may launch vaccine in Europe due to costly lawsuits and failure to get indemnification

According to Biosci's senior vice president of marketing, the company is considering launching their AIDS vaccine in Europe prior to introducing the product in the U.S. market. A front-page *New York Times* story said that Biosci warned that the climate for launching the AIDS vaccine in the United States might not be right because of potential costly lawsuits. The European Union, on the other hand, has made assurances to Biosci that the company would likely be freed from liability if it introduced the AIDS vaccine to their continent first.

However, the Biosci executive did not rule out bringing it to the United States first: "We are seeking indemnification from lawsuits, often stimulated by media sensationalism, so that we may better focus on what we as scientists do best—save lives."

April 13. Possible vaccine launch in Europe protested

As the situation's complexity increases and strategies continue shifting, activists march outside Biosci's offices demanding that the vaccine be available first in the United States. Pointing out that U.S. citizens made up the vast number of trial participants, they threaten to cease participation in existing AIDS vaccine trials if Biosci proceeds with its plan to launch the vaccine in Europe.

April 15. Deadline for launching NAVIP is missed, AIDS activists accuse president of bowing to political pressure

Holding a candlelight vigil in front of the White House, AIDS activists angrily ask, "Where is NAVIP?" Later, their spokesperson appears on ABC's *Nightline* saying, "The president promised the nation a program to vaccinate all Americans by April 15, and he has not delivered. Instead, he has bowed to political pressure, and meanwhile more people have died and become infected."

April 21. Biosci's chief scientist receives Presidential Medal of Freedom for pioneering work, but company accused of profiteering

The day after both NIH's AIDS team and Biosci's chief scientist receive the Presidential Medal of Freedom for their breakthrough development of NIH's original work, allegations are made from all parts of the spectrum that the drug company is looking out for its own bottom line. One spokesperson for a prominent black group states: "The black community has already sustained great losses of life due to the AIDS virus. We must curtail the possibility that the loss of black lives will be equally as great due to the irresponsible use of a vaccine that has not yet been proven to be sound or safe. Saving lives should be higher on the list of motives than profit-making." Several leading gay activists voice similar reservations. Later, several PTO leaders in Philadelphia argue at a news conference that "the safety of our children is more important than the drug company profits."

A Biosci spokesperson replies the next day that since the government is the major purchaser of the vaccine for its NAVIP program, all the company seeks with this guaranteed market is assurance that it will receive "fair compensation": "We will not 'push the envelope' by seeking high profits."

April 22. Congress debates indemnification as a "necessary compromise"

Discussion in Congress creeps toward indemnification with surprising support from the left. Noting the lack of incentives for manufacturers to market the AIDS vaccine in the United States, Congress opens a special floor debate on indemnification. Members from California, New York, and Massachusetts argue strongly for the "necessary compromise" of indemnifying the drug companies to prevent the further spread of AIDS. Democrats in both houses support a full-scale vaccination program. Massachusetts representative Barney Frank argues that indemnification must be provided now to save lives. Following debate, the Speaker of the House estimates that the indemnification process will take several weeks.

April 27. Biosci criticizes media for sapping public confidence in vaccine

The CEO of Biosci criticizes the media for reducing public confidence in the vaccine and whipping up an even more litigious atmosphere. He warns of more lives lost if indemnification is delayed. The media's magnification of problems—imagined for the most part, he adds—has created more public fear. He also complains of the distracting costs of lawsuits: "We are seeking indemnification from these often frivolous lawsuits stimulated by media sensationalism."

April 28. AMA backs indemnification

Leaders of the American Medical Association announce their support for manufacturer indemnification at a news conference on Capitol Hill. Organizers of the event state that indemnification is the only way to "protect the innocent against the ravages of AIDS." Nightly news programs suggest that indemnification is the only barrier to production of the vaccine.

May 1. FDA inspection finds vaccine manufacturing deficiencies at Biosci

An FDA memo leaked to the *Washington Post* describes a regular February site inspection of Biosci that resulted in a warning letter documenting several manufacturing violations. If the company fails to correct them, it will not be permitted to market production in the United States. The *Post* story concludes by questioning the feasibility of launching NAVIP due to this seeming setback.

May 3. President announces support for indemnification, Biosci admits FDA warning

Positive news also brings new worries. With Biosci's CEO at his side, the president urges the American people to support indemnification for the drug companies. He argues that the prospects of vaccinating all Americans against AIDS and other diseases will diminish unless developers of these products are ensured protection from burdensome lawsuits. The CEO responds to subsequent press questions about the FDA warning letter by saying that the company is in close contact with the FDA and calls the findings "routine" and no reason for alarm.

May 7. Minority group leader presses for completion of AIDS vaccine development

At a National Rainbow Coalition event, a visibly angered Jesse Jackson lashes out at the party leaders in Congress, claiming that the delay in funding is proof that they are more interested in protecting their political futures than protecting young African Americans from AIDS. "Find it now, develop it now, and stop getting distracted by red herrings like indemnification."

May 9. More financial concerns arise even among supportive scientists

New levels of complexity surface as analysis moves beyond costs and safety. Not only deficit hawks and conservatives but even a leading member of the medical community raise thorny issues of opportunity costs and efficiency. The medical director of Washington, D.C.'s Children's Hospital suggests that funding the AIDS vaccine program so aggressively and broadly may not be using scarce resources wisely: "There are many children in America who getting very sick and even dying because they are not getting the appropriate childhood vaccinations. And there are many elderly people dying of the common flu because the influenza vaccine is not getting to them. In light of the low rates of these essential vaccinations, I believe the nation's scarce resources would be better spent in these areas."

May 12. Conservatives pledge faster NAVIP approval if AIDS treatment funding shifted to prevention

There is livelier treatment debate as the prevention regime gets closer. Appearing on CNN's *Larry King Live,* the Speaker of the House reports that the votes are there to pass NAVIP legislation if the White House will agree to a reduction in AIDS treatment spending and HIV/AIDS medical research at the NIH. "With this AIDS vaccine, we now have a viable preventative for AIDS," the Speaker states. "To continue funding levels for HIV/AIDS treatment and medical research would be a misdirection of priorities and money. There are many other serious diseases that require money for medical research, particularly diseases like breast cancer. So let's put our money into those programs and eliminate government excess in other areas."

May 14. New AIDS cases down in general but growing among heterosexuals

There is mixed news, as is so often the case in the worlds of science and public policy: The CDC reports that new cases of AIDS are down overall but are up among heterosexuals. The CDC concludes that a vaccine is needed more than ever to prevent the epidemic from spreading with increasing rates.

May 18. NAVIP authorization possible by September, but vaccine shortages likely

Good news can also be bad news, as GAO report concludes that Biosci will not be able to meet the expected demand for the AIDS vaccine if the national AIDS inoculation program begins as expected at the start of the school year in September. Based upon the size of their manufacturing facility and the delays by Congress in authorizing NAVIP, GAO concludes that Biosci will not be able to produce enough vaccine in the limited time before school begins, adding:

"Congress should stop its foot dragging and approve NAVIP soon if the logistics are to work out for the goal of vaccinating all school-age children before the year is over."

May 20. At-risk groups debate priorities for who gets vaccine

AIDS activists declare in New York that they should be the targeted group for the vaccine if there is a shortage. They claim that bias against gays is the reason for the commission's "forgetting about the people whom AIDS has ravaged in the greatest numbers." But the head of the NAACP calls a press conference later that day to assert that there is a race and class bias in the emphasis that these largely middle-class white gays are receiving. He complains that "our black brethren are suffering in the shadows" while the media and the medical community are giving disproportionate attention to the suffering of mostly middle-class groups. Both gay and black leaders claim that a less at-risk group, teenagers, is getting too much priority attention at the expense of their more at-risk constituents.

May 24. Senator calls for more prevention efforts from Congress to match the current campaign for treatment

Tensions increase between treatment and prevention approaches. A senior senator from a key electoral state, which is the home of three celebrities who recently died from AIDS, calls for "bold, aggressive leadership from our energetic President. . . . And congressional action for a campaign of prevention at least as great as the current campaign for treatment. Trying to beat AIDS after someone is infected just doesn't match the power of prevention. Let's go whole hog to get this vaccine."

May 26. Conservatives deride NAVIP as "big government" and ask for more control by states

Comparing it to the president's defeated health care plan, the Speaker of the House and leading congressional conservatives criticize NAVIP as too bureaucratic: "The people of this nation know that if they want the best health care in the world and if they want to save their families from AIDS, they cannot trust the Washington bureaucracy to perform," the Speaker declared. "We ought to let the states decide how to spend this money and how to best protect their citizens."

Public health officials from eight states also appear at the press conference and push for control of AIDS vaccination in their states. They read this statement: "The federal government has mishandled vaccine initiatives from polio to swine flu to children's vaccines. The states ultimately are responsible for the heath and welfare of their citizens. In fact, the states are already responsible for vaccinating our children. Establishing NAVIP would funnel much-needed money and resources away from the states to federal bureaucracies, create duplicating vaccination missions, and therefore have a negative impact on the American public."

May 28. Polls show Americans favor NAVIP by more than 2 to 1, but are less willing to be vaccinated

The issue of who is actually at risk surfaces, and as people hear about the decline in the number of new AIDS cases, they begin to ask, "Why should I worry?" Polls show that more than 70 percent of Americans support the establishment of NAVIP even if it adds to the deficit. But they appear less certain they will participate: only 38 percent are willing to be vaccinated this year.

June 1. Tensions flare among AIDS activists as likely NAVIP passage prompts moves to protect treatment programs

NAVIP passage seems imminent, but support for treatment understandably will not go away because it is linked to an intensely invested interest group—those who are HIV-positive. In response to the Speaker's critical comments about continuing high levels of funding for treatment approaches, many AIDS activists hold marches throughout the country, demanding maintenance of funding levels for treatment programs and medical research.

Meanwhile, many staunch prevention advocates in the same activist community demand the vaccine now and give little attention to treatment issues. One of the two openly gay members of Congress says: "The most important thing this administration and members of Congress can do is authorize NAVIP now! The plague of AIDS must end as soon as possible, and vaccinating all Americans with Biosci's AIDS vaccine is the only way for this to happen."

June 3. Indemnification finally passes but companies seek further guarantee

Moving forward and sideways on the same day, Congress passes indemnification legislation for AIDS vaccine manufacturers in order to encourage vaccine production. The president then announces that he expects authorization for NAVIP is not far behind.

But Pharma, the drug industry trade group, announces that although pleased with these results, it still has concerns: "We are asking the Department of Justice to review the legislation, because our members like Biosci cannot afford it if this apparent victory is overturned later. We must ensure that in this legislation Congress has sufficiently protected the interests of AIDS vaccine manufacturers before wide-scale production and distribution occurs."

June 5. CNN town meeting on AIDS vaccine reveals both strong public support and continued controversy

CNN's primetime town meeting on the AIDS vaccine, broadcast from both San Francisco and New York, garners very high ratings. A call-in poll shows strong public support for the AIDS vaccine and NAVIP.

But during the show's final segment, debate erupts over a recently released public service announcement. The PSA features a famous actor who is HIV-positive. He urges viewers to press the government to act now on NAVIP: "Hundreds of millions of dollars were spent searching for an AIDS vaccine, billions of dollars have been spent treating HIV and AIDS, and hundreds of thousands of lives have been lost to this deadly disease. Now that there is finally a safe and effective vaccine, why are we not going to get our return on such a massive investment? Americans are owed the AIDS vaccine, especially since we now have one that works!"

But many in the audience criticize the PSA by noting that the HIV-positive actor was know for his wild lifestyle. The show ends with a young mother saying to panel members, "I have no problem with the government making this wonderful vaccine available for those who want to take it. But what if I as a mother do not want my child to have the vaccine? I do have a problem with the government trying to force me to get my kids vaccinated under the guise of NAVIP."

June 8. Activists stage nationwide protests criticizing delays but disagree on direction of action

Staging impromptu protests throughout Washington D.C., New York, and San Francisco, AIDS activists demand action on the vaccine. Interrupting congressional committee meetings, Wall Street trading, and wharf activities, the AIDS activists chant "Time is running out, release the AIDS vaccine!" In a press release, signed by groups like the Gay Men's Health Crisis, Project Inform, the ACLU, and the United Way, the activists report that they have "an army of volunteers" ready and willing to take the AIDS vaccine. Too many lives will be lost to AIDS waiting for the complete results of the field trials, the groups argue. If the AIDS vaccine is still being delayed by May, the group threatens to "unleash protests of the magnitude not seen since Vietnam."

June 10. World Health Organization to purchase Biosci's next vaccine but presses for Third World price reduction

Citing evidence that Biosci's AIDS vaccine is safe and effective, researchers at the World Health Organization (WHO) AIDS conference successfully persuade WHO to use the bulk of its funding to purchase Biosci's next vaccine. In a press release, the organization says that in light of the alarming growth of AIDS in the developing world, it feels that action must be taken to get the vaccine to the world's population. WHO also pressures Biosci to dramatically reduce its price for the third world.

For its part, Biosci says that this growing need has created such a market for their scientific breakthroughs that they now must shift their attention to development of an AIDS vaccine for the third world. They aim to create, no later than next year, a modified vaccine to account for differences in HIV strains. At that time the company and WHO will jointly fund trials in third world countries in Africa and Asia.

June 12. Plan to vaccinate all high school children raises questions about practicality and risk

The vaccine program widens its net as the HHS secretary announces a plan to vaccinate all high school children "because their combination of adolescent sexual curiosity and adolescent illusions of their own invulnerability makes them perhaps more at risk than almost any other segment of the population." At the news conference the surgeon general says, "I agree with the Secretary 100 percent because to do otherwise would probably be more comfortable for most of us, but it would be like sticking our heads in the sand and ignoring this potential teenage time bomb that it ticking away out there." At the end of the press conference, in response to aggressive media questioning about the risks of this plan and the practicalities of its implementation, the secretary adds that HHS will also stress a teenage education campaign for safe sex and admits that, with such coverage, vaccine shortages could develop .

June 17. Biosci confirms it will sell vaccine to the EU instead of U.S. government

At a press conference, Biosci's CEO confirms that they indeed plan to sell their AIDS vaccine to the EU: "At this point, we have been very impressed with the commitment of the European Union, and we anticipate finalizing a deal for their purchase of twenty million units of the AIDS vaccine sometime in the next two weeks." In the face of tough questioning, he later adds that "I have to protect the interests of our shareholders, and so we have two goals: first, develop an AIDS vaccine, which we have accomplished with tremendous dedication and hard work; and second, distribute the AIDS vaccine to as many people throughout the world as possible. So if the U.S. government is not interested in buying our product or is going to endlessly delay a decision, then we will find others to help us get the vaccine to ordinary people."

June 21. Senator moves to stop AIDS vaccine export and receives wide media coverage

Citing government development contributions, a liberal California senator announces that she has filed a bill that would stop Biosci from exporting the AIDS vaccine until it is distributed in the United States. Quoting the "millions of dollars" that the federal government spent in assisting Biosci's vaccine development efforts and the "countless resources" extended by the FDA and the NIH while reviewing the vaccine's safety and efficacy, this senator and other political critics of Biosci and the EU receive wide and sometimes heated coverage on the weekend TV news shows.

June 24. Administration steps up congressional lobbying

Pulling out all stops for the passage of NAVIP, several congressional committee chairs and ranking minority members are invited to the White House. It is reported that the president has promised to several pivotal Democrats fund-raising trips to their districts and support for key legislation. Republicans are promised support for items in their deficit reduction package.

June 27. Public wants Congress to act now before Biosci deals with EU

As signs indicate that the administration is coming close to the needed votes to pass NAVIP, a CBS/*New York Times* poll shows that nearly 75 percent of Americans support authorizing NAVIP. But 90 percent of them believe that Congress should act immediately before the supply is depleted by a deal with the EU.

June 30. NAVIP agreement reached but priority vaccination targets and other details not yet decided

A front-page *New York Times* story reports that Congress and the White House have reached an agreement on an NAVIP bill, with a July 4 bill signing planned at the White House. The two sides apparently agreed to gradually decrease AIDS treatment funding and NIH medical research at the rate of 10 percent a year.

The story also reports that specific details about NAVIP will be worked out by the CDC in the next two weeks. Apparently, both sides could not finish crafting the measure prior to the June 30 deadline that was imposed by the president. Issues that remain to be worked out by congressional and administration officials as well as public health experts are who will receive the AIDS vaccine first, whether or not the vaccine will be required for teenagers, and which government organization will have ultimate authority and oversight for the program.

July 4. "America will defeat AIDS with NAVIP!" president announces at White House ceremony

Standing alongside congressional leaders, Biosci executives, and public health officials, the president triumphantly signs the authorization of the national AIDS vaccine initiative program. He proudly says: "The end of the AIDS epidemic is clearly in sight. The American public will now have access to Biosci's remarkable AIDS vaccine. History will show how the spirit of America came to declare independence once more—in this case, from a horrible disease called AIDS. Through scientific innovation and cooperation between the public and private sectors, and in the revolutionary spirit of this great nation, we have taken a crucial step in overcoming a relentless enemy that has even withstood our arsenal of powerful drugs like protease inhibitors. The approval of the NAVIP will lead to the wide vaccination of the American public with the AIDS vaccine."

This bill places the responsibility for operating NAVIP in the hands of the Centers for Disease Control and Prevention's Vaccine Division. By mid-July, the CDC will release the details of the program. NAVIP is scheduled to begin in September, at the beginning of the new school year. Due to a limited initial supply of the AIDS vaccine, the plan is for high-risk individuals and teenagers to be vaccinated first.

July 5. Polls find that American public embraces president and AIDS vaccine program

Following the president's stirring Fourth of July announcement, nationwide polls report that the American public overwhelmingly supports NAVIP and the president. Nearly 80 percent of Americans approve of NAVIP, while the president's approval rating surpassed 70 percent.

July 8. NAVIP's rationing decisions criticized

Supporters are so diverse that differences quickly surface among them. The popular governor of a key electoral state complains that "needy states should have priority for receiving the AIDS vaccine. The citizens of our fine state have borne a disproportionate share of AIDS casualties over the past decade. We deserve to receive a lion's share of the first available AIDS vaccine." He adds that the state's lawyers are examining the feasibility of suing the CDC to receive the vaccine earlier.

July 10. Leading scientist disagrees about vaccine safety

Scientific controversy continues almost unabated. The same leading university scientist who previously had warned of the dangers of the AIDS vaccine appears on ABC's *20/20* with purported new evidence that "Washington has made a series of decisions that will sadly prove to be a danger to the health of the American public. We have allowed public pressure and Washington politics to override reasonable safeguards." He suggests that the vaccine is only partially effective against one strain of HIV, noting that because of the virus's high rate of mutation, new tests have shown that the Biosci vaccine does not protect against other HIV strains.

July 19. Religious leaders criticize plans to vaccinate children

Several leading Protestant evangelical ministers and Catholic cardinals condemn the planned vaccination of children: "Vaccinating minors against a sexually transmitted disease would be immoral and unnecessary. Foolish government policies such as wide distribution of condoms to teens and teaching sex education to elementary-age schoolchildren may have contributed to promiscuity. Thus, it is misguided to vaccinate children with an AIDS vaccine that has yet to stand the test of time."

July 24. Minority groups speak out—but not in unison—on vaccinating high-risk groups first

There is division among diversity: reflecting differences among minority groups, the Congressional Black Caucus (CBC) chairperson holds a press conference and states that inner-city black Americans will refuse to be "used as guinea pigs in this experiment." Noting that the American public health community has had a checkered past in providing care to blacks, especially in instances like the Tuskegee experiment, the CBC chair notes that "one could hardly blame the reluctance and mistrust of black citizens toward government plans to vaccinate them against AIDS. Attempting to select blacks as high-risk would be viewed as racist by the CBC."

Meanwhile, Hispanic community leaders present a petition to the CDC praising the government's effort to make the vaccine available to minority groups like Hispanics and call for increased funding for Spanish-language AIDS education.

August 2. Biosci announces they have retained four other firms to produce vaccine due to anticipated shortages

More warnings occur about good news being bad news. In a surprise announcement, Biosci executives report that if demand for the vaccine is high among the at-risk population, it is unlikely that they will be able to manufacture enough vaccine for NAVIP during the upcoming year: "We did not anticipate having the burden of producing so much vaccine so quickly. In order to ensure that the product is safe and effective, we will not rush to produce the vaccine faster than is scientifically possible. As a result, we have licensed the production of our vaccine to four other drug manufacturers. We believe that once these four manufacturers are operating, pent-up demand for the vaccine will be satisfied."

Meanwhile, the NAVIP Advisory Committee reports that supply problems from Biosci will prevent further expansion of the program for several months. Demonstrators in Chicago, Washington, D.C., and Key West demand that the government supply adequate amounts of the vaccine for the inoculation program. Most health clinics are to expect shortages lasting several weeks.

August 7. Religious organizations seek to block NAVIP with big fund-raiser

The 700 Club conducts a fund-raising and petition drive to block NAVIP, because they claim it will increase promiscuity and hasten societal decay. Initial reports indicate it is the most successful fund-raiser in the history of the organization.

August 11. Actual number who plan to be vaccinated looks less promising

Looking at the nitty gritty shows some slipping backward as an NBC/*Wall Street Journal* poll reports that 62 percent of Americans favor the vaccination program, but only 45 percent plan to be vaccinated themselves or encourage family members to be vaccinated.

August 17. Surprising support comes from father of modern conservatism

There is much adversity within each position. The *Washington Post* reports that the 1964 Republican presidential candidate, widely regarded as the father of modern conservatism, supports the vaccination program. In remarks to local media, he declares: "The most important function of government is to care for the welfare of the people of this nation and without prejudice. It is incumbent upon this president and members of the Republican Party to make this program work."

August 27. AIDS activists raise questions of priority and neglect of AIDS victims

More prevention and treatment tug of war occurs as AIDS activists and the AIDS Action Committee express their concern that those who continue to suffer from the disease have been neglected in the wake of the vaccine development. They reiterate their demand that money not be taken away from AIDS victims and stress the need for treatment research. Administration officials meet with them and promise to promote a bill that would guarantee funding for education and treatment of HIV individuals.

September 1. NAVIP launched throughout the U.S., vice president calls it the "last lap"

In Washington, D.C., the first lady and the vice president are vaccinated in front of cameras at the Whitman Walker Clinic. The vice president notes that he is glad to line up for the vaccine and hopes that many will get vaccinated and join what he calls " the last lap in this journey against a modern plague."

  Meanwhile, vaccinations are given to children in most schools, especially in big cities, as they return from summer vacation. Although not required like other vaccinations for children under the age of five, those not taking the AIDS vaccine need a letter from a parent, religious leader, or physician that excuses them from inoculation.

September 2. Poor management preparation causes big delays and long lines as vaccination begins

The start of NAVIP marks the beginning rather than the end of implementation problems. Public health officials in San Francisco and Los Angeles receive the first batches of the AIDS vaccine targeted for high-risk individuals. In both cities, coalitions of AIDS activists organize vaccination drives directed at the gay community, who they say urgently need the vaccine. In the first days, unanticipated tens of thousands flood understaffed public health centers, and there are waits of up to five hours.

September 4. Media fans fires of controversy with suicide story

A Miami man commits suicide after receiving the AIDS vaccine. Without any supporting data, the tabloid news program *A Current Affair* suggests a link between the vaccine and suicidal tendencies. Several mainstream news organizations pick up the story. However, the *New York Times* and other outlets point out that a high proportion of at-risk persons who are receiving the vaccine in these early days may have higher suicide rates because of the risk and stress they face. They also quote a researcher who says that those participating in the vaccine's original trials had a somewhat higher suicide rate.

September 5. President condemns media sensationalism of suicide

The president holds a news conference to condemn the media sensationalism of the AIDS vaccine and he specifically cites the suicide report. "If you use unsubstantiated rumors and outlandish suggestions as facts and scare the American people from being vaccinated," he tells the assembled media, "you bear significant responsibility for diverting people from this life-saving procedure."

September 7. More than a million vaccinated but large numbers remain unprotected

Another pendulum upswing occurs at NAVIP gets off to a successful start. By the end of the week, public health officials report that over one million people, including school-aged children and high-risk persons, have been vaccinated. But despite the fine start, public health officials warn that tens of millions more across the country also need vaccinations. With the help of community volunteers, the wait at most clinics is reduced to one hour.

September 11. Protesters taunt those getting vaccinated, administration says little

At several Philadelphia public health clinics, there is a new backlash with protesters from Christian political groups taunting people receiving the vaccine as being immoral. The White House and HHS say little, while congressional liberals complain about lack of leadership.

September 12. Some suburban groups protest for greater vaccine availability

Wide variance exists in support and dissent as vaccination priorities are debated.

In marked contrast to the hesitancy among other suburbanites, at the state capitol in Harrisburg, Pennsylvania, parents' groups from the upper-middle-class suburbs of Philadelphia protest the state's plan to vaccinate teenagers in the inner city before those in the suburbs. A group leader asks, "My child does not have to wait for his tetanus shot and there hasn't been tetanus here in decades, so why should he have to wait for an AIDS shot when the disease is all around us?"

September 18. Subcontracted manufacturer criticized for tainted vaccine

Management problems multiply as apparently tainted vaccine is identified at five of New York's busiest vaccination centers. The CDC blames Vacit, the company shipping it. But Vacit refuses comment until further investigations are conducted.

September 24. New HIV strain suspected among those vaccinated, but CDC is skeptical

There is another curve in the road as a new and apparently more deadly HIV strain is discovered in three people in San Francisco, all of whom received the vaccination at the start of the program in July. But officials at the CDC report that the likelihood of the AIDS vaccine causing a new HIV strain is minimal at most. Public health officials vow to conduct thorough testing of these individuals and the vaccine to ensure that this apparently "false alarm" is just that—false. In the meantime, the CDC reassures the public that it is indeed safe to continue receiving AIDS vaccinations. Nevertheless, network news reports cause alarm in several gay neighborhoods in San Francisco and New York. Doctors' offices and local health clinics are flooded with calls.

September 25. Drug company criticizes media coverage

Executives at Biosci are reportedly considering a defamation suit against several media outlets for "reckless" stories about their product and motives. A spokesman for the company said, "These sensationalistic stories about alleged side effects are harmful both to the nation and to a business whose goal is to save lives." Leaks to the media indicate that company executives are concerned about rumors that class action suits will be filed against Biosci because of alleged flaws in the vaccine.

September 27. NAVIP committee discusses poor job of targeting young adults

The NAVIP Executive Committee meets to discuss low vaccination rates among adults. Teenagers receive vaccinations in schools, but few focused efforts to vaccinate adults have been discussed. The percentage of adults who have been vaccinated only stands at 20 percent of the population. The lowest immunization rates, second only to the elderly, are among heterosexual men eighteen to forty years old.

September 29. AIDS victim admits fraudulent claim

Backtracking on his earlier allegations, the twenty-one-year-old man from New York who claimed he became HIV-positive after participating in a vaccine trial goes on the television program *A Current Affair* and suggests that he may have contracted the virus from a former girlfriend who has since died from a form of pneumonia associated with AIDS. The mainstream media largely ignores this development.

October 1. House defeats AIDS treatment and education program after debating costs

In a major defeat for the administration just prior to the midterm elections, the Republican-controlled House of Representatives rejects a bill promoted by the president that would have increased funding of AIDS treatment and education programs. Instead, the fiscally conservative House votes to eliminate AIDS education programs and reduce treatment services by one-third. The majority leader commented at a press conference that "due to the fact that NAVIP's costs appear to be headed to levels that exceeded the administration's plans and that AIDS is already taking up a disproportionate share of the nation's budget, we just did not feel we could ask the American public to burden themselves by paying for additional AIDS treatment and education programs."

October 3. AIDS activists picket clinics demanding more support for treatment programs

Protesters at clinics in New York City and Washington, D.C., carry signs calling for "Support of your brethren! Don't forget those who died for your freedom from AIDS! Support equal funding for treatment now!"

October 4. Former surgeon general and celebrity panel call for private fundraisers for treatment programs, stress that states are best equipped to carry them out

Speaking before a large crowd at Independence Hall in Philadelphia, former surgeon general C. Everett Koop, leading medical and education professionals, and several Hollywood actors call for privately funded support for AIDS treatment and education programs that the government will not be providing. "Congress has shirked its responsibility to the American people," Koop states. "It has left its public health responsibility in the waiting room. Cutting education efforts just at the moment they have a chance to truly pay off is wrong. We should be doubling our efforts to knock out this lethal enemy that is down and injured, once and for all." But he and other speakers stress that the states are best equipped to carry out such programs.

October 6. CDC internal memo reports that tainted vaccine may have been given to 2,000 people in New York

A *New York Times* front-page story reports that an internal CDC memo suggests as many as two thousand people may have received tainted AIDS vaccine at two New York health clinics. The agency has been reviewing the discovery of tainted vaccine in New York that was supplied by Vacit, a manufacturer subcontracted by Biosci. The CDC memo, dated September 18, does not offer any firm basis for the figure that was hypothesized.

October 7. Poll shows public confidence in NAVIP wanes

A Gallup poll reported on *CBS Evening News* indicates that public support for the vaccine program has fallen to only a 33 percent favorable rating.

October 8. Government scientists seek to calm fears raised by media

NIH officials accuse the media of unduly frightening the public and sensationalizing unfounded or unsubstantiated cases of AIDS related to the vaccine: "A preliminary internal CDC memo by no means should be considered the government's official finding. The memo in question was hypothesizing on the possible number of people who received tainted vaccine. After further investigation and retesting of those at-risk individuals who received the vaccine at these clinics, we are certain that no more than fifty people received a tainted AIDS vaccine shot. The problem with the manufacturer has been taken care of, and we do not anticipate any further problems."

But politicians go for the bait, and on the news that evening both Republican and Democratic members of congressional committees and commentators criticize the drug company's safeguards.

October 9. Levels of infection drop in first six months

Researchers at Johns Hopkins announce that the number of new HIV-positive cases dropped by 35 percent for the first six months of the year. They project that if recent trends continue, "it is possible that we may yet gain control of this disease through a combination of prevention, treatment, and now vaccination."

October 13. Comparing AIDS vaccine management to swine flu debacle, prominent conservative editor blasts administration

The editor of a weekly conservative magazine writes an op-ed piece, which appears in many newspapers across the country, that criticizes "the wastefulness and poor management of NAVIP" and asks where the strong presidential leadership has been. "They haven't learned anything since the swine flu scare in the 1970s. When will this president do something commonsensical to fix this problem?"

October 14. Low school-age immunization rates blamed on supply shortages

After school has been open for over a month, a congressional committee estimates that only 40 percent of all public school students (and only 15 percent of private school students) have received the vaccine due to supply and distribution problems.

October 15. PTO groups withdraw support for NAVIP

Because of the many reported problems with NAVIP, individual parents and PTOs begin refusing to have their children vaccinated in many schools throughout the nation. "Our children will no longer be subjects of any more experiments with the AIDS vaccine," declares the San Diego PTO.

October 17. Media reports of isolated cases of side effects continue to fuel fears

60 Minutes runs a special devoted to the AIDS vaccine. Mike Wallace interviews several people vaccinated with the tainted vaccine who are now experiencing vomiting and excessive fatigue. Wallace suggests that the government was negligent in testing the vaccine.

October 18. Preliminary study indicates "new" AIDS strain is not really new

Some good news for the vaccine is reported at the key level of scientific data as preliminary results of a Harvard AIDS Institute study appear in the *New England Journal of Medicine.* Researchers conclude that the new AIDS strain discovered in San Francisco is not the result of the vaccine. Instead, they find that this new form of the disease has existed in Africa for about a decade and is not connected with the vaccine.

October 19. As NAVIP's public and political support declines, administration seems to look for an exit

Scientific research and new data do not seem to be enough to counter the political pull away from NAVIP. On *Larry King Live,* the secretary of HHS seems to reluctantly agree with a prominent gay activist that the administration has been moving off its support of NAVIP: "We have to remember that the department must deal with many other health crises."

October 21. Liberals criticize administration's weak commitment to NAVIP, demanding more effort

There seems to be some movement countering these backlashes, but they may be too late. Congressman Henry Waxman and consumer advocate Ralph Nader decry the "Administration's paltry effort to ensure that the vaccine is safely delivered" to all American communities. "This is a war for America's health and sense of community," an impassioned Waxman exclaims. "And the president should act accordingly. But so far, this commander in chief has failed the American people."

October 23. Widespread confusion leaves many local officials feeling helpless

Local public health officials and mayors from across the country hold an emergency meeting in Washington. They seem confused and fearful of the latest developments surrounding the vaccine. They appeal to the CDC, NIH, and HHS for guidance and hint that they may close health clinics distributing the vaccine until they can be assured that the public is not at risk.

October 25. Victims appeal to courts to redress harm done by AIDS vaccine

A class action lawsuit is filed in federal court in New York on behalf of vaccinated persons allegedly suffering from vaccine side effects. They charge that the vaccine has caused a wide array of negative effects, including nausea, headaches, memory loss, and high blood pressure. They demand the creation of a multibillion-dollar fund to compensate victims of what they call "AIDS Vaccine Syndrome."

October 27. Calling for immediate cessation of the program, conservatives criticize administration for NAVIP blunders

The chairs of the House and Senate appropriations committees criticize NAVIP disorganization and announce their belief that the NAVIP program should be canceled because of grave doubts about the safety and efficacy of the AIDS vaccine and widespread public resistance.

October 28. Biosci appeals to president for renewed commitment

Biosci's CEO meets with administration officials at the White House, and news accounts report his frustration. Says one high-ranking official, "He is worried that the company cannot survive this sustained onslaught of negative, untruthful press attention and may have to stop producing the vaccine."

October 29. President's approval rating drops to four-year low

A *New York Times*/CBS poll shows the president's approval rating at the lowest level in four years. Most respondents criticize the administration's handling of the AIDS vaccine program, and 65 percent believe the administration has been unable to effectively fight the AIDS crisis.

October 30. President reported considering halt to NAVIP before midterm election

It is reported from the White House that the president is considering halting NAVIP before the midterm elections to give his party a chance at regaining some lost seats. The president will convene a cabinet meeting later in the week to determine the proper course of action.

October 31. Hospitals threaten to end vaccination program

Well-respected teaching hospitals in Los Angeles, New York, and Chicago threaten to stop administering the AIDS vaccine because of persistent rumors about its safety and widespread confusion among the populace.

November 2. President halts program after meetings with cabinet and NAVIP committee

Following a meeting of the cabinet and the NAVIP Executive Committee, the president decides that the AIDS vaccination program should be suspended until further notice. The president calls a press conference for later that afternoon to announce to the public the decision that he has reached: "Mistakes have been made in an effort to do what is best for the public health of the American people. Though intentions were well placed, some actions may have been off the mark. The risk of one innocent child's life for the sake of continuing a program whose safety is now in doubt is one I am not willing to have any American family take. Starting today, NAVIP is hereby suspended until a further scientific review is undertaken on the AIDS vaccine's safety and efficacy as well as on its necessity."

8

Curing the Disease: Prospects for Improving the Management of Public Health Initiatives

INTRODUCTION

When the nation faces a serious public health threat, all of the political and institutional resources of government are severely challenged. While the quality of executive management is critical to success, the unique characteristics of the disease itself and the specifics of its control are important factors in conditioning an appropriate response. Even so, improving the performance of public policy responses to and management of emerging disease threats relies to a great extent on understanding and anticipating the kinds of problems that all too typically undermine quick and effective responses. And program executives need to approach the program design and implementation role with strategic skepticism, mindful of the places where plans can go awry and initial assumptions can be tested. The previous chapters have provided a rich array of experience in the challenges of managing large-scale public health initiatives. The historical cases of five major public health efforts reveal the dimensions of public health management challenges that were first identified in Chapter 1; there is a striking similarity in the principal obstacles that threatened to derail them. This chapter is an effort to aggregate the lessons learned and the approaches that seem most promising for improving the management of future threats.

We started the book with the recognition that there is no magic bullet: the discovery is not the cure. The crises created by the threats of dangerous diseases face complex forces, some unique and idiosyncratic. Even a thorough investigation of historic lessons provides no immutable blueprint for success. But we believe that public executives can do better than they have, and as we have discussed, even small improvements in the management of large-scale public health programs can have significant impacts. Our contribution here is a modest though important one. It is an effort to identify and analyze the character of potential

176

obstacles and the style of thinking and managing likely to expose them in advance. Preparation for potential obstacles may allow us to avert or circumvent them or at least provide us with a plan to confront them, should they appear.

In the first part of the chapter, we will illuminate that style of thinking—the style that allows a program executive to undertake the kind of scenario building we illustrated in suggesting a likely result from the announcement of the discovery of an AIDS vaccine in Chapter 7. That scenario was generated through study of early experience with the AIDS crisis and an analysis of historic patterns visible in most of the public health efforts we have examined here. Although there is no single formula for success, there does seem to be a quality of thought likely to uncover relevant considerations for the manager prepared to seek them out.

The second part of the chapter will apply the lessons from that approach to the management of future efforts. We will attempt to suggest some generic types of responses that can be built in advance to prevent or confront predictable and typical program impediments. Uncertainty is high both in new areas of scientific discovery and in applications of existing technologies in new social and political settings. This is especially the case when quick application is required and large-scale production and distribution are undertaken hastily. Moving from the discovery of an effective treatment or vaccine to the implementation and management of a large-scale immunization or treatment program carries with it considerable risks. Having contingency plans recognizes the high degree of uncertainty that accompanies any effort of this size. Complex logistics in a multisector, intergovernmental effort combined with typical unpredictability in the early development and production of new medical interventions always raise the specter of error in forecasting, and the risk of being wrong is always high. The management challenge is therefore to prepare for these uncertainties and anticipate possible errors. The key, as we have discussed, is to know where prediction is weakest and where alternative plans should be available.

Finally, successful implementation is frustrated by a number of obstacles that plague most efforts we have examined, yet few anticipatory solutions are in place to confront them. If, for example, fears of liability remain a critical impediment to private market research and production, federal executives need to have protections at hand. It makes little sense to confront continual legislative crises that prevent timely implementation and have the added effect of reducing private investment in vaccine research. Federal executives need to have arsenal of approaches to allow them to balance public and private interests when time is short. These kinds of remedies will improve the climate for public health investments even while they improve the quality of program management. A number of typical challenges we have examined fit this type. Thus, an additional goal of this chapter will be to identify obstacles that constitute enduring challenges that could benefit from more generic institutional and policy solutions.

The chapter will be organized first to illustrate the kind of management thinking that informs managers and allows them to invent useful scenarios. These scenarios help to alert skeptical program executives to the kinds of difficulties they will face, often in a highly politicized environment. Managing relations with the private sector, scientific controversy and politics, intergovernmental relations, and the media are among some of the most endemic problems, but they are also frequently accompanied by problems, of public education, equity and rationing, financing, and declining public trust. We will review typical and predictable obstacles that executive managers need to be mindful of and the kinds of generic approaches available to confront them. Finally, following the framework presented in Chapter 1, we will illustrate the kinds of remedies that might prove helpful to future managers as they wade through the increasingly challenging environment of public health management. Many of these remedies derive from successful strategies illustrated in the previous chapters; perhaps as often, they derive from the negative results of historic efforts. We will also identify those obstacles that demand more generalized responses and that emanate from more fundamental institutional and policy arrangements.

LEARNING FROM THE PAST AND ANTICIPATING THE FUTURE

Designing a large, national public health effort under the threat of wide-scale illness and death taxes the capacities of even highly skilled managers, because the stakes are so high and time is often of the essence. To improve performance and avoid the trauma that we have observed in a myriad of high-stakes initiatives, most students of public administration recognize the essential necessity of learning from the past and anticipating the future.[1] Nevertheless, as we have already discussed, neither appears very easy to do in any effort of this scale. And the attempt to do so when the stakes are high has not been equal to the challenge.

> It has been inhibited by the priority that elected officeholders give to political and policy goals; by a constitutional tradition that casts doubt on the legitimacy of administrative power, making agencies the object of suspicion; and by deeply ingrained pragmatism in policy making. American lawmakers tend to believe, or act as if they believe, that there is no way of knowing what the effects of a law will be until it is tested. Then whatever turns out to need fixing can be fixed. There is a good deal to be said about this attitude. Realistically implementation has to respond to experience. Adjustments will be made successively as experience accumulates. However, extreme pragmatism increasingly becomes a luxury as government becomes more centralized, with power concentrated at the national level, and more active, with a widening range of responsibility. Under such conditions, the ramifications of error are so great that it becomes increasingly important to avert or limit the risks

if possible. Too many people are harmed when something is "broken" and the constant fixing takes a heavy toll in administrative turbulence.[2]

Cognitive limits and bounded rationality confront all comprehensive strategies.[3] Program planners always face the unanticipated consequences of their efforts; reducing all the risks inherent in complex large-scale initiatives is unrealistic. As we have argued elsewhere, successful managers do and should manage by adapting to the lessons of field-based learning.[4] Success often depends as much on how an executive responds to problems experienced in the field—drug side effects or political opposition—as it does on the initial design of the program itself. Nevertheless, it seems apparent that whatever the institutional and philosophical propensities that militate against a more comprehensive approach to program design, considerably more can be done to improve results. An understanding of historical patterns is one such approach. If program planners of the swine flu initiative had been better students of the polio vaccine experience, it seems certain that a host of implementation pitfalls would have been avoided. If they had questioned the explicit and implicit presumptions about the similarity and differences between the swine flu outbreak and the pandemic of 1918, their course of action and program design choices might have been better.[5]

In developing what most observers have viewed as a brilliant foreign policy success, capable of changing for the better the course of modern foreign relations, General George Marshall engineered the Marshall Plan by looking at his choices. But as Neustadt and May convincingly hypothesize, Marshall's choices "surely emerged from his looking toward the future with a long look at the past." Breathtakingly imaginative and unprecedented in character and scale, the Marshall Plan was the result of considerable prudence: "Underneath was cautious concern about *what might go wrong*, and underneath that . . . was deep *awareness of long running currents* in both American and European experience."[6]

Neustadt and May illustrate the value and technique of "thinking in time," reflecting ideas about how public officials and their aides might do their work. Using a set of mini-methods designed to prompt examination of the basis for decision-making, they assume that in the exercise of government power, particulars matter, marginal improvement is worth seeking, and *a little thought can help.* Drawing on history is important, but more important for would-be implementers is the ways and means of doing so: how to use experience in the process of deciding today. Better decision-making, they argue, draws on history to frame sharper questions and does so systematically, routinely. This can be done, they argue, by subjecting a decision based on history and experience to analysis that asks the public executive to determine what is known, unclear, and presumed. If this exercise in mini-methods were applied to any of the initiatives we have studied, no doubt decisions about program design and implementation would certainly have been different. This is especially the case if historical analogies had been more fruitfully used. The assumption—had it been explicit—that public health clinics and other medical providers of the poor would have been willing and able to screen infants for childhood immunizations surely would have revealed the weaknesses in the delivery system for these populations. Similarly, production capabilities of swine flu vaccine producers, which were historically impeded by liability issues and uncertainties in the conversion from the lab to large-scale production, would have identified more modest targets and thus drawn attention to the need to ration limited supplies. All these constraints on feasibility would have altered the means and goals, improving the credibility and performance of the swine flu immunization program. Indeed, they might have altered the assessment of the feasibility of a universal program itself.

SCENARIO BUILDING: THE ART OF UNDERSTANDING (AND PREPARING FOR) THE FUTURE

Scenario building in its essence uses history, experience, and careful analytic thinking to reveal likely futures. Different from predictions, scenarios provide a methodology for understanding risks and realities; they are vehicles for helping people learn. According to Peter Schwartz, "Scenarios allow managers to say, 'I am prepared for whatever happens.' It is this ability to act with a knowledgeable sense of risk and reward that separates both the business executive and the wise individual from a bureaucrat or a gambler."[7] Scenario building anticipates what can go wrong. Its goal is to invent plausible stories that alert the public executive to the most likely saboteurs to successful program implementation. From plausible stories can emerge important insights that help shape strategies.[8] Saboteurs may, indeed, be critical actors inside and outside of government. But public opinion, institutional or organizational arrangements, and unique political circumstances may also serve to sabotage program implementation. Skillful scenario building based on analysis and historical insight has the potential to reveal these possibilities in advance.

Sabotage implies an intentional effort to undermine program efforts, but sometimes actors or institutional obstruction is simply the consequence of individuals or groups pursuing what they view as their primary interests. The unwillingness of manufacturers to develop or produce needed vaccines or treatments is simply the consequence of their pursuing what they perceive to be their economic self-interest. Similarly, the resistance of state and local public health authorities to implementation of the swine flu program simply reflected their concerns about the efficacy and necessity of the effort. The consequence, however, was low immunization rates. Examination and analysis of the interests of important stakeholders, those whose cooperation or opposition can undermine even a well-conceived initiative, are crucial steps in development of strategies to prevent or circumvent potential saboteurs.

Stakeholder Mapping

One approach to gathering the necessary evidence from experience and history about the likely or potential behavior of important interests is called stakeholder mapping.[9] Stakeholders are all those claimants that have a vested interest and depend in part on the implementing organization for the realization of some of their goals. Stakeholders need not be individual actors but may be roles, occupational classes, social classes, institutions, or political units.[10] Stakeholder mapping is a systematic effort to first identify all explicit or implicit stakeholders inside and outside with the potential to affect program objectives and then to examine stakeholder positions: their motivations with reference to how the design of the effort is likely to effect their situations, both personally and organizationally.[11]

Often, oppositional forces organize to increase their influence. Conservative politicians and the Christian Coalition are good examples with their collective efforts to limit aggressive programmatic investments in the early campaign to fight AIDS. Identifying the likely alliances among stakeholders is an important anticipatory step in imagining potentially difficult political alliances that might oppose program initiatives. The goal of these efforts is to develop solutions—strategies to respond to or at least to neutralize potential opposition in advance. For example, identifying the relative power of supporting and opposing stakeholders can provide clues or insights about how to increase the power of supporters (perhaps through increasing information sharing or opportunities to organize) and undermine the influence of detractors.

Stakeholder mapping is one vehicle to increase insight into what can go wrong and suggest options available to preempt or reshape opinions or actions of needed participants. For example, sometimes it is possible to effect change in the *perceived* interests of potentially oppositional groups. Through interest conversion, players whose initial positions may be oppositional can be coopted through an organized effort to identify how their interest can be served by the preferred approach. Sometimes that means designing in advance incentives, sanctions, or protections for their active participation. Providing indemnity to needed manufacturers of childhood vaccines changed the economics of research and production and increased the number of pharmaceutical companies willing to enter the market. Similarly, increasing the financial benefits of participation in increasing immunization through subsiding vaccine costs increased the desire and willingness of states' efforts to participate in Clinton's Vaccines for Children program.

Additional Methods for Scenario Writing

Scenario building, aided by a number of methods for using history and information gathering and analysis (such as stakeholder mapping), allows managers to prepare themselves for the uncertainties inherent in public health management. In the process useful insights are gleaned, critical uncertainties revealed, driving forces recognized, and predetermined elements examined.[12] These are the building blocks of scenarios. In our AIDS scenario, the safety and effectiveness of a new vaccine represented a critical uncertainty that affected public and official support; recent FDA authorization for testing of the first AIDS vaccine in the United States and Thailand suggests how this uncertainty leads to scientific controversy, which accompanies virtually all new efforts, even when official sanction is given. The role of the media in publicizing (sensationalizing?) these controversies contributes to their significance, especially to a public unable to evaluate the merits of the arguments or the credibility of the dissenters.[13]

A critical force driving the AIDS scenario is the characteristics of the most visible victims, homosexuals and drug users, groups in society that evoke limited sympathy.[14] These forces have had a powerful impact on the social construction of the disease itself and on the associated politics of treatment and prevention. In developing our scenario they figure prominently in shaping the likely course of events in any effort to launch an AIDS vaccine immunization effort.

Finally, Schwartz advises a search for predetermined elements. Predetermined elements do not depend on any chain of events: they are certain no matter what scenario develops and thus represent basic assumptions. The current demographics, physical infrastructure, and development of resources are typical examples since they represent slow-growing phenomenon. Similarly, constrained situations like the federal budget and the allocations for public health or immigration policy that affects the movement of people from high-risk areas in the world to the United States condition the environment in which our scenario takes place, affecting the course of likely developments for the future. According to Schwartz, the critical uncertainties, however, may be about the strength of our assumptions about predetermined events. What if all immigration/travel from high-risk countries was banned? Under what circumstances could that happen? How might reduced risk of infection affect the future course of the AIDS crisis and current support for it? "Even the most unlikely events should be prepared for if the consequences are great enough. If scenario building is preparing for the future, then the builder's job is to simulate events as if she were already living them. . . . You train yourself to recognize which drama is unfolding. That helps you to avoid unpleasant surprises, and know how to act."[15] Further, "the role of scenarios is to arrange the factors so they illuminate the decision, instead of obscuring it."[16]

Anticipation is the key to the development of useful scenarios. In systems with significant interactions and interconnections, unanticipated consequences of actions are likely to arise. Robert Jervis maintains that "many policies are self-defeating because they provide information that allows third parties to take advantage of them."[17] Once an approach is identified, saboteurs can mobilize counteractions to undermine their effectiveness. But anticipation can help. Sometimes, merely envisioning negative consequences mobilizes ideas and resources to counter them in advance. What Albert Hirschman called "an action arousing gloomy vision" can and does serve to galvanize executives about impending danger and thus produce strenuous efforts to overcome it.[18]

LESSONS FROM SCENARIO WRITING

The scenario we constructed for an AIDS vaccine immunization program in many respects could also prove illuminating for other future efforts. The exploration of historical patterns and currents in American public health and management as well as unique political and environmental conditions facing efforts to control AIDS shape our vision. Yet a recent analysis of the capacities of the federal infrastructure to respond to a worldwide "chicken flu" pandemic revealed similar pessimism.[19] Most of our pessimism derives from a recognition of potent challenges facing public health policy-makers and managers when comprehensive, large-scale initiatives are undertaken. There are specific challenges that emanate in part from our mixed economy, federalist system, and political culture. Others derive from unique social conditions and professional imperatives. How well public managers are prepared for these possible challenges depends on their ability to anticipate them; to recognize where their plans are vulnerable, even when considerable uncertainty exists.[20] We have seen a well-documented history of where the management of public health initiatives is likely to face resistance. Whether it is an AIDS vaccine initiative or any other, successful implementers and managers will need to face their jobs with suspicious skepticism, anticipating the minefields.

MARKET FAILURES

In Chapter 1 we introduced the importance the market plays in carrying out important public purposes; nowhere is that role more evident than in public health. Public health organizations depend on a myriad of actors to advance their agendas. As we have discussed, managing a TB control program cannot be successful without the cooperation of private physicians to test patients who may visit their offices for other conditions and report positive cases to the proper public health authorities; hospitals that must retrofit their facilities and develop procedures for protecting the spread of infection to their patients and staff; and myriad public facilities where high-risk victims may be identified, reported, and tracked. In all the cases we have studied, nongovernmental actors figured prominently in carrying out or supporting the effort. Success often depends on how well program design considered the role, incentives, and behavior of these critical partners.

Partnerships between government and the private and nonprofit sectors in carrying out functions as diverse as space exploration (telecommunications), prisons, and child welfare are increasing throughout the economy at an accelerated rate.[21] Cooperation in these boundary-spanning efforts is more likely to be negotiated than mandated. Government's role in encouraging or inducing cooperation derives most often from relations and actions that provide mutual benefit to participating parties. These relationships are fundamental, and as we have observed, actions to facilitate public use of private interest must be anticipated and built in advance. Three key areas appear crucial for public health activities: encouraging pharmaceutical companies to invest in new drug development and timely and high-quality production of socially important vaccines and treatments; ensuring the participation and cooperation of private delivery agents at the state and local level, including private physicians, hospitals, and clinics; and ensuring the design and implementation of mechanisms for accountability and oversight of nongovernmental organizations. These areas require public executives to design strategies to change the risks, involve stakeholders, and focus on means to increase accountability and regulation.

The most immediate and compelling case before us now is to first facilitate the devleopment of an AIDS vaccine and then deliver it effectively. Critical market impediments can discourage needed private investment. To compensate for the socially inadequate incentives provided by the market, it is essential to strengthen the payoffs for greater private sector involvement in the AIDS vaccine development effort. Later, if a vaccine or improved treatments are discovered, private producers or partners may be needed for mass drug production or for other public-private efforts to deliver lifesaving treatments to infected individuals. Improving the willingness of private firms to invest in this market and carry out necessary public activities may involve developing strategies to reduce their costs and risks and to improve the payoffs from public collaboration.

The Public Use of Private Interest

The future success of the scientific race to cure or prevent AIDS lies in mobilizing private as well as public actors in the contest. Experiences with private producers of the swine flu vaccine and childhood vaccines suggest the kinds of incentives necessary to ensure their willingness to play an active role. Private and public interests should be better aligned so that they more readily coincide in such developments. A key impediment to implementing the swine flu vaccine program and later the childhood immunization initiatives was the behavior and participation of private drug developers and manufacturers. Pharmaceutical companies may be willing to play a necessary role when they perceive an economic benefit to do so, and public health initiatives that depend on their performance, as most do, must design programs that ensure their participation. This is an area where the development of interest conversion between public policy-makers and market actors is key. Interest conversion requires the development of patterns in which private and public interests coincide. Through executive actions, programs can be designed that recognize the significant role that private actors play and ensure that their interests—economic and public relations—are protected in exchange for performing important public purposes.

Success for public executives derives from striking a balance between the needs of private participants and the public good. For example, one obstacle to enlisting private manufacturers in large-scale vaccine production (production that may crowd out other manufacturing or may require new investment to increase capacity) for a national immunization effort is ensuring that vaccine produced according to government specifications will be purchased at an economic price. But guaranteeing purchases places the federal government at risk if immunization rates do not reach expected levels, a result that occurred in the swine flu program. Since flu vaccine shelf life is very limited due to the changes in flu strains from season to season, unpurchased vaccine may have no future market; without contracts to ensure its purchase, manufacturers are forced to bear the full risk. Successful cooperation depends on recognizing the legitimate concerns of producers and providing adequate protection against the risks of participation by sharing some of them. Public executives need to be cautious, however, about the proper balance and the legitimate concern that the public has about drug company profiteering. Bulk purchases at capped prices, such as those negotiated in the Clinton administration's Vaccines for Children initiative, represent one prototype.

In Chapter 1 we described the additional reluctance of private firms to invest in new drug development, especially vaccine development, even when there is enormous potential demand. When economic uncertainty is high and domestic markets cannot guarantee adequate return, firms may choose alternative investments. Vaccines, even when indicated for a general population, are usually administered once or twice with perhaps a booster in later years. When compared with drugs for chronic conditions, which may be prescribed for patients daily for many years, the economic returns favor investment in new drugs. Further, once developed, vaccines are ultimately sought in a world market, where often the greatest need is in developing countries in which manufacturers are generally forced to sell their products at reduced or below-market prices due to humanitarian pressures.[22]

In addition, as we have illustrated for the swine flu and childhood vaccines, when large populations are exposed to any vaccine, the risk of significant side effects in a healthy population is always expected in some portion of those vaccinated. The courts have allowed redress for such claims if a manufacturer is found to be responsible. Such suits frequently result in costly settlements or unlimited compensation.[23] These risks are difficult to predict, and because liability insurance is often unavailable or very costly, firms may fear entering these markets without some protection or indemnification. Fears of liability affect a firm's assessment of economic risk and willingness to invest in both R and D and production. In the 1980s, the costs associated with vaccine liability coupled with the attraction of more lucrative markets resulted in a virtual withdrawal of most childhood vaccine producers from the market. Not until 1986, when legislation for a victim's compensation fund financed by surcharges on vaccine sales provided a no-fault solution, were pharmaceutical companies willing to reenter the market.[24] Since then, the United States has experienced reinvestment in vaccine research and development resulting in new vaccines for chicken pox, hepatitis, and other diseases.[25]

Liability fears, costly lawsuits,[26] and calls for indemnification were important sources of distraction, delay, and production shortages in the swine flu program. The success of childhood immunization goals were also compromised by the declining investment of drug companies in new vaccine development marketing and sales. Since no-fault insurance and limited indemnification were ultimately required to ensure private participation in these socially important efforts, it is curious that legislative mechanisms to anticipate these market problems have not been developed in advance to speed and facilitate effective private-public partnerships. Relieving liability concerns will have the dual function of increasing the attractiveness of investing in vaccine development and willingness to meet the production needs of federal initiatives in times of crisis. Instead, however, uncertainty has inhibited R and D investments and necessitated emergency legislation when manufacturers have been reluctant to meet timely production needs. Indeed, additional measures to ensure markets for manufacturers agreeing to produce the necessary volume of vaccines on government schedule have also been required. Since manufacturers face the risk of production without the assurance of sales, contracts for guaranteed sales were necessary to protect producers in the polio immunization and swine flu programs.

The conditions necessary to create favorable environments for new drug development, marketing, and production are driven by the market, but they are often in conflict with important social objectives. Strategies to correct these market imperfections in the form of nontort protections for producers—a means to lower their costs and increase their incentives—have proved successful in developing the market for childhood vaccines, resulting in increased interest. A victim's compensation fund financed through a surcharge on vaccine sales is a means to share the costs of liability claims; so are contracts for guaranteed sales. Public policies must be available to change the incentives so that outcomes better reflect social goals. But these mechanisms must be in place *before* producers are needed. Legislation that allows Congress to trigger these mechanisms when conditions require them may be one way to improve the vehicles available to develop effective public-private cooperation without providing windfalls to private companies.[27]

Lessons from early efforts suggest that dealing with liability issues in advance may have significant benefits. If manufacturers were given assurances now, prior to their investment in the development of an AIDS vaccine, that they would be indemnified from future lawsuits over an FDA-approved vaccine, the economics of entering this market might be more favorable. Preindemnification serves two purposes. First, it will encourage more pharmaceutical and biotech companies to enter the race for discovering an AIDS vaccine. Second, it might well expedite and assure a smoother delivery of a vaccine to the market after FDA approval. These mechanisms could be put in place now, in advance, and legislation that allows Congress to trigger them when conditions are right may be one way to improve the vehicles available to develop effective public-private cooperation without providing windfalls to private companies.

By creating today, in advance, an alternative legal regime to govern eventual claims for vaccine-related injuries and deaths, we send a signal to vaccine manufacturers that they will be safe from unforeseeably large damage awards. The proactive legal changes may encourage more research and development. Specifically, a nontort system, similar to the effective resolution of liability concerns for childhood vaccines under the National Childhood Vaccine Injury Compensation Program, would likely result in a faster, better, and cheaper development of an AIDS vaccine. By utilizing relatively informal administrative procedures rather than civil trials, manufacturers' interests in stability and predictability could be balanced against consumers' interests in safety and adequate compensation.

The VICP is an example of the kind of model that policy-makers might consider in designing what regime to apply in the AIDS vaccine context. VICP served to respond to childhood vaccine manufacturers who had fled the market in 1986 in response to the declining profitability of vaccine development and production given the continual uncertainty over the potentially unlimited costs of liability claims. Using a similar approach for an AIDS vaccine might well avoid the delays and distraction, and indeed improve the climate for vaccine development in the first place.

Models exist to create greater public use of private interests, and others should be considered. For example, more public-private partnerships might be created between the National Institutes of Health (NIH) and pharmaceutical and biotechnology companies, as was the case in the successful discovery of AZT as a treatment for AIDS.

The interests of the government and drug companies in developing an AIDS vaccine coincide in various ways. But strong leadership is needed to demonstrate where collaboration serves both constituencies. Public-private research partnerships should be made more routine. Instead of discouraging drug companies by demonizing them, efforts could be made to get them invovled in bilateral drug development. The government can utilize the numerous resources that drug companies can offer in research and production. Simultaneously, drug companies could be made aware that government has plenty to offer them in return for their efforts, including cutting-edge scientific technology, intellectual capital, and other resources. Use of vehicles such as tax incentives (for targeted areas of R and D) that reduce the cost of investment while improving the economics, should new discoveries prove fruitful, is an additional means that might be explored when policy-makers seek to improve the environment for AIDS drug research.

Tax incentives might be particularly attractive to small biotech companies in early stages of development.

There is a precedent for these public-private partnerships and bilateral drug development—the case of AZT. Whatever the ultimate judgment on AZT's scientific and clinical merits, its successful development is one model for future public-private joint ventures. In 1985, National Cancer Institute scientist Sam Broder decided that it was necessary to create an AIDS drug. But he saw that he did not have the staff, funding, or facilities to create a drug that would be available to the rapidly expanding number of AIDS patients, so he lobbied private industry to get involved in the project.

Broder eventually got Burroughs-Wellcome and forty-nine other companies aboard by convincing them that their risk was minimal and their potential gain was large. He offered them an exclusive patent on discoveries as well as marketing rights. Pharmaceutical companies also would benefit from the test that Broder's lab had developed as well as their superior technology. By becoming a part of Broder's testing group, the pharmaceutical companies were donating raw materials to which the government did not have access, such as patented drugs for other ailments. In turn, they benefited from having NIH do the actual R and D. As we discussed in Chapter 6, Broder's group soon discovered that AZT, an undeveloped and unsuccessful former cancer treatment, demonstrated great promise against AIDS.

Although controversy still surrounds the price ultimately borne by patients for access to AZT ($10,000 annually) after Burroughs-Wellcome received the patent (a reward some claim they did not earn), much credit still attends the successful effort to enlist private firms in publicly desirable research, testing, and production. Examples of this sort suggest that recognition of market weaknesses necessitates creative and proactive strategies to respond to the unfavorable economics of some drug and vaccine development.

Private Stakeholder Involvement

A major blunder in the swine flu initiative and success in New York's initiative to control TB arose from how private actors were enlisted in the effort and how subsequent program imperatives were communicated to them. Stakeholder analysis, a major vehicle for scenario building, reveals critical actors potentially important for program success. Involving stakeholders addresses two significant challenges. First, including critical stakeholders early, before program design and development, provides an initial opportunity to understand their needs and possible problems. The failure to include private physicians and other private providers in the early design of the swine flu program represented a missed opportunity to understand and address their concerns. Indeed, the reluctance of private physicians and other health care providers to move quickly to advise their patients about the necessity of immunization severely constrained immunization rates. Private physicians remained unconvinced about the necessity for the vaccine and insufficiently briefed about emerging risks and changes in program strategy. In contrast, the New York City TB initiative, through its large-scale event, sought to include all critical stakeholders, using the occasion to identify the nature of the problem, each actor's role in its solution, and problems and concerns that program design and management could subsequently address. Ongoing task forces and communications were then focused on addressing concerns and building support from the ground up. Indeed, critical stakeholders became partners in designing the implementation plan and supporting program goals.

Cultivating critical stakeholders and addressing their concerns at the outset might have saved swine flu from unexpected delays and production shortages by exposing liability problems at the outset. Ironically, there was a conscious decision to ignore insurance companies, leaving needed producers to manage their own liability problems. This serious blunder resulted, of course, in serious production delays and the need for eventual legislative response. If a stakeholder analysis had revealed the potentially deleterious impact of insurance companies—a problem that surely would have been exposed as a consequence of earlier polio lawsuits—efforts to gain their cooperation might have been launched in advance.

Regulation and Accountability

In all the initiatives we have examined, a failure to adequately manage the performance and behavior of private actors created problems that threatened the credibility and legitimacy of the enterprises. Even the successful polio immunization program was threatened by questions of equity in the early distribution of scarce vaccine when physicians used their limited supply to vaccinate friends and family members first.[28] Similarly, the Cutter incident, which exposed innocent immunees to needless infection and almost derailed the program, resulted from a failure of Cutter Laboratories to adhere strictly to prescribed production methods that were inadequately monitored and regulated. Government oversight (resources and authority) was unable to ensure the integrity of the production process, and the traditional unwillingness to interfere with private medicine and the drug industry left the entire initiative vulnerable.

Superintended vaccine production and requirements for strict conformity to and accountability for government-specified production and testing protocols are more commonplace under modern public health arrangements. Nevertheless, risk of abuse and attendant scandals are still common and threaten the public trust. While public executives need to embrace the private sector as partners in large-scale public health enterprises, at the same time their designs need to ensure commitment and resources for relentless oversight of private firms serving public purposes. Clearly, part of the essential success of public-private ventures is in the quid pro quo that constitutes an appropriate interest conversion.

A critical vehicle for guaranteeing the public interest while protecting against private losses is the effectiveness of the accountability and regulatory mechanisms that ensure the fulfillment of contractual arrangements. Although significant programmatic experience has underscored the importance of these arrangements, only recently designs to ensure early childhood disease protection resulted in abuses and unintended consequences from a failure to develop accountability mechanisms.[29] Some of the most troubling accountability problems in VFC derive from a failure to properly regulate the behavior of private actors—like private physicians who stood to gain by purchasing vaccine at reduced prices but whose use of the low-cost vaccine for legitimate purposes could not be monitored. Equally disturbing was the failure to have in place any accountability mechanisms that made sure that states were using the low-cost federally purchased vaccine in the appropriate way for targeted groups. No enforcement mechanisms were designed through the legislation, and thus a means to evaluate program performance is limited. While much has changed in federal regulatory authority since the polio initiative, recent public health policies still lack a sufficient concern for management and the design of arrangements to ensure compliance and accountability.

MANAGING SCIENTIFIC CONTROVERSY

Threats to public health frighten ordinary citizens. Nowhere is "information asymmetry" (a term used by economists to describe a condition where markets cannot function efficiently) more of a problem. Without the help of experts, ordinary citizens cannot evaluate the seriousness of public health threats or the appropriate actions they should take. Ultimately, their willingness to take direction from public health authorities depends on their confidence in the strength and legitimacy of expert judgment; rarely, however, does expert judgment speak with one voice. And rarely do scientists and medical practitioners reach consensus on complex scientific matters. Scientists work in diverse settings dispersed throughout the country, and controversy is both prevalent and desirable in furthering scientific advances.

Nevertheless, policy decisions on public health matters that affect broad populations must seek out and consider the widest possible expert opinion. Policymakers have an obligation to ensure in advance that any decision capable of harming (as well as helping) healthy citizens has vetted all legitimate views. Politics figure prominently in these decisions, but, as we have described, a failure to include diverse scientific and medical opinions in a well-orchestrated process before designing a program has the effect of creating sabotage among dissenters quite willing to have their hearing in the press. President Ford was simply not well advised when he made the decision to go forward with a national immunization program for swine flu. The dissenters, had they been heard, might have produced a more cautious outcome, such as stockpiling. But if they had been heard, they surely would have aired the reasonable expectations for side effects, children's dosages, and production shortfalls. If CDC Director Sencer convinced President Ford to go ahead anyway, contingency planning and program design changes would surely have been made.

Efforts at creating broadly based deliberative groups of experts inside and outside of government risk exposing weaknesses and uncertainty in program approaches to public health crises; but the risks of failing to do so are much greater. Policy-makers who understand the concerns of dissenters have the additional advantage of planning ahead to address legitimate controversies through a well-informed and well-designed media and public education effort. Where acknowledged risks are assumed—such as the possible extent and severity of side effects—contingency plans can be developed and safeguards designed in advance. This effort to include a broad base of actors in the "large-scale event" is precisely what allowed Commissioner Hamburg to anticipate many of the program obstacles related to managing drug resistance in the final New York City TB program design.

Public executives face public health crises as politicians and as policy-makers. Seeking the airing of scientific controversy within a legitimate forum in advance of program design and marketing is both politically astute and manage-rially prudent. But crisis often demands quick and decisive action, while endless controversy risks inaction and stalemate, characteristics of the early efforts to stem the tides of AIDS though prevention. Balancing the need for full disclosure with the competing need for action is the key to successful management of sci-entific controversy. Some lessons seem clear, however.

Legitimate forums of appropriately constituted membership from various institutional settings need to be provided so that a well-managed discussion can take place. Executives can then develop properly orchestrated plans to address dissent and preempt damaging and sensational media exposés. Providing signif-icant data for scenario building, understanding where scientific conviction may be vulnerable allows the design of an initiative that recognizes the consequences of being wrong about any of the critical scientific and medical judgments (or for that matter any number of political, strategic, or logistical judgments).

Further, exposing interagency biases (CDC and NIH, for example) through open discussion of alternative approaches allows executives to design coordinat-ing mechanisms and institutional arrangements that are sensitive to potential resistance. Commissioner Hamburg understood that successfully confronting the TB crisis involved a complex system of interactions over a long period of time with many different agencies. Involving them in the solution was at the very core of her ambitious agenda and posed the most daunting obstacles. Although the Department of Health led the initiative, other agencies had the critical first point of contact with infected individuals. But once the approach was developed, ongo-ing interagency task forces were held accountable for meeting specific goals by defined dates. These arrangements to promote accountability served to manage scientific and interagency conflict through a disciplined, integrated, and operational approach.

FEDERALISM: MANAGING INTERGOVERNMENTAL COOPERATION

The development of a coordinated national immunization effort in fifty states and hundreds of thousands of localities is a daunting task. By tradition and law, public health efforts are locally designed and administered. The federal government's role has largely been restricted to providing financial resources and technical assistance to state and local departments of health. When a public health crisis is national (and international, in the case of AIDS) in scope and significance, command and control mechanisms to compel state and local actors to behave in prescribed ways are limited. Yet, without state and local health departments as partners, federal initiatives have little chance to succeed.

In virtually all the immunization and treatment programs we have analyzed, state and local performance has varied dramatically. A recent comparison of the success of TB control in New York and the disappointing progress in Washington, D.C., highlights the complex character of differing managerial, political, and technical capacities around the country. Dramatically different immunization rates for early childhood diseases nationwide similarly reflect variations in local will and capacity. The CDC can provide support and technical assistance to bolster local capacity, and financial incentives through grants and cost sharing can provide necessary inducements to pursue federal policy goals. Indeed, bulk purchases of childhood vaccines at federally negotiated capped prices served to underwrite some of the costs of Clinton's VFC initiative in the states. Even so, local actors often pursue agendas that compete with federal mandates, and scarce political capital is frequently reserved for what are perceived as more pressing local priorities. In many cases, local public health directors, unconvinced or uncertain about the necessity and risks of immunization, were not willing to invest in the federal swine flu initiative. Unevenness of immunization rates reflected this unwillingness; had a true pandemic developed, lack of state and local cooperation with federal policy would have been devastating.

One size does not fit all. State and local actors require discretion in the design and delivery of public health services to meet local needs. Conditions vary enormously and dictate variations in public health strategies and priorities; population profiles differ, affecting the nature of disease risk and incidence. Social conditions (for example, poverty, housing conditions, immigration, and age distribution) that affect health status and the appropriateness of different delivery modes also vary dramatically. In addition, local preferences and unique historical circumstances have resulted in unevenness in public health infrastructure, capacity, and expertise. While federal resources and technical assistance can be instrumental in moving reluctant local actors to willingly pursue national goals, federal actors need to design national initiatives that are sensitive to local differences and supportive of local efforts. Indeed, for any federal public health effort, state and local public health authorities are often the most important stakeholders, and they can represent the most formidable saboteurs.

The early AIDS experience is instructive because the incidence of the disease varied so dramatically around the country. Concentrated in urban areas where large numbers of homosexuals and IV drug users reside, the early crisis appeared to threaten very few states. Efforts to move quickly and decisively were undermined by a lack of federal leadership and imagination, stalled by the limited political support for unpopular victims, and constrained by the absence of support from a majority of states that saw no threat to their populations. Political risks may be taken when the stakes appear high, but the early AIDS crisis, which surely would have been controlled through bold and decisive preventive public health measures, met with a reluctant and indifferent intergovernmental public health system. Disinclined to embrace interventions that targeted intimate personal behavior, powerful interests—especially conservative politicians in states where the risk seemed remote and the political costs very heavy—ignored and then resisted the priority of launching an aggressive, coordinated preventive program managed by the federal public health authority to contain the deadly disease.

Efforts in scenario building would have predicted such a response as we did in Chapter 7 when anticipating federal and local response to a federal AIDS vaccine initiative. Such a prediction suggests that alternative means may be necessary to ensure that federal programming is embraced by local efforts, and that controversial approaches in the interest of public health need to be fashioned with the cooperation and involvement of those in a powerful position to contribute to their success. When Sencer and other federal executives ignored local public health officials in their design and planning for the implementation of the swine flu immunization effort, they contributed insurmountable obstacles nationally to an expeditious immunization campaign. Their strategy stands in stark contrast to Commissioner Hamburg's in New York, where a mechanism was designed at the outset which recognized that gaining understanding and commitment was essential for generating cooperation from diverse agencies, cooperation that would be essential to her success. If Sencer and others had engaged local officials at the outset, they might have understood their reluctance, designed an information and communication system to reassure them, and appreciated the need to market their strategy more effectively. Instead, they risked having large proportions of the population unprotected against what might have been a deadly flu pandemic.

Courting and cultivating state and local stakeholders—and giving them ownership of important public health strategies—are fundamental management dictates to ensure cooperation and coordination of federal policy directives. Formal participation in design and implementation strategies and creative incentive and participation mechanisms for critical local players are essential to creating partnerships among important intergovernmental actors. Nowhere does this need seem more important or formidable than for a potentially controversial initiative like an AIDS vaccine program. But the experience of TB control, childhood immunization efforts, and the swine flu program suggest that even for more prosaic threats, mobilizing and engaging the interests of local actors are essential requirements for successful public health efforts.

MEDIA MANAGEMENT

The media can be important partners or unrelenting detractors of public enterprises. Any effort that fails to consider in advance the role that the media can play and how the media can be best managed to aid in public education and public relations is bound to be the hapless victim of unanticipated and potentially damaging interference. "News coverage contributes directly to the opinions of policy makers, virtually all of whom read news publications and watch television news programs; it plays a role in setting the agenda of public concerns as a consequence of what is aired and what is left out; and it helps shape public opinion by continuous, reinforcing coverage of issues it deems interesting or important."[30]

As we have discussed, the failure of Sencer and the other federal executives managing the swine flu effort to plan and implement a media strategy from the outset placed them in a purely reactive position when questions were raised about the necessity and appropriateness of the program. When dissenters could not get a fair hearing in advance of program design, they took their objections to the press, where investigative reports revealed continual controversy about the wisdom of the program. Further, with no organized effort to educate local service providers and ordinary citizens about program developments—for example, side effects with children's dosages, production shortfalls, and no emerging cases of swine flu—criticism mounted in the press that undermined public and professional confidence in the effort.

In Chapter 1 we reviewed the media's critical role in shaping public opinion and providing, in effect, generalized information about highly complex scientific matters for public consumption. Although science reporters are increasingly well trained to understand and interpret growing scientific knowledge, they are also influenced by the business of news reporting, which increasingly values newsworthiness by the degree of controversy and sensationalism it provides. "Most journalists working for the daily press are constrained by competition, deadlines, budgets, and the need to cover complex subjects within limited time and space. They must attract and hold the attention of readers, and they must develop an angle that will define their writing as news."[31] In addition, reporters are particularly ill suited to evaluate evidence about risk. Since the basis on which decisions about intervention are made for many large-scale public health programs is assessments of the risk of infection and the probable safety and effectiveness of any treatment or vaccine, how the press deals with and communicates the notion of risk can have important effects on public confidence. Journalists are generally looking for definitive answers from scientists and public officials. But in cases of scientific uncertainty, there is a wide interpretation of risk—a fact that contributed to the decision to move ahead with a universal immunization program for swine flu. With few standards to guide analysis, scientists assessing risk frequently arrive at different conclusions, which creates a dilemma for journalists.[32] They often believe that balanced reporting requires opposing views even if their (and the public's) ability to assess the credibility of the sources is limited.

Establishing the necessity and the legitimacy of any public intervention is crucial to developing public trust and confidence. But nowhere is it more important than when federal authorities are asking ordinary citizens to undertake medical interventions where their health is at stake. The media play a crucial role in informing the public about important public health risks and in scrutinizing the public policy response. Thus, plans and briefing channels to educate the media about important public health threats and the appropriateness and necessity of an organized public health response must be carefully constructed—in advance. Once channels of communication are built, public health executives must be proactive in sharing developments and acting swiftly and responsively to anticipate press inquiries, especially in the face of unanticipated developments such as side effects or changing incidence patterns. Whenever controversy arises, absence of official sources of accurate and high-quality information leads investigative reporters and science journalists to seek alternative sources, many of whom are bound to be among those most skeptical about the efficacy of official approaches, or those who stand to benefit from delegitimizing the enterprise.

New York City's TB control initiative depended in large part on the development of a conscious and systematic effort to educate and brief the media. The active engagement of the press served, first, to raise public consciousness about the seriousness of the threat and, later, to provide timely and accurate information to underscore the city's initiative. The commissioner and her director of the Bureau of Tuberculosis Control provided timely and regular information to the press and briefing channels to ensure a check on sensationalism that might cause needless fear and alarm. The commissioner recognized the value of the legitimate press in mobilizing elite interests about the importance of TB control, an effort that had the dual function of reinforcing executive support within the mayor's office and building strong visibility for the program among needed outside actors. Recognizing the value of press coverage to mobilize attention and preempting aggressive investigative reports by providing timely and accurate sources—even when the news is unfavorable—as well as anticipating media interest and seizing control of what is released allow executives to provide their version of the facts and how they will respond rather than being at the mercy of sensational or inaccurate reporting.

Both the swine flu immunization program and the implementation plans for Clinton's VFC were victims of damaging investigative reports for which they were ill prepared to respond. If they had realized the importance of a well-designed media strategy and been prepared to anticipate rather than merely respond to damaging reports, the credibility of both efforts would have been improved. While good press relations cannot rescue an ill-conceived or poorly implemented program (and, indeed, provide no guarantees), they can save an initiative from distracting and needless criticism. (The public relations success of the polio immunization program represents a good example of how well-orchestrated efforts can assist program progress even when difficulties arise.)

In general, three key activities appear essential to a media management effort. First, the media need to be contacted and briefed in advance of program implementation decisions. An effort should be made to educate the press about the initiative's scientific basis and the justification and description of the program strategy. Where controversy exists, it should be exposed in advance, and the logic of the approach—including the probable risks—carefully explained. Second, regular briefings on an ongoing basis should be planned. Bad news should be anticipated and presented by the lead agency with an official position or explanation prior to any news reports. Third, the media should expect fair, timely, and accurate reports. Credibility and public interestedness are essential qualities in an executive; a suspicious press can be mollified by a conscious strategy to cultivate their belief in the integrity of the leadership and the legitimacy of the effort.

DISTRIBUTIONAL EQUITY

Even before a multiple antibiotic cure for TB was found, desperate patients and their families sought out the developers of promising new drugs, often reported in the press, begging for access even in advance of completed research on their safety and effectiveness. Similar efforts plagued the early polio immunization program when initial vaccine supplies were inadequate to ensure universal coverage. Scandals were exposed about physicians and other health care providers reserving scarce vaccine for their friends and families even when priority allocation was reserved for children. The development of priority allocation systems and appropriate means of enforcement is a significant management function in the design of large-scale public health efforts.

Americans are unusually loath to embrace explicit forms of rationing, which is suspect for most public services, and distributional questions are usually resolved in implicit ways. Even in areas where scarcity imposes serious social costs, such as in distribution of limited organs for transplants, efforts to design legitimate and equitable allocation criteria are subject to controversy and abuse. Whatever the political difficulty in the development of appropriate allocation criteria for scarce and potentially lifesaving treatments or vaccines, program experience confirms the importance for management and politics of determin-ing—in advance—treatment priorities.

Public health presents a classic public goods problem. Most private transac-tions represent a bargain between buyer and seller, the benefits of which accrue to the individuals involved. Not so with public health activities. The behavior of one individual, whether he takes his TB medication or not, affects the well-being of others, since untreated TB—or worse, undertreated TB—can be spread to con-tacts of an infected person. Thus, social costs of individual behavior can be great, particularly for contagious diseases.

Public health responds to this market failure by substituting public services for private action. However, public health officials are often victims of budget constraints or limited availability of lifesaving preventive agents or treatments. In a crisis, production shortfalls or excessive costs of universal coverage often limit access to needed treatments or vaccine protection. Scarce resources or sup-plies require policies that serve to maximize the health of the public and satisfy the political demands that inevitably result. In the absence of explicit, defensible, and enforceable allocation policies, however, program goals can be needlessly compromised, and incentives for abuse by powerful interests can result. Worse, suspicions of manipulation by powerful interests that often accompany limited access can have serious consequences for public perceptions about the integrity of the entire enterprise.

Distributional equity has two separate management dimensions. The first deals with judgments and subsequent policies about which societal groups should have priority access to treatment or prevention resources. When children's dosages in the swine flu program required two immunizations instead of one, production capacity limited supplies of the vaccine. Since timely inoculation was crucial to provide adequate immunity before the start of the flu season, it became clear that not enough vaccine would be available for universal distribution. Even though rationing was a predictable necessity, unrealistic production targets obscured the importance of planning ahead for such an inevitability. When the shortages became clear, however, federal officials paid inadequate attention to developing and enforcing a priority distribution system. Indeed, priorities were developed that favored politically powerful groups like the elderly, even though their risk may have been lowest due to prior immunity developed through exposure to the pan-demic of 1918. If a true swine flu epidemic had appeared, prime-aged adults and children might have been at far greater risk of serious illness or death.

Withholding preventtive agents or treatments requires a powerful rationale, one that must withstand the scrutiny of both professional judgment and political pressure. Federal directives need to find and build support in myriad local juris-dictions on whom they depend to deliver services. Rationing policies, therefore, are unsuitable candidates for quick and expedient decisions made under severe time pressures. Historical analysis and scenario building would reveal these as key contingencies likely to emerge in large-scale public health efforts. Plans could be ready in case they were required, and means to ensure accountability and enforcement could be determined in advance.

But rationing cannot be accomplished by fiat even if the logic of selection is self-evident (which it seldom is). If targeting high-risk groups is an important criterion for the development of a priority system, attention must be given to how to ensure that high-risk groups actually receive services. Otherwise, any initiative will implicitly allocate on a first-come, first-served basis, leaving it to local service providers to manage demand. Education and resources would then be the implicit determinants of service delivery, a fact that seems clear from the analysis of immunization rates for young children, where middle-class parents with regular sources of care are more likely to understand the necessary value and process of getting their kids immunized.

Targeting high-risk groups and ensuring that they receive services, we have observed, require a service delivery strategy that combines focused public education on targeted groups and methods of service delivery likely to find and attract hard to reach groups. These efforts require significant coordination and cooperation within state and local public health systems. Strategies like directly observed therapy, so critical to the success of the New York City TB control program, were provided through the financial and personnel support of the CDC. Thus, financial and technical assistance efforts on rationing and targeting need to be coordinated with federal policies to ensure that the resources and incentives to comply with federal policies are strong.

FINANCING

Earlier in this chapter we suggested some useful methods for scenario building proposed by Schwartz.[33] One such method is to identify predetermined events, those factors or conditions that appear fixed over the relevant time frame in question. Budgetary resources are one category of constraints. During the 1980s, for example, when the federal budget deficit loomed large in any public policy debate, financing a new initiative became a serious constraint on implementation and shaped the environment for decision-making. Nevertheless, even within constrained budgets, financing options represent important independent choices for program design. A program whose goals gain significant public support often faces opposition based entirely on the choice of financing.

Financing decisions—who pays and who benefits—raise fundamental issues of fiscal federalism. When do public health policy choices represent local tastes and preferences and a responsiveness to local needs or, in the case of widespread communicable disease, a federal responsibility? Most public health activities have traditionally been financed through federal cost sharing and grants in aid to the states. Even when there is a pressing national interest in ensuring universal immunization, such as in the Clinton administration's VFC program, federal vaccine purchases at below-market prices were offered to states for repurchase, not financed entirely by federal dollars. While such financing arrangements allow cost sharing, they also risk undermining the goal of universal coverage, since states always have the option to opt out.

Financing issues also heighten awareness of public perceptions about the worthiness of the groups at risk, the determinants of disease, and whether ability to pay should have a bearing. For wide-scale epidemics where the burden of risk is equally shared, there is more support for federal financing. When disease incidence varies by demographic group, jurisdiction, or individual behavior, questions of redistribution are raised, and consensus is more difficult to achieve. Indeed, financing issues confront underlying social, political, and economic values.

The recent rejection of efforts to secure continued federal funding for needle exchange programs in states and localities represents a particularly vivid example. The debate reflected the tension between means and ends. Clean needle programs represent a relatively safe, effective, and inexpensive means to stem the tide of AIDS infection by intravenous drug users, a significant and growing group among newly infected HIV victims. Considerable research and experience suggest the effectiveness of the approach.[34] Nevertheless, the distribution of needles to IV drug users confronted significant opposition from conservatives and antidrug forces who saw the initiative as one that reinforced drug use and undermined social sanctions. Here, important social taboos confronted public health practice, and the debate was played out through federal financing. State and local governments would remain free to fund needle exchange programs with their own resources.

There are no blueprints for shaping federal financing arrangements. Successful programs like the polio immunization effort relied little on federal financing arrangements. In contrast, the swine flu initiative, at significant federal expense, was ultimately judged a costly failure. Program design, however, must anticipate the way in which the financing debate serves as a lightning rod for many contentious social and political tensions. A failure to participate in early program development with a feasible and politically viable financing plan risks introducing costly delay to programmatic efforts where time is often of the essence. Building initial support for federal public health initiatives and creative financing arrangements represents a formidable task involving federal officials in highly politicized bargaining with legislators and state and local officials. A considerable investment of managerial resources is required in the politics of negotiating financing arrangements, but experience demonstrates the importance of developing consensus on an agreement early in the program design phase.

THE DECLINE OF PUBLIC TRUST

As we have illustrated in our analysis of five large-scale public health initiatives over forty years, successful federally led efforts for protection or treatment of disease rely on the cooperation of myriad actors inside and outside government. But nowhere is program success more vulnerable than in its efforts to recruit ordinary citizens. The key to success is developing confidence among millions of potential participants in the public health prescriptions—whether they be behavioral changes, vaccination, or treatment. Indeed, the ability of public health authorities to successfully implement any public health effort depends principally on the degree of trust that multiple publics place in public authority and public agencies.

Consider the extraordinary faith that ordinary citizens must place in public authority when they submit to vaccination, exposing themselves and their children to injection with foreign agents. Few citizens have the knowledge or experience to evaluate the risks involved. When vaccines have a long track record and the risks and rewards are well known, it is far easier to reassure reluctant participants. But even then, confidence in the integrity of the enterprise is essential to getting citizens to willingly submit to public exhortations. Public executives have some means to effect public confidence in their performance; a well-managed effort that provides high-quality services and successful public education to diverse groups can induce high levels of voluntary compliance. But as we have discussed, successful management of these efforts has been hard to achieve. And even effective public managers cannot single-handedly transform a more generalized mood of suspicion and distrust emanating from history and the current environment.[35]

Public perception of government and trust in its agents has been declining for some time,[36] posing a fundamental challenge to any large-scale public health effort. If we accept Schwartz's methodology for scenario building, predetermined events, fixed in the short term, constrain the environment and thus affect the plausible realities we can invent. We have called on public executives to approach the management challenge with strategic skepticism. We ask them to question their assumptions, their expectations, and the likelihood that events will unfold as planned. We ask them to be prepared for the worst, even as they move expeditiously to implement a well-designed effort.

Ordinary citizens have adopted a similar approach to public enterprise. They are skeptical of the competence and goodwill of public officials and the efficacy of public policy initiatives. We view this skepticism not as a serious threat to effective governance but as a predetermined event—an underlying assumption—of effective public health management. While scholars argue about the strength and significance of declining public trust,[37] public managers must operate in an environment that is increasingly inhospitable to public intervention even for public health. Recent efforts to gain tighter regulation over foreign and domestic food supplies to control increasingly dangerous food-borne disease have met with significant resistance in gaining budget authority for increased inspection and regulatory activities. This is the case even though the FDA enjoys higher levels of public confidence than most other federal agencies.[38] The recent backlash of private citizens to managed care and calls for more regulation of their activities, however, may suggest a greater role and trust in government in the protection of health "entitlements," if not in their provision.[39.]

Public executives face their roles in difficult times. Their most powerful tools lie in building the integrity and legitimacy of their enterprise and using their managerial skills to establish the competency and effectiveness of their initiatives. Media relations is one vehicle we have discussed with the potential to assist in establishing the merits of their programs. For example, efforts to call attention to and bring recognition for potential AIDS discoveries through the development of a prestigious prize for an AIDS vaccine discovery might provide a crucial adjunct, both to facilitating scientific interest and public support. The use of a public relations effort of this sort to elevate both the race for a discovery and the respect with which a potential scientist might be held could serve to generate valuable public support, much like that afforded to Jonas Salk, even as it provides an added incentive for researchers.

While developing effective public relations provides an important adjunct to sound management, public health executives can no longer count on an electorate they found during the polio immunization program—trusting in the competence and goodwill of the NFIP. In an environment of suspicion and mistrust, program managers have the added responsibility of building confidence and respect for their enterprises step by step. Efforts like the New York City TB control program found effective vehicles to mobilize diverse constituents in a common initiative for which most took some ownership. A strategic management approach anticipated the need to build commitment and confidence in the program at the outset. Success derived from designing innovative means to problem-solve with multiple stakeholders in an environment of collective mission. Thus, citizens, advocates, service providers, and public servants shared responsibility and an investment in the program, and a blind faith in the beneficence of public enterprise was not required.

CONCLUSION

The AIDS crisis remains a significant challenge for public health, and continued identification of new global threats suggests that it may be only the first modern challenge among many to follow.[40] Recent threats from "superbugs" suggest that public health officials can no longer remain complacent, even against historically widespread and benign infections.[41] Developing mutations causing drug-resistant strains (themselves a result of lapses in treatment management) pose serious challenges to public health officials.

Increasing investment of public and private resources in research and new drug development for AIDS and more prosaic diseases continues unabated. Even so, recent assessments of progress in finding a vaccine or the development of long-term effective treatments for AIDS remain increasingly elusive.[42] Nevertheless, the management challenges facing efforts to improve prevention and to manage the delivery of available treatments to HIV- and AIDS-infected people persist. Prevention still remains the most effective means to control HIV and AIDS, but prevention programs like sex education, condom distribution, and needle exchange have run up against the timidity of government and community leaders who fear the conservative backlash of clergy and political opponents. Worse, fearing political fallout from the antidrug lobby, the Clinton administration failed to reverse a nine-year ban on the use of federal resources to fund state needle exchange programs even after Donna Shalala, his secretary of health and human services, provided evidence of their effectiveness.[43]

Widespread use of treatments like protease inhibitors faces significant financing issues as well as variations in intergovernmental commitment to fund their use under the Medicaid program. Some populations do not seek care, while others are denied drugs in the belief that some patients cannot manage the protocols, thereby risking the development of drug-resistant strains that can be spread to others.[44] Unevenness in professional education has resulted in inadequate knowledge of their use among dispensing physicians, since new drugs and increased experience are changing the preferred protocols quite rapidly. Public health and professional education have been inadequate to keep up with the changes. The result is that access to lifesaving treatments is inequitably distributed, favoring those who have access to the most sophisticated and experienced physicians and those whose income, insurance, or state Medicaid programs can cover the high costs of care.[45] Thus, issues of financing and distributional equity undermine any comprehensive federal approach, and continued management of the AIDS crisis relies largely on state and local initiative supplemented by federal grants.

If an effective vaccine were available tomorrow, all indications are that it would meet considerable obstacles in being effectively produced, marketed, and universally administered. The continued uncertainty facing private manufacturers about future markets, liability protection, and profitability serve to undermine aggressive investments in comparison to more profitable alternatives. The scenario for an AIDS vaccine initiative built in Chapter 7 was developed using strategic skepticism, an effort to anticipate the likely sources of management obstacles and threats. Informed by historical insight and stakeholder analysis, we painted a picture of conflict and delay that frustrated efforts to bring a lifesaving vaccine to millions. Recent official analysis of national and international readiness to meet a far more benign viral threat concluded that the CDC and public health officials were no more ready to launch a universal vaccination program against the "bird flu," should it represent a true international pandemic, than they had been in responding to the threat of swine flu.[46] The conclusion suggests that little progress has been made in anticipating the inevitable management challenges confronting large-scale public health efforts and acting in advance to ameliorate or circumvent them.

Management matters. Indeed, the previous chapters have made a strong case for the independent importance of management even when safe and effective treatments or vaccines are available and policy decisions favor comprehensive programs. Even so, most public health executives, like other public executives, focus on policy with limited success. As we have argued elsewhere, policy choices are point decisions and are fundamental. But "having a goal and a vehicle to achieve it is not the same as creating and sustaining the actual apparatus, both human and technical, to launch, steer, and see it through. . . . [success] depends on line decisions—complex processes of assemblage, coordination, and bargaining among many independent actors that take place after the initial point decision. These line decisions are the multiple and critical implementation steps that give life to the larger ideas generated by a policy decision."[47]

Management of complex systems in times of crisis is seldom routine, but as we have discussed, generic threats to program design can be identified in advance, and contingency planning can assist when likely or possible obstacles emerge. We have emphasized the category of threats that typically arise and the type of preemptive actions likely to deter them. But more important, we have argued that approaching the management challenge with strategic skepticism informed by preemptive scenario building is the executive strategy most likely to reveal the potential minefields and arm program managers with contingent plans. Rather than providing a set of blueprints, we offer a way of conceptualizing and approaching the management role.

We began the book by arguing that the discovery is not the cure—even safe and effective treatments or vaccines do not in themselves ensure the elimination of disease. The missing link in disease control is management. As we await the critical scientific breakthroughs that will allow us to contemplate the potential victory over AIDS, we urge greater public health investment in the strategies of management we have identified here. A change in understanding about the contributions of management and the opportunities to improve executive strategies will allow us to envision different scenarios in the future.

Notes

1. TAMING THE MANAGEMENT BEAST

1. Sheryl Gay Stolberg, "Superbugs: The Bacteria Antibiotics Can't Cure," *New York Times Magazine,* August 2, 1998.

2. Allan Brandt, *No Magic Bullet: The Social History of Venereal Disease in the United States Since 1880* (New York: Oxford University Press, 1985). The social history of venereal disease in the United States provides a fascinating case of the tenuous relationship between scientific discovery of a cure and disease control.

3. Lawrence Altman, "'Bird Flu' Reveals Gaps in Plans for Possible Global Outbreaks," *New York Times,* January 6, 1998. Even efforts to control new flu threats are met with delay and conflict, revealing a profound lack of readiness and appropriate planning. The current outbreak demonstrates that many of the lessons of the swine flu threat of 1976 have gone utterly unheeded.

4. Frank Ryan, *Virus X: Tracking the New Killer Plagues out of the Present and into the Future* (Boston: Little, Brown, 1997).

5. Deborah Sontag and Lynda Richardson, "Doctors Withhold HIV Pill Regimen from Some," *New York Times,* March 2, 1997.

6. Lynda Richardson, "Experiment Leaves Legacy of Distrust of New AIDS Drugs," *New York Times,* April 20, 1996.

7. Aaron Wildavsky, *Searching for Safety* (New Brunswick, N.J.: Transaction Publishers, 1989).

8. While an important sponsor of research, the federal government funded only 45.6 percent of basic and applied research in 1994, with most of it paid for and carried out by industry, universities, and other nonprofit institutions. If development funds are included, the federal funds as a proportion of total R and D drop to 36.1 percent. United States Science Foundation, *National Patterns of R and D Resources,* Annual Report, 1994.

9. U.S. Health Care Financing Administration, *Health Care Financing Review* (Spring 1996).

10. Bruce G. Weniger and Max Essex, "Clearing the Way for an AIDS Vaccine," *New York Times,* editorial page, January 4, 1997. The authors are, respectively, a member

of the board of the presidential Advisory Commission on HIV and AIDS. and a professor of virology at Harvard and chairman of the Harvard AIDS Institute.

11. An excellent analysis of the NIH can be found in Natalie Davis Spingarn, *Heartbeat: The Politics of Health Research* (Washington, D.C.: Robert B. Luce, 1976).

12. The various rivalries and blunders attendant to these two lead agencies in the early days of AIDS drug development are well described in Peter Arno and Karyn Feiden, *Against the Odds: The Story of AIDS Drug Development, Politics and Profits* (New York: HarperCollins, 1992).

13. Coordination, Christopher Foreman reminds us, is important but at least with AIDS policy it does not approach the importance of a simple lack of knowledge in explaining weak public responses. A considerable amount of coordination is now found at HHS, and President Clinton has appointed an AIDS "czar," but even giving someone the authority and responsibility for coordinating federal agencies and resources for AIDS cannot solve the problem of inadequate scientific knowledge. See Foreman, "AIDS and the Limits of Czardom: Why We Can't Coordinate an End to the Epidemic," *The Brookings Review* (Summer 1993): 18–21.

14. Spingarn, *Heartbeat.*

15. Robert N. Proctor, *Cancer Wars: How Politics Shapes What We Know and Don't Know About Cancer* (New York: Basic Books, 1995), p. 8.

16. Ibid.

17. Recent interest by the Clinton administration in AIDS vaccine research is predicted to increase funding and perhaps shift the emphasis. However, even recent executive budget proposals are widely viewed to be inadequate for the task. See Alison Mitchell, "Clinton Calls for AIDS Vaccine as a Goal," *New York Times,* May 19, 1997.

18. Brandt, *No Magic Bullet;* Charles E. Rosenberg, *The Cholera Years* (Chicago: University of Chicago, 1962); Elizabeth Fee and Daniel M. Fox, eds., *AIDS: The Burdens of History* (Berkeley: University of California Press, 1988); Arien Mack, ed., *In Time of Plague* (New York: New York University Press, 1991); Susan Sontag, *Illness as Metaphor* (New York: Vintage, 1979).

19. Disease constituencies have an especially palpable effect on public policy interest and budget allocations. There are literally thousands of diseases, and organized interests have an important role in defining research priorities and funding levels. See, for example, Abraham B. Bergman, *The Discovery of Sudden Infant Death Syndrome: Lessons in the Practice of Political Medicine* (New York: Praeger, 1986).

20. Allan Brandt, "AIDS and Metaphor: Toward the Social Meaning of Epidemic Disease," in Mack, *In Time of Plague,* pp. 95–96.

21. Anne Dievler, "Plans and Politics—Fighting Tuberculosis in the 1990s: How Effective Is Planning in Policy Making?" *Journal of Public Health Policy* 18, no. 2 (Summer 1997): 167–87.

22. Increasingly, intergovernmental cooperation means global cooperation, since origins of the emerging viral "killer plagues" appear to be related to changes in worldwide ecosystems through climactic changes and development activities threatening the rain forests and other previously undisturbed homes to most viral hosts. "Plague viruses know no country. There are no barriers to prevent their migration across international boundaries or around the 24 time zones" (Richard M. Krause, quoted in Ryan, *Virus X,* p. 221).

23. Christopher H. Foreman, *Plagues, Products, and Politics* (Washington, D.C.: The Brookings Institution, 1994), p. 76.

24. Ibid., p. 21.

25. Stephen Klaidman, *Health in the Headlines* (New York: Oxford University Press, 1991).

26. Proctor, *Cancer Wars*, points out in analyzing controversy over cancer risks that competing interest groups have much at stake in what the public believes. Fear drives the solicitation of funds, just as complacency favors many commercial interests. The result is that experts quarrel over the gravity of specific hazards, and the media are ill suited to evaluate the relative merits of the arguments.

27. See Gina Kolata, "In Inplant Case, Science and the Law Have Different Agendas," *New York Times*, July, 11, 1998.

28. "Health risk issues are especially manipulable because of the high level of uncertainty that is typical of them. But scientific uncertainty can be used by the media to transmute scientific uncertainty into political reality" (Klaidman, *Health in the Headlines*, p. 234).

29. James Kinsella, *Covering the Plague: AIDS and the American Media* (New Brunswick, N.J.: Rutgers University Press, 1989), p. 264. On August 30, 1983, *CBS Evening News* incorrectly reported a blood product factor that was contaminated and recalled, causing panic among hemophiliac users of the product.

30. Gordon Chase and Elizabeth Reveal, *How to Manage in the Public Sector* (Reading. Mass.: Addison-Wesley, 1993). Rather than simply responding to bad news, Chase and Reveal argue that public managers should anticipate it and "beat the media to the punch when possible." This allows agency executives to control what is released and to provide their own version of the facts and how they will respond rather than being the victims of sensational or inaccurate reporting.

31. Klaidman, *Health in the Headlines*, p. 230, reports the sucessful strategy of William Ruckelshaus, who made a visit to CBS anchorman Dan Rather even before he assumed the directorship of the EPA. The visit reportedly was designed to make clear, in advance, his agenda for the agency. This kind of strategy is typical of other public figures who are attentive to media considerations. See also: Chase and Reveal, *How to Manage in the Public Sector.*

32. Chase and Reveal, *How to Manage in the Public Sector.*

33. While the Reagan administration was clearly unwilling to focus its political and policy resources on an epidemic thought to infect gay males through sexual activity, the mainstream media demonstrated a similar reluctance to cover what was clearly a growing epidemic. See Kinsella, *Covering the Plague.*

34. Charles L. Schultze, *Public Use of Private Interest* (Washington, D.C.: The Brookings Institution, 1977), and Arthur M. Okin, *Equity and Efficiency* (Washington, D.C.: The Brookings Institution, 1975). Schultze argues that American public policy has been particularly loath to impose solutions that violate the dictum "do no direct harm." Instead, harm is often induced indirectly where distributional rules are not explicit but distributional outcomes are.

35. Richard M. Titmuss, *The Gift Relationship* (London: Allen and Unwin, 1971). The moral consequences of market mechanisms for such activities are well illuminated in an analysis of the private market for blood.

36. Sheryl Gay Stolberg, "AIDS Drugs Elude the Grasp of Many of the Poor," *New York Times,* October 14, 1997.

37. Recent criticism of the CDC's lack of readiness for new threats of flu pandemics specifically points out the failure to develop a triage plan for priority distributions for the inevitable shortages of vaccine supplies. See Altman, "'Bird Flu' Reveals Gaps."

38. Immigrants have been a particularly hard to reach group for immunization and treatment since they fear exposing their identity to public officials and therby compromising their status. The success of preventive health education against AIDS is significantly related to the effectiveness of programs to target and design culturally relevant programs for different subgroups. See Melinda K. Moore and Martin L. Frost, eds., *AIDS Education: Reaching Diverse Populations* (Westport, Conn.: Praeger, 1996).

39. See National Commission on Civic Renewal, transcript, first plenary session, January 25, 1997; Steve Kelman, *Making Public Policy* (New York: Basic Books, 1987); Andrew Kohut, *Deconstructing Distrust: How Americans View Government* (Washington, D.C.: The Pew Research Center, March 1998); and Robert Putnam, "Turning In, Turning Out: The Strange Disappearance of Social Capital in the United States," *PS: Political Science and Politics* 28, no. 4 (December 1995): 664–83. See also National Commission on Civic Renewal, *Final Report,* Washington, D.C., 1997, especially working papers, Scholars' Working Group on Civil Society, and E. J. Dionne, "Why Civil Society? Why Now?" *Brookings Review* 15, no. 4 (Fall 1997): pp. 5–8.

40. Seymour Martin Lipset and William Schneider, *The Confidence Gap* (New York: Free Press, 1983). More recent surveys document that there is still a problem of confidence in the federal government. Two-thirds of the American public believe that the American system is good, but that the people who are running it are incompetent. This confirms trends that have been documented for the last two decades. See National Commission on Civic Renewal, transcript, especially discussion by James Davison Hunter, who reports on his survey with the Gallup Corporation.

41. Jeffrey Goldfarb, *The Cynical Society* (Chicago: University of Chicago Press, 1991).

42. Kohut, *Deconstructing Distrust.* Trust in state and local government enjoys a greater following than the federal government and confidence has edged up for both since the economic recovery expanded in 1994. The period from 1982 to 1994 experienced far lower confidence ratings—21 percent compared to 37 percent in 1997. Public opinion following the presidential scandal of January 1998 showed a five-point slip. See David S. Broder, "Trust in Government Edges Up," *Washington Post,* March 10, 1998.

43. Robert Jervis, *System Effects: Complexity in Political and Social Life* (Princeton, N.J.: Princeton University Press, 1996), documents the uncertainty of effects that result in systems where there are many interactions and interconnections. "The result is that systems often display nonlinear relationships, outcomes cannot be understood by adding together units of their relations, and many of the results of actions are unintended" (p. 6).

44. Stephen Linder and B. Guy Peters, "A Design Perspective on Policy Implementation: The Fallacies of Misplaced Prescription," *Policy Studies Review* 6, no. 3 (February 1987): 459–75; Eugene Bardach, *The Implementation Game* (Cambridge, Mass.: MIT Press, 1979); Jeffrey Pressman and Aaron Wildavsky, *Implementation* (Berkeley: University of California Press, 1973); G. Majone and Aaron Wildavsky, "Implementation as Evolution," in *Policy Studies Review Annual,* vol. 2, ed. H. E. Freeman (Beverly Hills, Calif.: Sage, 1978).

45. Aaron Wildavsky, *Speaking Truth Power* (Boston: Little, Brown, 1979).

46. Eugene Bardach, "On Designing Implementable Programs," in *Pitfalls of Analysis,* ed. G. Majone and E. S. Quade (New York: John Wiley, 1980).

47. This is a method adopted from I. I. Mitroff and R. O. Mason, "A Logic for Strategic Problem Solving: A Program of Research and Policy Planning" (unpublished) and cited in Center for Applied Research, "Stakeholder Mapping," an internal working paper, Philadelphia, 1993. It is based, however, on a number of sources including I. Mitroff and James R. Emshoff, "On Strategic Assumption-Making: A Dialectical Approach to Policy and Planning," *Academy of Management Review* 4, no. 1 (1979): 1–12.

48. Louise K. Comfort, ed., *Managing Disaster: Strategies and Policy Perspectives* (Durham, N.C.: Duke University Press, 1988).

49. Andrew Campbell and Marcus Alexander, "What's Wrong with Strategy?" *Harvard Business Review* (November/December 1997): 42–49.

50. Erwin C. Hargrove and John C. Glidewell, *Impossible Jobs in Public Management* (Lawrence: University Press of Kansas, 1990).

51. Naomi Rogers, *Dirt and Disease: Polio Before FDR* (New Brunswick, N.J.: Rutgers University Press, 1992). This was not always the case. The social construction of polio in the early part of the century stigmatized the poor and their lifestyle, thought to be related to the risk of the disease.

2. THE SUCCESSFUL MANAGEMENT OF POLIO

1. Naomi Rogers, *Dirt and Disease: Polio Before FDR* (New Brunswick, N.J.: Rutgers University Press, 1992).

2. Allan Chase, *Magic Shots: A Human and Scientific Account of the Long and Continuing Struggle to Eradicate Infectious Diseases by Vaccination* (New York: William Morrow, 1982), p. 297.

3. Jane Smith, *Patenting the Sun: Polio and the Salk Vaccine* (New York: William Morrow, 1990).

4. All of the money went to the Warm Springs Foundation, and none was used for the repayment of his personal loan of $200,000 to the organization. Richard Thayer Goldberg, *The Making of Franklin D. Roosevelt: Triumph over Disability* (Cambridge, Mass.: ABT Books, 1981), pp. 154–55.

5. Smith, *Patenting the Sun,* p. 70.

6. The NFIP was established in 1934 and continued until 1958.

7. Richard Carter, *Breakthrough: The Saga of Jonas Salk* (New York: Trident Press, 1962).

8. Saul Benison, book review of Naomi Roger's *Dirt and Disease: Polio Before FDR,* in *Journal of the History of Medicine and Allied Sciences* 9, no. 2 (April 1994): p. 305. See also John Paul's description of the NFIP as taking on the functions of "a bureau of health education" (*History of Poliomyelitis* [New Haven: Yale University Press, 1971] p. 319).

9. Chase, *Magic Shots,* p. 526 n. 8.

10. Goldberg, *The Making of Franklin D. Roosevelt,* p. 31.

11. Ibid.

12. Paul, *History,* p. 371.

13. Smith, *Patenting the Sun,* pp. 74–76.

14. Paul, *History,* p. 308.

15. Carter, *Breakthrough,* p. 26.

16. Smith, *Patenting the Sun,* pp. 131–32.

17. Paul, *History,* pp. 423–35.

18. Smith, *Patenting the Sun,* p. 193.

19. Carter, *Breakthrough,* p. 144.

20. Ibid., p. 26.

21. Rogers, *Dirt and Disease,* p. 185.

22. Carter, *Breakthrough,* pp. 214–15.

23. Harry A. Dowling, *Fighting Infection* (Cambridge, Mass.: Harvard University Press, 1977), p. 211; quoted in Rogers, *Dirt and Disease,* p. 184.

24. Jesse Green, "Who Put the Lid on gp120?" *New York Times Magazine,* March 26, 1995, and Frank Ryan, *The Forgotten Plague* (Boston: Little, Brown, 1993).

25. Salk had already injected five thousand children in the Pittsburgh area with the vaccine, but a statistically relevant trial was necessary to satisfy medical researchers of the vaccine's safety and effectiveness. See Paul, *History,* pp. 420, 426.

26. Smith, *Patenting the Sun,* pp. 230–34. Some estimates of volunteer workers numbered 150,000; the National Congress of Parents and Teachers estimated twice that many had been involved.

27. Saul Benison, *Tom Rivers: Reflections on a Life in Medicine and Science* (Cambridge, Mass.: MIT Press, 1967), pp. 534–35. See also, Smith, *Patenting the Sun,* pp. 226–28.

28. There is considerable fragmentation of authority in the provision of public health, a fact that adds to the management challenges of responding to large disease threats. The federal government's role is generally acknowledged to be one of policy coordination, research, and funding. While the federal role has been growing, day-to-day protection and promotion of health have traditionally been state functions, which many states devolve to local public health authorities. States have this authority under the Constitution under what is traditionally known as "police power"—the power reserved for states to take necessary action to promote public health and welfare, to foster prosperity, and to maintain public order. See Larry Gostin, "Traditional Public Health Strategies," in *AIDS and the Law: A Guide for the Public,* ed. M. Dalton and S. Burns (New Haven: Yale University Press, 1989), pp. 47–54.

29. Smith, *Patenting the Sun,* p. 283.

30. *Extension of the Poliomyelitis Vaccination Assistance Act,* 84th Cong., 2d sess., H.R. 8704, January 24, 1956, p. 2.

31. Smith, *Patenting the Sun,* pp. 221, 247. See also Rogers, *Dirt and Disease,* p. 178.

32. O'Connor was concerned that those "Polio Pioneers" who participated as the control group in the field trials be given the vaccine as a first priority and that others received a booster shot as needed. See Rogers, *Dirt and Disease,* p. 178.

33. Smith, *Patenting the Sun,* p. 360.

34. Carter, *Breakthrough,* p. 319.

35. Smith, *Patenting the Sun,* p. 366.

36. Bert Spector, "The Great Salk Vaccine Mess" *Antioch Review* 38, no. 3 (Summer 1980): 299–300.

37. Paul, *History,* pp. 435–36.

38. Rogers, *Dirt and Disease,* p. 180.

39. Smith, *Patenting the Sun,* 364–67.

40. For an opposing view, see Carter, *Breakthrough,* p. 311, where he argues: "If the sole concern of the Public Health Service had been public health, the tragedy could not have occurred. But other factors were involved. Scheele's budget, his procedures, and the size and disposition of his staff were regulated by law and tradition to ensure minimum interference with private medicine and the drug industry, the compulsions of which do not necessarily coincide with those of public health. This arrangement antedates Scheele."

41. George Rosen, *A History of Public Health* (New York: MD Publications, 1958), p. 467.

42. Spector, "The Great Salk Vaccine Mess," p. 293.

43. Paul, *History,* p. 435.

44. See Smith, *Patenting the Sun,* chap. 11.

45. Carter, *Breakthrough,* p. 302.

46. Smith, *Patenting the Sun,* p. 352. See also Spector, "The Great Salk Vaccine Mess," for a discussion of Hobby's advice to wait and see what the states decided to do before committing federal money.

47. Gerald W. Johnson, "Polio and Principles," *New Republic* 133 (July 4, 1955): 15.

48. "How 'Shots' Are Going in Canada," *U.S. News and World Report* 38 (June 3, 1955): 32.

49. Ibid.

50. Smith, *Patenting the Sun,* p. 366.

51. Spector, "The Great Salk Vaccine Mess," p. 302.

52. See, for instance, Aaron Klein, *Trial by Fury: The Polio Vaccine Controversy* (New York: Scribner, 1972), and similar complaints by Paul, *History,* and Paul de Kruif, *The Fight for Life* (New York: Harcourt Brace, 1962), that the NFIP hastily pushed field trials. However, no children were harmed by the vaccine during the field trials.

53. In fact, Dr. Rivers told Saul Benison that Dr. Francis's "evaluation of the Salk vaccine was a superb achievement" (Benison, *Tom Rivers,* p. 550).

54. Smith, *Patenting the Sun,* p. 353.

55. Spector, "The Great Salk Vaccine Mess," pp. 294–96.

56. Carter, *Breakthrough,* p. 312.

57. See Paul, *History,* for condemnation of the NFIP for seeking attention from the media.

58. Benison, *Tom Rivers,* p. 549.

59. Smith, *Patenting the Sun,* p. 257.

60. Rogers, *Dirt and Disease,* p. 178.

61. Ibid., p. 179.

62. Quoted in Carter, *Breakthrough,* p. 327.

63. Ibid.

64. "Truth About the Polio Scare," *U.S. News and World Report* 38 (May 13, 1955): 21.

65. Smith, *Patenting the Sun,* p. 363.

66. Carter, *Breakthrough,* p. 319.

67. Ibid., p. 302.

68. Ibid., pp. 303–4.

69. Ibid., p. 304.

70. Carter, p. 307.

71. Ibid.

72. Notes from the author's interview with Ken Jones, Boston, July 1994.

73. Kenneth Jones, "The Case of the Salk Polio Vaccine," *St. John's Symposium* (1992) 26.

74. Carter, *Breakthrough,* p. 302.

75. Ibid., p. 307.

76. See Smith, *Patenting the Sun,* p. 351.

77. H.R. 6286, 84th Cong., 1st sess., May 27, 1955.

78. Smith, *Patenting the Sun,* p. 351.

79. Carter, *Breakthrough,* p. 305.

80. Jones, "The Case of the Salk Polio Vaccine," p. 31.

81. Ibid., p. 33. Table 2 illustrates the low immunization rates as of April 1960: only 71 percent of the population younger than twenty and 40 percent of those ages twenty to forty were fully protected.

82. Smith, *Patenting the Sun,* p. 371.

83. For example, legal issues of informed consent currently required both to conduct field trials and to undertake a vaccination program are far more complex and the law more highly developed than it was in 1955. These and myriad other technical implementation questions plague current efforts. See Robert E. Stein, "The Development of an HIV Vaccine: Legal and Policy Aspects," in *Vaccine Research and Developments,* vol. 1, ed. Wayne C. Koff and Howard R. Six (New York: Marcel Dekker, 1992).

84. Gordon Chase, "Implementing a Human Services Program: How Hard Will It Be?" *Public Policy* 27, no. 4 (Fall 1979): 385–435.

3. THE SWINE FLU IMMUNIZATION PROGRAM

1. Victoria Harden, *Inventing the NIH: Federal Biomedical Research Policy, 1887–1937* (Baltimore: Johns Hopkins University Press, 1986), discusses the emergence of the cultural authority of the medical profession in the 1920s, enabling public health practitioners to emphasize personal health and hygiene as a means of preventing illness. The federal government, as well as the American Medical Association and the American Public Health Association, developed this idea into policy through the organization of public health campaigns targeting prevention rather than treatment. (A June 27, 1977, General Accounting Office [GAO] report adds that preventive medicine—with its inherent element of risk—was the underlying justification for the swine flu program.)

2. In schools of public policy and public management all over the United States, students use a five-part teaching case based on the analysis by Richard E. Neustadt and Harvey Fineburg, *The Epidemic That Never Was: Policy-Making and the Swine Flu Affair* (New York: Vintage Books, 1983). This analysis still constitutes a classic example of the difficulties and dilemmas of policy development and management. At the request of HEW Director Joseph Califano, Neustadt and Fineburg were charged with a review and analysis

of the swine flu program. Many of the historical details are based on that analysis as well as a 1977 GAO report to Congress.

3. The largest mass vaccination in history, six million in twenty-eight days, occurred in a smallpox outbreak in New York City in 1948. Inoculation rates for polio, for example, were significantly lower, only six million in over twelve weeks; it took over two years to vaccinate sixty million. See Monroe G. Sirken and Berthold Brenner, "Population Characteristics and Participation in the Poliomyelitis Vaccination Program," *Public Health Monograph,* no. 6, U.S. Public Health Service Publication no. 723 (Washington, D.C.: Government Printing Office, 1960).

4. Neustadt and Fineburg, *The Epidemic That Never Was,* p. 18. Arthur M. Silverstein, *Pure Politics and Impure Science: The Swine Flu Affair* (Baltimore: Johns Hopkins University Press, 1981), adds that only after the influenza virus had been isolated in the 1930s was the link between influenza and various respiratory ailments (and some pneumonia cases) fully appreciated.

5. Silverstein, *Pure Politics and Impure Science,* p. 17.

6. Neustadt and Fineburg, *The Epidemic That Never Was,* build this argument citing Nic Masurel and William M. Marine, "Recycling Asian and Hong Kong Influenza A Virus Hemagluttins in Man," *American Journal of Epidemiology* 97 (1973): 48–49; Silverstein, *Pure Politics and Impure Science,* cites W. I. B. Beveridge, *Influenza, The Last Great Plague* (New York: Prodist, 1977) and Edwin D. Kilbourne, ed., *The Influenza Viruses and Influenza* (New York: Academic Press, 1975).

7. Silverstein, *Pure Politics and Impure Science,* p. 19.

8. Letter from Comptroller Jack Young to Henry Waxman, House of Representatives, "The Swine Flu Program—An Unprecedented Venture in Preventive Medicine" (HRD-77-115), U.S. General Accounting Office, HEW report to Congress, Washington, D.C., 1977. Others report that Kilbourne considered the swine flu virus a genuine threat, though not as likely a candidate as Victoria-A strains.

9. Ibid., p. 9.

10. Ibid., p. 10.

11. More cautious approaches were advocated by Dr. Russell Alexander, a member of ACIP, Dr. Martin Goldfield, assistant commissioner and chief epidemiologist, New Jersey Department of Public Health, and Dr. J. Anthony Morris, a research virologist at the Bureau of Biologics, among others. Nevertheless, when Ford recessed the meeting, he indicated that he would be in the Oval Office to hear private doubts; no one came (Silverstein, *Pure Politics and Impure Science,* p. 48). Subsequent opposition included Dr. Sidney Wolf of Ralph Nader's Health Research Group and Dr. Albert Sabin, who partially recanted his support in May 1976.

12. See Sencer memorandum, Appendix D in Neustadt and Fineburg, *The Epidemic That Never Was,* pp. 198–205. It is clear from the way in which these assumptions are presented that Sencer is biased in favor of action and is seeking to justify this action. Silverstein, *Pure Politics and Impure Science,* p. 37.

13. Sencer memorandum, Appendix D in Neustadt and Fineburg, *The Epidemic That Never Was,* pp. 198–205.

14. Ibid.

15. The manufacture of a particular batch of vaccine takes about two months. The swine flu vaccine production method involves inoculating fertile eggs with seed virus.

After several days, the embryonic fluids are harvested and the virus is purified, concentrated, and inactivated. The inactivated virus is then diluted to a specific strength (a specific amount of viral antigen per dose). Thus, the dose yield per egg depends not only on the biological process of virus developing in the embryo, but also on the strength specified (U.S. General Accounting Office, "The Swine Flu—An Unprecedented Venture in Preventive Medicine," p. 50).

16. Excluding the thirty million doses on hand that would be made bivalent for high-risk groups but including those needed for the armed forces.

17. U.S. General Accounting Office, "The Swine Flu—An Unprecedented Venture in Preventive Medicine," p. 48.

18. Based on the mistaken assumption that manufacturers could extract more than one dose per egg. See Neustadt and Fineburg, *The Epidemic That Never Was,* p. 58, and Silverstein, *Pure Politics and Impure Science,* p. 77.

19. Neustadt and Fineburg, *The Epidemic That Never Was,* p. 90. In this case, the same batch of Parke-Davis vaccine was involved. Parke-Davis had earlier produced six million doses using a different strain, further impeding production and consuming egg supplies.

20. Ibid., 92. The surveillance centers established by the CDC had anticipated temporally related deaths, and Neustadt suggests that earlier announcements had been discussed but not acted upon until deaths occurred. Silverstein, *Pure Politics and Impure Science,* adds that once the story broke, reporters found it impossible to reach the CDC in Atlanta for clarification.

21. Several notable officials received public immunizations to encourage support, although with questionable success. At his health station, Maine governor James B. Longley criticized the effort to sell the mass immunization campaign like toothpaste or soapflakes. See *New York Times,* September 10, 1976.

22. The statistical probabilility of contracting Guillain-Barré syndrome was eleven times greater among those inoculated with the swine flu vaccine.

23. Officially, the program was funded through July 1977. At the state and local level, personnel and vaccine purchases were committed through this date although the program was officially halted in February 1977.

24. U.S. General Accounting Office, "The Swine Flu—An Unprecedented Venture in Preventive Medicine," p. 55.

25. Neustadt and Fineburg, *The Epidemic That Never Was,* p. 51, identify PHS Assistant Secretary for Planning and Evaluation William Morrill as Cooper's crucial ally in the decision to expedite the program without these elements. According to Silverstein, *Pure Politics and Impure Science,* p. 40, Nelson Rockefeller may have been correct in thinking that logistics experts in the armed services might do a better job than those at HEW.

26. In the days following Ford's announcement, reporters observed that some members of Congress reportedly believed they should have been included in the consultation before the decision was made. See Harold M. Schmeck Jr., "Tests of Flu Vaccine Expected in April," *New York Times,* March 26, 1976.

27. To further exemplify this conflict, Neustadt and Fineburg, *The Epidemic That Never Was,* p. 53, note that "the states looked to Millar . . . while the Washington press mostly went to Meriwether." See also Silverstein, *Pure Politics and Impure Science,* p. 77.

28. Such research would include study of flu viruses in the swine population and the instances of swine-to-man transmission; studies of antibodies and adverse reactions to vaccines produced and determining dosage and usage; determining the protection provided by swine flu vaccine in population groups; and testing the technology for producing and using live flu vaccine during pandemics and collecting data for comparing live-virus vaccines with killed-virus vaccines made of whole viruses, split viruses, or surface antigens of the virus.

29. Neustadt and Fineburg, *The Epidemic That Never Was*, p. 54.

30. U.S. General Accounting Office, "The Swine Flu—An Unprecedented Venture in Preventive Medicine," p. 57.

31. Ibid., p. 58.

32. See Joel Shurkin, *The Invisible Fire* (New York: G. Putnam, 1979). More recent examples of the unevenness of local efforts discussed in Chapter 5 are the comparative performances of cities seeking to control reemergent tuberculosis.

33. This approach would also ensure realistic goals. For example, two observers commented on New York City's immunization plan, which was restricted by existing budgets: "Using the [Department of Health's] 21 injector guns, which can vaccinate about 300 persons per hour, department workers could vaccinate one million people in five weeks. At that rate, it would take one year to vaccinate eight million (New York's total population)" (John Marr and Gwenyth Cravens, editorial, *New York Times*, April 22, 1976).

34. Neustadt and Fineburg, *The Epidemic That Never Was*, p. 94; see also Silverstein, *Pure Politics and Impure Science*, p. 139. Both authors suggest that the lack of informed local-level physicians was the cause of disappointing vaccination. Of the 1,900 physicians expected to participate in one city, only 400 requested vaccine (106 requested fifty doses or less); in three counties of one state, fewer than 200 of about 1,500 physicians requested vaccine. U.S. General Accounting Office, "The Swine Flu—An Unprecedented Venture in Preventive Medicine," p. 66.

35. Ibid., p. 67.

36. Ibid., p. 62.

37. Ibid., p. 67.

38. Ibid., p. 68.

39. Ibid., p. 42.

40. Neustadt and Fineburg, *The Epidemic That Never Was*, p. 63.

41. Ibid.

42. U.S. General Accounting Office, "The Swine Flu—An Unprecedented Venture in Preventive Medicine," p. 43.

43. Silverstein, *Pure Politics and Impure Science*, p. 112.

44. Additionally, the Department of Defense requested doses of 400 CCA-units (double dosages requiring more than one egg per dose) for the military population, imposing an additional strain on limited supplies; ibid., p. 83.

45. U.S. General Accounting Office, "The Swine Flu—An Unprecedented Venture in Preventive Medicine," p. 21.

46. Neustadt, 41.

47. U.S. General Accounting Office, "The Swine Flu—An Unprecedented Venture in Preventive Medicine," p. 49. Actually, these were verbal agreements; contracts were not officially signed until after the suspension of the program.

48. Neustadt and Fineburg, *The Epidemic That Never Was*, p. 85.

49. Ibid., p. 79.

50. The memo argued for, among other things, a decision on the secretary's part to pursue legislation for public management of vaccine-associated disability that would relieve the apprehension and anxiety of public health and medical professionals and of biologics producers. Ibid., p. 72.

51. A statement prepared by HEW's general counsel noted that since states are sovereigns, most state and local governments are immune from tort liability, and most local governments are not liable for employee negligence in the administration of vaccine in programs regarded as government functions. However, when a state or local government purchases liability insurance, immunity from tort liability is generally waived to the extent of the coverage. See U.S. General Accounting Office, "The Swine Flu—An Unprecedented Venture in Preventive Medicine," p. 73.

52. Ibid., p. 74.

53. For example, Cutter was ordered by the courts to compensate 204 victims of tainted polio vaccine, three-quarters of whom had become paralyzed and eleven of whom died.

54. U.S. General Accounting Office, "The Swine Flu—An Unprecedented Venture in Preventive Medicine," p. 24. Silverstein, *Pure Politics and Impure Science,* p. 109, adds that for a variety of important reasons the final consent form pleased almost no one.

55. The CDC drafted another form in January, which was scheduled to be reviewed in February to coincide with a resumption of the immunization program for high-risk individuals. See U.S. General Accounting Office, "The Swine Flu—An Unprecedented Venture in Preventive Medicine," p. 24.

56. Ibid., p. 69. Later, Senator Ted Kennedy would point out that 13 percent of those vaccinated had not signed informed consent forms; half of these merely signed a register while the other half signed nothing or could not remember. See Lawrence K. Altman, "Health Officials Get More Reports of Rare Paralytic Syndrome in U.S.," *New York Times,* December 18, 1976.

57. In addition to program officials being unable to reach CDC when vaccine deaths were discovered, Dr. Lowell E. Bellin, New York City's health commissioner, reported that when vaccine delivery was over one million doses less than requested, his staff could not get any firm information on why the allocations were changing. See David Bird, "Bellin Says Flu Vaccine Allotment Is Insufficient to Check Disease," *New York Times,* September 30, 1976.

58. Neustadt and Fineburg, *The Epidemic That Never Was,* p. 48.

59. U.S. General Accounting Office, "The Swine Flu—An Unprecedented Venture in Preventive Medicine," p. 65.

60. See Harold M. Schmeck Jr., "Tests Find Swine Flu Vaccines Satisfactory for Majority of Adults but Less Acceptable for Children," *New York Times,* June 22, 1976, and Schmeck, "Delay in Flu Shots for Young Likely," *New York Times,* June 23, 1976.

61. Stuart Auerbach, "Ford Asks for Nationwide Flu Shots," *Washington Post,* March 25, 1976.

62. See David E. Rosenbaum, "Flu Immunization Backed by House," *New York Times,* April 7, 1976. Other unchecked misinformation included ingesting several grams of vitamin C during the expected swine flu epidemic. See Linus Pauling, "On Fighting Swine Flu," *New York Times,* June 5, 1976.

63. Stuart Auerbach, "Vaccine Producer Seeks Insurance," *Washington Post,* June 16, 1976.

64. Deliberately exposing six volunteers to the swine flu virus, this study concluded that the Fort Dix outbreak may have been an isolated event and that the swine flu virus will not become established in man. The editorial added that the swine flu virus did not seem to be very good at infecting man and may have died out as a result. See editorial, *New York Times,* July 20, 1976.

65. Stuart Auerbach, "Vaccines for Swine Flu Flunk Tests in Children," *Washington Post,* June 22, 1976.

66. Boyce Rensberger, "U.S. Aide Doubts Flu Toll," *New York Times,* July 2, 1976.

67. Victor Cohn and Judith Valente, "Local Doctors Act in Face of Pa. 'Mystery Disease,'" *Washington Post,* August 5, 1976.

68. Deaths were either connected or disassociated with the vaccine in five articles in the *New York Times* on October 13, five articles on October 14, three on October 15, and so on.

69. Neustadt and Fineburg, *The Epidemic That Never Was,* p. 94. As early as April, a *New York Times* editorial by John Marr, director of the Bureau of Preventable Diseases in New York City, and novelist Gwyneth Cravens (April 22, 1976) on the early federal mismanagement of the swine flu program warned that, as with most important events, misinformation will proliferate.

70. U.S. General Accounting Office, "The Swine Flu—An Unprecedented Venture in Preventive Medicine," p. 64.

71. Ibid., p. 63.

72. Ibid., p. 63.

73. Neustadt and Fineburg, *The Epidemic That Never Was,* p. 94.

74. Among commuters, 61 percent thought the vaccinations were unnecessary, 13 percent were afraid, and 17 percent were advised against them by physicians. Among inner-city residents, 48 percent thought the vaccinations were unnecessary, 38 percent were afraid, and 11 percent were advised against them by physicians. See Ronald Sullivan, "New York City Residents Resist Flu Shots and a Poll Learns Why," *New York Times,* November 21, 1976.

75. Neustadt and Fineburg, *The Epidemic That Never Was,* p. 53.

76. The Victoria A vaccine was presented at the first ACIP meeting as a standard immunization strategy for the elderly; the doses were already in production. Additional questions arose concerning the viability of making the vaccination bivalent to include the swine flu strain.

77. In the report on federal regulation and regulatory reform conducted by the Oversight Subcommittee of the House Interstate and Foreign Commerce Committee, Representative John E. Moss, chairman of the subcommittee, cited the example that over 50 percent of the Nixon and Ford administrations' appointments to regulatory jobs during the previous five years were people who formerly had been employed by the regulated industry. See David Burnham, "Nine Agencies Found to Regulate Poorly," *New York Times,* October 3, 1976.

78. Nixon resigned after allegations of his connection to the Watergate scandal in 1974. Threatened with impeachment, he was subsequently pardoned by Ford shortly after

Ford assumed the presidency. Although this action was supported by the public, later polls suggest that it undermined Ford's public support.

79. Lawrence K. Altman, "The Lingering Effects of the Swine Flu Failure," *New York Times,* December 26, 1976.

80. Silverstein, *Pure Politics and Impure Science,* p. 112.

81. Neustadt and Fineburg, *The Epidemic That Never Was,* p. 94.

82. Adding that "the possibility that hundreds of thousands, perhaps millions, of Americans dying of swine influenza was hinted at unless their unprecedented mass vaccination program was carried out" (editorial, *New York Times,* July 3, 1976).

83. Editorial, "Light on Swine Flu," *New York Times,* July 20, 1976.

84. Dan Morgan, "Flu Vaccine Makers See Compliance with Deadline," *Washington Post,* April 2, 1976.

85. Dr. J. Anthony Morris, a research virologist at the Bureau of Biologics who called the immunization program "a big waste," was fired from his job in a move that led to "years of argument and litigation" (Silverstein, *Pure Politics and Impure Science,* p. 168). Bruce Dull at the CDC and Dr. Martin Goldfield in New Jersey also would be replaced before the end of the program.

86. U.S. General Accounting Office, "The Swine Flu An Unprecedented Venture in Preventive Medicine," p. 38. These figures neglect to address the absence of neuraminidase. Normally active in flu vaccines, this antigen was inactive in the vaccine produced for swine flu. Although scientific controversy exists as to whether this antigenic component is crucial to vaccine effectiveness, CDC and HEW officials believed their vaccine might provide adequate protection without it (p. 45).

87. Such recommendations required a second dose, information that, according to program officials, may not have been conveyed to parents; ibid., p. 43.

88. A group of government virologists who reviewed flu experiences between 1957 and 1972 simply concluded that "on some occasions the vaccine has worked and on others it has not. . . . Protection rates are clearly influenced by features peculiar to the vaccine, the virus, and the host—and by methods used by the investigators" (ibid., p. 40).

89. Ibid., p. 13.

90. Ibid., p. 10. In April, the World Health Organization met in Geneva to discuss the significance of the Fort Dix outbreak. Countries with the necessary capabilities were encouraged to initiate production of a vaccine for the Fort Dix strain that could be stockpiled as an emergency measure, combined with currently recommended vaccines, or administered it as an individual vaccine. Poorer countries were advised to create contingency plans.

91. The evidence also suggested that the new strain lacked the ability to compete successfully against other flu strains, especially Victoria, which was more likely to be dominant during the 1976–1977 flu season; ibid., p. 13.

92. Ibid., p. 14.

93. Robin Maranz Henig, *A Dancing Matrix: Voyages Along the Viral Frontier* (Alfred A. Knopf, 1993), and June Osborne, ed., *History, Science, and Politics: Influenza in America 1918–1976* (New York: Prodist, 1977).

94. See Neustadt and Fineburg, *The Epidemic That Never Was,* Silverstein, *Pure Politics and Impure Science,* and Osborne, *History, Science, and Politics.*

95. Robin Maranz Henig, "Flu Pandemic," excerpt from *New York Times Magazine,* November 29, 1992.

4. CLINTON'S CHILDHOOD IMMUNIZATION POLICY

1. Martin A. Levin and Mary Bryna Sanger, *Making Government Work* (San Francisco: Jossey-Bass, 1994).

2. James Q. Wilson, "What Is to Be Done?" unpublished paper.

3. The original administration proposal did call for some investments in infrastructure, tracking, and surveillance. Universal entitlement to free vaccine, however, was always the centerpiece of the Clinton initiative.

4. Outbreaks of measles that hit many U.S. cities between 1989 and 1992 resulted in 5,500 cases and 132 measles-related deaths.

5. Centers for Disease Control and Prevention, *Morbidity and Mortality Weekly Report* 43, no. 39 (October 7, 1994). These figures are for 1993.

6. Excluding the newly recommended Hepatitis B vaccine.

7. Some have argued that rates are already reaching desired levels and that 1992 figures available to the HHS secretary demonstrate this change. See Robert Goldberg, "The Gang That Couldn't Give Shots Straight," *Wall Street Journal,* June 20, 1994.

8. Some have argued, however, that abandoning basic data collection efforts in all areas of federal activities was a conscious decision of the Reagan administration for both budgetary and political reasons. Indeed, during a time of retrenchment and reduced government services, there was a conscious recognition that data collection which must reflect unfavorably on the effects of government policy ought to be abandoned.

9. D. Shea, "The Current Climate of Immunization: What's Happening, What Needs to Be Done?" in *Children: Our Future,* proceedings of the American Academy of Pediatrics Conference for Media, July 23, 1991, Chicago.

10. The first campaign to prevent the spread of communicable disease into the United States began in the late 1700s. Early legislation included the Act of 1799, which placed the management of quarantine under the supervision of the secretary of the treasury; the Act of 1878, which attempted to prevent the introduction of communicable diseases into the United States; and the Act of 1893, which gave the U.S. Public Health Service responsibility over foreign and interstate quarantine. The Virus Serums and Toxins Act of 1902 involved the federal government in the licensing and regulating of vaccines and their manufacturers in accordance with standards established by an interagency board under the secretary of the treasury. See U.S. House of Representatives, Subcommittee on Health and the Environment of the Committee on Energy and Commerce, *Childhood Immunizations: A Report* (Washington, D.C.: Government Printing Office, September 1986).

11. Data were provided on seven federal titles from 1955–1991. See Centers for Disease Control and Prevention, "Appropriations for Selected Health Programs, FY1980–91," and the Children's Defense Fund, "Medicaid and Childhood Immunizations: A National Study, 1994." The aggregate dollars are somewhat misleading since immunization-related activities constitute only a portion of all of the relevant federal titles. However, CDC figures for each title that separate vaccine-related funding from all others and that include Medicaid-related immunization expenditures are not available. Nevertheless, the general point is still quite clear.

12. In addition to federal legislative efforts to fund state and local immunization efforts and underwrite the cost of vaccine for the poor, the federal government, aware of

the decline in research and production of vaccines by major manufacturers, passed additional legislation in 1986. Designed to head off the consequences of the liability crisis that was driving manufacturers out of the market and increasing the costs of vaccines to compensate for anticipated litigation costs, the National Childhood Vaccine Injury Act of 1986 (P.L. 99-660) provided for a no-fault system to compensate the victims of unavoidable adverse effects of vaccination. Establishing the National Childhood Vaccine Injury Compensation program, the act ensured the stability of vaccine supplies and helped assuage some of the major legal and economic concerns, including increasing prices and reduced market participation by a large number of pharmaceutical companies. This was an important federal action to support the federal immunization efforts. Funded by an excise tax on vaccines, it had the effect of reducing the number of suits filed against manufacturers from 225 in 1985 to 18 in 1991.

13. Calculations are based on data provided by the American Academy of Pediatrics and Centers for Disease Control and Prevention, cited in "Childhood Immunizations," *CQ Researcher* 3, no. 23 (June 18, 1993): 529–52.

14. The American Academy of Pediatrics and the Centers for Disease Control and Prevention recommend five vaccines to protect against nine early childhood diseases, each of which involves multiple injections over a period of months or years. They include DPT, which requires five shots for complete immunizations; OPV, which requires four shots; MMR, which requires two shots; Hib, which requires four shots; and Hep. B, which requires three shots. These vaccines collectively immunize children against diphtheria, pertussis, tetanus, polio, measles, mumps, rubella, hemophilus influenza type B, and hepatitis B.

15. The final legislation calls for vaccine prices to be capped at the contract price the CDC paid when it purchased childhood vaccines from manufacturers in 1991–1992.

16. Eleven states currently buy vaccines for all children.

17. Recent cost data provided by the CDC National Immunization Program, July 1996. Total immunization funding from grants, direct operations, section 317, and VFC combined represented $878 million in FY 96.

18. Robert Pear, "Clinton Official Defends Plan for Vaccines," *New York Times,* May 31, 1994, and Pear, "Clinton Criticized as Too Ambitious with Vaccine Plan," *New York Times,* May 30, 1994.

19. Robert Goldberg, *Removing the Barriers: A New Look at Raising the Immunization Rates* (Waltham, Mass.: Brandeis University, The Gordon Public Policy Center, 1993).

20. "Childhood Immunization: Opportunities to Improve Immunization Rates at Lower Cost" (HRD-93-41), U.S. General Accounting Office, March 24, 1993; Mark V. Nadel, associate director of national and public health issues, U.S. General Accounting Office, letter to Honorable John D. Dingell, chairman of Committee on Energy and Commerce, House of Representatives, July 21, 1993; Goldberg, "Removing the Barriers.

21. Figures taken from GAO survey data provided by eight of the ten states that provide free vaccine.

22. Gary L. Freed, Clayton Bordley, and Gordon H. Defriese, "Childhood Immunization Programs: An Analysis of Policy Issues," *Milbank Quarterly* 71 (1993): 65–96; Alan R. Hinman, "What Will It Take to Fully Protect All American Children with Vaccines?" *American Journal of Diseases of Children* 147, no. 5 (1991): 536–37; Goldberg, "Removing the Barriers." In addition, several studies of inner-city children in Los Angeles,

Baltimore, Rochester, and Philadelphia published as recently as 1993 revealed shockingly low rates of coverage at twenty-four months. See U.S. General Accounting Office, "Vaccines for Children: Critical Issues in Design and Implementation" (GAO/PEMD-94-28), July 1994, p. 7.

23. The Children's Defense Fund Report, "Medicaid and Childhood Immunizations: A National Study," 1992.

24. Freed, Bordley, and Defriese, "Childhood Immunization Programs"; Kenneth Jost, "Childhood Immunizations," *CQ Researcher* 3, no. 23 (June 18, 1993): 531–51; Georges Peter, "Childhood Immunizations," *New England Journal of Medicine* 327, no. 25 (December 17, 1992): 1794–1800; "The Public Service Action Plan to Improve Access to Immunization Services," *Public Health Reports* 107, no. 3 (May–June 1992): 242–51; Felicity T. Cutts, Elizabeth Zell, Dean Mason, Roger Bernier, Eugene Dini, and Walter Orenstein, "Monitoring Progress Toward U.S. Preschool Immunization Goals," *Journal of the American Medical Association* 267, no. 14 (April 8, 1992): 1952–55.

25. Hinman, "What Will It Take to Fully Protect All American Children with Vaccines?" pp. 559–62.

26. Regular sources of care among all children are very high. A national medical expenditure survey sponsored by the U.S. Agency for Health Care Policy Research showed that 80 percent of black and 92 percent of white infants had a regular source of care. The poor were less likely than middle-class respondents to have regular sources of care (82 percent versus 94 percent); for poor children under the age of one, the percentage with a regular source of care is even lower.

27. Freed, Bordley, and Defriese, "Childhood Immunization Programs," report on the results of a recent Gallup survey on parental knowledge and attitudes about immunizations. Of those interviewed, 47 percent did not know that a second measles immunization was necessary. Many were unaware of the new Hib recommended immunization, and 75 percent identified their physician as their major source of information on immunizations. Further, low-income inner-city parents and rural poor reported that work, food, and shelter are of higher priority than immunizing their children.

28. W. A. Orenstein, W. Atkinson, D. Mason, and R. H. Bernier, "Barriers to Vaccinating Preschool Children," *Journal of Health Care for the Poor and Underserved* 1, no. 3 (1990): 315–29.

29. See K. M. Farizo, P. A. Stehr-Green, L. E. Markowitz, and P. A. Patriarca, "Vaccination Levels and Missed Opportunities for Measles Vaccination: An Audit in a Public Pediatric Clinic," *Pediatrics* 89 (1992): 589–92, and K. M. McConnochie and K. J. Roghmann, "Immunization Opportunities Missed Among Poor Urban Children," *Pediatrics* 89 (1992): 1019–26.

30. National Vaccine Advisory Committee, "The Measles Epidemic: The Problems, Barriers, and Recommendations," *Journal of the American Medical Association* 266 (1991): 1547–52.

31. Testimony of the National Association of Community Health Centers, *Comprehensive Child Immunization Act of 1993: Joint Hearing Before the Senate Committee on Labor and Human Resources and the House Subcommittee on Health and the Environment of the Committee on Energy and Commerce,* 103d Cong., 1st sess., April 21, 1993.

32. The National Center for Clinical Infant Programs reports that problems of infant mortality have resulted in fifteen states implementing high-risk infant tracking programs

to identify infants with special health and developmental needs. Further, Early Periodic Screening and Diagnostic Testing Programs attempt to monitor the preventive services received by children on Medicaid. These programs are prototypes and are designed to identify and assist mothers and infants felt to be at risk. The Robert Wood Johnson Foundation is experimenting with models like the one used in North Carolina to implement an electronic birth certificate program from which data can be transferred to the central immunization registry. See B. C. Williams and C. A. Miller, "Preventative Health Care for Young Children: Findings from a Ten-Country Study and Directions for United States Policy." *Pediatrics* 89 (suppl.) (1992): 983–98.

33. Hinman, "What Will It Take to Fully Protect All American Children with Vaccines?"

34. Goldberg, "Removing the Barriers."

35. Freed, Bordley, and Defriese, "Childhood Immunization Programs."

36. F. T. Cutts, W. A. Orenstein, and R. H. Bernier, "Causes of Low Preschool Immunization Coverage in the United States," *Annual Review of Public Health* 13 (1992): 385–98; P. G. Szilagyi et al., "Improving Influenza Vaccination Rates in Children with Asthma: A Test of a Computerized Reminder System and an Analysis of Factors Predicting Vaccination Compliance," *Pediatrics* 90, no. 6 (December 1992): 871–75.; K. Tollestrup and B. B. Hubbard, "Evaluation of a Follow-up System in a County Health Department's Immunization Clinic," *American Journal of Preventive Medicine* 7, no. 1 (1991): 24–28.

37. Representative Marge Roukema (R–N.J.) introduced H.R. 1840, *The Childhood Immunization Incentive Act,* which would have prevented parents from collecting any welfare until they demonstrated that their children were immunized; Representative Dave Camp (R–Mich.) introduced H.R. 2432, *Responsible Parent Immunization Plan Act of 1993,* which sought to provide monetary incentives for welfare parents who get their children immunized and to reduce the grants of those who do not.

38. Joint hearing, *Comprehensive Child Immunization Act of 1993,* p. 46.

39. The final legislation includes a provision that prevented this potential abuse.

40. See note 37.

41. Martha Derthick, *Agency Under Stress* (Washington, D.C.: Brookings Institution, 1990).

42. Ibid., p. 175.

43. Ibid., p. 176.

44. See Levin and Sanger, *Making Government Work,* chap. 2, and Martin Levin and Marc Landy, *The New Politics of Public Policy* (Baltimore: Johns Hopkins University Press, 1993).

45. See Levin and Sanger, *Making Government Work.*

46. In this case it was considered and ignored. There was a view that implementation issues could be figured out later.

47. Although the states' role has been growing, day-to-day protection and promotion of public health have traditionally been their function. States have this authority under the Constitution under what is traditionally known as "police power"—the power reserved for states to take necessary action to promote public health and welfare, to foster prosperity and to maintain public order. See M. Dalton and S. Burns, eds., *AIDS and the Law: A Guide for the Public* (New Haven: Yale University Press, 1989), especially chap. 4, "Traditional Public Health Strategies."

48. Section 317 is a program that is designed to set the goals and provide states with considerable flexibility to meet them. It does not, however, provide any accountability for states to meet measurable outcomes.

49. National Commission on the State and Local Public Service, *Hard Truths/Tough Choices: An Agenda for State and Local Reform* (Albany, N.Y.: The Nelson A. Rockefeller Institute of Government, State University of New York at Albany, 1993); Lawrence Lynn, "Innovation and the Public Interest: Insights from the Private Sector," paper prepared for the Innovations and Organizations Conference, University of Minnesota, Minneapolis, September 1992.

50. Levin and Sanger, *Making Government Work.*

51. Ibid.

52. Thomas Peters and Robert Waterman, *In Search of Excellence* (New York: HarperCollins, 1982).

53. National Performance Review, *From Red Tape to Results: Creating a Government That Works Better and Costs Less* (Washington, D.C.: Government Printing Office, 1993).

54. National Commision on the State and Local Public Service, *Hard Truths/Tough Choices.*

55. A recent issue of the leading public policy and management journal was devoted entirely to exploring new roles for the nonprofit sector, particularly as their activities become more commercial. Both the nonprofit and the private sectors are undertaking historically public roles in service provision of all kinds. See *Journal of Policy Analysis and Management* 17, no. 2 (Spring 1998): 175–313.

56. This perception is often incorrect since many policy changes can dramatically reduce expenditures—reducing entitlements and changing the distribution of services—and often changes in program management are actually important policy initiatives. New York City's management agenda, which includes dramatic reductions in some services for low-income constituents and freezes or relative increases in middle-class services, must be seen as an important policy initiative.

57. U.S. General Accounting Office, "Vaccines for Children: Critical Issues in Design and Implementation," July 1994.

58. U.S. General Accounting Office, "Vaccines for Children: Reexamination of Program Goals and Implementation Needed to Ensure Vaccination," June 1995.

59. See letter to Congressman Waxman, chairman of the Subcommittee on Health and the Environment, August 12, 1994.

60. U.S. General Accounting Office, "Vaccines for Children: Critical Issues."

61. Goldberg, "The Gang That Couldn't Give Shots Straight."

62. U.S. General Accounting Office, "Vaccines for Children: Reexamination of Program Goals."

63. An interview with Walter A. Orenstein, director of the CDC national immunization program, has revealed that the CDC's prime basis for program success is not improved immunization rates, but the building of a long-term financing system of both today's and tomorrow's vaccines. See "Ask the Experts: The Vaccines for Children Program, One Year Later," *Infectious Diseases in Children* 8, no. 10 (October 1995): 26–27.

64. This and other examples of potential program distortions were provided off the record by congressional counsels of one of the important health subcommittees involved in developing and amending VFC legislation.

65. Centers for Disease Control and Prevention, *Morbidity and Mortality Weekly Report* 45, no. 7 (February 23, 1996).

66. U.S. General Accounting Office, "Vaccines for Children: Reexamination of Program Goals."

67. A win-win policy is one capable of achieving both liberal and conservative goals simultaneously. See Stuart S. Nagel, "Win-Win Policy," *Policy Studies Journal* 23, no. 1 (Spring 1995): 181–82.

5. CONTROLLING REEMERGENT TB

1. By 1990, almost half of all TB hospitalizations in New York City were also the result of HIV infection, and these hospitalizations are 50 percent longer than those associated with TB alone. See Peter Arno, Christopher J. L. Murray, Karen Bonuck, and Philip Alcabes, "The Economic Impact of Tuberculosis in Hospitals in New York City: A Preliminary Analysis," *Journal of Law, Medicine, and Ethics* 21, nos. 3–4 (Fall–Winter 1993): 317–23.

2. Indeed, many attribute the steadily and improving rates of decline in TB incidence in previous decades almost exclusively to the improvement in social and economic conditions and very little to public health control programs during the period. See Victor W. Sidel, Ernest Drucker, and Steve Martin, "The Resurgence of Tuberculosis in the United States: Societal Origins and Societal Responses," *Journal of Law, Medicine, and Ethics* 21, nos. 3–4 (Fall–Winter 1993): 303–16.

3. Frank Ryan, *The Forgotten Plague* (Boston: Little, Brown, 1993).

4. Gordon Chase, "Implementing a Human Services Program: How Hard Will It Be?" *Public Policy* 27, no. 4 (Fall 1979): 385–435.

5. Many obstacles to discovery, as well as delivery, are not necessarily scientific; often the most important impediments are social, political, economic, or institutional.

6. Thomas B. Brock, *Robert Koch: A Life in Medicine and Bacteriology* (New York: Springer Verlag, 1988), quoted in Ryan, *The Forgotten Plague*, p. 10.

7. TB has the capacity for gouging large holes in bones, especially spinal bones and vertebrae. Thus skeletal remains of ancient people revealed the existence of TB as early as 4000 B.C. Further evidence of tuberculosis in the skeleton of a young man from a neolithic grave near Heidelberg was dated at 5000 B.C. See Ryan, *The Forgotten Plague*, p. 5.

8. Sheila M. Rothman, "The Sanitorium Experience: Myths and Realities," in special report, *The Tuberculosis Revival: Individual Rights and Societal Obligations in a Time of AIDS* (New York: United Hospital Fund, 1992).

9. Although pulmonary TB is the most common presentation of the disease, it can also take a number of other forms. Extrapulmonary TB is not contagious through the airborne route but is disseminated in the lung causing small seedlike lesions or life-threatening meningitis. It travels through the bloodstream from the lungs to other parts of the body. HIV-infected individuals and children are most susceptible. See U.S. Congress, Office of Technology Assessment, "The Continuing Challenge of Tuberculosis," 1993, p. 30.

10. While active TB can be very contagious, it requires closeness or intimacy of contact with an actively infected person for an extended period of time. The probability of infection is greatly increased in close quarters with minimal air movement, little ventilation,

and no sunlight. See G. W. Comstock and G. M. Cauthen, "The Epidemiology of Tuberculosis," in *Tuberculosis: A Comprehensive International Approach,* ed. L. B. Reichman and E. S. Herrshfield (New York: Marcel Dekker, 1993).

11. Ryan, *The Forgotten Plague,* p. 289.

12. H. Williams, *Requiem for a Great Killer* (London: Health Horizon, 1973).

13. While little organized national research was specifically funded by any governments, the British in the 1930s were engaged in a variety of large-scale treatment, support, and education activities by both public and philanthropic means. See Ryan, *The Forgotten Plague.*

14. Lawrence K. Altman, "Failed Tests on Monkeys Frustrate Hopes for AIDS Vaccine," *New York Times,* July 3, 1998.

15. "Treatment of Pulmonary Tuberculosis with Para-aminosalicylic Acid and Streptomycin: A Preliminary Report," *British Medical Journal* ii (1949): 1521; cited in Ryan, *The Forgotten Plague,* p. 331.

16. Ryan, *The Forgotten Plague,* p. 327. The research was reported in "Streptomycin Treatment of Pulmonary Tuberculosis: A Medical Research Council Investigation," *British Medical Journal* ii (1948): 769–82.

17. Ryan, *The Forgotten Plague,* chap. 20.

18. Interviews with H. Corwin Hinshaw were provided to Frank Ryan and were reported in Ryan, *The Forgotten Plague.*

19. Ibid.

20. Merck was reported by both Waksman and Hinshaw, two notable participants in the research effort of the time, to have relinquished the patent rights in order to help encourage faster and better development for worldwide production at a reduced price by allowing competition among companies. George Merck himself thus added to his previous generosity of providing free quantities of streptomycin for research, a loss of millions of dollars in potential profit. See Ryan, *The Forgotten Plague,* p. 339.

21. Ibid., p. 275.

22. In our research on childhood immunization, for example, we demonstrated in Chapter 4 the significant importance of legislation that reduced drug company liability for vaccine-related side effects in increasing research and vaccine production. This development, however, required a significant act of public policy that protected the dual interests of consumers and private industry.

23. See Allan Brandt, "AIDS in Historical Perspective: Four Lessons from the History of Sexually Transmitted Diseases," *American Journal of Public Health* 78 (April 1988): 367–71.

24. House Committee on Energy and Commerce, *The Tuberculosis Epidemic,* 103d Cong., 1st sess., March 29, 1993, 1–59.

25. House Committee on Energy and Commerce, *Tuberculosis Control Program Reauthorization, H.R. 4097,* 101st Cong., 2nd sess., February 22, 1990, 1–41; House Committee on Energy and Commerce, *The Tuberculosis Epidemic,* 1–59.

26. Directly observed therapy, we will see, is an effort to ensure that cases with a high risk of failure to complete treatment are given drugs under supervision of public health personnel.

27. House Committee on Energy and Commerce, *Tuberculosis Control Program,* 100th Cong., 1st sess., March 25, 1987, 100–132.

28. Thomas Frieden, director, New York City Bureau of Tuberculosis Control, New York City Department of Health, interview by the author, New York City, July 24, 1995.

29. "Tuberculosis in New York City: 1995 Information Summary" (New York: New York City Department of Health, 1995).

30. By 1992, it was estimated that more than 40 percent of New York City tuberculosis cases were also HIV or AIDS infected. See "Tuberculosis in New York City: 1992 Information Summary" (New York: New York City Department of Health, 1993).

31. F. Kramer et al., "Delayed Diagnosis of Tuberculosis in Patients with Human Immunodeficiency Virus Infection," *American Journal of Medicine* 89 (1990): 451–56.

32. The federal government's role is generally acknowledged to be one of policy coordination, research, and funding. Although the federal role has been growing, day-to-day protection and promotion of public health have traditionally been a state function. New York City is unique in that both the state and the city departments of health report directly to CDC.

33. These data refer to the cost of drugs alone and do not include other treatment costs. See U.S. Congress, Office of Technology Assessment, *The Continuing Crisis of Tuberculosis,* OTA-H-574 (Washington, D.C.: Government Printing Office, 1993).

34. Ongoing research on DOT continues to demonstrate its cost-effectiveness. Research on savings conducted by the Institute for Health Policy Studies at the University of California–San Francisco provides strong evidence that DOT saves three to four dollars in hospital costs for each dollar invested. As such, it is the management strategy of choice. See Statement of Alan Hinman, M.D., CDC Director, in his testimony before the House Committee on Energy and Commerce, *Tuberculosis Control Program Reauthorization, H.R. 4097,* 1–41.

35. R. A. Torres et al., "Human Immunodeficiency Virus Infection Among Homeless Men in a New York City Shelter: Association with Mycobacterium Tuberculosis Infection," *Archives of Internal Medicine* 150 (1990): 2030–36, and E. Nardell et al., "Exogenous Reinfection with Tuberculosis in a Shelter for the Homeless," *New England Journal of Medicine* 315, no. 25 (1986): 1570–75.

36. In 1979, estimates from the current population survey placed the poverty rate in New York City at 20.2 percent. By 1990 the rate was 25.2 percent, and by 1993 it had increased to 27.3 percent. Data provided by the Community Service Society, updated poverty tables, July 1995.

37. Obviously these changes are related. As drug policy shifted over the decade of the 1980s from a treatment to a punitive model, there was a 254 percent increase in drug-related arrests; 70–80 percent of the new arrests tested positive for drug use. In the jail system in New York City in 1990, 80 percent tested positive for some form of drug use, and 18.5 percent tested positive for HIV. See Steven Safer et al., "Tuberculosis in Correctional Facilities: The Tuberculosis Control Program of the Montefiore Medical Center Rikers Island Health Services," *Journal of Law, Medicine, and Ethics* 21, nos. 3–4 (Fall–Winter 1993): 342–51.

38. All population data provided by the New York City Mayor's Office of Management and Budget.

39. Brian R. Edlin et al., "An Outbreak of Drug-Resistant Tuberculosis Among Hospitalized Patients with the Acquired Immunodeficiency Syndrome," *New England Journal of Medicine* 29, no. 2 (June 1992): 1514–21.

40. Bruce Lambert, "Health Chief and AIDS: A Chant of Critics Amid Praise," *New York Times,* August 30, 1988.

41. Commissioner Joseph had one major TB initiative during this period. Recommending and receiving changes in the health code, he initiated a requirement for all new school entrants to receive a TB test (PPD) prior to enrollment. This approach proved to be costly and target-inefficient, and as the only significant TB strategy, it uncovered few new cases of TB while incurring the costs of testing 120,000 at low risk of infection. The description of the initiative is found in Stephen C. Joseph, "Comment: New York City, Tuberculosis, and the Public Health Infrastructure," *Journal of Law, Medicine, and Ethics* 21, no. 3–4 (Fall–Winter 1993): 372–75.

42. Michelle Lord, former deputy director for human services, Mayor's Office of Operations, and director of the Mayor's Office of Health Policy, interview by the author, New York City, August 2, 1995.

43. Jeanne Kassler, "Drug-Resistant Tuberculosis Is Surging," *New York Times,* June 2, 1991.

44. Thomas R. Frieden et al., "Drug-Resistant and Nosocomial Tuberculosis, New York City, 1991," Department of Health and Human Services, U.S. Public Health Service, Centers for Disease Control, 1991.

45. New York City Office of Management and Budget, executive budget, fiscal year 1990.

46. The City of New York is legally bound to have a balanced budget, so any potential gaps must be closed by reducing expenditures or increasing revenues.

47. This view of the budget process and the perceptions of various agencies was confirmed by interviews with Health Commissioner Margaret Hamburg, a senior Office of Management and Budget official in the Dinkins administration, and several high-level officials in the Mayor's Office of Operations at the time.

48. A number of interviewees suggested that this was especially a concern of Barbara Sabel, commissioner of the Human Resources Administration.

49. A number of critical studies about the scope and nature of the growing threat accompanied by rising numbers of cases reported by the city health department and the CDC provided irrefutable evidence on the dimension and seriousness of the problems. See, for example, Frieden et al., "Drug-Resistant and Nosocomial Tuberculosis, New York City, 1991"; K. Brudney and J. Dobkin, "Resurgent Tuberculosis in New York City: Human Immunodeficiency Virus, Homelessness, and the Decline of Tuberculosis Control Programs," *American Review of Respiratory Disease* 144 (1991): 745–49; and Torres et al., "Human Immunodeficiency Virus Infection Among Homeless Men in a New York City Shelter," pp. 2030–36.

50. Frieden et al., "Drug-Resistant and Nosocomial Tuberculosis, New York City, 1991."

51. The initial draft of the blueprint released for public comment was designed to provide a framework for all relevant agencies to develop their action plans. It was dated September 21, 1992, and formally released on October 8, 1992. See City of New York, "Tuberculosis Blueprint: Goals and Objectives," draft, October 8, 1992.

52. The FY 1993 budget had a projected $1.3 billion gap to be closed.

53. Barbara Turk, former deputy director, Mayor's Office of Management and Budget, Dinkins administration, interview by the author, New York City, July 25, 1995. Turk

acknowledged that TB was "in a class by itself in getting the city's attention" and transcended other mayoral initiatives. OMB wanted to place no limit on the prescription—even given limited resources—but needed a coherent plan to know "what we need to do." Thus, public health officials, principally Margaret Hamburg, were given enormous respect and authority.

54. Robert W. Jacobs, *Real Time Strategic Change* (San Francisco: Berret-Koehler, 1994). Jacobs was a consultant to the Fund and describes the method and how it has worked in a range of private, nonprofit, and public settings, including at the New York City Health and Hospitals Corporation in their effort to move to a managed care model.

55. Mary McCormick, president, Fund for the City of New York, quoted in Jacobs, *Real Time Strategic Change,* p. 260.

56. All actors identified the resistance and extreme skepticism of Barbara Sabel, New York City Human Resources Commissioner, about both the planning process and the appropriateness and ability of HRA to undertake major TB control efforts.

57. Thomas Frieden, director, Bureau of Tuberculosis Control, New York City Department of Health, interview by the author, New York City, New York, July 24, 1995. Of all those interviewed, Dr. Frieden was the least salient about the value of the effort. Nevertheless, Deputy Budget Director Barbara Turk reported that OMB would never have allocated the resources in the absence of the planning process.

58. Barbara Turk, interview, July 25, 1995.

59. These demands grew out of an advocates' suit originally brought in federal court in 1982, which forced the city to provide adequate health services at Rikers Island. It was settled in various stages. The suit in 1991 after the outbreak of MDR-TB in upstate prisons represented a motion for supplemental relief. After filing the motion, the Legal Aid Society negotiated for an expansion of who would be included under a consent decree, which coincided with the city's long-range plan for respiratory isolation units. In early 1992, federal judge Morris E. Lasker ordered the Department of Corrections to complete the first phase of the communicable disease isolation units in ninety days. Because of the time frame and the need to finance the design of a state-of-the-art facility, the city spent close to $500,000 per cell. By 1993, 140 were completed. See Safer et al., "Tuberculosis in Correctional Facilities," pp. 342–51.

60. Most of the evidence on the nature and impact of the city's control program has come from interviews with the commissioner of health, the director of the department's Bureau of Tuberculosis Control, published and unpublished department data, and a recent special article in the *New England Journal of Medicine* documenting the city's success and providing the research evidence to support it. See Thomas R. Frieden et al., "Tuberculosis in New York City—Turning the Tide," *New England Journal of Medicine* 333, no. 4 (July 27, 1995): 229–33.

61. Although the incidence around the country has decreased since 1993, there are questions about whether the reported decline is the result of TB control activities or changes in reporting procedures and AIDS surveillance case definition. See "Control of Tuberculosis in the United States," *American Review of Respiratory Disease* 146, no. 6 (December 1992): 1623–33; U.S. General Accounting Office, report to the ranking minority member, House Committee on Commerce, "Tuberculosis: Costly and Preventable Cases Continue in Five Cities" (Washington, D.C.: Government Printing Office, 1995); and Office of Technology Assessment, "The Continuing Challenge of Tuberculosis."

62. "Expanded Tuberculosis Surveillance and Tuberculosis Morbidity—United States, 1993," *Morbidity and Mortality Weekly Report* 43 (1994): 361–65. This rate of decline in one year was significantly higher than in other cities with a serious increase in the numbers of TB and MDR-TB in the years 1985–1992. See U.S. General Accounting Office, "Tuberculosis: Costly and Preventable Cases Continue in Five Cities" (GAO/ HEHS-95-11), March 1995.

63. M. D. Iseman, "Treatment of Drug-Resistant Tuberculosis," *New England Journal of Medicine* 329 (1993): 784–91.

64. Budget data are from the Department of Health and the Mayor's Office of Management and Budget.

65. Two-thirds of the funds are federal, but as emphasized earlier it was the city's release of previously frozen funds through the granting of "post-audit status" to the Department of Health that dramatically increased initial staffing. This proved more important than the absolute amount provided by the city.

66. Frieden et al., "Tuberculosis in New York City—Turning the Tide."

67. S. A. Maloney et al., "Efficacy of Control Measures in Preventing Nosocomial Transmission of Multidrug-Resistant Tuberculosis to Patients and Health Care Workers," *Annals of Internal Medicine* 122 (1995): 90–95.

68. This analysis was reported in Frieden et al., "Tuberculosis in New York City—Turning the Tide," p. 231. The recent data on the growth of MDR-TB in hospitals reinforce this concern.

69. New York City Task Force on Tuberculosis in the Criminal Justice System, *Final Report* (New York: New York City Department of Health, June 1992).

70. Frieden et al., "Tuberculosis in New York City—Turning the Tide," p. 232.

71. Department of Health laboratories do free TB diagnostic and drug susceptibility testing for suspected and confirmed TB cases in their own clinics and for private physicians. Many other laboratories do testing.

72. Research had established that 90 percent of the increase in cases resulted from a reactivation of a previous infection. See "The Use of Preventive Therapy for Tuberculosis Infection in the United States: Recommendation of the Advisory Committee for the Elimination of Tuberculosis," *Morbidity and Mortality Weekly Report* 39 (1990): 9–12.

73. Recent revelations about problems of incentives in the pharmaceutical industry, however, suggest that future control may be impeded by lack of current investment in the commercial development and marketing of new antibiotics. At a recent meeting sponsored by *Lancet,* the international medical journal reported in the *New York Times,* participants claimed that new drugs have been developed and are ready for testing, but the investment costs to bring the drugs to market are too high for pharmaceutical companies, given their profit potential. See Lawrence K. Altman, "As TB Surges, Drug Producers Face Criticism," *New York Times,* September 18, 1995.

74. Frieden et al., "Tuberculosis in New York City—Turning the Tide," p. 232.

75. Office of Technology Assessment, "The Continuing Challenge of Tuberculosis," p. 81.

76. Frieden et al., "Tuberculosis in New York City—Turning the Tide."

77. Dr. Hamburg is one of the only commissioners whose tenure has spanned both the Dinkins and the Giuliani administrations. Nevertheless, while there has continued to be an extraordinary maintenance of effort, TB control has not captured the attention of the current administration as a front-burner issue.

78. While there are conspicuous examples of scientific and legal controversy in the TB case regarding the appropriate protection of health care workers and the appropriate use of DOT and involuntary detention, standard TB control efforts generally are fairly uncontroversial. See Office of Technology Assessment, "The Continuing Challenge of Tuberculosis." These controversies also were identified in interviews with Frieden and others. See also Lawrence O. Gostin, "The Resurgent Tuberculosis Epidemic in the Era of AIDS: Reflections on Public Health, Law, and Society" *Maryland Law Review* 54, no.1 (1995): 1–131.

79. This finding is consistent across a large number of public health initiatives that we have studied, including smallpox, polio, swine flu, and childhood disease immunization programs.

80. Chase, "Implementing a Human Services Program."

81. Dr. Thomas Frieden identified a conscious and systematic effort to brief and educate the media in order to ensure accurate but timely reporting of the city's initiative and provide public education about the seriousness of the epidemic while keeping a check on sensationalism that might cause needless fear and alarm; interview with author, July 1995. An interview with Dr. Hamburg further identified the importance of the legitimate press, especially the *New York Times,* in serving to mobilize elite interests about the importance of TB control. Thus, press relations and management were critical.

82. Throughout my interview with the commissioner, it was clear that she saw all the risks of her strategy but felt that in its absence the chances for the success of such a massive undertaking in the short time available were very slim. While she applauded the outcomes of the process, she was not completely convinced of the necessity of all the "process oriented" activities involved in deciding what needed to be done and detailing what different pieces would be done by whom.

83. Robert Behn, "The Big Questions of Public Management," *Public Administration Review* 55, no. 4 (July–August 1995): 313–24.

84. In his model of social policy implementation, Laurence Lynn, "Policy Achievement as a Collective Good," in *Public Management*, ed. Barry Bozemen (San Francisco: Jossey-Bass Publishers, 1993), provided the rationale for noncooperative behavior and the tendency for goal displacement. Drawing on game theory, principal agent theory, and positive political theory, he identifies the dilemmas for managers as those imposed by strategic conflict and the economy of incentives in bureaucracies that leave public managers with few satisfactory resolutions if they seek cooperative outcomes. However, the theory of motivation that underlies his analysis differs from ours and from Behn's.

85. Behn, "The Big Questions of Public Management," p. 319. As Behn also points out, another assumption is that if people have a role in deciding what goals to pursue and how to pursue them, they will work harder to pursue them.

86. This approach is common to many successful and innovative public initiatives. See Martin A. Levin and Mary Bryna Sanger, *Making Government Work* (San Francisco: Jossey-Bass, 1994), chap. 9.

87. As we argue elsewhere, "Constraints loosen in a crisis because there tends to be more acceptance of the need for radical change, and this provides considerable freedom to innovate. . . . Crisis often quiets natural opposition and provides the political and organizational support for change" (Levin and Sanger, *Making Government Work,* p. 132).

88. Nevertheless, the Department of Health has sustained only minimal budget cuts

during a period of extraordinary fiscal constraint when other city agencies have experienced significant contraction.

89. This case analysis also supports similar conclusions about how other successful innovators manage. See Levin and Sanger, *Making Government Work.*

6. THE EARLY MISMANAGEMENT OF THE AIDS CRISIS

1. Epidemiologists at the CDC had an important role in defining the new syndrome prior to isolating a putative causal agent. They first developed a causal model based on "lifestyle": "Epidemiology, unlike virology, has a strong social dimension in that it explicitly incorporates perceptions of a population's social relations, behavior patterns, and experiences into its explanation of disease processes. Given their training, epidemiologists fairly consistently defined HIV infection as a biological process occurring within a determinate social matrix. That the infection was first identified among young, male homosexuals and intravenous drug users certainly reinforced that professional proclivity" (see Gerald Oppenheimer, "In the Eye of the Storm," in *AIDS: The Burdens of History,* ed. Elizabeth Fox and Daniel M. Fee [Berkeley: University of California Press, 1988]).

2. Charles E. Rosenberg, "*Disease and Social Order in America: Perceptions and Expectations,*" in Fox and Fee, *AIDS: The Burdens of History,* pp. 28–29.

3. Charles Perrow and Mauro F. Guillen, *The AIDS Disaster: The Failure of Organizations in New York and the Nation* (New Haven: Yale University Press, 1990).

4. Rodger Streitmatter, *Unspeakable: The Rise of the Gay and Lesbian Press in America* (Boston: Faber and Faber, 1995), pp. 252–59.

5. Randy Shilts, "Gay Freedom Day Raises AIDS Worries," *San Francisco Chronicle,* May 27, 1983.

6. Dennis Altman, *AIDS in the Mind of America* (Garden City, N.Y.: Anchor Press/Doubleday,1986), p. 149.

7. "Garage Sale Marks Closing of Baths," *Gay Community News,* September 10, 1983, p. 2.

8. Randy Shilts, *And the Band Played On* (New York: St. Martin's Press, 1987), p. 416.

9. Quoted in John-Manuel Andriote, *Victory Deferred: How AIDS Changed Gay Life in America* (Chicago: University of Chicago Press, 1999), p. 79.

10. Brian Jones, "Community Plan to Regulate Baths," *Bay Area Reporter,* September 27, 1984.

11. Shilts, *And the Band Played On,* p. 489.

12. Ibid., p. 306.

13. Quoted in Andriote, *Victory Deferred,* p. 81.

14. Erwin Hargrove and John C. Glidewell, *Impossible Jobs in Public Management* (Lawrence: University Press of Kansas, 1990).

15. Albert R. Jonsen and Jeff Stryker, eds., *The Social Impact of AIDS in the United States* (Washington, D.C.: National Academy Press, 1993), p. 91.

16. Margaret A. Fischl et al., "The Efficacy of Azidothymidine (AZT) in the Treatment of Patients with AIDS and AIDS-Related Complex: A Double-Blind, Placebo-Controlled Trial," *New England Journal of Medicine* 317 (1987): 185–91.

17. Lawrence K. Altman, "New Study Questions Use of AZT in Early Treatment of AIDS Virus," *New York Times,* April 1, 1993.

18. Peter S. Arno and Karyn L. Feiden, *Against the Odds: The Story of Drug Development, Politics, and Profits* (New York: HarperCollins, 1992), p. 98.

19. U.S. House of Representatives, Committee on Government Operations, *AIDS Drugs: Where Are They?* (Washington, D.C.: Government Printing Office, 1988).

20. Arno and Feiden, *Against the Odds,* p. 58.

21. Larry Kramer, *Reports from the Holocaust: The Making of an AIDS Activist* (New York: St. Martin's Press, 1989), pp. 140–44.

22. Michael Callen, "Remarks," April 24, 1987; courtesy of PWA Health Group, New York City.

23. Douglas Crimp with Adam Rolston, *AIDS Demographics* (Seattle: Bay Press, 1990), pp. 76–83.

24. NIAID AIDS Clinical Trials Advisory Group, *Final Report,* January 22, 1988, p. 4.

25. House of Representatives, *AIDS Drugs: Where Are They?*

26. Michael Callen, *Surviving AIDS* (New York: HarperCollins, 1990), p. 121.

27. Quoted in Andriote, *Victory Deferred,* p. 191.

28. Quoted in Arno and Feiden, *Against the Odds,* p. 174.

29. Kramer, *Reports from the Holocaust,* pp. 287–88.

30. Arno and Feiden, *Against the Odds,* p. 175.

31. Ibid., p. 176.

32. Jonsen and Stryker, *The Social Impact of AIDS,* p. 96.

33. Andriote, *Victory Deferred,* p. 200.

34. Ibid., p. 202.

35. Robert M. Wachter, *The Fragile Coalition: Scientists, Activists, and AIDS* (New York: St. Martin's Press, 1991).

36. Larry Kramer, *The Destiny of Me* (New York: Penguin, 1993), p. 17.

37. Centers for Disease Control, *HIV/AIDS Surveillance Report,* June 30, 1998.

38. H. Miller, C. Turner, and L. Moses, *AIDS: The Second Decade* (Washington, D.C.: National Academy Press, 1990).

39. Darrell E. Ward, *The AmFAR AIDS Handbook* (New York: W. W. Norton, 1999), p. 191.

40. A. Greig, "Harm Reduction in the U.S.: A Movement for Change," *Canadian HIV/AIDS Policy Law* 3–4 (Winter 1997–1998): 22–28.

41. Ward, *The AmFAR AIDS Handbook,* p. 192.

42. Centers for Disease Control, "Update: Syringe Exchange Programs—United States, 1997," *Morbidity and Mortality Weekly Report* 47 (August 14, 1998).

43. Public Law 102-394, Sec. 514.

44. P. G. Lurie, E. Drucker, and A. Knowles (Center for AIDS Prevention Studies), *Int Conf AIDS* 12 (1998, abstract no. 33403): 670.

45. Warren E. Leary, "Report Endorses Needle Exchanges as AIDS Strategy," *New York Times,* September 20, 1995.

46. American Public Health Association, *The Nation's Health* (March 1996): 10.

47. Katharine Q. Seelye, "AMA Backs Drug-User Needle Exchanges," *New York Times,* June 27, 1997.

48. Unsigned editorial, "Clean Needles, No Money," *Washington Post,* April 23, 1998.

49. Unsigned editorial, "Federal Funds for Clean Needles," *New York Times,* February 22, 1997.

50. Fox News Online, "GOP Rips Clinton on AIDS Needle Exchange," April 22, 1998.

51. Amy Goldstein, "Clinton Supports Needle Exchanges But Not Funding," *Washington Post,* April 21, 1998.

52. Unsigned editorial, "Cowardice on Clean Needles," *New York Times,* April 22, 1998.

53. Sheryl Gay Stolberg, "President Decides Against Needle Programs," *New York Times,* April 21, 1998.

54. David Kocieniewski, "New Jersey's Hard Line on Needle Exchanges," *New York Times,* February 2, 1999.

55. Unsigned editorial, "Elation, and Deflation, over AIDS," *New York Times,* July 13, 1996.

56. Lawrence K. Altman, "Deaths from AIDS Decline Sharply in New York City," *New York Times,* January 25, 1997.

57. Richard Lacayo, "Hope with an Asterisk," *Time* 148/149 (30 December 1996–6 January 1997).

58. Larry Kramer, "A Good News/Bad News AIDS Joke," *New York Times Magazine,* July 14, 1996, p. 26.

59. S. Deeks et al., "HIV-1 Protease Inhibitors: A Review for Clinicians," *Journal of the American Medical Association* 277 (1997): 145–53.

60. C. D. Holtzer and S. G. Deeks, "Impact of HIV-1 Protease Inhibitors on the Cost of Treating HIV/AIDS Patients," *Drug Benefit Trends* 10, no. 1 (1998): 27–31.

61. David R. Haburchak, "The Economics of AIDS in America," *The AIDS Reader* 7, no. 5 (1997): 155–60.

62. "Medicaid Managed Care for People with HIV/AIDS," *Drug Benefit Trends* 9, no. 7 (1997): 12.

63. "Study Underscores Need for Increased ADAP Funding," *AIDS Policy Law* 12, no. 14 (August 8, 1997): 6–9.

64. S. C. Johnson, A. Hageman, H. Wing, M. Grodesky, P. Romfh, and W. Williams, *Int Conf AIDS* 12 (1998, abstract no. 42211): 815.

65. "ADAP Funding Seen as Insufficient; Increases Sought," *AIDS Policy Law* 12, no. 8 (May 2, 1997): 6.

66. Lawrence K. Altman, "With AIDS Advance, More Disappointment," *New York Times,* January 19, 1997.

67. Associated Press, "Setbacks for Many on Drugs for AIDS," *New York Times,* September 30, 1997.

68. Mark Sullivan, "Study Finds Many Miss Doses of HIV Medicine," *Washington Blade,* December 19, 1997.

69. Reuters news wire, "U.S. HIV Patients Admit They Don't Take Drugs—Survey Results," May 5, 1998.

70. Deborah Sontag and Lynda Richardson, "Doctors Withhold HIV Pill Regimen from Some," *New York Times,* March 2, 1997.

71. P. S. Bozek, P. J. Weidle, B. E. Perdue, and R. E. Everson, "The Use of Anti-retroviral Therapy in Association with Evolving Standards of Practice," abstract no. 257, Fourth Conference on Retro Viruses and Opportunistic Infections, January 22–26, 1997.

72. Michele Crespo-Fierro, "Compliance/Adherence and Care Management in HIV Disease," *Journal of the Association of Nurses in AIDS Care* 8, no. 4 (July/August 1997): 43–54.

73. Bill Valenti, "Which Came First . . . Adherence or Effective Medical Therapy?" Medscape online coverage from the Twelfth World AIDS Conference, June 29—July 2, 1998.

8. PROSPECTS FOR IMPROVEMENT

1. Martha Derthick, *Agency Under Stress* (Washington, D.C.: The Brookings Institution, 1990), p. 216.

2. Ibid.

3. Charles Lindbloom, "The Science of Muddling Through," *Public Administration Review* (September 1959): 79–88.

4. Martin Levin and Mary Bryna Sanger, *Making Government Work* (San Francisco: Jossey-Bass), 1994.

5. Richard Neustadt and Ernest May, *Thinking in Time: The Uses of History for Decision Makers* (New York: Free Press, 1986), pp. 52–56.

6. Ibid., p. 250; emphasis added.

7. Peter Schwartz, *The Art of the Long View* (New York: Doubleday, 1990), pp. 6, 7. While Schwartz's notion of scenario is more future-oriented than ours he is suggesting a very similar approach. Used initially as a method for military planning in World War II, scenario building was since the 1960s a favorite approach of futurist Herbert Kahn as a tool for business prognostication.

8. Andrew Campbell and Marcus Alexander, "What's Wrong with Strategy?" *Harvard Business Review* (November/December 1997): 42–49.

9. Center for Applied Research, "Stakeholder Mapping," internal working paper, Philadelphia, 1993. The approach is principally the work of James R. Emshoff and Edward R. Freeman but relies significantly on the work of I. I. Mitroff, R. L. Ackoff, Chris Argyris, D. Schon, H. Minzberg, and others. The authors would like to thank Professor Ellen Schall for originally suggesting this literature.

10. I. I. Mitroff and R. O. Mason, "A Logic for Strategic Problem Solving: A Program of Research on Policy and Planning" (unpublished).

11. The approach recognizes that the impact can be on personal values (security, power, survival, status, achievement) and organizational values (efficiency and effectiveness), but that personal values will usually dominate in influencing stakeholders' attitudes. See Center for Applied Research, "Stakeholder Mapping," p. 4.

12. Schwartz, *The Art of the Long View*, pp. 106–23.

13. Lawrence K. Altman, "FDA Authorizes First Full Testing for HIV Vaccine," *New York Times*, June 4, 1998.

14. Two recent surveys have documented the degree to which the American public holds unfavorable views toward homosexuals even at a time when tolerance for other

group differences appears to be growing. See Alan Wolfe, *One Nation, After All* (New York: Viking, 1998), and Carey Goldberg, "Acceptance of Gay Men and Lesbians Is Growing, Study Says," *New York Times,* May 31, 1998.

15. Schwartz, *The Art of the Long View,* p. 200.

16. Ibid., p. 201.

17. Robert Jervis, *System Effects: Complexities in Political and Social Life* (Princeton, N.J.: Princeton University Press), p. 262.

18. Albert Hirschman, *A Bias for Hope: Essays on Development in Latin America* (New Haven: Yale University Press, 1971). See also discussion of the Lijphart effect in Jervis, *System Effects,* p. 263.

19. Lawrence K. Altman, " 'Bird Flu' Reveals Gaps in Plans for Possible Global Outbreaks," *New York Times,* January 6, 1998.

20. Strategies to manage disaster have many of the same challenges characterized by uncertainty, interaction, complexity, and time. Risk assessment and error correction are as central to disaster management as they are to managing public health initiatives. See Louise K. Comfort, "Designing a Policy for Action: The Emergency Management System," in *Managing Disaster: Strategies and Policy Perspectives,* ed. L. Comfort (Durham, N.C.: Duke University Press, 1987), pp. 1–21.

21. Paul Light, *The True Size of Government* (Washington, D.C.: Brookings Institution, 1999), has demonstrated that while the number of public servants in government may be decreasing, they have been more than replaced by private and nonprofit sector employees whose principal functions are as contractors providing goods and services for government.

22. A recent example is the United Nations AIDS program's negotiations with Glaxo Wellcome for a substantial cost reduction in the AIDS drug AZT for distribution to thirty thousand pregnant women in eleven African countries. The negotiated price represents 2.5 percent of the normal cost for a course of treatment. See Lawrence K. Altman, "UN Plans to Treat 30,000 HIV-Infected Pregnant Women," *New York Times,* June 30, 1998.

23. Fear of court-ordered settlements has recently induced four pharmaceutical companies to settle with thousands of hemophiliacs who contend they were infected with the AIDS virus from blood-clotting products.. The companies offered $620 million to 6,200 hemophiliacs even though they claimed they had no way of knowing at the time how AIDS was transmitted. Settlement was offered in order to avoid even more costly court judgments had they been found at fault. This kind of risk affects investment strategies.

24. The National Childhood Vaccine Injury Compensation program was established by an act of Congress (P.L. 99-660) in 1986 to provide a no-fault system to compensate the victims of unavoidable adverse affects of vaccination; see Chapter 4; note 12.

25. In addition, other recently developed vaccines approved by the FDA for field tests or sales include those for AIDS, TB, and Lyme disease.

26. Significant additional costs to defend a liability claim are the legal bills, which accumulate since even a successful defense may take years before a claim is adjudicated. Cases against the Cutter Corporation following the polio immunization program took nearly a decade to settle.

27. These triggers have precedents. Laws designed to respond to economic downturns have provided for federal increases in the length of unemployment insurance benefits and funds to the states, which often have been triggered by increases in unemployment

rates based on certain formulas. Similar formulas related to disease incidence, epidemic levels, or severity might represent an analagous model.

28. Without the established authority or development of appropriate regulatory apparatus in the Eisenhower years, local health departments were left on their own to manage the increasing outcry about controlling distribution. With nothing but a voluntary priority system, the New York City health commissioner tried to embarrass physicians who had violated the priority system. Indeed, the New York City Board of Health was so indignant about the violations that it amended the health code, requiring every medical prescription for vaccine to require the indication of the patient's age. See Richard Carter, *Breakthrough: The Saga of Jonas Salk* (New York: Trident Press, 1966), p. 305.

29. See U.S. General Accounting Office, "Vaccines for Children: Reexamination of Program Goals and Implementation Needed to Ensure Vaccination," June 1995.

30. Stephen Klaidman, *Health in the Headlines: The Stories Behind the Stories* (New York: Oxford University Press, 1991).

31. Dorothy Nelkin, *Selling Science: How the Press Covers Science and Technology* (New York: W. H. Freeman, 1987), p. 111.

32. Ibid., pp. 126–28.

33. Schwartz, *The Art of the Long View.*

34. Helen Mathews Smith, "The Deadly Politics of AIDS," *Wall Street Journal,* October 25, 1995. The National Commission on AIDS endorsed needle exchange programs as early as 1991. See also David Kirp, "Needle Exchange Comes of Age," *Nation* 256. no. 16 (April 16, 1993): 559–60, and Benedict Carey et al., "Needle Swaps Not Boosting Drug Use," *Health* 8, no. 1 (January 1994): pp. 25–26. A more recent finding from a government panel of scientists confirmed that providing clean needles to IV drug users did not increase drug use but could save lives. See Christopher Wren, "$1 Million Pledged for Needle Exchanges," *New York Times,* April 14, 1998.

35. Recent surveys document the low level of trust that citizens place in elected officials. Government workers fare better, but evidence suggests that there are significant variations in the confidence that citizens have in particular federal agencies and that these views reflect their experience with actual agency performance. See Andrew Kohut, *Deconstructing Distrust: How Americans View Government* (Washington, D.C.: Pew Research Center for People and the Press, 1998).

36. While the robust economy explains a quite recent upswing in confidence in government, the aggregate figure of 37 percent remains low, and recent presidential scandals recorded a 5 percent decline as recently as February 1998. See Kohut, *Deconstructing Distrust.*

37. See National Commission on Civic Renewal, final report, 1997, especially working papers, Scholars' Group on Civil Society.

38. Morian Bunos, "President to Push for Food Safety," *New York Times,* July 4, 1998. Also see Kohut, *Deconstructing Distrust.*

39. Lizette Alvarez, "Eye on Policy, GOP Unveils a Patient's Bill," *New York Times,* July 16, 1998.

40. Frank Ryan, *Virus X* (New York: Little, Brown, 1997).

41. Sheryl Gay Stolberg, "Superbugs: The Bacteria Antibiotics Can't Kill," *New York Times Magazine,* August 2, 1998.

42. Lawrence K. Altman, "AIDS Meeting Ends with Little Hope of Breakthrough," *New York Times,* July 5, 1998.

43. Sheryl Gay Stolberg, "Clinton Decides Not to Finance Needle Program," *New York Times,* April 21, 1998, and "Cowardice on Clean Needles," *New York Times,* April 22, 1998. Susan F. Hinley, Damien J. Jolley, and John M. Kaldor, "Effectiveness of Needle-Exchange Programmes for Prevention of HIV Infection," *Lancet* 349, 9068 (1997): 1797–1800, report that in twenty-nine cities worldwide, HIV infection dropped by almost 58 percent a year through needle exchange programs (NEPs) compared to fifty-two cities without them where annual infection rates increased by almost 59 percent. The average annual change in seroprevalence was 11 percent in cities with NEPs. The surgeon general, Dr. David Satcher, says that 40 percent of all new HIV infections are caused directly or indirectly by contaminated needles; also see note 34 above.

44. Sheryl Gay Stolberg, "AIDS Drugs Elude the Grasp of Many of the Poor," *New York Times,* October 14, 1997.

45. Robert Pear, "Expense Means Many Can't Get Drugs for AIDS," *New York Times,* February 16, 1997.

46. Altman, " 'Bird Flu' Reveals Gaps."

47. Levin and Sanger, *Making Government Work.*

Index

Accardi, Sal, 123
Access, 78, 102, 188
　improving, 82
　problems with, 47, 80–82, 83, 168
Accountability, 8, 91, 93, 184, 198
　democratic, 94
　drug company, 102
　promoting, 192
　regulation and, 189–90
ACIP. *See* Advisory Committee on Immuniza-
　tion Practices
Ackoff, R. L., 234n9
ACLU (American Civil Liberties Union), 150,
　161
ACTG (AIDS Clinical Treatment Group), 132
Acts of 1799, 1878, and 1893, 219n10
ACT UP. *See* AIDS Coalition to Unleash Power
ADAPs (AIDS drug assistance programs), 137
Advisory Committee on Immunization Prac-
　tices (ACIP)
　mass immunization and, 53
　swine flu virus and, 52
　Victoria A vaccine and, 217n76
Aerosol pentamidine, 129, 130, 131
AFDC, 82
AIDS
　deaths from, xv, xvi, 136, 140
　eradication of, 117
　etiology of, 4, 119, 120, 139
　fear of, 123
　human/economic costs of, 4
　management challenges for, 3–6
　myths about, x
　politics of, xi, 135, 139
　social construction of, 3, 5, 11, 29, 120, 121,
　139

social response to, 120, 150
spread of, 104–5, 120, 124, 235n23
TB and, 95, 105, 113
treatments for, xi, 3
AIDS Action Committee, 167
AIDS activists
　AZT and, 130
　interests of, 133
　NAVIP and, 155
　pressure from, vii, viii
　treatment programs for, 170
　vaccine and, 144, 145, 152, 161, 167
AIDS Advisory Commission (NIH), AIDS vac-
　cine and, 146
AIDS Clinical Treatment Group (ACTG), 132
AIDS Coalition to Unleash Power (ACT UP)
　Burroughs Wellcome and, 129
　demonstration by, 129
　FDA and, 130
　New York, Treatment and Data Committee
　of, 132
AIDS crisis, 41, 123, 177, 193
　black community and, 156, 157
　challenge of, xiii, 97, 174, 201
　early years of, 122
　management of, 6, 26, 121, 126, 127, 139,
　140, 202
　media and, 207n33
　public health and, 5–6, 103
　responding to, 10, 17, 23, 24, 51, 119
AIDS drug assistance programs (ADAPs), 137
AIDS Physicians and Economists for Smart
　Policy, 150
AIDS-Related Complex, AZT and, 128
AIDS Research Advisory Committee (NIAID),
　143

AIDS Research at the NIH: A Critical Review,
   132
AIDS Research Program Evaluation Working
   Group (Levine Committee), 132
AIDS Treatment Data Network, 137
AIDS vaccine, 3, 97, 100, 118, 201
   confusion about, 174
   delays for, 4
   development of, vii–viii, xviii, 9, 28, 46, 99,
      122, 131, 140, 184, 186, 187, 194
   discovery of, xv, 177, 187
   effectiveness of, viii, xi, 144, 175
   evaluation of, ix, xiii, 146
   funding for, 150
   implementation of, viii, x, xiii–xiv, 22, 28,
      47
   interagency coordination and, 57
   management of, 172
   opposition to, 148, 165, 202
   planning for, 115, 143–44
   rationing, 18, 164, 165
   researching, 11, 187, 206n17
   safety of, 144, 149, 151, 152–53, 165, 175
   scenarios about, 27–28, 183
   side effects of, 151, 173–74
   supply problems and, 37
   support for, 142, 145–46, 161
   tainted, 169, 171
   testing, 149, 151, 155, 182
AIDS Vaccine Commission (AVC), 143
   AIDS vaccine and, 144, 146, 147, 148
   Biosci and, 144, 148
   problems at, 148–49
Alexander, Russell, 213n11
Allegheny County Health Department, flu shots
   and, 55
Allocation
   criteria for, 196–97
   TB drug, 101
   See also Rationing
AL-721, 129
Altman, Lawrence K., on protease inhibitors,
   137
AMA. *See* American Medical Association
American Academy of Pediatrics, 78, 220n14
American Civil Liberties Union (ACLU), vac-
   cination and, 150, 161
American Drug Manufacturing Association,
   vaccination and, 39
American Insurance Association
   AIDS vaccine and, 153
   Cooper and, 60
American Medical Association (AMA)
   AIDS vaccine and, 147
   indemnification and, 157
   NAVIP and, 155
   needle exchange and, 134

   prevention/treatment and, 212n1
   Sabin at, 33
American Public Health Association, preven-
   tion/treatment and, 212n1
Americans for Democratic Action, 150
Annual United States Immunization Survey, 75
Antibiotics, 1, 2, 98–99
Anticipation, 25, 182
Antigenic shifts, 69, 70, 71
Antimyces, 99
Antiviral Drug Division (FDA), 131
Argyris, Chris, 234n9
Asian flu epidemic (1957), vaccine for, 70
At-risk groups, ix
   politicization of, 5
   vaccination for, 159, 165, 168, 198
   worthiness of, 199
AVC. *See* AIDS Vaccine Commission
AZT (azidothymidine), 131, 235n22
   access to, 188
   AIDS-Related Complex and, 128
   approval of, 127, 129
   clinical trials for, 128
   delivering, 122
   development of, 127
   FDA and, 129, 130
   problems with, 139
   public-private partnership for, 187, 188

Bacterial meningitis, 79
Bathhouses
   closing, viii, 12, 122–26
   sex at, 122, 123–24, 125
Bay Area Reporter, on bathhouses, 123
Bayer, TB drugs and, 101
Behavioral factors, 82–84
Behn, Robert, 116, 117, 230n84
Bellin, Lowell E., 216n56
Benison, Saul, Salk vaccine and, 211n53
Biosci Company, 174
   AIDS vaccine by, 141, 142, 147, 158–59,
      160, 161, 162, 164
   AVC and, 144, 148
   criticism of, 156, 165
   EU and, 162–63
   FDA and, 143, 157
   indemnification for, 151–52
   lawsuit against, 153
   lobbying by, 145
   media and, 154, 155, 156, 169
   NAVIP and, 156
   Phase II trials for, 152
   production by, 166
   safety questions and, 154
   testing and, 151
   Vacit and, 171
Bird flu, xiv, 122

Birthday Balls, 31
Black community, AIDS crisis and, 156, 157, 159, 165
Block grants, 77, 103
BoB. *See* Bureau of Biologics
Brandt, Edward, on AIDS, 4
Breakthrough: The Saga of Jonas Salk (Carter), quote from, 33–34
British Medical Council, PAS and, 99
Britt, Harry, AIDS researchers and, 123
Broder, Samuel
    AIDS drug research and, 127, 188
    AZT and, 188
Budget crisis, 91
    reinventing government and, 90
Budget Reconciliation Act (1993), 85
Bureau of Biologics (BoB), 59
    interagency coordination and, 56
    swine flu and, 54
Bureau of Tuberculosis Control (NYC), 106, 195
    budget of, 112
    MDR-TB and, 109
Burroughs Wellcome
    ACT UP and, 129
    AIDS research and, 127
    AZT and, 127, 128–29, 188
Bush, George, 128, 131

Califano, Joseph, 55, 212n2
Callen, Michael, 129
    on CRI, 130
Camp, Dave, H.R. 2432 and, 222n37
Campbell, Jack, 125
Carter, Richard
    on cost, 45
    on Public Health Service, 211n40
    on Sabin/Salk, 33–34
Categorical grants, 77
CBC (Congressional Black Caucus), 165
CBS Evening News
    on AVC, 147
    on public confidence, 171
CBS/*New York Times* poll
    on NAVIP, 163
    on vaccine, 153–54
CCC (County-Community Consortium), 130, 131
CCG (Community Constituency Group), 132
CDC. *See* Centers for Disease Control
CDF. *See* Children's Defense Fund
CDUs (communicable disease isolation units), 111, 113
Center for AIDS Prevention Studies, needle exchange and, 134
Centers for Disease Control (CDC), viii, 6, 8, 58, 78, 85, 88, 173, 191, 202
    AIDS cases and, xvii–xviii, 133, 158
    AIDS vaccine and, 43, 143, 147, 165, 166
    assistance from, 12
    contingency plans and, 62
    Cutter vaccine and, 38
    DOT approach and, 105
    education and, 14
    free vaccines and, 80
    grants from, 105, 112, 219n11
    HIV and, 169
    immunization and, 66, 75, 94, 216n55, 219n11, 223n63
    implementation and, 61
    interagency coordination and, 56
    liability protection and, 60–61
    National Immunization Program, 220n17
    NAVIP and, 164
    needle exchange and, 133, 134
    and NIH compared, 11
    PERT and, 54–55
    practical/applied orientation and, 9
    publicity campaign by, 61–62
    study by, xv, xvii
    supply problems and, 55
    support/technical assistance from, 192
    surveillance centers by, 214n20
    swine flu vaccination and, 52, 59, 64, 71
    tainted vaccine and, 169, 171
    TB and, 103, 198
    vaccine deaths and, 216n57
    VFC and, 93
Chase, Gordon, xii
    planning strategy and, 115–16
    on program implementation, 115
    on public managers/media, 207n30
    on risk prediction, 49
    on service delivery programs, 96
    TB control initiative and, 114
Chiasson, Mary Ann, on AIDS deaths, 136
Chicken flu, 183, 202
Chicken pox, 121, 186
Childhood diseases, xi, 139, 230n79
    immunization against, 6, 12, 25, 192
    incidence of, 77
    lessons from, xi
Childhood Immunization Incentive Act, The (H.R. 1840), 222n37
Childhood immunization programs, 3, 17, 18, 49, 97, 140, 184, 194
    Clinton and, 73
    crisis in, 87
    funds for, 85
    history of, 76–78
    legislative debate over, 84–86
    screening for, 180
    seizing, 75–76
    success of, 186

Children's Defense Fund (CDF)
on poverty/health care, 78
social welfare and, 87
Christian Coalition, AIDS crisis and, 181
Clean needle programs. *See* Needle exchange
programs
Clinical trials, 68, 144
Clinton, Bill
AIDS issue and, 206nn13,17
CDF and, 87
childhood immunization and, 25, 84, 86
health care reform and, 86, 87
immunization rates and, 75
needle exchange and, 134, 135
vaccination program and, 80
VFC and, 73, 181, 192
Clinton, Hillary, 75
CNN/*USA Today* poll, on AIDS vaccine, 154
Combination treatment therapies
cost of, 137
maintaining, xv–xvi
Communicable disease isolation units (CDUs),
111, 113
Community Constituency Group (CCG), Fauci
and, 132
Community Research Initiative (CRI)
aerosol pentamidine and, 130
Presidential Commission on the HIV Epidemic and, 131
Competition, 48
interagency, 14, 132
intergovernmental, 30, 56, 132, 140, 145
professional, 30
scientific, 99–100
Complacency
managing, xv
risks of, xvi–xvii, 104–6, 118
Compliance, xiv, xvi, 13, 83
ensuring, 82
Compound S. *See* AZT
Comprehensive Child Immunization Act
(1993), 76
Concord Coalition, inoculation and, 147
Condoms, 3, 12, 202
Confidence, 30, 208n42
Congressional Black Caucus (CBC), AIDS vaccine and, 165
Congressional Budget Office, on liability pay-
ments/litigation costs, 59
Consequences
dangers of, 93–94
envisioning, 182–83
Contingency planning, 21, 27, 51, 55, 66, 191,
203
lack of, 62
problems with, 25, 72
Controversy, 10, 14, 48, 195

effectiveness, x, 15, 22
See also Scientific controversy
Cooper, Ellen, 131
Cooper, Theodore, 52, 60, 61, 65, 214n25
swine flu and, 53
Cooperation, 4, 11, 13, 14, 21, 116, 185
building, 122, 140, 184
challenge of, 58, 104, 107–8
ensuring, 193–94
global, 206n22
importance of, 96
interagency, 118
intergovernmental, 192–94, 206n22
limited, 13
politics of, 121
public-private, 186, 187
state-local, 198
Coordination, 13, 14, 206n13
challenge of, 104, 107–8
developing, 4
ensuring, 193–94
federal government and, 210n28
interagency, 56–57, 118
policy, 88
state-local, 198
Costs, 48
access and, 78
immunization and, 25, 78, 79, 88
public-private, 126
research, 120
role of, 78–80
total, 46, 47
treatment, 120
vaccine, 80, 85, 86, 87, 94, 190
See also Prices
County-Community Consortium (CCC), 130, 131
Cravens, Gwyneth, 217n69
CRI. *See* Community Research Initiative
Curran, Jim, 123
Current Affair, A, 168, 170
Cutter incident, 47, 189
federal leadership and, 40
media and, 43
NFIP and, 40, 42–43
Cutter Laboratories, 43, 44, 189
cases against, 235n26
polio immunization and, 16, 216n53
protocols by, 38
supply shortages and, 37–38

DdI, 131
Delays, xii, 38, 57, 205n3
criticism of, 152, 161
implementation, 93
liability, 66
management conflicts and, x
problems with, 186

production, 58, 65
swine flu vaccine, 59–60, 64
Delivery, 184
challenges in, 74, 82, 89
local/private sector, 80
problems with, 57, 83, 168–69
scenario involving, 173
silver bullets and, 2–3
social conditions and, 192
Delivery agents
mobilization problems with, 58
participation/cooperation of, 184
Department of Corrections (NY), MDR-TB
and, 107
Department of Health (DOH)
education by, 117
MDR-TB and, 107–8, 109, 191
planning by, 110, 112–13
priorities by, 116
TB control and, 106, 108, 114, 115
Department of Health, Education, and Welfare
(HEW), 39
budget cuts for, 230n88
interagency coordination and, 56
media and, 63
National Commission and, 61
production/distribution and, 60
scientific opposition and, 69
support/cooperation and, 58
swine flu program and, 54, 68–69, 70
TB testing and, 229n71
Department of Personnel (NYC), 111
Derthick, Martha, on administrative success, 86
Destiny of Me, The, 132
Development
disincentives for, xiii
investment in, 185
phases of, 131
public-private partnerships for, 188, 201
success with, 20, 22
Dextran Sulfate, 129
Dickey, Nancy, needle exchange and, 134
Dinkins, David, TB outbreak and, 106–7
Diptheria, immunization against, 67, 220n14
Directly observed therapy (DOT), xviii, 2, 3,
103, 112, 114, 115
CDC and, 105
efficacy of, 113
Discovery, xiii, 2–3
cure and, 1
Disease control
management and, 3
scientific discovery and, 205n2
Distribution, xiv, 85
controlling, 8, 39, 60, 236
difficulties with, 44–45
large-scale, 177

planning, 38
policies for, 18, 19
problems with, 30, 36, 37, 45, 48, 93
Distributional equity, 17–19, 65–66, 178
dealing with, 196–98
financing and, 18–19
management dimensions of, 197
questions of, 120
DOH. See Department of Health
DOT. See Directly observed therapy
DPT, 75, 79, 220n14
Drug cocktails, 136, 140
Drug companies, 89, 229n13
AIDS vaccine and, 187
court-ordered settlements and, 235n23
FDA and, 128
indemnification for, viii, xiv–xv, 22, 37,
160–61
insurance companies and, 153
investment by, 184
liability for, 7, 225n22
licensing, 77
media and, 169
profit/accountability of, 102
R and D costs for, 79
social benefits and, 7
supply problems and, 55
TB drugs and, 101–2
Drug-resistant strains, 1, 2, 111
Drug users
clean needles for, 199
HIV and, 135
needle sharing by, 133
social sympathy for, 182
Dull, Bruce, 60, 63

Early Periodic Screening and Diagnostic Testing Programs, 222n32
Ebola virus, 1
"Economics of AIDS in America, The" (Haburchak), 137
Edelman, Marian Wright, 87
Education, xvii, 48, 62, 178, 225n13
AIDS, xi, 14, 123
focusing on, 198
funding for, 167
HIV, xviii
importance of, 81, 170, 171, 198
information and, 15–16
marginalized groups and, 64–65
media and, 14, 43, 69, 72, 115
parental, 83, 85
public, 16, 17, 191, 202
public relations and, 194
sex, 3, 12, 162, 202
Spanish-language, 166
TB, 117

Effectiveness, vii, xvi, 16, 57, 126
　assessing, 28, 30, 69
　controversy over, 15, 22
　decline in, 78
　importance of, 6, 195, 200
　scenario considering, 182
　storage/packaging/shipping, 93
Eisenhower, Dwight D.
　distribution problems and, 44–45
　HEW and, 39
　Hobby and, 40, 41
　leadership/managerial failure by, 41
Eleventh International Conference on AIDS,
　　drug cocktails and, 136
Eliot, Martha M., 39–40
Emshoff, James R., 234n9
Enders, John, 33
Epidemics, responding to, 119, 121

Family First, 150
Fauci, Anthony
　on clinical trials, 131
　drug approval process and, 121
　innovations by, 132
　interagency competition and, 132
FDA. See Food and Drug Administration
Federal Emergency Management Agency, plan-
　　ning by, 22, 55
Federal government
　coordination/research/funding and, 210n28,
　　226n32
　trust in, 19, 208nn40,42
Federalism, 11–12, 13, 36, 192–94
　fiscal, 19
　lack of, 50
　limitations of, 51
　problems with, 89
Feinstein, Dianne, 124
Ferels, Jim, 124
Ferrosan, 102
Field trials, 34, 35, 38, 44, 55, 212n83
　polio vaccine, 36–37
Financing, 91, 157–58, 178
　distributional equity and, 18–19
　questions of, 120
　shaping arrangements for, 198–99
Fineburg, Harvey, 64, 212n2
　on acceptance rates, 65
Fire alarms, 14, 15
Fluconazole, 129
Folsom, M. B., 36
Food and Drug Administration (FDA), 6, 9
　aerosol pentamidine and, 130, 131
　AIDS vaccine and, 141–42, 143, 145, 146
　approval by, vii, viii, 121, 130, 182, 187
　AZT and, 127, 129, 130
　Biosci and, 143, 157, 163

breast implants and, 16
　drug companies and, 128
　drug development and, 27, 126–33
　IND and, 128
　on NIH/scientific research, 145
　public confidence in, 200
　regulation by, 126, 129
　swine flu and, 54
Food, Drug, and Cosmetic Act (1938), 126
Ford, Gerald R.
　management problems and, 56, 63
　swine flu program and, 10, 52, 53, 55, 60,
　　63, 65, 67, 69, 190–91
Foreman, Christopher, 206n13
Forgotten Plague, The (Ryan), 97
Fort Dix strain, 50, 51, 62, 69, 217n64
　vaccine for, 218n90
　WHO and, 218n90
Francis, Thomas, Jr., 35
　coordination by, 36
　killed virus and, 33
　Salk vaccine and, 211n53
Francis Report, 42
Frank, Barney, 156
Freeman, Edward R., 234n9
Frieden, Thomas, 110, 228n57, 230n81
　MDR-TB and, 109
Fund for the City of New York, coordination
　　by, 109–10
Future, anticipating, 178–83

Gallup Polls, 83, 171, 208n40
GAO. See General Accounting Office
Gay community
　bathhouses and, 124, 125
　promiscuity in, 123, 125
　sexual freedom and, 123–24
　treatment/prevention and, viii
　unfavorable views of, 182, 234n14
Gay Men's Health Crisis (GMHC), 138, 161
General Accounting Office (GAO)
　accountability and, 93
　letter from, 75–76
　needle exchange and, 134
　VFC and, 15, 92
General Services Administration (GSA), 15, 79,
　　88
　distribution and, 92, 93
　VFC and, 92
Giuliani, Rudolph, 91
Glaxo Wellcome, UN AIDS program and,
　　235n22
GMHC. See Gay Men's Health Crisis
Goldfield, Martin, 63, 213n11
Goldwater, Barry, 39
Gore, Al, National Performance Review and,
　　90

Gp120 vaccine, viii, xiv
GSA. *See* General Services Administration
Gudakunst, Don, 33
Guillain-Barré syndrome, 55, 69, 214n22

Haburchak, David R., 137
Hamburg, Margaret, 193, 227n47, 228n53
  McCormick and, 109–10
  TB control and, 91, 104, 107, 108, 109, 110,
    112, 114, 115, 116, 117, 191, 229n77,
    230n81
Hanta virus, 1
Harvard AIDS Institute, study by, 173
Health and Hospital Corporation (HHC), TB
  control and, 107, 108, 115
Health care reform, 86
  CVF and, 87
Health Resources and Services Administration
  (HRSA), 65
Hemophilus influenza type B, immunization
  against, 220n14
Hepatitis B, 79, 186
  vaccine for, viii, 3, 220n14
Heroin addiction, treatment for, xi–xii
HEW. *See* Department of Health, Education,
  and Welfare
HHC. *See* Health and Hospital Corporation
HHS, 168, 173
  VFC and, 79
  warehousing/distribution and, 92
Hib, 83, 220n14, 221n27
High-risk groups. *See* At-risk groups
Hinshaw, H. Corwin, 225n20
  allocation decisions by, 18
  TB drugs and, 101
Hirschman, Albert, 182–83
History of Poliomyelitis (Paul), 32
Hitt, R. Scott, 135, 136
HIV
  drop in, xv, xvi, 172, 202, 237n43
  drug-resistant, xvi, xviii, 99, 100, 138–39,
    147, 169
  drug users and, 134, 135, 237n43
  eradication of, xvii, 117
  etiology of, 119
  increase in, 104–5
  nature of, x
  needle sharing and, 133
  in NYC, 106
  research on, 158
  TB and, 95, 103, 105, 112, 113, 224nn1,9,
    226n30
  treatment for, xv, 127, 138–39
HIV vaccine, 34, 97
  developing, 99, 127
Hobby, Oveta Culp, 211n46
  criticism of, 40, 47

Eisenhower and, 41
  vaccine distribution and, 44–45
  vaccination program and, 39, 45
Hoffman La Roche, TB drugs and, 101
Hong Kong flu epidemic (1968–1969), vaccine
  for, 70
Hothouse, 123
House Committee on Energy and Commerce,
  letter to, 75–76
House Committee on Government Operations,
  130
"How to Have Sex in an Epidemic" (brochure),
  125
HRSA (Health Resources and Services Admin-
  istration), 65
Human Resources Administration (HRA), 108
  TB control and, 107, 115, 228n56
Hunter, James Davison, 208n40

Immunization, 221n27
  funding, 219n11, 219n12
  large-scale, 27, 31, 35, 46, 47, 53, 57, 177,
    185, 214n21
  local, 82
  misinformation about, 81
  protocols for, 81–82
  public, 54, 214n21
  regular, 81
  as right, 84, 86
  stockpiling for, 70
  universal, 140
Immunization Committee, divisions within,
  33
Immunization programs, vii, 57, 212n83,
  217n76
  blueprint for, xi
  circumstances for, 34–35
  implementation of, 53
  initiation of, 20–21
  management of, 76
  planning/designing, 13
  restrictions on, 215n33
  universal, xv, 5, 20, 77, 218n82
  unnecessary, 217n69
Immunization rates, 18, 30, 47, 58, 94, 169–70
  childhood, 75, 76, 77, 78, 192
  costs and, 78, 79
  decline in, 80, 87
  as health crisis, 92
  improving, 65, 77–78, 84, 93, 223n63
  poverty and, 79
  studying, 80, 82, 83, 198
  supply shortages and, 172
Immunization schedules, 82, 83
  monitoring, 81
Immunology, 100, 120
Imperato, Pascal, 65

Implementation, xi, 17, 27, 47, 74, 189
   CDC and, 61
   challenges of, xii, 29, 88, 198
   considering, vii, xv
   delays in, xii, xiii–xiv, 19, 92–94
   insurance companies and, 61
   literature on, 21
   management and, xi, 39–41, 73
   media and, 196
   problems with, 22, 24–25, 30, 39–41, 51, 55,
      58, 179
   realistic, 178
   scenarios for, 22
   steps to, xiii, 203
   strategies for, 47, 193–94
   successful, 177
IND. *See* Investigational new drug
Indemnification, viii, xiv–xv, 51, 186–87
   calls for, 186
   debating, 156
   importance of, 22
   passage of, 160–61
   providing, 7
   scenario involving, 151–52, 155, 157
   for swine flu vaccine, 60
Individual rights, public health and, 124
Influenza pandemics, 62, 70, 197
   CDC and, 208n37
   hypothesizing about, 52
   impact of, 51–52, 66
Influenza virus
   information on, 52
   respiratory ailments and, 213n4
Influenza Viruses and Influenza, The (Kil-
      bourne), 52
Information
   asymmetry, 190
   gathering/analyzing, 181
   negative, 64
   public education and, 15–16
   See also Misinformation; Sensationalism
Infrastructure
   lack of, 82
   public health, 30, 104
Injecting drug users. *See* Drug users
In Search of Excellence, 90
Institute for Health Policy Studies, research by,
      226n34
Institutional arrangements, 178
   problems with, 4
Insurance companies
   drug companies and, 153
   implementation and, 61
   indemnification and, 60
Interagency conflict
   managing, 192
   promoting, 11

Intergovernmental relations, 30, 132, 140
   managing, 178
   problems of, 89
   scenario about, 145
Investigational new drug (IND), 127
   FDA and, 128
   NIAID and, 131
Isoniazid, 99, 101

Jackson, Jesse, 157
Jervis, Robert, 182
Johnson, Gerald, 40
Johnson, Roger, 92
Joseph, Steven
   AIDS crisis and, 106
   TB initiative and, 227n41

Kahn, Herbert, 234n7
Kaiser Family Foundation, 137
Keefer, Chester, 39
Kefauver, Estes, 43
Kennedy, Ted, 216n56
Kilbourne, Edwin D.
   on influenza outbreaks, 52
   program implementation and, 58
   on swine flu virus, 213n8
Killed-virus versus live-virus debate, 33
Koch, Robert, 98
Koop, C. Everett, 171
Kramer, Larry, 129, 140
   Destiny and, 132
   on Fauci, 131
   on protease inhibitor, 137
Kruif, Paul de, 42

Lancet, 229n73
   on swine flu program, 62–63
Langmuir, Alexander, 38
Larry King Live, 158, 173
Lasker, Morris E., 228n59
Lawsuits, vii
   protection against, 151–52
   threats of, viii, 186
Leadership, lack of, 41, 50
Legal Aid Society, 107, 228n59
Legionnaire's disease, 63, 70
Lehmann, Jorgen, 99, 102
Levine Committee (AIDS Research
      Program Evaluation Working Group),
      132
Liability, 7–8, 51, 216n51, 220n12
   CDC and, 60–61
   defense against, 22
   federal, 61
   problems with, 25, 186–87
   proliferation of, 37
   protection against, 151–52

swine flu vaccine, 59–60
tort, 60, 216n51
Licensing, 36, 37, 39, 77
Lindsay, John, xii
Littlejohn, Larry, 123
Live-virus versus killed-virus debate, 33
Local actors, engaging interests of, 193–94
Local agencies
  federal agencies and, 12
  federal immunization and, 21
  success rates for, 57
Local government
  culture/politics of, 12
  tort liability and, 216n51
  trust in, 208n42
Longley, James B., 214n21
Lorch, Paul, 123
Lyme disease, 14, 235n25
Lyphomed, 130

Mad cow disease, 1
Magic bullets, 176
  delivery systems and, 2–3
Management, xii–xiii, 5–6, 47, 51, 85, 201
  centrality of, 89
  challenges of, 3–20, 23, 24, 27, 29, 88, 94,
    96, 114–15, 116
  consistency in, 73–74
  constituency for, 90–92, 94
  crisis, 22, 91, 92, 117
  delays and, vii, x
  disease control and, 3, 96, 102, 203
  effective, x, 21
  entrepreneurial approach to, 116
  federal, 13
  future, 177–78
  immunization policy, 76
  implementation and, xi, 73
  importance of, 122, 197, 203
  improving, 26, 28, 82, 90, 94, 97
  media relations and, 64
  methods for, 20–23, 203
  policy and, 73, 74–75, 86–87, 90, 92, 94
  polio vaccine and, 46
  problems with, xiv, 26, 47, 48, 51, 55, 56,
    69, 86, 87–90, 94, 118, 167
  program, 16, 21, 73, 92–94
  public, xi, 5, 13, 23, 139, 212n2
  service delivery and, 74
  strategy for, xv, 20–21, 81
  swine flu program, 71, 72
Mantle, Mickey, 18
March of Dimes, 24, 30, 32, 36
Market mechanisms, 6–8
  dealing with, 183–90
  moral consequences of, 207n35
  private investment and, 184

public health and, 197
Marr, John, 217n69
Marshall, George, Marshall Plan and, 179
Mason, James
  on Fauci, 131
  parallel track and, 131–32
Mathews, David, 52
  American Insurance Association and, 60
  swine flu and, 53
May, Ernest, 179
Mayo Clinic
  allocation decisions by, 18
  TB drugs and, 101
Mayor's Office of Operations (NYC), 110
McCormick, Mary, 109–10
MDR-TB. See Multiple-drug resistant TB
Measles
  deaths from, 219n4
  immunization against, 67, 220n14, 221n27
  outbreak of, 219n4
Media
  adversarial role for, 64
  AIDS vaccine and, 142, 146, 152, 207n33
  Biosci and, 154, 155, 156, 169
  Cutter incident and, 43
  education and, 14, 43, 69, 72, 115
  help from, 16–17
  HEW and, 63
  implementation and, 196
  management of, 43–44, 64, 71, 115, 178,
    194–96
  NFIP and, 34, 42
  NIH and, 171
  problems with, 10, 15, 16, 48, 61–62, 142,
    143–44, 145, 168, 169, 172
  public health and, 41–44
  safety question and, 149
  Salk vaccine and, 41, 42
  sensationalism by, vii, x–xi, 16, 22, 117,
    140, 155, 156, 168, 171
  swine flu program and, 62, 63–64, 67–68,
    194, 196
  TB drugs and, 100–101
Medicaid, 78, 80, 93, 202
  eligibility for, 85
  HIV/AIDS and, 137, 139
  immunization and, 83
  TB and, 103
Merck
  streptomycin and, 102, 225n20
  swine flu vaccine and, 60
Merck Sharp & Dohme, manufacture/distribu-
    tion by, 54
Meriwhether, Delano, 56, 214n27
Merrell National
  manufacture/distribution by, 54
  swine flu vaccine and, 60

Methadone, implementation challenges for, xi–xii
Meyer, Harry, Jr., 54
Millar, Donald, 56, 214n27
Mine Shaft, closing, 125
Minority community
    AIDS vaccine and, 165, 166
    treatment/prevention and, ix
Minzbcrg, H., 234n9
Misinformation, 30, 48, 70
    dangers of, 63–64
    about immunizations, 81
    media, 16
    See also Information
Mismanagement. *See* Management, problems with
Mitroff, I. I., 234n9
MMR, 75, 79, 220n14
Monitoring, xv, 81, 82, 83, 84
    improving, 85
Moral issues, ix, 19, 145
Morgan, James, 146, 147
Morrill, William, 214n25
Morris, J. Anthony, 213n11
    on immunization program, 218n82
Moss, John E., 217n77
Multiple-drug resistant TB (MDR-TB), 105, 116–17, 126, 137, 191
    challenges of, 94
    growth of, 106, 111, 112–13, 229n68
    management and, 114
    outbreak of, 107, 228n59
    policy response to, 97
    scope of, 108–9
    threat from, 95, 102–4
    victims of, 119
Mumps, immunization against, 220n14

NAACP, AIDS vaccine and, 159
Nader, Ralph, 173
National Academy of Sciences
    AIDS vaccine and, 143
    on drug users/HIV, 134
    on FDA/AZT, 127
National AIDS Vaccine Inoculation Program (NAVIP), 152, 175
    AIDS activists and, 155
    AMA and, 155
    authorization for, 145, 158–59
    Biosci and, 156
    costs for, 170
    creation of, 146–47, 167
    criticism of, 148, 150, 153, 154, 159–60, 166, 172, 174
    feasibility of, 157
    public confidence in, 171
    rationing by, 164–65

supply problems and, 166
    support for, 149, 160, 161, 163, 164, 173
    vaccination rates and, 169–70
National Alliance of State and Territorial AIDS Directors, 137
National Cancer Institute (NCI), 128, 188
    AZT and, 127
National Center for Clinical Infant Programs, 221n32
National Childhood Vaccine Injury Act (1986), 220n12
National Childhood Vaccine Injury Compensation, 220n12, 235n24
National Commission for the Protection of Human Subjects of Biomedical and Behavioral Research, 61
National Commission on AIDS, NEPs and, 236n34
National Commission on the State and Local Public Service, 90
National Foundation for Infantile Paralysis (NFIP), 41, 44
    competence/goodwill of, 201
    coordination by, 36
    Cutter incident and, 40, 42–43
    establishment of, 209n6
    field trials and, 35, 36–37
    media and, 33, 34, 42
    patient care and, 24, 30
    polio vaccination and, 30
    propaganda techniques of, 32
    public relations effort by, 24
    public support and, 31, 32–33, 43
    research efforts and, 24, 30, 47
    role of, 31–32
    Salk and, 42
    supply problems and, 36–37
    vaccination by, 37, 44, 45
National Immunization Program (CDC), 220n17
National Institutes of Allergy and Infectious Diseases (NIAID), 9, 59, 132, 143
    AIDS vaccine and, 131, 141, 142, 146
    AZT and, 128
    clinical trials program and, 130
    drug approval process and, 121
    IND and, 131
    interagency coordination and, 56
    swine flu and, 54
National Institutes of Health (NIH), 6, 8, 173, 191
    academic culture of, 9
    AIDS vaccine and, 141, 142, 143, 144, 146
    Biosci and, 163
    and CDC compared, 11
    decreased funding for, 163

media and, 171
partnership with, 187
R and D by, 188
swine flu and, 54
TB and, 103
trials review by, 145
National Organization for Women, vaccination and, 150
National Rainbow Coalition, AIDS vaccine and, 157
National Task Force on AIDS Drug Development, 132
National Tuberculosis Association, 32
NAVIP. *See* National AIDS Vaccine Inoculation Program
NBC Evening News, on safety, 152–53
NBC/*Wall Street Journal* poll, on AIDS vaccination, 166
NCI. *See* National Cancer Institute
Needle exchange programs (NEPs), viii, x, 3, 12, 106, 133–36, 202
funding for, 134, 135, 199
opposition to, 199
support for, 134, 236n34
Neuraminidase, absence of, 218n86
Neustadt, Richard E., 64, 212n2
on acceptance rates, 65
Marshall Plan and, 179
New England Journal of Medicine, 173, 228n60
New Republic, criticism in, 40
New York City
MDR-TB in, 44, 95, 96, 97, 104, 106, 107–8, 111, 113, 117–18, 126, 191, 192
public health needs in, 13
social conditions in, 106–7
stakeholders in, 189
TB in, 114, 195, 198
New York Times
on AZT, 129
on CDC/AIDS vaccine, 171
on Joseph, 106
on needle exchange, 135
on protease inhibitors, 136, 137, 138
on scare propaganda, 67
on Scheele/Cutter incident, 43
on TB control, 230n81
on vaccination, 168
Whitman in, 135
New York Times/CBS poll
on AIDS vaccine, 142
on NAVIP, 174
New York Times Magazine, on protease inhibitors, 137
NFIP. *See* National Foundation for Infantile Paralysis

NIAID. *See* National Institutes of Allergy and Infectious Diseases
Nightline
on AIDS vaccine, 149
on NAVIP, 150, 155
NIH. *See* National Institutes of Health
NIH Revitalization Act (1993), 132
Nixon, Richard M., 217n78
No-fault system, 186, 235n24

O'Connor, Basil
implementation strategy and, 39
NFIP and, 24, 31, 32
polio fight and, 30, 33, 210n32
Salk vaccine and, 34
supply problems and, 36–37
Office of AIDS Research, Levine Committee of, 132
Office of General Counsel, interagency coordination and, 56
Office of Management and Budget (OMB)
interagency coordination and, 56
planning and, 110
TB and, 109, 228n53
Organized constituents, 89
Ostrow, David, 125
Outreach, 46–47, 48, 83
importance of, 81, 84
improving, 47, 85
marginalized groups and, 64–65
Oversight Subcommittee (House Interstate and Foreign Commerce Committee), report by, 217n77

Para-aminosalicylic acid (PAS), 99, 100, 102
Parales, Caesar, 108–9
Parallel track, support for, 131–32
Parental responsibility, 82–84
vaccine costs and, 85, 86
Parent Teacher Organization (PTO), 148, 156
Parke-Davis, 214n19
manufacture/distribution by, 54
swine flu vaccine and, 60
PAS. *See* Para-aminosalicylic acid
Past, lessons from, 178–80
Paul, John, 32
Pentamidine, 130, 131
Perceived interests, changes in, 181
PERT (Program Evaluation Review Technique), 54–55
Pertussis, immunization against, 220n14
Pharma, concerns of, 160–61
Phase I trials, 126
Phase II trials, 126, 141
Phase III trials, 126, 144, 152
waiving, 128
Plague viruses, migration of, 206n22

Planning, 108–11, 117, 179
  appropriate, 205n3
  contingency, 21, 25, 27, 51, 55, 62, 66, 72, 191, 203
  criticism of, 40
Pneumocystis carinii pneumonia, 129, 130, 131
Policy, 8, 178
  changes in, 226n37
  coordination of, 88
  management and, 73, 74–75, 86–87, 90, 94
  public doubts about, 10
Policy-making, 51, 70
  official timidity/short-term politics of, 12
  scientific controversy and, 10
Polio, xiii, 6, 119, 139, 230n79
  eradication of, 45
  impact of, 29, 32
  inoculation rates for, 213n3
  priority system for, 44
  response to, 23
  social construction of, 29, 209n51
Polio immunization, 17, 67, 72, 97, 186, 201, 220n14
  federal mismanagement of, 39–41
  lessons from, xi, 31, 47–48
  management lessons from, 49
  problems with, 235n26
  progress of, 41
  safety/effectiveness of, 20
  success of, 20, 23–24, 50, 88, 196
Poliomyelitis Vaccination Assistance Act (1955), 45, 46, 47, 76–77
Polio Pioneers, 42, 44
Polio Surveillance Unit, 38
Polio vaccine, x, 75, 121, 179
  controversies about, 15
  cost of, 45–46
  research/development of, 33
  tainted, 216n53
Politics, 8, 197
  AIDS and, 139
  managing, 178
  problems with, 4, 41
  public health and, 133
Poverty
  AIDS and, 105–6
  health care and, 78
  immunization rates and, 79
  in NYC, 226n36
  TB and, 106
  vaccine costs and, 87
Presidential Advisory Council on HIV/AIDS, 136
Presidential Commission on the HIV Epidemic, CRI and, 131
Presidential Task Force on Regulatory Relief, 128

Prevention, 4, 18, 26, 46, 172, 202
  AIDS, 12, 191
  support for, 159
  swine flu program and, 52–54
  treatment and, ix, 212n1
Prevention education programs, xvi, 208n38
Prices, 75
  federally capped, 92
  See also Costs
Priority, 196–97
  at-risk groups and, 198
  funding, 103
  violations of, 45
Private sector
  public use of, vii, 8, 22, 120–21, 184–85
  relations with, 178
Production, 189
  large-scale, 177
  managing, 8, 37–38
  problems with, 25, 30, 34–35, 40, 48, 58, 60, 180, 185, 186
  regulating, 35, 39, 77
Program Evaluation Review Technique (PERT), 54–55
Program management, 16, 21
  decision-making and, 73
  flaws in, 92–94
Project Inform, AIDS vaccine and, 161
Promiscuity, 123, 125, 150
Prontosil, 100
Protease inhibitors, xvii, 136–39
  distribution of, 18
  effectiveness of, 139
  financing, 45
  hope of, 15, 140
  implementation/compliance problems of, 139
  side effects from, 136
  success for, 4
  using, xiv, xvi, 137
  withholding, 138
Providers, 89
  AIDS infection from, ix–x
  private/nonprofit, 6
  uncertainty for, 8
PTO (Parent Teacher Organization), 148, 156
Public confidence, decline in, 67, 91, 156, 171
Public consciousness, raising, 195
Public health, 193
  AIDS and, xv, 4
  education and, 202
  externalities of, 17
  federal authority in, 11–12
  individual rights and, 124
  investments in, 177
  management of, 7, 178, 200
  market failure and, 197

media and, 41–44
policy and, 70, 203
politics and, 133
problems with, 26, 51
protecting, 43, 222n47
as public goods problem, 197
response by, 119
successes in, 26, 96
Public health crises, 73, 191, 195
challenges of, 176
childhood immunization and, 76
managing, 2, 5, 6, 19–20, 97
responding to, 21, 23, 121
timeline/constraints for, 17
Public health initiatives, 89, 96, 97
consensus on, 118
designing/implementing, 22, 178
managing, xv, 5, 7–8, 25, 28, 176, 183
obstacles for, 20–22
safety/effectiveness of, 9
understanding, 15–16
Public health institutions
AIDS crisis and, 5–6
problems with, 1
Public health officials
competence/goodwill of, 200
reemergence of, 102
TB and, 103, 104
vigilance of, 2
Public Health Service (PHS), 131, 132
CDC/NIH and, 11
legacy of, 14
swine flu and, 54
Public Health Service Act (1966), 77
Public interest
guaranteeing, 190
polio and, 32
private interests and, vii
Publicity, negative, 62, 64
Publicity campaigns
federal, 64
state, 65
for swine flu vaccine, 61–62
Public opinion, shaping, 194–95
Public policy initiatives, 5, 176, 212n2
acceptance/trust for, 68
efficacy of, 200
Public-private partnerships, 28, 186, 188, 189
developing, 187
Public purposes, private interests and, 8
Public relations, 196
developing, 201
dynamics of, viii
education and, 194
Public support, 30, 31, 201
NFIP and, 32–33
Public trust

decline of, 19–20, 66–68, 72, 178, 199–201
misunderstanding, 67
NFIP and, 43
undermining of, 50
PWA Health Group, AL-721 and, 129

Quarantine, 77, 219n10

R and D, 7, 103, 186, 187
development funds for, 205n8
investment in, 185
private roles in, 121
Rather, Dan, 207n31
Rationing, 17–18, 101, 178, 196
policies for, 18
problems with, 48, 197–98
scenario involving, 164–65
See also Allocation
Rayburn, Sam, 36
Real Time Strategic Change, 110
Regulation, 201
accountability and, 189–90
problems with, 4
Reinventing government
budget crisis and, 90
opportunities for, 89
Religious organizations
AIDS crisis and, 181
NAVIP and, 166
Renslow, Chuck, 125
Research, 49
AIDS, 121, 158
Responsible Parent Immunization Plan Act of
1993 (H.R. 2432), 222n37
Reveal, Elizabeth, 207n30
Rheumatic fever, 100
Rikers Island Prison, 111, 113
Risks, 49, 82, 179
cancer, 207n26
distribution of, 17
preparation for, 16
Rivers, Thomas
Falk vaccine and, 211n53
killed-virus and, 33
on media, 42
Robert Wood Johnson Foundation, 222n32
Rockefeller, Nelson, 214n25
Roosevelt, Eleanor, 98
Roosevelt, Franklin D.
media and, 42
NFIP and, 31
polio and, 29
Roper Survey, on federal government/trust, 19
Roukema, Marge, 222n37
Rubella, immunization against, 220n14
Ruckelshaus, William, 207n31
Ryan, Paul, 97, 101

Sabel, Barbara, 227n48
Sabin, Albert, 9
    criticism by, 34, 213n11
    live-virus vaccine and, 33
Sabin vaccine, and Salk vaccine, compared, 33,
    34
Sabotage, 180
Safe sex, xvi
    campaign for, 3, 124, 162
Safety, 16, 61
    concerns about, 15, 18, 22, 28, 30
    importance of, 195
    scenario involving, 149, 151, 152–53, 154,
        165, 174, 175, 182
Salk, Jonas, 9, 29, 41, 43, 142, 201
    on Cutter protocols, 38
    discrimination against, 34
    killed-virus and, 33
    NFIP and, 42
    work of, 20
Salk vaccine, 24
    demand for, 40, 41, 47
    development/testing/licensing of, 29, 37
    distribution of, 40
    field trials for, 32, 35
    media and, 41, 42
    problems implementing, 20, 37
    and Sabin vaccine compared, 33, 34
    safety of, 43
    support for, 34
    threats to, 30
San Francisco
    AIDS in, 123
    bathhouse closures in, 122–26
San Francisco Chronicle, 123
Scarlet fever, 100
Scenario building, 27–28, 140, 141–75, 180–83
    efforts in, 193
    future and, 182
    lessons from, 183
    methods of, 181–82
Schall, Ellen, 234n9
Schatz, Albert, 99
Scheele, Leonard, 211n40
    Cutter incident and, 41, 42–43
    Cutter vaccine and, 38
    vaccination program and, 43
Schon, D., 234n9
Schultze, Charles L., 207n34
Schwartz, Peter, 180, 182, 234n7
    scenario building by, 198, 200
Science, culture of, 8–10, 68–69
Scientific controversy, 30, 33–34, 35, 153–54
    managing, 8–10, 178, 190–92
    persistence of, 10
    policy-making and, 10
    polio immunization and, 68

TB and, 99–100
Scientific progress, 15, 25, 68
    disease control and, 205n2
    implementation/management and, 2–3
    politics of, 10–11
Seal, John
    on split vaccine, 59
    swine flu and, 54
Sencer, David, viii, 54, 193
    immunization plans and, 57
    interagency coordination and, 56
    media strategy and, 194
    preventive health agenda and, 10
    program implementation and, 58
    replacement of, 55
    swine flu and, 10, 52, 53, 60, 61, 63, 191
Sensationalism, 43, 48, 182
    controlling, 195
    criticism of, 168
    scenario involving, 140, 155, 156, 168, 169,
        171
    about TB, 100–101
Sentinel, on bathhouses/sex clubs, 122
Sex clubs, 122, 123
Sex education, 12, 202
Shalala, Donna, 92, 202
    needle exchange and, 134
    on universal entitlement, 84
Shilts, Randy, 123, 125
Shortages, 37–38, 100, 172, 180, 186, 197
Side effects, vii, 169, 172, 173–74, 194
    liability for, 225n22
    negative, 64, 66
    problems with, viii, 25, 69, 191
    TB drug, 100, 105
Silicone breast implants, 16
Silverman, Mervyn, 123, 124
60 Minutes, on AIDS vaccine, 143, 172
Skepticism, 34, 100, 143
    increase in, 68
    strategic, 22, 23
Smallpox, 230n79
    responding to, 121
    vaccination for, 57, 213n3
Smart organisms, dealing with, 100–101
Social conditions, 7, 68, 121
    delivery and, 192
    in NYC, 106–7
Socialized medicine, fear of, 45
Social Security Administration, 39
    administrative failure in, 86
Split vaccines, 59
Squibb, TB drugs and, 101
Stakeholder mapping, xiv, 22, 26
    described, 133, 181
Stakeholders
    courting/cultivating, 193–94

involvement of, 188–89
relative power of, 181
undermining interests of, 180
State government
tort liability and, 216n51
trust in, 208n42
"Strategic Plan for the Elimination of TB in the United States" (CDC), 103
Streitmatter, Rodger, 123
Streptomycin, 99, 102
limits of, 101
MDR-TB and, 100
research, 225n20
shortage of, 100
side effects of, 100
Success rates, 64–65, 67
Superbugs, threats from, 201
Supply
immunization rates and, 172
problems with, 30, 48, 55, 59, 168–69, 196
scenario involving, 166
Swine flu, xiii, 6, 10, 16, 121, 139, 140
deaths from, 218n82
as false alarm, 69–70
lessons from, xi
predicted, 197
threat of, 57, 63, 67, 202, 205n3
Swine flu program, 49, 51, 74, 86, 97, 194, 195, 197
coordination problems for, 56
design of, 188
end of, 55
failure of, 73
federal mismanagement of, 217n69
goals of, 66
lessons of, 122
liability concerns for, 7
media and, 67–68, 194, 196
prevention and, 52–54
problems for, 50, 57, 62, 88, 172, 179
public support for, 67
Swine Flu Tort Claims Act, 61, 63
Swine flu vaccine, 13, 47, 215n28
children's dosages of, 59
field trials for, 59
manufacture of, 213n15
problems with, viii, 22, 24–25
shortages of, 180, 186
side effects from, 55, 191
Syndromes, defining, 231n1

TAG (Treatment Action Group), 132
TB. See Tuberculosis
Technical Advisory Committee, Cutter vaccine and, 38
Tetanus, immunization against, 220n14
Therapies, self-implementing, 3

Thiosemicarbazones, 99, 101
Tort liability, 216n51
immunity from, 216n51
states and, 60
Treatment, 26, 172
costs of, 19, 120
distribution of, 18
effective, 4
funding for, 170–71
implementation of, 3
large-scale, 177
managing, xvii, 113
prevention and, ix, 212n1
support for, 150–51, 159, 170, 171
Treatment Action Group (TAG), 132
Treatment and Data Committee (ACT UP/New York), 132
Troast, David W., 135
Tuberculosis (TB), xi, xiii, xvii, 49, 121, 139, 140, 151
blood-borne, 98
contagiousness of, 224n10
controlling, 1, 2, 17, 95, 102, 105, 107, 194, 195, 198
decline in, 102, 224n2
described, 97–99
drug development for, 17–18
drug-resistant, xvi, 1, 12, 15, 26, 96, 99, 100, 105
elimination of, 113–14, 116–17, 118
etiology of, 99
extrapulmonary, 224n9
famous victims of, 98
funds for, 103, 109
HIV/AIDS and, 95, 103, 105, 112, 113
hospitalization for, 224n1
HRA and, 228n56
management of, 26
nonpulmonary, 98
OMB and, 228n53
poverty and, 106
prophylactic remedies for, 116–18
public health infrastructure for, 104
pulmonary, 224n9
R and D funds for, 103
reemergence of, 2, 6, 12, 17, 26, 98, 106, 113, 118
research on, 103
roots of, 97
social conditions for, 106
spread of, 26, 98, 107
testing for, 115, 227n41, 229n71
treating, 12, 26, 196, 197
Tuberculosis control program
described, 111–13
implementation of, 114
managing, 183

Tuberculosis control program, *continued*
  in NYC, 201
  odd bedfellows for, 133
  operational demands of, 115
Tuberculosis hospitals, 102, 104
Turk, Barbara, 227n53, 228n57
20/20, on safety concerns, 165

Unanticipated events, anticipating, 21, 121
Unemployment insurance, 235n27
United Nations AIDS program, Glaxo Well-
  come and, 235n22
United Way, AIDS vaccine and, 161
United We Stand America, inoculation program
  and, 147
U.S. Agency for Health Care Policy Research,
  221n26
USA Today, on AIDS vaccine, 154
U.S. News and World Report
  on planning/implementation, 40
  on Salk vaccine, 43

Vaccination programs. *See* Immunization programs
Vaccination rates. *See* Immunization rates
Vaccine Division (CDC), NAVIP and, 164
Vaccine Injury Compensation Fund, 79
Vaccines
  administering, 7
  cost of, 25, 75, 79, 80, 85, 86, 94, 190
  development of, 85
  effective, xiii
  entitlement to, 219n3
  excise taxes on, 220n12
  free, 19, 77–94
  licensing/regulating, 219n10
  live-virus/killed-virus, 215n28
  research on, 11
Vaccines for Children (VFC), 12, 19, 78, 84,
  91, 92, 181, 185, 192
  accountability problems in, 190
  compromises on, 85
  costs for, 79, 93
  developing/amending, 73, 223n63
  effectiveness of, 93
  financing, 198–99
  health care reform and, 87
  GSA and, 92
  implementation of, 25, 196
  mismanagement of, 15, 74–75, 88, 94

outreach and, 47
  as policy response, 74–75
  state participation problems with, 13
Vacit, tainted vaccine and, 169, 171
Vaxgen vaccine, xiv
Venereal disease, 1
  social history of, 205n2
  vaccine for, 3
VFC. *See* Vaccines for Children
VICP, 187
Victim's compensation fund, 186
Victoria A vaccine, 66, 213n8, 217n76, 218n91
Virology, 120, 231n1
Viruses, dealing with, 70–71
Virus Research Committee, 42
Virus Serums and Toxins Act (1902), 219n10

Wachter, Robert M., 132
Wallace, Mike, 172
Wall Street Journal, on Biosci/AIDS vaccine,
  145
Warm Springs Foundation, 31, 209n4
Washington Post
  on AIDS vaccine, 141, 142, 166–67
  on FDA/Biosci, 157
  on Fort Dix outbreak, 62
  on NAVIP, 148
  on swine flu program, 63, 68
Waxman, Henry, 173
Weiss, Ted, 128
White, Ryan, x, 149
Whitman, Christine Todd, 135
Whitman Walker Clinic, vaccinations at,
  167
WHO. *See* World Health Organization
WIC, 82
Winchell, Walter, 42
Wolf, Sidney, 213n11
Workman, Cassy, 138
World Health Organization (WHO)
  AIDS vaccine and, 162
  DOT and, 105
  Fort Dix outbreak and, 218n90
Wyeth
  manufacture/distribution by, 54
  swine flu vaccine and, 60

Young, Frank, 129

Zingale, Daniel, 135